In this book Nicholas Grene explores political contexts for some of the outstanding Irish plays from the nineteenth century to the contemporary period, including *The Playboy of the Western World* and *The Plough and the Stars*, with the famous riots they provoked. The politics of Irish drama have previously been considered primarily the politics of national self-expression. Here it is argued that Irish plays, in their self-conscious representation of the otherness of Ireland, are outwardly directed towards audiences both at home and abroad. The political dynamics of such relations between plays and audiences is the book's multiple subject: the stage interpretation of Ireland from *The Shaughraun* to *Translations*; the contentious stage images of Yeats, Gregory and Synge; reactions to revolution from O'Casey to Behan; the post-colonial worlds of *Purgatory* and *All that Fall*; the imagined Irelands of Friel and Murphy, McGuinness and Barry. In reinterpreting its politics, Grene offers a new conception of Irish drama.

NICHOLAS GRENE is Professor of English Literature at Trinity College, Dublin. Grene has lectured widely on Irish literature and is the author of *Synge: A Critical Study of the Plays* (1975); *Shakespeare, Jonson, Molière: The Comic Contract* (1980); *Bernard Shaw: A Critical View* (1984) and *Shakespeare's Tragic Imagination* (1992).

CAMBRIDGE STUDIES IN MODERN THEATRE

Volumes for Cambridge Studies in Modern Theatre explore the political, social and cultural functions of theater while also paying careful attention to detailed performance analysis. The focus of the series is on political approaches to the modern theatre with attention also being paid to theatres of earlier periods and their influence on contemporary drama. Topics in the series are chosen to investigate this relationship and include both playwrights (their aims and intentions set against the effects of their work) and process (with emphasis on rehearsal and production methods, the political structure within theatre companies, and their choice of audiences or performance venues). Further topics will include devised theatre, agitprop, community theatre, para-theatre and performance art. In all cases the series will be alive to the special cultural and political factors operating in the theatres examined.

Books published

Brian Crow with Chris Banfield, *An introduction to post-colonial theatre*
Maria DiCenzo, *The politics of alternative theatre in Britain, 1968–1990: 7:84 (Scotland)*
Jo Riley, *Chinese theatre and the actor in performance*
Jonathan Kalb, *The theater of Heiner Müller*
Richard Boon and Jane Plastow, eds., *Theatre matters: performance and culture on the world stage*
Claude Schumacher, ed., *Staging the Holocaust, The Shoah in drama and performance*
Philip Roberts, *The Royal Court Theatre and the modern stage*
Nicholas Grene, *The politics of Irish drama: plays in context from Boucicault to Friel*
Anatoly Smeliansky, *The Russian theatre after Stalin*

The politics of Irish drama

Plays in context from Boucicault to Friel

Nicholas Grene

PUBLISHED BY THE PRESS SYNDICATE OF THE UNIVERSITY OF CAMBRIDGE
The Pitt Building, Trumpington Street, Cambridge, United Kingdom

CAMBRIDGE UNIVERSITY PRESS
The Edinburgh Building, Cambridge CB2 2RU, United Kingdom
http://www.cup.cam.ac.uk
40 West 20th Street, New York, NY 10011–4211, USA http://www.cup.org
10 Stamford Road, Oakleigh, Melbourne 3166, Australia

First published 1999

Printed in the United Kingdom at the University Press, Cambridge

Typeset in Trump Mediaeval and Schadow BT, [CE]

A catalogue record for this book is available from the British Library

Library of Congress cataloguing in publication data
Grene, Nicholas.
The politics of Irish drama: plays in context from Boucicault to Friel / Nicholas Grene.
p. cm. – (Cambridge studies in modern theatre)
Includes bibliographical references and index.
ISBN 0 521 66051 3. – ISBN 0 521 66536 1 (paperback)
1. English drama – Irish authors – History and criticism.
2. Boucicault, Dion, 1820–1890 – Political and social views.
3. Politics and literature – Ireland – History – 19th century.
4. Politics and literature – Ireland – History – 20th century.
5. Political plays, English – History and criticism.
6. Friel, Brian – Political and social views.
7. Theatre – Political aspects – Ireland. I. Title. II. Series.
PR8795.P64G74 1999
822.009'358–dc21 99–10289 CIP

ISBN 0 521 66051 3 hardback
ISBN 0 521 66536 1 paperback

For Antoinette, Brendan and Terence

Contents

Acknowledgements

I would like to acknowledge, with more than merely formal gratitude, a year's leave of absence from Trinity College, Dublin, in 1997–8 during which this book was written. It was, however, while teaching a graduate seminar on Irish drama in Brazil in 1993 that I first had the idea for such a study. I am most grateful to Munira Mutran of the University of São Paulo for her invitation to teach that course and her warm-hearted hospitality while I was there. A version of chapter 6 was given as a lecture at the annual conference of IASAIL-Japan at Shikoku University in 1996 and published in *The Harp: IASIL-Japan Bulletin*, XII (1997); chapter 8 is adapted from an essay published in *Literature and Nationalism*, edited by Vince Newey and Ann Thomson (Liverpool: Liverpool University Press, 1991). As Director of the Synge Summer School in Rathdrum, Co. Wicklow, since 1991, I have gained enormously from lectures delivered there in ways beyond specific acknowledgement. I want to thank all of the many speakers at the School who have helped to shape my understanding of Irish drama. Adrian Frazier, reading early chapters of the book in draft, gave me warm encouragement when it was most needed. Lucy McDiarmid's generous response and constructive commentary on a somewhat later version of chapter 2 were equally welcome. This is the first book of mine to have been read in manuscript both by my father David Grene and my mother Marjorie Grene. I am extremely pleased that they both thought well of it, and have benefited a great deal from their criticisms of its style and substance. The book is affectionately dedicated to Terence Brown, Brendan Kennelly and Antoinette Quinn whose company as colleagues and friends has meant so much to me over the years.

Chronology

Dates given for plays are those of first production at Abbey Theatre, unless otherwise indicated; titles given **in bold** are analysed in detail in the book.

DATE	THEATRICAL EVENTS	POLITICAL EVENTS
1860	Boucicault, *The Colleen Bawn* (Laura Keene's Theatre, New York)	
1864	Boucicault, *Arrah-na-Pogue* (Theatre Royal, Dublin)	
1867		Fenian rising
		Execution of 'Manchester martyrs'
1869		Disestablishment of the Church of Ireland
1874	**Boucicault, *The Shaughraun*** (Wallack's Theatre, New York)	
1879		Establishment of Land League
1880		Parnell elected leader of Irish parliamentary party
1886		First Home Rule Bill

DATE	THEATRICAL EVENTS	POLITICAL EVENTS
1890		Parnell divorce case
1891		Death of Parnell
1893		Second Home Rule Bill
1894	**Yeats, *The Land of Heart's Desire*** (Avenue Theatre, London)	
1897	Establishment of Irish Literary Theatre	
1899	First season of Irish Literary Theatre	
1902	**Yeats and Gregory, *Kathleen ni Houlihan*** (St Teresa's Hall, Dublin)	
1903	Irish National Theatre Society founded	Wyndham's Land Act
	Synge, *The Shadow of the Glen* (Molesworth Hall, Dublin)	
1904	Opening of the Abbey Theatre	
	Shaw, *John Bull's Other Island* (Court Theatre, London)	
1905		Establishment of Sinn Féin
1907	**Synge, *The Playboy of the Western World***	
1909	Death of Synge	
1910	**Gregory, *The Travelling Man***	
1912		Third Home Rule Bill
		Ulster Covenant against Home Rule
1913		Dublin lockout
1914		Home Rule enacted but suspended for duration of war

Year	Theatre	History
1916		Easter Rising
1919		Establishment of Dáil Eireann
		Beginning of War of Independence
1920		Introduction of 'Black and Tans'
1921		Anglo-Irish Treaty
1922		Establishment of Irish Free State
		Outbreak of Civil War
1923	**O'Casey, *The Shadow of a Gunman***	End of Civil War
1924	**O'Casey, *Juno and the Paycock***	
1926	**O'Casey, *The Plough and the Stars***	
1928	O'Casey's *The Silver Tassie* rejected by the Abbey	
	Establishment of Gate Theatre Company, Dublin	
1929	**Johnston, *The Old Lady Says 'No!'*** (Gate Theatre Company, Peacock Theatre)	
1932	Death of Gregory	Fianna Fail government of De Valera
1937		New Irish Constitution
1938	**Yeats, *Purgatory***	
1939	Death of Yeats	
1949		Ireland declared Republic
1950	Death of Shaw	
1951	Abbey Theatre destroyed by fire	
1953	Establishment of Pike Theatre, Dublin	
1954	**Behan, *The Quare Fellow*** (Pike Theatre)	

DATE	THEATRICAL EVENTS	POLITICAL EVENTS
1956–62		IRA Border campaign
1957	**Beckett, *All that Fall*** (Broadcast BBC, Third Programme)	
1958	**Behan, *The Hostage*** (Theatre Royal, Stratford East, London)	
1961	Murphy, *A Whistle in the Dark* (Theatre Royal, Stratford East)	
1964	**Friel, *Philadelphia Here I Come!*** (Gaiety Theatre, Dublin)	
1966	New Abbey Theatre opened	
1967	**Friel, *Lovers*** (Gate Theatre)	
1968	Murphy, *Famine* (Peacock Theatre, Dublin)	
1969	**Murphy, *A Crucial Week in the Life of a Grocer's Assistant***	Beginning of violence in Northern Ireland
1972		Bloody Sunday, Derry
1973	Friel, *Freedom of the City*	Ireland joined EEC
	Leonard, *Da* (Olympia Theatre, Dublin)	Sunningdale agreement for power-sharing executive in N. Ireland
1974	**Murphy, *On the Outside/On the Inside*** (Peacock Theatre)	Power-sharing executive brought down by Ulster Workers' Council action
1975	Establishment of Druid Theatre Company, Galway	
1977	Kilroy, *Talbot's Box* (Peacock Theatre)	
1979	Friel, *Faith Healer* (Longacre Theatre, New York)	

1980	Establishment of Field Day Theatre Company	
	Friel, *Translations* (Field Day, Guildhall, Derry)	
1981		Hunger strikes in N. Ireland
1983	Murphy, *The Gigli Concert*	
	Reid, *Tea in a China Cup* (Lyric Theatre, Belfast)	
1984	Parker, *Northern Star* (Lyric Theatre)	
1985	**Murphy, *Bailegangaire*** (Druid Theatre)	Anglo-Irish agreement
	Murphy, *A Thief of a Christmas*	
	McGuinness, *Observe the Sons of Ulster Marching Towards the Somme*	
1986	Kilroy, *Double Cross* (Field Day, Guildhall, Derry)	
1987	Parker, *Pentecost* (Field Day, Guildhall, Derry)	
1988	McGuinness, *Carthaginians* (Peacock Theatre)	
1990	Friel, *Dancing at Lughnasa*	
1994	Carr, *The Mai* (Peacock Theatre)	
1995	**Barry, *The Steward of Christendom*** (Royal Court Theatre Upstairs, London)	
1996	McDonagh, *The Beauty Queen of Leenane* (Druid, Town Hall, Galway)	
1997	McPherson, *The Weir* (Royal Court Theatre Upstairs)	
1998		Good Friday agreement

Abbreviations

The following abbreviations are used for frequently cited texts.

Barry	Sebastian Barry, *The Steward of Christendom* (London: Methuen, 1995, repr. 1997).
Beckett, *CDW*	Samuel Beckett, *The Complete Dramatic Works* (London: Faber, 1986).
Behan	Brendan Behan, *An Giall*, ed. and trans. Richard Wall / *The Hostage*, ed. Richard Wall (Washington D.C.: Catholic University of America Press; Gerrards Cross: Colin Smythe, 1987).
Boucicault	Dion Boucicault, *Plays*, ed. Peter Thomson (Cambridge: Cambridge University Press, 1984).
Friel, *Lovers*	Brian Friel, *Lovers* (Dublin: Gallery Books, 1984).
Friel, *SP*	Brian Friel, *Selected Plays* (London: Faber, 1984).
Gregory, *CP*, I–IV	Lady Gregory, *Collected Plays*, ed. Ann Saddlemyer, 4 vols. (Gerrards Cross: Colin Smythe, 1970).
Gregory, *SW*	Lady Gregory, *Selected Writings*, ed. Lucy McDiarmid and Maureen Waters (Harmondsworth: Penguin, 1995).
Johnston, *Old Lady*	Denis Johnston, *The Old Lady Says 'No'!*, ed. Christine St. Peter (Washington D.C.: Catholic University of America Press; Gerrards Cross: Colin Smythe, 1992).
McGuinness	Frank McGuinness, *Observe the Sons of Ulster Marching Towards the Somme* (London: Faber, 1986).

Murphy, *P1*	Tom Murphy, *Plays: One* (London: Methuen, 1992).
Murphy, *P2*	Tom Murphy, *Plays: Two* (London: Methuen, 1993).
Murphy, *P4*	Tom Murphy, *Plays: Four* (London: Methuen, 1997).
O'Casey, *A*, I–II	Sean O'Casey, *Autobiographies*, 2 vols. (London: Macmillan, 1963; repr. New York: Carroll & Graf, 1984).
O'Casey, *SP*	Sean O'Casey, *Seven Plays*, ed. Ronald Ayling (Basingstoke: Macmillan, 1985).
Shaw, *CPP*, I–VII	Bernard Shaw, *The Bodley Head Bernard Shaw: Collected Plays with their Prefaces*, 7 vols. (London: Max Reinhardt, 1970–4).
Synge, *CW*, I–IV	J.M. Synge, *Collected Works*, 4 vols. (London: Oxford University Press, 1962–8).
Yeats, *CPl*	W.B. Yeats, *Collected Plays* (London: Macmillan, 2nd ed. 1952).
Yeats, *VP*	W.B. Yeats, *The Variorum Edition of the Poems of W.B. Yeats*, ed. Peter Allt and Russell K. Alspach (New York: Macmillan, 3rd ed. 1966).

Introduction

As long as there has been a distinct Irish drama it has been so closely bound up with national politics that the one has often been considered more or less a reflection of the other: the most recent work on twentieth-century Irish drama is subtitled *Mirror up to Nation*.[1] It is understandable that it should be so. The Irish national theatre movement was an integral part of that broader cultural nationalism of the turn of the century which sought to create for a long-colonised Ireland its own national identity. There were those sharp encounters over *The Playboy of the Western World* and *The Plough and the Stars* which gave dramatic expression to the charged relationship of Irish theatre and national politics. Irish drama since the time of the early Abbey has remained self-consciously aware of its relation to the life of the nation and the state. The aim of this book, however, is to suggest that there is more to the politics of Irish drama than merely a theatrical mimesis of the national narrative. A three-way set of relationships between subject, playwright and audience has to be considered in the complex act of negotiation which is the representation of Ireland on the stage. This could be called a poetics of Irish drama in so far as it is concerned with the way the playwright addresses his/her subject; in considering the interaction of dramatic image and audience, it could be identified as a dynamics of Irish drama. But given the political dimensions of both poetics and dynamics in the representation of Ireland, it seems reasonable to call the whole the politics of Irish drama.

The politics of Irish drama, then: *all* the politics? *All* Irish drama? Necessarily not. The book focuses on that Irish drama which is self-consciously concerned with the representation of Ireland as its main subject. It excludes as a result the plays of Farquhar and

Goldsmith, all of Wilde and most of Shaw, with the exception of *John Bull's Other Island*; Beckett is represented only by *All that Fall*. This is not to deny the Irishness of such playwrights: Shaw's Irishness has never been in question, and increasingly critics have demonstrated the significance of Wilde's and Beckett's nationality in reading their work. I am not trying to construct a canon of national drama excluding plays by Irish playwrights that are not directly concerned with Ireland. *The Importance of Being Earnest*, for all its English setting, *Waiting for Godot* with its placeless country road, may well be illuminated by an awareness of their authors' Irish background. But the subject of my book is that particular tradition of Irish drama which is constituted around its Irish subject and setting. In taking Dion Boucicault's *The Shaughraun* as the chronological starting-point for that conspectus, I intend to show that this self-conscious stage representation of Ireland antedated the Irish national theatre movement as such. Ireland, from at least as far back as Boucicault, was a marketable phenomenon, a space, a place which *needed* to be represented and represented truly. This book is concerned with the politics of such representation.

A subject so defined marches on the much broader area of cultural self-representation in the expanding field of Irish studies. A number of recent books here have been very influential: Declan Kiberd's *Inventing Ireland*, which brings postcolonial theory to bear on the full range of Irish writing in the modern period; Luke Gibbons's *Transformations in Irish Culture*, which identifies crucial signs in the visual fields of modernising Ireland; Joep Leerssen's two magisterial volumes, *Mere Irish and Fíor-Ghael* and *Remembrance and Imagination*, charting the complementary English and Irish imagological traditions in representations of Ireland down to the end of the nineteenth century.[2] In the context of these wide-ranging studies, to narrow down to just the drama, and a selected number of dramatic texts at that, may seem unduly limited and limiting. However, there are benefits in such a restricted focus. To start with, the Irish dramatic tradition treated in this book has been a notably cohesive one, with its own special intertextual lines of descent, and these forms of filiation will be a part of my subject. More generally, though, concentration on the reading of selected dramatic texts may allow us to come in closer to the phenomenon of representing Irishness than more theoretically inflected analyses of broader cultural manifestations. A theatrical script, as a set of signs for potential stage realisation, constitutes an extraordinarily rich subject for interpretation. The images created before a live audience are representation in action, the negotiation of meanings through the words of the playwright, the real bodies and voices of the actors, the *mise en scène* of director and designer, all operating within the field of the spectators' preconceptions and prejudices, likes and dislikes. The words of the text bear a specially close scrutiny, not primarily for their authorial authority, but as they reach out towards theatrical embodiment. They are signs in search of an audience, not necessarily or only the audience for which the play is first written. An awareness of the potential, implied audience is the more important for this book because it is a basic tenet of my argument that Irish drama is outward-directed, created as much to be viewed from outside as from inside Ireland. Even where the plays are produced wholly within an Irish theatrical milieu, the otherness of Ireland as subject is so assumed by the playwrights as to create the effect of estranging exteriority.

The Politics of Irish Drama considers in some detail about two dozen Irish plays out of the many thousands which have been produced since the last half of the nineteenth century. It does not attempt to duplicate the historical coverage and chronological order of works such as Christopher Murray's *Twentieth-Century Irish Drama*, D.E.S. Maxwell's *Modern Irish Drama 1891–1980* or Christopher Fitz-Simon's *The Irish Theatre*.[3] The texts selected have been chosen as they provide key illustrations of the specific issues being addressed in the politics of Irish drama, not because I judge them to be the outstanding achievements of that tradition. I am very conscious of the many major playwrights omitted and the limited sample of the work of those included. So, for instance, only two of Synge's texts are considered, and I have not found room for what I still regard as Brian Friel's greatest play, *Faith Healer*, nor his most successful to date, *Dancing at Lughnasa*. Although most of the plays chosen are indeed among the central works of modern Irish drama, that is not the reason why they are in this book. My object is not evaluation but a critical analysis of the political interplay of dramatic text and context.

Instead of following the line of a single thesis, I have preferred to vary the angle of approach for each chapter, making connections backwards and forwards within the overall argument rather than locking each part into one linear chain. So the long first chapter maps out the subject by considering three plays of Boucicault, Shaw and Friel as they represent different versions of the stage interpretation of Ireland. Chapter 2 examines the themes and variations played upon the motif of strangers in the house by Yeats, Gregory and Synge, where chapter 3 concentrates on just the one text – *The Playboy* – and the one event, its politically explosive reception. Looking at issues of class and space in relation to O'Casey in chapter 4 makes for a different perspective on his first two Abbey plays, while *The Plough* is considered in chapter 5 with the later reactions to revolution of Denis Johnston and Brendan Behan. Two plays of Yeats and Beckett are analysed in chapter 6 as they reveal both their contrasting versions of post-Independence Ireland and the affinity which distinguishes them from other Irish playwrights. Chapter 7 is taken up with the theatrical effects of some early plays of Friel and Tom Murphy and their reception outside Ireland, illustrating their contrasted negotiation with the mode of pastoral. Murphy's Ireland as represented in the rich and resonant *Bailegangaire* is the subject of chapter 8. The last chapter is concerned with the politics of imagining the other in recent plays by Frank McGuinness and Sebastian Barry. The aim of the book as a whole is to extend and alter the sense of what constitutes the politics of Irish drama, and by doing that to reconceive the nature of Irish drama itself.

1 Stage interpreters

Here, for the first time, is the real Ireland on stage:

> Ireland, so rich in scenery, so full of romance and the warm touch of nature, has never until now been opened by the dramatist. Irish dramas have hitherto been exaggerated farces, representing low life or scenes of abject servitude and suffering. Such is not a true picture of Irish society.
>
> (Playbill for the first production of Dion Boucicault's *The Colleen Bawn*, New York, 1860)[1]

> We will show that Ireland is not the home of buffoonery and of easy sentiment, as it has been represented, but the home of an ancient idealism. We are confident of the support of all Irish people, who are weary of misrepresentation.
>
> (Manifesto for the Irish Literary Theatre, 1897).[2]

> the neo-Gaelic movement ... is bent on creating a new Ireland after its own ideal, whereas my play is a very uncompromising presentment of the real old Ireland.
>
> (Preface to *John Bull's Other Island*, 1907)[3]

> apart from Synge, all our dramatists have pitched their voices for English acceptance and recognition ... However I think that for the first time this is stopping ... We are talking to ourselves as we must and if we are overheard in America, or England, so much the better.
>
> (Brian Friel, on the Field Day production of *Translations*, 1980)[4]

Authenticity and authority have been issues in Irish drama as far back as Boucicault, as far forward as Friel. Every dramatist, every dramatic movement, claims that they can deliver the true Ireland which has previously been misrepresented, travestied, rendered in sentimental cliché or political caricature. And they can so produce an unprecedentedly authentic Ireland because they really know what they are talking about: they have the Irish credentials to do so. *The Colleen Bawn* is 'Founded on a true history First told by an Irishman and now Dramatized by an Irishman.'[5] The manifesto writers of the Irish Literary Theatre are confident of the support of the Irish people who are 'weary of misrepresentation', and who will be able to confirm their country as the 'home of an ancient idealism'. Shaw contests this idealism as a Utopian fantasy: *John Bull's Other Island*, by contrast, presents the 'real old Ireland'. Irish playwrights of Brian Friel's generation are no longer going to pitch 'their voices for English acceptance and recognition', 'we are talking to ourselves'.

'We will *show* that Ireland is not . . .' Who is to be shown this? For whose benefit is this theatrical revisionism undertaken? The answer varies from case to case, but it is never unambiguously clear. On the one hand, there is the appeal to those who know, who share the authority of the dramatists and can corroborate their versions of Ireland as truth. On the other hand, the audiences, almost by definition, are those who need to have their images of Ireland revised, who have been so conditioned by false stageland versions that they will find the truth startingly new and unfamiliar. The drama is directed simultaneously at those who know Ireland as the dramatists claim to know Ireland, and at those who do not: it is an act of expression and an act of interpretation. Ireland is at once here, our own, held in common between playwright and audience, and elsewhere, out there to be imagined and, with difficulty, understood.

Three plays may stand as representative examples of this process of the stage interpretation of Ireland and the way it has changed over time: Boucicault's *The Shaughraun* (1874), Shaw's *John Bull's Other Island* (1904) and Friel's *Translations* (1980). Each of these plays had a specific political context and was written as a more-or-less direct, more-or-less self-conscious, intervention in that context. The playwrights' interpretations of Ireland offered a political vision of the country to challenge contemporary thinking on the subject. They suggested answers to the 'Irish question' or at least set out to re-formulate the question. But as significant as the plays' national politics is their internal politics of interpretation. In each of the texts there is at least one figure who stands as interpreter, interpreting between characters, between stage and audience, reading and explaining Ireland on behalf of the dramatist creator. The function and nature of these stage interpreters change from play to play, often as part of the process of discrediting past interpretations, reinvesting authority in new and different versions of Irishness. What is one play's authentic spokesman becomes the next play's stage Irishman, acting out the false stereotypes of foreign expectations. How, though, do the various onstage interpreters within the plays relate to the business of intrepretation which the plays themselves transact? *The Shaughraun*, *John Bull* and *Translations* were all performed, for the most part highly successfully, in England and America as well as Ireland, and they are designed to speak to non-Irish as to Irish audiences. The analysis of the stage interpretations of Ireland in the three plays may bring into focus the varying role of the dramatist as interpreter, for whom he interprets and to what end.

The Shaughraun

The Shaughraun was the third of Boucicault's Irish melodramas, but the first to have a contemporary, or near-contemporary, setting. *The Colleen Bawn* (1860) appears to have been set in the 1790s for costume purposes, though 1819 was the date of the actual murder on which Gerald Griffin based his 1829 novel *The Collegians*, Boucicault's acknowledged source. *Arrah-na-Pogue* (1864) has a 1798 rebellion plot, featuring Boucicault as Shaun the Post singing 'The Wearing of the Green'. The events following the abortive Fenian rising of 1867, the trial of the 'Manchester martyrs' and the explosion at Clerkenwell prison, led to 'The Wearing of the Green' being banned throughout the British Empire. It was in this period of Fenian activity and its aftermath that Boucicault set *The Shaughraun*. Although the playbill for the first New York production at Wallack's Theatre in November 1874 specifies that the time of the action is 'The Present',[6] the references in the text seem to suggest a time back in the winter of

1867–8. The villain Kinchela plans to use the current political situation to justify his murder of the escaped Fenian convict Robert Ffolliott by the police: 'The late attack on the police van at Manchester [September 1867], and the explosion at Clerkenwell prison in London [December 1867], will warrant extreme measures.'[7]

For what sort of audience and towards what kind of political sympathies was *The Shaughraun* directed? In writing a play with a Fenian hero for production in New York, it seems plausible that Boucicault was courting Irish-Americans in the country where the Fenian movement began. And it is true that at the end of its smash-hit four-months' run, the playwright was given an official presentation by the Irish community of New York for his services to Irish drama. Replying to the tribute (and the gift of a statue of Tatters, Conn the Shaughraun's never-seen offstage dog) Boucicault claimed the play's significance was its patriotic exposure of English misrepresentations: 'let me disclaim any pretension as an actor to excel others in the delineation of Irish character. It is the Irish character as misrepresented by the English dramatists that I convict as a libel.'[8] With the profits of the play he bought himself a steam-yacht, and considered sailing it to England and running up the rebel Irish flag,[9] following the example, no doubt, of the belated American brig laden with arms, pathetically misnamed *Erin's Hope*, which arrived in Ireland in 1867 when the Fenian rising had already petered out.[10]

Yet, in spite of such Anglophobic attitudes on Boucicault's part, *The Shaughraun* was every bit as successful in London when it was produced in Drury Lane in the autumn of 1875. This followed the pattern of Boucicault's other Irish plays which had enjoyed equally rapturous receptions in New York, London and Dublin. *The Colleen Bawn*, like *The Shaughraun* a New York hit which transferred to London, had been a special favourite of Queen Victoria, and had made a lionised star out of Boucicault in his native Dublin. The highly successful opening of *Arrah-na-Pogue* in Dublin was a tryout for London where, at the Princess's Theatre, it went on to achieve a run of 164 nights.[11] Although Boucicault was adept at recasting his plays to suit local conditions – as most famously with *The Streets of New York* transformed into *The Streets of Liverpool*, *The Streets of London* etc. etc. – there is no sign that he altered the political complexion of his

Irish plays to suit his several audiences.[12] The romantically pro-Fenian *Shaughraun* which New York applauded was the same *Shaughraun* which London loved.

Boucicault made of that very universality of acclaim of *The Shaughraun* the basis of his public appeal to Disraeli for the release of Fenian prisoners in an open letter to the press in January 1876.[13] By that stage, Boucicault argued, most of the chief Fenian leaders were already at liberty, and it was for the relatively few, relatively rank-and-file prisoners he appealed. He cited the 200,000 people who had seen the play in London and who had all cheered sympathetically the news of a Fenian amnesty as evidence of public opinion on his side. What is more, he imagined an even more dramatic reunion of hearts for twenty million Americans,

> hearts that sincerely respect their mother country, and would love her dearly if she would let them. One crowning act of humanity would be worth a dozen master-strokes of policy; and the great treaty to be established with the United States is neither the Canadian fisheries nor the border-line on the Pacific Ocean – it is the hearty cohesion of the English and the American people.[14]

Disraeli failed to recognise this version of Churchill's Anglo-American 'special relationship' ahead of its time, and ignored Boucicault's appeal. It was treated by the British press with scepticism as one more publicity stunt by the arch-showman: 'One word for the Fenian Prisoners, and how many for the "Shaughraun?"', runs the caption to a cartoon of Boucicault holding up a placard labelled 'Petition & Advt The Shaughraun' behind a studiously cold-shouldering Dizzy.[15] But the appeal, Utopian and theatrical as it was, rightly represented the Utopian and theatrical politics of the play.

The action opens with a mock passage of arms between the English officer Captain Molineux and the Irish Claire Ffolliott whom he takes, in the style of *She Stoops to Conquer*, for the dairymaid.

> MOLINEUX. Is this place called Swillabeg?
> CLAIRE. No. it is called Shoolabeg.

MOLINEUX. Beg pardon; your Irish names are so unpronounceable. You see I am an Englishman.
CLAIRE. I remarked your misfortune; poor crature, you couldn't help it. (Boucicault, 173)

After some flirtatious by-play between them in which Molineux snatches a kiss and they churn the butter together in suggestive intimacy, Claire gets in a parting shot before calling her cousin Arte O'Neal:

CLAIRE. . . . What's your name again? (*looking at card*) Mulligrubs?
MOLINEUX. No! Molineux.
CLAIRE. I ax your pardon! You see I'm Irish, and them English names are so unpronounceable! (Boucicault, 174)

Ireland 2: England nil. The bantering over national difference here sets up the expected trope of a romance to come: the bumbling but honorable Englishman falling in love with the witty and charming Irishwoman, she in spite of her prickly patriotism unable to resist his decency, uprightness and sincerity. By the end of the action Irish and English will join in a marriage of complementary equals not in colonial subordination.[16]

In the imagination of this national romance, class is crucially important. In revenge for his mistaking her for the dairymaid, Claire deliberately distorts the aristocratic Molineux into the ludicrous Mulligrubs. But he is to prove his class affinity with her in the next scene. When the villainous 'squireen' Corry Kinchela appears, Molineux bristles with social antagonism. Two speeches by Kinchela are enough to provoke the aside 'This fellow is awfully offensive to me' (Boucicault, 176) and Kinchela's self-introduction is insultingly rejected. It is this instinctive hostility to the social 'bounder' which seals Claire's alliance with Molineux as he takes his leave, making formal apology for his initial mis-classing of her:

MOLINEUX. . . . I ask your pardon for the liberty I took with you when I presented myself.
CLAIRE. (*offering her hand*) The liberty you took with him

> [Kinchela] when he presented himself clears the account.
> (Boucicault, 176)

Class solidarity, the identification of a Molineux with a two-f Ffolliott against a Kinchela, is here established as a decisive bond beyond national difference.

The upper-class Arte O'Neal and Claire Ffolliott are cousins, and their kinship is made to stand for a pre-Cromwellian alliance of Old Irish and Old English gentry. Father Dolan reminds the would-be dispossessing Kinchela of the curse upon the usurpers of Suil-a-more:

> When these lands were torn from Owen Roe O'Neal in the old times, he laid his curse on the spoilers, for Suil-a-more was the dowry of his bride, Grace Ffolliott. Since then many a strange family have tried to hold possession of the place; but every year one of that family would die; the land seemed to swallow them one by one – till the O'Neals and Ffolliotts returned, none other thrived upon it. (Boucicault, 178)

Colonial expropriation is here figured as the standard Gothic family melodrama; the details of history are blurred or elided. Owen Roe O'Neill, Gaelic leader for the Confederation of Kilkenny at the Battle of Benburb in 1646, is a rebel figure sufficiently removed historically to make a respectable ancestor 'in the old times'. The role of the English in the confiscation of Irish lands is tactfully omitted (not to mention the fact that the real-life Ffolliotts seem only to have come to Ireland in the seventeenth century as Ulster plantation settlers in Fermanagh[17]) so that it may appear that the original 'despoilers', as well as the 'strange families' who tried to seize Suil-a-more since, were all hated Irish 'middle-men' like Corry Kinchela.

The middleman is a great man to blame in these matters. The agent who stands between the landlord and tenant, unscrupulously exploiting both, the rackrenter who sublets at extortionate rates the lands he himself leases rather than owns, the half-educated 'half-sir' who rises through the middle-class professions to ape or oust the Ascendancy family, these are all the favoured villains of nineteenth-century Irish fiction. The unsettled state of Ireland and its chronic land problems need not be attributed to the colonial connection or the inequities of land tenure when there are the middlemen to blame. And hand-in-glove with the middleman in this rogues' gallery is the informer: in the case of *The Shaughraun*, Harvey Duff.

Harvey Duff is not only an informer but an *agent provocateur*, employed not by the police but by Corry Kinchela for his own nefarious ends. He protests when Kinchela tries to fob off his demands for more money for his evidence against the Fenians:

> KINCHELA. Were you not handsomely paid at the time for doing your duty?
> DUFF. My jooty! was it my jooty to come down here amongst the people disguised as a Fenian delegate, and pass meself aff for a head centre so that I could swear them in and then denounce them? Who gave me the offis how to trap young Ffolliott? (Boucicault, 190)

Robert Ffolliott has been transported to Australia on the strength of Duff's evidence, but it remains doubtful in just what, if any, Fenian activity he engaged. He is first mentioned by Captain Molineux who (with wild implausibility for an English officer) refers to him as 'a distinguished Fenian hero' (Boucicault, 174). An air of the disguised rebel on the run is as much Fenianism as Robert needs. The Fenian movement itself is made to seem a fabrication of the Harvey Duffs and the Corry Kinchelas, a wicked chimera devised to further their own heinous ends. The middlemen, the squireens and informers, stand between and *misinterpret* relations which would otherwise be amicable and co-operative, the relationship of landlord and tenant, of English and Irish. Land wars and Fenian liberation movement alike are products of such wilfully contrived misunderstanding.

It is significant in this emollient picture of Irish politics that the priest Father Dolan is emphatically on the side of the angels. When Arte O'Neal explains the impoverished position of herself and her cousin Claire, Molineux attributes it to *Castle Rackrent*-ish high living in the family: 'You have to suffer bitterly, indeed, for ages of family imprudence, and the Irish extravagance of your ancestors.' Arte retorts with pride: 'Yes, sir; the extravagance of their love for their country, and the imprudence of their fidelity to their faith' (Boucicault, 175). The O'Neals and the Ffolliotts are, it seems, allied not only by class and political allegiance but by their common Catholicism. However, no further inconvenient signs of their faith are forthcoming in the play, and their priest is a most reassuring figure. In the wake of the disestablishment of the Church of Ireland in 1869 and with the growing power of an increasingly modernised and well-organised Catholic Church in Ireland, he might well not have been so reassuring for English (or Irish) Protestant audiences. Boucicault took care not only to stress Father Dolan's personal loyalty, and his exemplary standards of honour – he is unable to give the assurance Molineux demands that Robert is not hiding in his house, whereupon Robert gives himself up to spare his priest the sin of perjury – but also his class subordination.

Father Dolan's speech varies through the play. He can rise to the high register of melodrama rhetoric as in his account of the curse on Suil-a-more quoted earlier. But he is also given the telltale dialect vowels which place him in the brogue-speaking classes. He recoils in horror at Kinchela's proposal that he should marry Arte: 'I'd rather rade the service over her grave and hear the sods falling on her coffin than spake the holy words to make her your wife' (Boucicault, 178). While the recruitment of priests from the peasant class, their close involvement in grassroots local politics, were to make them a formidable part of the Land League organisation in the 1880s for all the disapproval of the hierarchy, Boucicault reads Father Dolan's relatively humble status as a guarantee of political loyalty. As the uncle of Moya, the peasant heroine who will eventually marry Conn the Shaughraun, as somewhere between priest and faithful retainer to the upper-class O'Neals and Ffolliots, he is no threat to the dream of Utopian political harmony towards which the action tends.

Conn the Shaughraun himself has the key role in the engineering of this politically happy-ever-after denouement. In plot terms, the Shaughraun is the exemplary opposite of the middleman. Corry Kinchela and Harvey Duff, as magistrate and police spy, are the ostensible agents of law and order who are in fact deeply subversive; Conn the lawless vagabond is the incarnation of true loyalty. The middlemen deceive, misrepresent, misinterpet. They suppress letters (Corry Kinchela has intercepted Robert's prison letters home to Arte O'Neal), they bear false witness, they wrongfully imprison the innocent and the good. Conn is the communicator, using his songs outside Robert's prison walls for coded messages, the liberator who frees his master not once but repeatedly.[18] (And if Conn's story of how he hitched shiprides to Australia and enabled Robert to escape sounds fantastic, it is hardly less so than the real-life rescue of Fenian prisoners from their Australian penal settlement by the Catalpa expedition later in the year that *The Shaughraun* closed in London.)[19] While Kinchela has the traditional villain's combination of financial and sexual predatoriness, Conn facilitates the two politically and socially correct marriages of Arte with Robert, Molineux with Claire, and is to be rewarded with his own union with Moya – provided the audience 'go bail for' him. In an artful version of the traditional *plaudite*, Conn appeals to his public:

> You are the only friend I have. Long life t'ye! Many a time you have looked over my faults. Will you be blind to them now, and hould out your hands once more to a poor Shaughraun?
>
> (Boucicault, 219)

The Shaughraun/Boucicault here invites applause and approval not only for his starring performance, but for the reconciliatory happy ending which he has brought about and the Irish drama which he has presented and epitomised.

The Shaughraun was offered as 'an entirely New and Original Play ... illustrative of Irish Life and Character'[20], and the Shaughraun himself was cast as the greatest illustration and illustrator. In the Dramatis Personae he is listed as 'CONN (the shaughraun, the soul of every fair, the life of every funeral, the first fiddle at all weddings and patterns)' (Boucicault, 171). Conn is here associated with the Irish genre scenes which it is the design of the play to display as it displays the much-featured Irish scenery. He is the essence of Irishness as it is manifested in fairs and funerals, wakes and weddings, but he is also the showman who produces and stars in them. In this regard Boucicault's special position as actor/author/producer is significant. There was nothing unusual about having the lead actor in the comic part rather than the role of the nominal hero/juvenile lead: the phenomenon was familiar back to the time of Molière and before. Equally traditional is the key role as contriver and controller given in comedy to normally subordinated figures; Boucicault's comic Irish servants are legitimate descendants of the tricky slaves of Plautus and Terence. But there is a particular piquancy in having the illiterate Conn played by the man who wrote the whole play, and an added dimension as a result to the *faux naiveté* of the clever/foolish dialect-speaking clown who presides over the action.

Boucicault apparently insisted on the play's title, in spite of the protests by the theatre manager Lester Wallack that the New York public would not be able to pronounce, much less understand, it.[21] It seems to have been his policy in the titles of all his Irish plays (including the later unsuccessful *The Amadan*) to use the estranging novelty of an Irish-derived word or phrase. It was a part of what he had to purvey, the otherness of Ireland, like the romantic scenes and place-names which he marketed in such abundance, at times regardless of geography. (*The Shaughraun* appears to move the Blaskets from the Dingle peninsula to the coast of Sligo, while *The Colleen Bawn* combines the Limerick setting implied by its subtitle *The Brides of Garryowen* with the full benefit of the Kerry lakes of Killarney.[22]) It is a composite idea of Ireland which Boucicault offers to his audience, its picturesque scenery, its dialect, its traditional music, all of them equally strange and yet thoroughly familiar in their strangeness. The Shaughraun is there as audience sponsor to inhabit and comfortably interpret the Irish scene.

The wake is one of the great set-pieces of the play, as it was one of the most distinctive and commented-on customs of the Irish. Molineux acts as English straight man to be baffled by the practices of what he constantly calls 'you Irish'. 'In the name of Bedlam,' he exclaims at Conn's mother's plans for the wake, 'does she propose to give a dance and supper-party in honour of the melancholy occasion?' (Boucicault, 208). An audience may be supposed to smile at the Englishman's ignorance of the practice of the wake, to side with Claire in her impatient refusal to be stereotyped as 'you Irish'. Yet it is very important to the wake-scene that we know *in advance* that Conn is not really dead. The strong curtain of Act II closes on the fallen figure of the Shaughraun who has given his life for his master, with all the added pathos of dying in front of the moonlit broken shrine of St Bridget. But in the very next scene the incorrigible, unmurderable

Conn is back, disclosing himself to his allies, furthering the next stage of the plot, yet refusing to undeceive his mother, bent instead on returning to play his part as the corpse: 'Would you have me spile a wake? Afther invitin' all the neighbours!' (Boucicault, 209). The audience goes into the wake-scene thus prepared to enjoy the spectacle as pure comedy.

The wake and the keen were potentially frightening, awe-inspiring, as the customs of an archaic, even a barbaric culture. The abandoned uninhibitedness of the keen was striking to as late and sympathetic an observer as Synge. Boucicault opens his scene with the picturesqueness of a formal genre painting, 'TABLEAU OF AN IRISH WAKE', and domesticates the keen into a recognisable ballad format with alternating male and female choruses. Conn exploits the comedy of the undead corpse for all its worth, with the stage business of stealing the head keener's whiskey and amused wonderment at his miraculously improved reputation: 'It's a mighty pleasant thing to die like this, once in a way, and hear all the good things said about you afther you are dead and gone' (Boucicault, 212). As a result, what is strange and potentially disturbing about the spectacle of the wake is neutralised by having it turned into a comic version of itself. With Conn the conman, the audience can enjoy the wake as pure grotesque.

The scene acts similarly to mime and defuse other threatening images as well. With Molineux's revelations of the iniquities of Kinchela and Harvey Duff, the keeners are suddenly transformed into a lynch-mob, as they bay for the blood of the informer:

> BIDDY seizes axe. MRS. O'KELLY crosses to fire for poker. DONOVAN gets scythe and file. PEASANTS rush for various implements that are about the stage. MOLINEUX comes on BIDDY with axe, backs to MRS. O'KELLY with poker, turns to DONOVAN with scythe, whom he eyes with his glass.
>
> (Boucicault, 213)

In the iconography of terror there is a special place for the crowd released into anarchic violence by the peasants' revolt, armed with the agricultural implements of their labour. Here, though, Molineux the English officer, who might be expected to be the victim of Irish peasant rage, is actually on their side. The momentary discomfort of being surrounded by angry people brandishing axe, poker and scythe is made ludicrous by Molineux's monocle and the confident knowledge that he is not their intended scapegoat. The men they are really out to get are – of course – the offstage middlemen, Kinchela and Duff. And though the fury of the mob is used to drive Duff to a suicidal leap from the cliff, Kinchela is rescued from lynching by a single command from Father Dolan: 'Stand back! D'ye hear me? Must I speak twice?' at which 'The crowd retire, and lower their weapons' (Boucicault, 218). Violence in *The Shaughraun* is localised, controllable by the authority of the priest, directed not against the colonising British or the true landowning classes of O'Neals and Ffolliotts but only at the limited and eradicable class of the villainous middlemen.

Boucicault's Irish plays were produced in fashionable theatres to largely middle-class audiences, though they could be popular with the working classes also.[23] For such audiences, the social conservatism of the plays' politics, the reassuring picture of a pseudo-feudal bond of gentry and loyal peasants allied against greedy and unscrupulous bourgeois ambition offered 'an optimistic myth of reconciliation'[24] in the colonial context of Ireland. In the magic space of melodrama the realities of Fenian politics, of power struggles at agrarian and national level, are susceptible of domestic solution. The Utopian idyll represented by the line-up at curtain close of *The Shaughraun*, Conn and Moya flanked by Mrs O'Kelly and Father Dolan, with the two couples, Robert/Arte, Molineux/Claire at either end, and not a Kinchela or a Duff to be seen, could be appreciated equally by American, English or Irish audiences. It could appeal to the inherited sentimental patriotism of Irish-Americans, allay the fears of the English and satisfy the national self-esteem of the Irish. This flexibility of appeal, the winning charm of the version of Ireland produced by *The Shaughraun*, were made possible by its simultaneous inside/outside perspective. Boucicault as Conn the Shaughraun interpreted Ireland as an actor interprets his role, embodying, impersonating the part he plays, but always with the consciousness of an outer, other audience with its preconceptions and prejudices. That stance came to be despised as stage-Irishry, castigated for its inauthenticity, condemned for its ingratiating 'blarney' and 'bootlicking'.[25] Political disapproval apart, the Shaughraun is indeed a stage Irishman, designed to live in the theatre as a representative type 'illustrative of Irish life and character'. The concern of the rest of this chapter is with how later dramatists developed the political business of interpreting and reinterpreting Ireland for audiences at home and abroad, and how the figures of stage interpreter, Irish genre scene and English/Irish marriage initiated by Boucicault are redeployed by Shaw and Friel.

John Bull's Other Island

The politics of *John Bull*, its genesis, production and performance history, is a more complicated story than that of *The Shaughraun*, partly because it extended over a longer period of time. Shaw's ideas about Irish and English national character were simmering as far back as 1897 when he let off a volley at a meeting of the London Irish Literary Society in response to a fatuous paper on 'Irish Actors of the Nineteenth Century'.

> It is a mistake to think an Irishman has not common sense. It is the Englishman who is devoid of common sense ... It is a mistake to think the Irishman has feeling; he has not; but the Englishman is full of feeling. What the Irishman has is imagination; he can imagine himself in the situation of others.[26]

Shaw's target here is the Arnoldian polarity of the emotional Celt and the practical Saxon, and the design of his 'play on the contrast of Irish and English character'[27] which (at Yeats's prompting) he undertook to write for the Irish Literary Theatre was to reverse these stereotypes.

In its resistance to stereotyping, Shaw's play accorded with the aims of the Irish Literary Theatre to escape from the misrepresentations of Ireland on the English stage, and Yeats was no doubt pleased to get the promise of a play from a playwright of Shaw's standing for what by 1904 was about to become the Abbey Theatre. However, from the beginning the play was written from within an English rather than an Irish theatrical context. All through the summer of 1904 while at work on the play, Shaw fired off a series of all but daily letters to Harley Granville Barker about the casting and staging of the projected production at the Court Theatre, while one equivalent letter to Yeats enquiring whether the Dublin theatre had a hydraulic bridge – 'It seems to me that as you will deal in fairy plays you may have indulged yourself with hydraulic bridges' – indicates an unfamiliarity both with the modesty of the Abbey Theatre then being fitted up, and the nature of Yeats's 'fairy plays'.[28] The Dublin production seems to have been very much secondary to the London one in his mind, and he cannot have been too much concerned when, in October 1904, Yeats came to the conclusion that the play was beyond what the Abbey could manage or afford. *John Bull*, on the other hand, was integral to the pioneering work of the Vedrenne–Barker management at the Court: 'we shall have to play off the piece as a very advanced and earnest card in the noble game of elevating the British theatre'.[29]

Shaw had in mind also a British political context for the reception of his play. In August he wrote to Granville Barker proposing a delay in the production of what was then still called *Rule Britannia*:

> It has only just occurred to me that it would be very bad business to produce Rule Britt. before parliament meets again. In fact, it mustn't be done. You will sell a lot of stalls to the political people; and the Irish M.P.s will fill the pit.[30]

(It is interesting to note the differentiation of the Irish MPs from the 'political people', and the assessment of their different means in terms of the price of the tickets they would buy.) In the event, Shaw was proved exactly right and the play drew enormous political interest, with Prime Minister Balfour, who had previously been Irish Secretary, attending five performances in all, bringing (on separate occasions) two future Liberal leaders, Campbell-Bannerman and Asquith, as his guests.[31]

Shaw's reputation as a leading Fabian – it was Beatrice Webb who brought Balfour to *John Bull* initially – ensured him the attention from the British political establishment which Boucicault with his appeal to Disraeli so signally failed to achieve. But *John Bull* had in any case a much more specific, much more seriously topical political argument to advance than *The Shaughraun*. The year 1903 had seen the passing of Wyndham's Land Act, one of the most important in the series of legislation that allowed Irish tenant farmers to buy their land and that resulted ultimately in the wholesale expropriation of the

Irish landlord class. Though the first of these Land Acts had been the doing of Gladstone's Liberal administration in 1870, Wyndham's Act had been brought in by the Tory government as part of their policy of 'killing Home Rule with kindness'. For many people it represented some sort of ultimate triumph of that policy: by solving the land question, it effectively solved the 'Irish question'. The design of Shaw's play was specifically to challenge that assumption, to argue that an Ireland of small-farm owner–occupiers was no nearer the end of its problems than the Ireland of persecuted and summarily evicted tenants. 'I have taken,' said Shaw in the wake of the play's production, 'that panacea for all the misery and unrest of Ireland – your Land Purchase Bill – as to the perfect blessedness of which all your political parties and newspapers were for once unanimous; and I have shown at one stroke its idiocy, its shallowness, its cowardice, its utter and foredoomed futility.'[32] It is not clear how far the play may have influenced the Irish policies of Balfour (who was to be defeated in the next General Election) or of the incoming Liberals, but certainly they sat up and took notice.

John Bull got a lukewarm critical press on its first production in London, but it attracted great political interest and was a real popular success, culminating in the Royal Command Performance in March 1905 where, famously, Edward VII broke the outsize royal chair laughing. The play folded after just two weeks in New York where the critics castigated its preachiness: 'a thick, glutinous and impenetrable four-act tract'.[33] To the surprise of many, however, it was given a very warm reception in Dublin when it was staged there in November 1907 in a touring version of the Vedrenne–Barker production, and it was to prove an enduring favourite at the Abbey for many years after it was (belatedly) staged there in 1916.[34] In 1907, the year of *The Playboy*, there was apparently a great deal of nervousness about the reception *John Bull* would get, so much so that the Theatre Royal had police on duty to deal with potential disturbances. In the event, they were not needed and the play was as successful in Dublin as it had been in London. Joseph Holloway, the Abbey Theatre architect and obsessive theatre-goer, whose sympathies were always on the nationalist side and who was still sore with the Abbey over the *Playboy*, commented triumphantly in his journal: 'I have been hearing since the play saw light at the Court that a Dublin audience would wreck the theatre if produced here and yet the event has taken place and the Royal stands unruffled where it stood.' He gleefully imagined the Abbey directors' chagrin at the success of the play they had turned down: 'I wonder how Yeats felt as he sat in the box with Lady Gregory and witnessed the play being thoroughly appreciated by a £300–0–0 house at least!'[35]

A part of the reason why *John Bull* was so appreciated in Dublin was its even distribution of political satire. Irish nationalists could enjoy the exposure of Tim Haffigan, the fake stage-Irishman, and revel in the absurdity of Tom Broadbent, one of the greatest comic stage-Englishmen ever created. And yet the play also gave a caustically satiric picture of Rosscullen, the Irish small town. In fact, the debate between Hodson the English valet and Matt Haffigan the Irish small farmer on their relative sufferings was apparently turned into an Ireland versus England political contest, with alternating rounds of applause from the dress-circle and the gallery.[36] It is extraordinary to imagine Unionists (presumably) in the fashionable dress-circle seats applauding Hodson's socialist attack on the Irish tenant-farmers as less disadvantaged than the English working classes, but equally bizarre that nationalists should have rallied to the cause of the politically myopic Mat Haffigan. Where Synge had incensed the specifically nationalist audiences of the Abbey with a grotesque vision of the sacrosanct West of Ireland peasantry in their own supposedly national theatre, Shaw provided a mixed Dublin audience at the more fashionable Theatre Royal with something for everyone. If the universality of Boucicault's appeal was based on a policy of general conciliation, *John Bull* made its way with the English and the Irish, nationalists and Unionists, by a strategy of even-handed provocativeness and iconoclasm.

The play was directed at both English and Irish audiences and its theatrical design was to move the audience from England to Ireland. Granville Barker, in despair at a play which ran for more than three and a half hours and could only be played in an extended matinée, suggested to Shaw that the first act should be cut and a first scene substituted 'in Cork, with Broadbent already in tweeds on Irish soil'; Shaw insisted that it 'would be about ten minutes longer than the existing first act, and would do its work worse'.[37] The work of the first act was to show Broadbent on home English territory, thoroughly taken in by the stage Irishman Tim Haffigan. Broadbent, preparing for his visit to Ireland, proposes to take Haffigan as his 'Irish Secretary' to 'come with me and help to break the ice between me and your warmhearted, impulsive countrymen'.[38] Haffigan is to play the part of Irish interpreter for Broadbent, the part of Boucicault's Shaughraun, and he plays it to the life: roguish, deferential, whiskey-drinking, brogue-spouting, giving the gullible Englishman top of the morning with an air. Shaw no doubt intended his English audience to be as taken in by this performance as Broadbent, and to be equally taken aback when it is revealed that Haffigan is 'not an Irishman at all' (Shaw, *CPP*, II, 905).

Shaw had a first go at the Boucicaultian stage Irishman in a review of *The Colleen Bawn* in 1896. 'I have lived to see The Colleen Bawn with real water in it; and perhaps I shall live to see it some day with real Irishmen.' Shaw's argument there, elaborated in *John Bull*, is that the stage Irishman was not a misrepresentation of the Irish by the English, but a meretricious invention of the Irish to suit English tastes. 'Of all the tricks which the Irish nation have played on the slow-witted Saxon, the most outrageous is the palming off on him of the imaginary Irishman of romance.'[39] And so in *John Bull* he produces Larry Doyle as the real Irishman to expose the unreality of Haffigan and to take over from him the job of stage interpreter of the Irish. Larry is described in the stage directions in terms which no English audience, reared on images of rollicking shaughrauns, would associate with Ireland:

> Mr Lawrence Doyle is a man of 36, with cold grey eyes, strained nose, fine fastidious lips, critical brows, clever head, rather refined and goodlooking on the whole, but with a suggestion of thinskinnedness and dissatisfaction that contrasts strongly with Broadbent's eupeptic jollity.
>
> (Shaw, *CPP*, II, 901–2)

It is Larry who provides the full-scale denunciation of the stage Irishman. When the flabbergasted Broadbent protests that Tim Haffigan spoke and 'behaved just like an Irishman', Larry explodes:

> Like an Irishman!! Man alive, dont you know that all this top-o-the-morning and broth-of-a-boy and more-power-to-your-elbow business is got up in England to fool you, like the Albert Hall concerts of Irish music? No Irishman ever talks like that in Ireland, or ever did, or ever will. But when a thoroughly worthless Irishman comes to England, and finds the whole place full of romantic duffers like you, who will let him loaf and drink and sponge and brag as long as he flatters your sense of moral superiority by playing the fool and degrading himself and his country, he soon learns the antics that take you in. (Shaw, *CPP*, II, 905–6)

Larry's de-authentication of the Boucicault-like stage Irishman helps to establish his authority as real Irishman, as true interpreter of Ireland. In the first act he functions as Shavian spokesman for his creator's own theories of national character, voiced already in the 1897 speech at the Irish Literary Society. The notion of national character was problematic for Shaw. He was utterly opposed to any racial or ethnic concept of Celticism: once again Larry voices his views (expounded at length in the 'Preface for Politicians'):

> When people talk of the Celtic race, I feel as if I could burn down London. That sort of rot does more harm than ten Coercion Acts. Do you suppose a man need be a Celt to feel melancholy in Rosscullen? Why, man, Ireland was peopled just as England was; and its breed was crossed by just the same invaders. (Shaw, *CPP*, II, 908)

Shaw was enough of a cultural materialist, sufficiently formed by his reading of Marx, to distrust any essentialist explanation of human behaviour. And yet he was committed to the idea that there *was* a fundamental difference between English and Irish character. His own persona as GBS, quizzical, sharp-eyed and sharp-tongued Irish commentator on the ways of the thick-witted English, depended on a bold antithesis of national difference. His solution was to adopt the environmental/climatic theory of nationality which Larry airs in the great 'dreaming' speech of *John Bull*.

When Broadbent maintains that the ennui of life in the country is much the same in England as in Ireland, Larry earnestly contradicts him:

> No, no: the climate is different. Here, if the life is dull, you can be dull too, and no great harm done. (*Going off into a passionate dream*) But your wits cant thicken in that soft moist air, on those white springy roads, in those misty rushes and brown bogs, on those hillsides of granite rocks and magenta heather. Youve no such colors in the sky, no such lure in the distances, no such sadness in the evenings. Oh, the dreaming! the dreaming! the torturing, heart-scalding, never satisfying dreaming, dreaming, dreaming, dreaming!
>
> (Shaw, *CPP*, II, 909)

Though the idea of climate as cultural determinant starts as some sort of paradoxical challenge to racial/ethnic essentialism, it soon transmutes into the romantic cult of landscape which even those Irish writers most allergic to national nostalgia find hard to escape. And Larry's analysis of the Irish imagination is actually a version of Arnoldian Celticism, with a fierce twist of self-hatred rather than a patronising or self-congratulatory admiration. 'An Irishman's imagination never lets him alone, never convinces him, never satisfies him; but it makes him that he cant face reality nor deal with it not handle it nor conquer it' (Shaw, *CPP*, II, 909). This is the Celtic resistance to the 'despotism of fact' seen as a miserable disability not a spiritual and creative asset. Doyle's speech stresses all the things an Irishman's imagination unfits him for:

> He cant be religious. The inspired Churchman that teaches him the sanctity of life and the importance of conduct is sent away empty; while the poor village priest that gives him a miracle or a sentimental story of a saint, has cathedrals built for him out of the pennies of the poor. He cant be intelligently political: he dreams of what the Shan Van Vocht said in ninety-eight. If you want to interest him in Ireland youve got to call the unfortunate island Kathleen ni Hoolihan and pretend she's a little old woman. (Shaw, *CPP*, II, 910)

The Irishman's imagination leaves him fantasy-fed, permanently dissatisfied with a world of impoverished facts; but still more pernicious is the dark obverse of this imagination, the disposition to begrudging laughter which provides the peroration of Larry's speech:

> And all the time you laugh! laugh! laugh! eternal derision, eternal envy, eternal folly, eternal fouling and staining and degrading, until, when you come at last to a country where men take a question seriously and give a serious answer to it, you deride them for having no sense of humour, and plume yourself on your own worthlessness as if it made you better than them. (Shaw, *CPP*, II, 910–11)

The first act of *John Bull* with its theatrical highpoint of Larry's aria on Irish imagination prepares an audience to travel to Ireland with whetted appetite and new eyes: the stage Irishman is left behind in England, and the credibility of Doyle as interpreter is constantly enhanced by the solemn obtuseness of Broadbent. Yet the opening scene of Act II, the first vision we are given of Ireland, all but restores the scenic romanticism of Boucicault.

> Rosscullen. Westward a hillside of granite rock and heather slopes upward across the prospect from south to north. A huge stone stands on it in a naturally impossible place, as if it had been tossed up there by a giant. Over the brow, in the desolate valley beyond, is a round tower. A lonely white high road trending away westward past the tower loses itself at the foot of the far mountains. It is evening; and there are great breadths of silken green in the Irish sky. The sun is setting.
>
> (Shaw, *CPP*, II, 922)

This is giving an audience brought up on Boucicault just what they might expect from Ireland, and it is significant that the New York critics who hated *John Bull* reserved their only praise for the scenery.[40] Shaw, for all his denunciation of the stage Irishman, was working within the theatrical idiom of the Boucicaultian Irish Romance, as Martin Meisel was the first to demonstrate.[41] Though Rosscullen is purely fictional and Shaw does not exploit the scenic glamour of the real places of Boucicault's plays, Killarney, Glendalough, Sligo, his is a generically Irish mise-en-scène combining the wildly picturesque landscape with the Round Tower borrowed from *Arrah-na-Pogue*. Shaw does not deny to his audiences the romantic spectacle of Ireland they are used to; he seeks rather for them to re-read and reinterpret it.

Broadbent is there as cultural tourist to mimic and mock that business of interpretation. Guide-book in hand, he is prepared to be 'deeply interested' in the antiquities: 'Have you any theory as to what the Round Towers were for?' he asks Father Dempsey eagerly. Father Dempsey is offended: 'A theory? Me! ... I have a knowledge of what the Roun Towers were, if thats what you mean. They are the forefingers of the early Church, pointing us all to God' (Shaw, *CPP*, II, 932–3). The allusion here is to the debate which raged through much of the nineteenth century between those who argued for a pre-Christian origin of the round towers, including (notoriously) the claim that their phallic shape was evidence of their use in pagan fertility cults, and the historical scholarship which placed them as medieval structures with a defensive function. At stake was nothing less than the very idea of national identity, as Joep Leerssen has so tellingly shown.[42] While for Broadbent this is the stuff of theorising, for Father Dempsey it is dangerous nonsense, threatening the authority of the Church. As Corny Doyle so devastatingly puts it, 'Father Dempsey is the priest of the parish, Mr Broadbent. What would he be doing with a theory?' (Shaw, *CPP*, II, 933). Broadbent is the outsider who theorises, generalises, interprets – like Molineux with his 'you Irish' – and whose interpretations are always rebuked by the reality on the ground, the reality of Father Dempsey and Corny Doyle, of Aunt Judy and Nora Reilly.

A dimension to the reality of Rosscullen which Shaw contrasts with preconceptions of Ireland is the changed political and social situation of 1904. The generic threat in any number of nineteenth-century melodramas was the threat of dispossession, of the about-to-be-foreclosed mortgage. Boucicault gave to this a specially Irish cast in *The Shaughraun* by having the beleaguered heroines the already dispossessed Arte O'Neill and Claire Ffolliott. The threat of the villain Corry Kinchela is to complete that process of dispossession by driving them from the tiny remains of their property. The happy ending thus not only reassuringly removes the threat of immediate expropriation but acts as an imagined reversal of the colonial expropriations of the past. In *John Bull* the foreclosure of the mortgage, so often threatened and never effected in melodrama, has already happened before the action starts, and is indeed the occasion of the action. Larry Doyle is upset to hear that the Rosscullen landowner has lost his estate, as he explains to Broadbent in the first act:

> Your foreclosing this Rosscullen mortgage and turning poor Nick Lestrange out of house and home has rather taken me aback; for I liked the old rascal when I was a boy and had the run of his park to play in. I was brought up on the property.

To this the businesslike but quite unvillainous Broadbent merely shrugs his shoulders: 'But he wouldnt pay the interest. I had to foreclose on behalf of the Syndicate' (Shaw, *CPP*, II, 906). In Shaw's 1904 Rosscullen, the dispossession of the landed gentry, the feared threat of Boucicault's melodramas, is an accomplished political fact of life.

Here and throughout Shaw coolly rewrites and de-melodramatises Boucicault. In place of the all-but-demonic middleman Corry Kinchela, his land agent is the glumly realised Corny Doyle, a small man trapped in a system he does not begin to understand. The understanding, the authority to interpret what is happening, is given instead to his son Larry. It is Larry who voices Shaw's political reading of Ireland in Act III, as he was given Shaw's deconstruction of the stage Irishman in Act I. Wyndham's 1903 Land Act had gone a long way towards the transfer of the land from landlord to tenant farmer – a process that was to be completed by the 1909 Act which brought in powers of compulsory purchase. This tacit admission by the British government of the illegitimacy of centuries of colonial acquisition represented a nation-wide act of restoration. But Shaw, through Larry, questions whether the replacement of landlord by peasant farmer will result in a social system of greater equity and less exploitation. Larry rounds on Matt Haffigan, the newly independent landholder:

> Do you think, because youre poor and ignorant and half-crazy with toiling and moiling morning noon and night, that youll be any less greedy and oppressive to them that have no land at

> all than old Nick Lestrange, who was an educated travelled gentleman that would not have been tempted as hard by a hundred pounds as youd be by five shillings?
>
> (Shaw, *CPP*, II, 962)

Shaw here lends to Larry his own socialist perspective in which a nation of small farmers is that worst of all worlds, a nation of small capitalists.

Larry Doyle speaks with his author's authority in interpreting the Irish political scene: in his opposition to separatist nationalism – 'I want Ireland to be the brains and imagination of a big Commonwealth, not a Robinson Crusoe island' (Shaw, *CPP*, II, 914); in his diagnosis of the power of the Catholic Church beyond state control; in his views on the perniciousness of Ireland's exportation of cheap labour to Britain. Larry acts as Shaw's sponsor in his de-mythologising interpretation of Irish politics. And yet nobody on stage, either English or Irish, can be brought to share his views. His most extended exposition of his ideas is the third-Act speech which ensures that he will *not* become Member of Parliament for Rosscullen. In Shaw's version of stage interpretation the truth about Ireland is what the Irish, as much as the English, refuse to see. Where Boucicault's romance was intended to bring all his characters, of whatever class and nationality, to a point of understanding and mutual goodwill amplified out into the audience, Shaw's strategy is to authorise what the mass of his stage figures obtusely fail to recognise.

Larry Doyle, piercingly perceptive as he is, consistently loses out to the fatuously uncomprehending Broadbent. He loses the seat in Parliament to him, and he loses Nora Reilly. The marriage of Nora and Broadbent is Shaw's impish version of the national romance imaged in the love between Molineux and Claire Ffolliott. Where Boucicault's pair succumbed to the irresistible attraction of difference, Nora and Broadbent's relationship is the hilarious product of complete miscomprehension. Shaw preemptively undoes the image of the Irish colleen in his introductory stage description of Nora:

> A slight weak woman . . . she is a figure commonplace enough to Irish eyes; but on the inhabitants of fatter-fed, crowded, hustling and bustling modern countries she makes a very

> different impression. The absence of any symptoms of coarseness or hardness or appetite in her, her comparative delicacy of manner and sensibility of apprehension, her fine hands and frail figure, her novel accent, with the caressing plaintive Irish melody of her speech, give her a charm which is all the more effective because, being untravelled, she is unconscious of it . . . For Tom Broadbent therefore, an attractive woman, whom he would even call ethereal.
>
> (Shaw, *CPP*, II, 927)

So much so that Broadbent proposes within two minutes of meeting her by the Round Tower at twilight. The two 'love-scenes' between Nora and Broadbent are wonderful elaborations on a comedy of cross-purposes, the Englishman sentimentally infatuated with a wholly illusory romantic projection, the Irishwoman baffled and bewildered but finally overborne by his ludicrous solemnity and self-importance. It is very funny but hardly the basis for an idyllic marriage.

The deeper version of the national romance in *John Bull* is not the marriage of Broadbent and Nora but the partnership of Broadbent and Doyle.[43] Broadbent's engagement to Nora is an act of acquisition by the 'conquering Englishman', as Keegan calls him only half ironically: 'Within 24 hours of your arrival you have carried off our only heiress, and practically secured the parliamentary seat' (Shaw, *CPP*, II, 1010). Larry too accounts for Broadbent's greater success in love in terms of national difference:

> Nora, dear, dont you understand that I'm an Irishman, and he's an Englishman. He wants you; and he grabs you. *I* want you; and I quarrel with you and have to go on wanting you.
>
> (Shaw, *CPP*, II, 1008)

Larry says this 'nervously relapsing into his most Irish manner' and it is not clear if he means it; rather it seems from other things he says that he has contrived for Broadbent to take her off his hands. Certainly there is no equivocation as to which is the deeper attachment from his point of view in the triangular relationship he imagines for the future:

> LARRY. . . . we must be friends, you and I. I dont want his marriage to you to be his divorce from me.

> NORA. You care more for him that you ever did for me.
> LARRY. (*with curt sincerity*) Yes of course I do: why should I tell you lies about it? (Shaw, *CPP*, II, 1008–9)

The 'marriage' of Broadbent and Doyle, figured in their partnership and their bachelor household together in the first act, is the complementary pairing of equal opposites exemplified by the national romance of Boucicault's Claire and Molineux. They need one another, and depend on one another: Broadbent needs Doyle for his brains, his ideas, his imagination; Doyle needs Broadbent for his certainty, his experience of the world, his resolute energy. For Shaw it may seem to be an exemplary partnership which has been compared, quite plausibly, to his own relationship with Sydney Webb.[44] And yet Doyle's part in that partnership suggests the psychological dependence of the colonised even in the formal tribute he pays to Broadbent:

> it is by living with you and working in double harness with you that I have learnt to live in a real world and not in an imaginary one. I owe more to you than to any Irishman.
> (Shaw, *CPP*, II, 913)

Doyle here acknowledges the superior 'reality' of the metropolitan colonial centre over the mere imaginings of the Irish. He expresses the dilemma of the expatriate Irishman in terms of a conventionally Arnoldian contrast of Celtic 'dream' and Saxon 'fact'.

> Live in contact with dreams and you will get something of their charm: live in contact with facts and you will get something of their brutality. I wish I could find a country to live in where the facts were not brutal and the dreams not unreal. (Shaw, *CPP*, II, 919)

In default of such a country, Doyle has allied himself to the brutal facticity of Broadbent's England, a brutality which he will help to impose on Rosscullen as though in revenge for the unreality of its charm. The business syndicate which Broadbent and Doyle represent, he tells Keegan with a sort of sadistic triumphalism in Act IV, 'will grind the nonsense out of you, and grind strength and sense into you' (Shaw, *CPP*, II, 1014).

One of the most striking features of the action of *John Bull* is the way in which the role of stage interpreter moves from Doyle to Keegan and the changed perspective which that shift produces. Boucicault in *The Shaughraun* had made of Father Dolan a reassuringly subordinate order-figure, allaying anti-Catholic fears of the power of the priesthood in Ireland. Shaw makes no bones of the political influence wielded by his Father Dempsey, the parish priest of Rosscullen who confidently presides over the meeting to select the next parliamentary candidate. Larry in his argument for the establishment of the Catholic Church, Shaw in the 'Preface for Politicians' forecasting an anti-clerical movement of both Catholics and Protestants in a post-Home Rule Ireland, suggest ways in which the power of the Father Dempseys might be curbed. But in Peter Keegan Shaw created a priest figure of a quite different order of dignity and authority, a dignity and authority enhanced, it has to be said, by his being an unfrocked priest.[45]

He appears first as part of that romantic tableau at the beginning of Act II which gives the audience its first sight of Ireland; and a fittingly romantic figure within it he is. 'A man with the face of a young saint, yet with white hair and perhaps 50 years on his back, is standing near the stone in a trance of intense melancholy, looking over the hills as if by mere intensity of gaze he could pierce the glories of the sunset and see into the streets of heaven' (Shaw, *CPP*, II, 922). Shaw's rhetorical description here sets the tone for Keegan: the saintliness, the alienation, the far-seeing vision. In the first scene of Act II the ex-priest's credentials of culture and education are clearly established not only in his training and travels from Salamanca to Rome, from Oxford to Jerusalem, but in the class indicators of his speech. If Boucicault intermittently dropped Father Dolan's speech down into dialect by way of placing him below the social level of the audience, Shaw underlines the fact that with Keegan a brogue is 'the jocular assumption of a gentleman and not the natural speech of a peasant' (Shaw, *CPP*, II, 922). It is this gentleman ex-priest, this 'mad' visionary, who provides a secular/sacred interpretation of Ireland which upstages and transforms the previously trustworthy readings of it by Larry Doyle.

Among other things, Keegan unmasks the neo-colonial future

planned for Ireland by the likes of Broadbent and Doyle. Up until Act IV, Broadbent's antics in Rosscullen are the subject of comfortable comedy, of spectacular misunderstanding constantly corrected by Larry's superior knowledge. But as Keegan (implausibly but effectively) exposes the business strategies of the Broadbent and Doyle syndicate, they begin to look much more like the conventionally conniving villains of melodrama. The syndicate which already owns most of Rosscullen will take complete control of the rest of it, trapping the small farmers and merchants into overmortgaging their property. Matt Haffigan will be dispossessed again from his hard-won farm; the limited independence achieved by the ex-agent Corny Doyle will be lost. And Rosscullen will be turned into a theme park, with its charm and its antiquities a marketable bonus for the tourists who come for its golfing hotel. Broadbent and Doyle's gospel of capitalist efficiency is denounced by Keegan at his most priest-like:

> when at last this poor desolate countryside becomes a busy mint in which we shall all slave to make money for you, with our Polytechnic to teach us how to do it efficiently, and our library to fuddle the few imaginations your distilleries will spare, and our repaired Round Tower with admission sixpence, and refreshments and penny-in-the-slot mutoscopes to make it interesting, then no doubt your English and American shareholders will spend all the money we make for them very efficiently in shooting and hunting, in operations for cancer and appendicitis, in gluttony and gambling; and you will devote what they save to fresh land development schemes. For four wicked centuries the world has dreamed this foolish dream of efficiency; and the end is not yet. But the end will come. (Shaw, *CPP*, II, 1018)

Shaw, here through Keegan, prophesies the neo-colonial era of global capitalism which will render the long-contested issue of national independence obsolete and irrelevant.

But if Keegan is given this dystopic prevision of Ireland's future, he voices also, for some impossibly distant time beyond, a Utopian dream of heaven:

> In my dreams it is a country where the State is the Church and the Church the people: three in one and one in three. It is a commonwealth in which work is play and play is life: three in one and one in three. It is a temple in which the priest is the worshipper and the worshipper the worshipped: three in one and one in three. It is a godhead in which all life is human and all humanity divine: three in one and one in three. It is, in short, the dream of a madman. (Shaw, *CPP*, II, 1021)

Whatever we are to make of this highly heterodox Trinitarianism, so remote from anything recognisable as Catholicism or even Christianity, what is suggestive is its special relation to Ireland. Although Keegan disclaims any interest in national boundaries – 'My country is not Ireland nor England, but the whole mighty realm of my Church' (Shaw, *CPP*, II, 1019–20) – he attacks Larry Doyle fiercely in defence of Ireland as 'holy ground', 'holy ground which such Irishmen as you have turned into a Land of Derision' (Shaw, *CPP*, II, 1019). If it is the function of Larry in the play to demystify Ireland by exploding the stereotypes of stage Irish and the misconceptions of Irish politics, it is the role of Keegan to remystify it. As Shaw says in the 'Preface for Politicians', '"The island of the saints" is no idle phrase. Religious genius is one of our national products; and Ireland is no bad rock to build a Church on' (Shaw, *CPP*, II, 837). The saintly Keegan is a specifically Irish saint and his pantheistic vision privileges Ireland as sacred site.

The ending of *John Bull*, like so much of the play, is remarkable for its poised balance. If the strategy of the action throughout involves the equitable distribution of satire, a playful iconoclasm which never becomes politically partisan, the conclusion affords to an audience a held doubleness of feeling and thought. With Keegan's exit, Broadbent and Doyle are left in possession, literally and metaphorically. Their uncomprehending exchanges, Broadbent's last line – 'Come along and help me to choose the site for the hotel' (Shaw, *CPP*, II, 1022) – provide a coda of ironic diminuendo. Keegan's marginal status as mad dreamer and the inevitability of the syndicated Rosscullen which he has forecast seem to be underscored by these final moments. Yet significantly, for all Keegan's denunciations of the Land Development

Syndicate and what it stands for, he tells Broadbent that 'I may even vote for you' (Shaw, *CPP*, II, 1015). There is a hint here of Shavian socialist meliorism, the belief that social and political progress must come through the development of capitalism, predatory and soul-denying as it inevitably is. But for all that, as Keegan 'goes away across the hill' (Shaw, *CPP*, II, 1021), he continues to command the high ground of Ireland and the Round Tower. He gives the promise of a perspective beyond the colonial present of John Bull's other island, beyond the immediate future to be controlled by Broadbent and Doyle. 'Every dream is a prophecy: every jest is an earnest in the womb of Time' (Shaw, *CPP*, II, 1021). If the play's dialectic counterpoints the imagined Ireland of a Boucicault with a sharply etched Shavian reality, it also allows the audience the inspiration of some transcendent future Ireland of the mind.

Translations

Translations, unlike *The Shaughraun* and *John Bull*, is set almost 150 years back in time, but even more than the other two plays it was a product of the contemporary situation in which it was composed. Writing a play around a 1830s Irish hedge-school centring on the loss of the Irish language and the Anglicising Ordnance Survey mapping of Ireland, Friel in 1979 was highly aware of the unfinished business of the English–Irish colonial connection represented in the violence of Northern Ireland, which had then been continuing for ten years. The joint decision by Friel and Stephen Rea to set up the Field Day Theatre Company to tour the play in both parts of Ireland, with an opening in Derry, was also animated by cultural politics. Given their status as internationally recognised playwright and actor, this was a very significant gesture by Friel and Rea, challenging the cultural hegemony of Dublin and Belfast in Ireland as the Irish Literary Theatre had challenged the theatrical authority of London by its seasons in Dublin eighty years before. Friel's play and the Field Day movement which it started sought to provide new ways of thinking about Ireland, of giving expression to the unexpressed in Ireland, in the face of the depressingly intractable Irish political situation.

Translations was a massive national and international success. Whereas Friel's more polemical *The Freedom of the City* had received a hostile press reception in Britain, and *Faith Healer* (his immediately previous play) had crashed catastrophically in New York, everyone loved *Translations*, critics and audiences alike. They loved it, though, for significantly different reasons, as Marilynn Richtarik has helpfully shown in her analysis of the reviews of the first production in Northern Ireland, the Republic and Britain.[46] In Northern Ireland generally, and in Derry in particular, there was simply delight that it was happening at all – and happening there. It was a measure of the low morale of the time that nationalists and unionists, Protestants and Catholics, were deeply grateful for such a cultural initiative taking place in the deprived and depressed town of Derry. They were prepared to regard the politics of the play as uncontentious, or indeed to disregard the fact that the play had a politics at all. Not so the reviewers from the southern part of the island; in the papers there the play was acclaimed for the way it showed 'the rape of the local culture by the imported one', 'a rural community with the hands of an empire at its throat and the boot of an imperial power at its chest'.[47] Perhaps unsurprisingly, British reviewers failed to see it in quite this light, but they were equally approving. In London *Translations* was valued for its lack of political polemic, for its wonderful dramatic rendering of the hedge-school, and the openness of its ending was stressed. With the play going on to successful production in America and many other countries and languages, Friel had created an Irish drama almost universally admired.

Such political resistance as there was to the play came not from theatre audiences or reviewers but from academics, literary critics and historians. Objections were made to Friel's inaccuracies and misrepresentations. It was pointed out that the hedge-schools were not taught exclusively through Irish as shown in *Translations*; indeed English was one of the most sought-after subjects in such schools as parents tried to ensure that their children acquired the means to progress in an Anglophone world. The National School system, instituted in the 1830s in Ireland, was not a malign instrument of British colonial policy to do away with the hedge-schools and eradicate the Irish language, as it appears to be in Friel's play. Above all, the Ordnance Survey map was not the process of Anglicising cultural appropriation, akin to eviction, which the play suggests.[48]

The map-makers tried specifically to establish place-names as close as possible to Irish originals and employed for this purpose John O'Donovan (equivalent to Owen in the play), one of the great scholars of the Irish language in his generation. In fact, rather than being, as Friel implies, a barely concealed military operation oblivious to local culture, the OS project began with a wildly over-ambitious project (as it turned out) to record all the place-related folklore of the country. No officer in the unarmed Royal Engineers conducting the survey could possibly have threatened the series of reprisals, evictions, the burning of houses and slaughter of stock which Captain Lancey does for the murder of Yolland in *Translations*.

Friel stuck to his guns on the issue of historical inaccuracy. He claimed his rights as a dramatist to alter facts: 'Drama is first a fiction, with the authority of fiction. You don't go to *Macbeth* for history.' He apologised only for the 'tiny bruises inflicted on history in the play'.[49] Some critics, however, refused to accept that only 'tiny bruises' were involved. The historian Sean Connolly claimed that '*Translations* represents a distortion of the real nature and causes of cultural change in nineteenth-century Ireland so extreme as to go beyond mere factual error.'[50] The argument here was not to do with the historical inaccuracy of the play itself but with the political consequences of giving authority to a quite fallacious idea of Ireland's past. In a similar vein, Edna Longley attacked the play for its failure to demythologise the nationalist reading of history: 'the play does not so much examine myths of dispossession and oppression as repeat them'.[51] It is not my concern here to enter into this controversy over the play's historical accuracy, but rather to pursue the question of how it constructs its interpretation of Ireland and for what potential audiences.

The quotation from Friel about *Translations* at the beginning of this chapter is a striking one in relation to the strategy of the play:

> apart from Synge, all our dramatists have pitched their voices for English acceptance and recognition ... However I think that for the first time this is stopping ... We are talking to ourselves as we must and if we are overheard in America, or England, so much the better.

By invoking Synge with its metaphor of overhearing, there seems to be an association of ideas with the famous/infamous passage in the 'Preface' to *The Playboy* which caused so much trouble:

> When I was writing *The Shadow of the Glen*, some years ago, I got more aid than any learning could have given me, from a chink in the floor of the old Wicklow house where I was staying, that let me hear what was being said by the servant girls in the kitchen.[52]

Nationalist critics seized on this image of the gentleman eavesdropper as it defined Synge's externality to the life he dramatised. Friel, in positing himself and the newly self-confident Irish dramatists of 1980 as 'talking to ourselves', overheard by London and New York, is claiming a new insider status with the servant girls in the kitchen, and no longer merely listening in.

The opening scene of *Translations* does indeed present itself without an outside interpreter. There is, initially, no Captain Molineux to misconceive and misconstrue, no Broadbent needing to be educated out of gullible belief in stage Irishry, just the community of the hedge-school, pupils and teachers, Sarah and Manus, Maire, Bridget and Doalty and finally Hugh the master himself. *Translations* begins by imagining from within the Irish hedge-school looking outward, rather than using a malcomprehending outsider as a way in. But the dramatic present of the scene is heavily conditioned by any audience's knowledge of it as an irretrievable past. The characters in casual expository conversation reach out to the local news, the opening of a National School in the neighbourhood, the coming of the map-making sappers to their area, new news to them but already loaded with consequences for those watching in a late twentieth-century theatre. The pathos and the irony of their unknowing is accentuated in the exchanges over the 'sweet smell', the feared harbinger of potato blight. Maire, the moderniser, the advocate of English and progress, protests in spirited terms at the gloomy prognosticators:

> Sweet smell! Sweet smell! Every year at this time somebody comes back with stories of the sweet smell. Sweet God, did the potatoes ever fail in Baile Beag? Well, did they ever – ever?

> Never! There was never blight here. Never. Never. But we're always sniffing about for it, aren't we? – looking for disaster.[53]

Some audiences may have had little knowledge of the National Schools or the Ordnance Survey, but everyone would have been aware of the Famine, the 'Great Hunger' as it had become widely known from the title of Cecil Woodham-Smith's 1962 popular history.[54] Pressing on Maire's brave resistance, therefore, is the doomed sense that the potato blight *will* hit Baile Beag, like all the other poor western seaboard areas where the famine was most acute, and that the disaster-mongers are to be proved all too right. In associating the Famine with the Ordnance Survey (the 'sweet smell' is detected 'just beyond where the soldiers are making the maps'), and both with the coming of the National Schools, Friel conjoins various factors which together were to bring about the destruction of Irish-speaking Ireland. The awareness of that coming destruction pre-interprets, as it were, the scene of the hedge-school. We are not watching here a vanishing Ireland like that of Synge – 'in Ireland, for a few years more, we have a popular imagination that is fiery and magnificent, and tender' (Synge, *CW*, IV, 54); this is a vanished Ireland.

Friel himself was apparently taken aback at the tendency to read his play as idyll.

> Several people commented that the opening scenes of the play were a portrait of some sort of idyllic, Forest of Arden life. But this is a complete illusion, since you have on stage the representatives of a certain community – one is dumb, one is lame and one is alcoholic, a physical maiming which is a public representation of their spiritual deprivation.[55]

This is a forceful point, and there is no doubt that opening the play with the almost dumb Sarah trying to say her name is a potent image for a nearly stifled Irish-speaking community. But surely the emphasis is on the positive efforts of Manus to enable her to speak, and the partial success of those efforts. The hedge-school is idyll in so far as it imagines a site where education is for all, for all ends and all capacities, from the remedial linguistics of Sarah's needs, through the elementary rudiments scratched out by Bridget and Doalty, to the

Latin and Greek which the very mature student Jimmie Jack reads for enjoyment and companionship. Whatever the deficiencies of the drunken Hugh – and his drunkenness is treated with great indulgence almost as a grace rather than a disability – the hedge-school is idyll for a contemporary audience in as much as it is pre-colonial and pre-modern, before the fall into Anglicised institutionalisation. This is a school such as the de-schooling idealists of the 1960s might have dreamed it, the archaism of its rote-learning and catechetical method given charm and attractiveness by the sportive good humour of both teachers and taught.

The easy awareness of classical literature among the people of the hedge-school, their fluency in Greek and Latin, provided openings for cultural self-congratulations on the part of Irish nationalist audiences, and there is some simple point-scoring off the supposedly monoglot English officers. If Boucicault's Captain Molineux talking of 'a distinguished Fenian hero' in the 1860s is one kind of implausibility, an 1830s Captain Lancey who cannot tell Latin from Irish is almost as hard to swallow. There is, though, a broader appeal to the idea of a pan-European culture represented in the hedge-school than merely a one-upping exercise for the Irish over the English. The supposedly unself-conscious juxtaposition of Gaelic and classical culture, a Grania with a Helen, Cuchulain with Apollo, suggests deep structures of significance that predate the colonial English–Irish polarity. In response to Yolland's naive enthusiasm for what he has found in the hedge-school, the fluency in Latin and Greek, the classical etymologies of the Irish place-names, Hugh replies: 'We like to think we endure around truths immemorially posited' (Friel, *SP*, 418). There may well be irony here; it is in this scene, according to the stage direction, that 'one has the sense that [Hugh] is deliberately parodying himself' (Friel, *SP*, 416–17). But the hedge-school culture, as imagined in *Translations*, does give renewed authority to the idea of an unchanging pre-colonial Celtic past dating back to time immemorial, the idea which in the nineteenth century was symbolised (in one view of things) by the round towers.

The attractiveness of this imagined past is enhanced by being apparently pre-Christian as well as pre-colonial and pre-modern. There must have been a priest to christen Nellie Ruadh's baby in the offstage action of Act I; there will need to be one to bury the poor infant in Act III. But the only direct reference to such a figure is when Hugh, as applicant for the post of schoolmaster in the new National School, goes off to get 'a testimonial from our parish priest – a worthy man but barely literate' (Friel, *SP*, 417). There is no equivalent to Boucicault's reassuringly benevolent Father Dolan in *Translations*, no counterpart to Shaw's politically powerful Father Dempsey. We hear nothing of one of the main objectives of the National School system, which was to set up a non-sectarian form of education, nor yet of the strong and in the end successful campaigns by all the churches to resist that objective and ensure that they controlled the schools. The hedge-school is a secular, if not a pagan place. Friel's Baile Beag is Edenic in so far as it dramatises a community not yet affected by the guilt of Christian religion or the knowledge of modernity. However roseate Yolland's view may be, he registers something of an audience's feelings when he speaks of his coming to Baile Beag as a revelation, 'of experience being of a totally different order. I had moved into a consciousness that wasn't striving nor agitated, but at its ease and with its own conviction and assurance' (Friel, *SP*, 416).

Friel does not provide the romantic Irish landscapes of round towers and ruined abbeys of Boucicault and Shaw, but he gives instead a genre scene of the hedge-school which is picturesque, archaic, truly rural. The setting, with its improvisatory cowbyre-turned-school, the disused farming paraphernalia in sight, adds to the charm. Though we see none of the ritual communal set-pieces equivalent to the wake in *The Shaughraun*, we are aware of them as actions off: the drunken christening and wake for Nellie Ruadh's baby, the crossroads dance attended by Yolland with such disastrous consequences. Friel, in disgust at the way in which audiences had consumed the hedge-school as kitsch, wrote his farce *The Communication Cord* as antidote, satirising bourgeois modern nostalgia for the cowbyre as primitive source of origin. But it is hard to imagine how a production of *Translations* could avoid rendering its scene as more-or-less picturesque, given its pastness, its difference, its Irishness.

The opening sequence of *Translations* may be unmediated, uninterpreted, drama, but the interpreter is to arrive shortly, and interpretation is of course the play's main theme. The transformation of the historical John O'Donovan into the play's Owen is the one piece of misrepresentation for which Friel was fully apologetic, and in significant terms:

> I read into O'Donovan's exemplary career as a scholar and orthographer the actions and perfidy of a quisling. (The only excuse I can offer for this short-lived delusion is that the political situation in the North was particularly tense about that time.) Thankfully that absurd and cruel reading of O'Donovan's character and career was short-lived. But it soured a full tasting of the man. And O'Donovan appears in the play as a character called Owen.[56]

Owen enters the hedge-school as the returning son, hail-fellow-well-met, with the good word for everybody. But his social skills and bonhomie are suspect in contrast with the gauche earnestness of his brother Manus, and his role as interpreter is stigmatised from the beginning. In the cleared theatrical space of a pause, he announces his position with the army almost as a confession: 'I'm on their payroll.' Though he laughs aside the idea he has enlisted as a soldier – 'I'm employed as a part-time, underpaid, civilian interpreter' (Friel, *SP*, 403–4) – there is a strong sense that he has gone over to the other side. When we see him in operation 'translating' Lancey's bureaucratic government humbug into palatable terms which mask its real meaning to the people of Baile Beag, the traditional equation 'translator=traitor' is given a new political force.

In terms of the succession of stage interpreters considered in this chapter, the characterisation of Owen comes as a striking shift. Though Owen may have some of the theatrical attractiveness of Conn the Shaughraun, his structural position is closer to that of the hated middleman. 'Isn't this a job for the go-between?' (Friel, *SP*, 408) he says ironically, as he introduces English to Irish at the end of Act I. The part of go-between, so reconciliatory in Boucicault's Conn, has become in Owen a kind of trimming pander. Owen understands Baile Beag, as Larry Doyle understood Rosscullen, but that understanding is not given the authority it had with Doyle. Owen is hardly represented as a villain, though nationalist reviewers were to see him as just that: there is in him none of that bitter self-hatred turned to destructiveness against his home country which Shaw diagnoses as the psychopathology of the returned emigrant in Larry. He acts, as he thinks, practically, rationally, with no ill-will to anyone. There is apparent good sense in his response to Yolland's guilty feelings about the nature of the Ordnance Survey:

> YOLLAND. . . . It's an eviction of sorts.
> OWEN. We're making a six-inch map of the country. Is there something sinister in that? (Friel, *SP*, 420)

Yet this is only apparent good sense. The play as a whole supports Yolland's view; the mapping and re-naming of the Irish landscape *is* an eviction of sorts, and there is nothing anyone can do to stop it.

What has changed from Boucicault or Shaw to Friel is a new scepticism about interpretation itself, especially in a colonial context. George Steiner's *After Babel*, one of Friel's major sources for the play's ideas about language, stressed the all but impossibility of translation/interpretation.[57] Friel borrows phrases and adapts sentences from Steiner in the text, including Hugh's final doubtful and reluctant agreement to teach Maire English:

> I will provide you with the available words and the available grammar. But will that help you to interpret between privacies? (Friel, *SP*, 446)

If, as Steiner maintains, there is an element of translation in any speech-act even within a shared native language, and thus 'all communication "interprets" between privacies',[58] what chance is there of true interpretation in an acquired language, a language imposed from without by a colonial power? *Translations* depends on a tragic vision of an historically determined colonial process which is to leave the Irish people spiritually and psychologically dispossessed, through the loss of a language unable any longer to say who they are and where they are. In these terms Baile Beag becomes radically uninterpretable, and the efforts of such as Owen to interpret between English and Irish are at best misguided, at worst a betrayal.

It is a similar belief that informs the version of national romance exemplified by Maire and Yolland leading to the play's tragic climax and catastrophe. Between Maire and Yolland there are not just the very superficial tokens of national difference easily overcome by Claire and Molineux, nor even the cultural cross-purposes of Nora and Broadbent; there is instead an unbridgeable gap, severing communication. In their one love-scene together, they can only express their mutual attraction in an antiphonal recitation of the Irish place-names learned by Yolland in his map-making. This is suggestive of the attachment to place which so frequently serves as marker for national identity within Irish literary and dramatic representation, an identity which escapes from political and sectarian definition. It acts as ritual invocation of that spirit of place felt as some sort of authentic site and origin of being. But as a means of communication it can only have its fragile moment before it is destroyed by the violent forces of history. The pathos of the scene lies in its very brevity, the sense of its ultimate impossibility. Within the colonial context the dream of intermarriage is like the attempt at interpretation, a hopeless hope. If *The Shaughraun*'s upbeat ending of marriages and reconciliation all round may be said to typify the age of Empire in which it was written, if *John Bull* with its more quizzical and ironic version of national interrelationship was produced for a time that still had hopes of Home Rule, the tragedy of *Translations* speaks to something like a postcolonial orthodoxy in which the colonial connection is seen retrospectively as a 'doom', vitiating everything and everyone, coloniser and colonised alike.

The paradox of *Translations* is that a play asserting the irrecoverable and uninterpretable nature of the pre-colonial past should have acted as such a readily available interpretation of the Irish experience for so many diverse audiences both in Ireland and outside. One key to that paradox is the central theatrical device by which the supposedly Irish-speaking characters on stage in fact speak English, just as the English do. This, in a sense, enacts the consequences of what the play dramatises: Irish *was* destroyed as Ireland's mother-tongue, so that by 1980, even within the Republic of Ireland after nearly sixty years of state-sponsored language revival, Irish-speaking characters could only be intelligible to most audiences by having them speak English. But by a sort of sleight of hand the play's practice of this device allows the dramatist to have it both ways: to register incomprehension and cultural impenetrability while achieving lucid, subtle and skilful communication.

Friel employs the English-for-Irish convention selectively, according to the practical requirements of the individual scene. So, for instance, in Act II Manus, who has deliberately and obtusely refused to speak English 'for the benefit of the colonist' Yolland, appears to switch languages when he communicates the good news of the job he has been offered in Inis Meadhon. At this high point of hope and good humour in the play, Friel dispenses with the need for Owen as interpreter. Equally, in the scene somewhat earlier in the act where Hugh talks to Yolland about the nature of Irish culture and language, he is presumed to be talking English to be directly understood. But it is exactly the same English as that which he speaks when he is speaking 'Irish', an English sufficiently fluent and capacious to include pieces of George Steiner's prose without sounding specially odd:

> You'll find, sir, that certain cultures expend on their vocabularies and syntax acquisitive energies and ostentations entirely lacking in their material lives. I suppose you could call us a spiritual people.[59] (Friel, *SP*, 418)

The difference between Hugh's 'English' English and his 'Irish' English can be so readily effaced, his speech can carry such intellectual formality without strain, because the language of the hedge-schoolmaster is really English from the beginning.

The hedge-schoolmaster as literary character was first created by William Carleton in his *Traits and Stories of the Irish Peasantry.* Carleton's Matt Kavanagh in 'The Hedge School' is a comic character who advertises his learning by the pedantic formality of his speech. The hedge-schoolteacher, as imagined by Carleton, proclaims his mastery by his use (and misuse) of the 'tall, high-flown English'[60] which parents hope their children may acquire from him. It is in this tradition that Friel is working with his figure of Hugh, drunkenness included; for, as Carleton says of hedge-schoolmasters, 'one of their strongest recommendations to the good opinion of the people, as far as their literary talents and qualifications were concerned, was an inordinate love of whiskey'.[61] Hugh's language is ballasted with a Latinate vocabulary – 'verecund', 'conjugation', 'acquiesce' – which is used to display his authority and provides the basis for the quiz game of etymologies by which he keeps his pupils on their toes. But that authority, even the quiz game, is dependent on the language used being English. It is in English that the formal inflation of Latinity is registered as inflation; it is in that high style of Latinate English that the proximity of words to their classical roots is most apparent. And it is into such a prolix and pedantic English style that Friel can plausibly introduce the intellectual rhetoric of George Steiner, leaving it poised somewhere between straight and ironic statement.

Translations translates what is by the play's own terms of definition untranslatable; its supple and eloquent English speaks the lost and hidden language of Irish. An outside audience is allowed to understand an inside situation which is unintelligible to outsiders. What is more, they may understand it in different ways according to taste and inclination. There is a strong nationalist strain in the play starting with Manus's approval of Doalty's sabotage of the soldiers' surveying: 'It was a gesture [...] Just to indicate ... a presence' (Friel, *SP*, 391). The map-making is seen as an act of colonial dispossession to be resisted, the translation of place-names into English a cultural conquest, 'an eviction of sorts'. This metaphorical eviction is followed in swift and logical succession in the play by Lancey's threat of a very literal one, no less than the complete devastation of Baile Beag. Here Friel has coalesced, in his chosen time of 1833, the forms of colonial violence of later and earlier periods: the scorched-earth policies of a Cromwell and the atrocious system of reprisals of the Black and Tans in 1920–1 to create a single starkly dramatic image. It is, in some ways, no wonder that the play should have been approved by *An Phoblacht*, the Sinn Fein paper,[62] nor that it should have been accused by some critics of nationalist propaganda.[63]

And yet the vision of *Translations* can also be construed as one more of pity than of anger. The resistance struggle of the offstage proto-Provo Donnelly twins, who haunt the edges of the action and are responsible for the (presumed) death of Yolland, is certainly not endorsed. Rather, the Donnellys, and the silence in the community which falls on the mention of their names, are seen as part of the inevitable cycle of violence and intimidation which is endemic in the colonial process. Owen, translator/traitor that he is, receives more sympathy as the play goes on when he learns, too late, the implications of the mapping and his function in it. One turning-point comes as he disavows to Yolland his English alias of Roland: 'George! for God's sake! *My name is not Roland!* ... My name is Owen' (Friel, *SP*, 421). The shock of Yolland's abduction and of Lancey's fiercely punitive response, which Owen has to translate for the Irish-speakers, this time with absolute accuracy, move him a stage further towards an implied abandonment of the Ordnance Survey suggested in the stage direction: 'Owen picks up the Name-book. He looks at it momentarily, then puts it on top of the pile he is carrying. It falls to the floor. He stoops to pick it up – hesitates – leaves it' (Friel, *SP*, 442). When Hugh refers to the Anglicised place-names of the Name-book and says, 'We must learn these new names ... We must learn where we live. We must learn to make them our own. We must make them our new home', Owen replies defiantly: 'I know where I live' (Friel, *SP*, 444–5). By this point in the play, however, the gesture seems impotent and unconvincing. Owen's problem was that he has not known where he lived, not known what it was to live in Baile Beag until Baile Beag, partly through his agency, is too far gone in destruction to be saved.

In this concluding section of the play, the drunken schoolmaster Hugh moves into the position of authority which the mad ex-priest Keegan occupied in *John Bull*, their visions given all the more weight in the theatre because of the damaged and marginal social positions they occupy. Hugh's cautionary reminiscence of the abortive expedition he and Jimmie Jack undertook to join the '98 rebellion sponsors a humanist distrust of the heroics of revolution. This is no *Kathleen ni Houlihan* in which the country will be transformed by the blood-sacrifice of her patriots. Instead Hugh speaks its political ethics of doubt: 'My friend, confusion is not an ignoble condition' (Friel, *SP*, 446). What is more, the hedge-schoolmaster, the very representative of the Irish-speaking culture which is being destroyed, articulates the inevitability of that destruction and of the need to accommodate to it. In Act II he reminded Yolland that 'words are signals, counters. They are not immortal. And it can happen [...] that a civilization can be imprisoned in a linguistic contour which no longer matches the landscape of ... fact' (Friel, *SP*, 419). It is this thinking which gives the decisive force of political policy to his statement 'We must learn these new names.'

Keegan's prophetic position at the end of *John Bull* was Utopian, impossibilist, envisioning a future beyond imagining, certainly far beyond the short-term future of Rosscullen in the neo-colonial hands of Broadbent and Doyle. Hugh, speaking out of the imagined past of 1833, looks sadly forward to a future which is the known present of Friel's audience. The play's final political position is represented in Hugh's very moving, repeated, recitation of the lines from Virgil's *Aeneid*: '*Urbs antiqua fuit* – there was an ancient city which, 'tis said, Juno loved above all the lands' (Friel, *SP*, 446). The use of the Rome/Carthage, England/Ireland analogy here places an audience, like Virgil's Augustan readership, looking back from an achieved present at the terrible but distant struggles of the history which brought it about. Virgil's special melancholy imperialism, plangent with the awareness of loss in the triumphant progress of empire, here perfectly suits Friel's purpose. It affords Ireland's grim colonial history the amplifying dignity of the classical epic. It suggests the arbitrariness of the configurations of power in which one culture flourishes at the expense of another's ruin, Rome by the annihilation of Carthage, Britain by the colonisation of Ireland. And we in the audience, remote from the point of origin dramatised, must live however remorsefully with the consequences of the imperial, the colonial, condition.

This, in the play's dying fall, is the politically quietist strain in *Translations* which no doubt helped to make it popular with British audiences and reviewers. At the same time, the brilliant balancing-act of the text allowed nationalists the glory of their lost language and culture, indignant outrage at its violent extinction. *Translations*, in its very different way like *The Shaughraun* or *John Bull*, offers an interpretation of Ireland to suit a wide variety of interpretees, making of the potential contentiousness of its subject a multi-dimensional asset. In highlighting the issue of language, however, Friel makes of his tragic drama of destruction and loss a manifestation of triumphant success. This is, in one sense, a text in which the empire writes back, an Irish playwright uses the English language to commemorate the Irish culture of which the English colonists deprived him and his. Yet this is no deliberately hybridised English which the dramatist uses to undermine and challenge the hegemony of metropolitan received standard forms. Irish itself appears in the text only in the magical incantation of place-names; dialect and regional colloquialisms are used quite sparingly to add colour and texture to the dialogue. Instead Friel addresses metropolitan audiences in their own language handled with the assurance and skill of mastery. And so, for all that *Translations* was first staged in Derry, toured through the town halls and improvised stages of both parts of Ireland North and South, it is written with a confidence of being not only 'overheard' but understood and applauded in London and New York.

The politics of staging Ireland

This extended reading of three plays has been intended to illustrate the varying forms of Irish stage interpretation which they represent. What are the general features of the business of staging Ireland which emerge, and what are their implications for the politics of Irish drama which it is the object of this book to explore? To start with, there is the fact that Ireland continues to be matter for interpretation, a space, a place, a people needing explanation, 'an *explicandum*'.[64] There is a problematics of Ireland which makes dramatic interpretation marketable, Ireland as somewhere with ongoing political difficulties, Ireland as somewhere different within the English-speaking world. The phenomenon of the Fenians, the issues of land purchase and Home Rule, the Northern Troubles, provided Boucicault, Shaw and Friel with an occasion and an audience for drama. But beyond the immediate topicality of this or that political question of the day is the abiding sense that Ireland, in part because of its vexed colonial history, demands representation and understanding.

That history has also helped to provide the audience for Irish drama abroad as well as at home. While in Ireland there is the preoccupation with national identity of a colonised people, the worldwide diaspora of Irish emigrants, the huge populations of people of Irish descent particularly in North America and in Britain has made for a potentially global interest in plays on Irish themes. It was to such a market that Boucicault's Conn the Shaughraun was already catering. But even where a theatre is explicitly directed towards Irish audiences, the Irish Literary Theatre in 1897, Field Day in 1980, it is doubtful how far Irish playwrights are ever merely 'talking to ourselves' in Friel's phrase. Theatre is a metropolitan phenomenon and the larger the metropolis the more significant the success. And so, although *John Bull* may possibly have been written as 'a patriotic contribution to the repertory of the Irish Literary Theatre' (Shaw, *CPP*, II, 808), it was simultaneously planned as a major production in the repertory of the Court Theatre, London. Field Day was given enormous impetus not just by the warm reception of *Translations* throughout Ireland but by the international attention which went with that reception, and the high-profile productions outside Ireland that followed. Even plays and companies which originate in Ireland are given new validity and authority by travelling on to London and New York.

Ireland exists as interpretable matter for Irish playwrights partly for political, social and demographic reasons; theatrical markets make for an outward dynamic beyond Ireland itself. However, such a situation, the fact that Ireland is a subject for dramatic interpretation, has created an internal structure for Irish drama with inbuilt interpretative modes. It is not just that *The Shaughraun*, *John Bull* or *Translations* are skilfully constructed to appeal to a range of different sorts of audiences, English, Irish, American, nationalist and Unionist, Protestant and Catholic. Such plays interpret Ireland, not solely for a given group or mixture of groups in New York, London or Derry, but for a hypothetical audience of anyone with ears to hear and eyes to see. Ireland is always being more or less self-consciously staged for somebody's benefit. In this sense it could be said that all dramatised Irish men and women are stage Irish men and women. Pejorative associations of misrepresenting for profit aside, there is always a show of Ireland which is there to show people what Ireland characteristically, typically, is like.

Theatre renews itself recurrently by rejecting as stereotype the conventions of representation of a previous theatrical generation. In Irish drama this process of revisionism has tended to have a heavily political loading. The misrepresentations of stage Irishry are often linked (explicitly or implicitly) to the mistreatment of Ireland, and claims for a new realism and authenticity are commonly couched in the language of national self-assertion. Ireland requires not only interpretation, but reinterpretation to escape from the misconceptions of the past and indeed the present. Onstage interpreters in Boucicault, Shaw and Friel function variously in relation to this process of interpretation and its political imperatives: from Conn the facilitating, ingratiating creator of Utopian happy endings, through Larry Doyle with his emotionally maimed understanding replaced by the visionary wisdom of a Keegan, to the translator–traitor Owen paired with the comic/tragic meditations of Hugh. But always, whatever his relation to the interpreting characters within the action, the dramatist himself retains the position of master-interpreter in relation to the audience.

There is here a politics of the representation of Ireland as a space to be shown and decoded. The structural relations of such representation imply an audience who both know and do not know the scene represented, a playwright of superior authority, presumably more intimately familiar with Irishness than his audience, yet detached enough from the scene to be able to stand off and expound it. This is a complementary crossover of inside and outside perspectives. Ireland has to be recognisably Ireland, whether the scene is the picturesque landscape of Boucicault, the Round Tower of *John Bull* or the hedge-school of *Translations*. The attraction of such scenes is at once their strangeness, their difference and yet their identifiable and known Irishness. An audience must be extrinsic enough to appreciate the picturesque quality of Irish genre scenes, and yet be made to feel at home in them and with them. The playwright speaks to that double position with a doubleness of his own. Whether through the sponsorship of a character/interpreter or by unmasking such a figure as misinterpreter, the author's authority is grounded in a claimed knowledge of the reality represented on stage. Yet the staging is an act of mediation, going out to an audience with however limited an awareness, with whatever preconceptions and prejudices, and negotiating with them. Ireland is the space between dramatist and spectators, an area already known and yet needing the play to be understood. It is that space, in its varying forms over the last hundred years, which it is the business of the following chapters to explore.

2 Strangers in the house

BRIDGET. What was it put you wandering?
OLD WOMAN. Too many strangers in the house.
(*Kathleen ni Houlihan*[1])

'The author of "Kathleen Ni Houlihan" appeals to you.'[2] So Yeats in 1907 sought to win over the hostile audience of anti-*Playboy* protesters at the Abbey by a reminder of his nationalist credentials. But was he the author of *Kathleen ni Houlihan*, and were the stirring emotions generated by that play his work? Now that it has been clearly established that *Kathleen ni Houlihan* was a fully collaborative work in which Gregory had no less a part than Yeats, traditional readings of it as reflecting *his* creativity, *his* aesthetics or politics, have to be seriously revised.[3] But beyond that is the issue of what determines the political effect of a play such as *Kathleen ni Houlihan*, to what extent meaning is invested in the material from which the play is created, how far it is controlled by its author(s), or is a product of performance, audience, context. The political reaction to Synge's *The Shadow of the Glen*, staged just a year later, was as vehemently negative as the reaction to *Kathleen ni Houlihan* had been positive. Was it conceived as an ironic antidote to the idealising *Kathleen*, or were Synge's very different intentions wrested towards politics by the Dublin audiences and the nationalist press?

Both plays work with a very basic, a very simple theatrical trope, that of the stranger in the house, which reappears not only in *Kathleen ni Houlihan* and *The Shadow of the Glen* but in a wide range of the one-act plays of the early national theatre movement.[4] There were no doubt practical, contingent reasons why. The stranger-in-the-house pattern involves the very simple dramaturgy appropriate to novice playwrights and a beginning theatre movement. A three-walled set to represent a country-cottage kitchen, a family group, one major entrance and the ensuing complications and catastrophe were just about what the then skills of the dramatists and the resources of the theatre movement could run to, however much aesthetic and ideological considerations may have helped to determine the choice of peasant setting and uncomplicated staging. Within this context, however, two plays, Yeats's *The Land of Heart's Desire* and Gregory's *The Travelling Man*, may be set beside *Kathleen ni Houlihan* and *The Shadow of the Glen*, by way of exploring the different uses made of the strangers in the house by the first three Abbey directors, and their different political outcomes.

A room within a house, a family in the room, stand in for normality, for ordinary, familiar life; into the room there enters a stranger, and the incursion of that extrinsic, extraordinary figure alters, potentially transforms the scene. This pattern appears in no less than three of Ibsen's later plays, which can be used to illustrate a range of its potential theatrical effects to compare with the Irish versions of a similar theme. The status of the stranger who comes from without may be questionable: does he/she belong to the same 'real' world as the ordinary figures within the house or to some supernatural otherworld? So there is a held ambiguity about the nature of the stranger whose arrival is so dreaded/anticipated by Ellida Wangel throughout *The Lady from the Sea*; and when in *The Master Builder* Ellida's stepdaughter Hilde arrives punctually on cue at the house of Solness just as he is expressing his metaphorical anxiety about 'youth coming knocking at the door', we are left initially wondering whether she is more than a dream-projection. The sinister rat-wife in *Little Eyolf* is again a figure somewhere between mundane social actuality – the rodent-exterminator of her time – and a creature of folklore on a different plane from Allmers, Rita and the two 'little Eyolfs', Asta the sister(in-law), and Eyolf the lame child. In each case the stranger who comes from outside is, in his/her strangeness, the representative of an uncanny other, the *unheimlich* which contrasts with the home entered. Yet he/she is also an agent testing that 'home', finding out its hidden weaknesses or malaise, drawing away one or more of its family members to danger or death outside. An Ellida may resist the lure, a Solness or an Eyolf succumb, but survival or destruction alike are suggestive of meanings between the social/psychological realm of the house and the symbolic/spiritual dimension that lies beyond.

The varying uses to which the pattern of the strangers in the house is put by Yeats, Gregory and Synge extend the spectrum of significance set by the Ibsen plays. There are in the Irish cases mythological as well as folkloric sources and the possibility of mythopoeic meanings. Christian and pagan systems of belief overlap and clash in Yeats's and Gregory's texts as they hardly do in Ibsen's. What in Ibsen is no more than a suggestion of supernatural apparition moves in *Kathleen ni Houlihan* and *The Travelling Man* towards full theophany. Above all, within the context of the Irish national theatre movement, the Irish plays took on the status of typical, representative or even allegorical images. The Irishness of Kathleen ni Houlihan and the exemplary young man Michael who is prepared to give his life for her was ecstatically applauded; the Irishness of Synge's Nora Burke who goes out with the Tramp was as fiercely contested. Whatever the intentions of their creators, these dramatic strangers in the house were bound to be construed politically in the context of the time. The dramatic motif of the stranger in the house brings into play axes of inner versus outer, the material against the spiritual, familial, domestic life opposed to a life of individually chosen destiny. The strategy of this chapter is to look at the chosen quartet of plays, first of all in order to tease out the different imaginative cast brought to this pattern in *The Land of Heart's Desire*, a solo work of Yeats, as against *The Travelling Man* (which began as a collaborative piece but ended up as a more or less single-authored play by Gregory) and thus to illuminate the mixed effect of the jointly created *Kathleen ni Houlihan*. The political impact of the Yeats–Gregory allegory may then be the more tellingly contrasted with that of Synge's ironic realism in *The Shadow of the Glen*.

The Land of Heart's Desire

The Land of Heart's Desire is a staged version of the drama of the changeling latent in Yeats's earlier lyric 'The Stolen Child'. The poem is set entirely in the outer world of the fairies, the night landscape of Sligo round Lough Gill:

> Where dips the rocky highland
> Of Sleuth Wood in the lake . . .
>
> Where the wave of moonlight glosses
> The dim grey sands with light,
> Far off by furthest Rosses
> We foot it all the night . . .
>
> Where the wandering water gushes
> From the hills above Glen-car . . .[5]

In the first three verses, the refrain wooing the child away 'to the waters and the wild' floats in from the natural world animated by the fairies. Only in a single brilliant phrase in the final verse is the stolen child actually seen:

> Away with us he's going,
> The solemn-eyed[.] (Yeats, *VP*, 88)

On this fulcrum of the suddenly very human toddler, the poem changes direction and it is the homely sounds and sights that the child is leaving which materialise in the following lines:

> He'll hear no more the lowing
> Of the calves on the warm hillside
> Or the kettle on the hob
> Sing peace into his breast,
> Or see the brown mice bob
> Round and round the oatmeal-chest. (Yeats, *VP*, 88)

With this retro-thrust, the poem becomes a lyric of loss, and in the final refrain the escape into the sorrowless world of the fairies is an image of abduction, their world only sorrowless because inhuman.

> *For he comes, the human child,*
> *To the waters and the wild*
> *With a faery, hand in hand,*
> *From a world more full of weeping than he can understand.*
> (Yeats, *VP*, 88–9)

The Land of Heart's Desire reverses the perspective of 'The Stolen Child' by its setting within the homely interior into which the enticing fairy will come. Yeats makes possible an elaborated drama of conflict and choice by having the central figure not a mute child but a newly married bride, another traditional target for the fairies.[6] Mary Bruin, living for the first time in her husband's family home, is at a liminal point of transition, a state echoed at seasonal level by the play's setting on May Eve. Around are the figures that represent the normalities of her new life and its future: cross mother-in-law Bridget, complacent father-in-law Maurteen, the benevolent priest Father Hart. They are characterised only just enough to represent the types which are *not* there in the Land of Faery about which she reads:

> Where nobody gets old and godly and grave,
> Where nobody gets old and crafty and wise,
> Where nobody gets old and bitter of tongue.[7]

Placed ahistorically back in 'a remote time', the play is typically 'Celtic twilight' in picturing a scene where the mythology and folk belief of a pagan past are marginal memories in a Christian and materialist present. The story Mary reads of Princess Edain and her enchantment by the fairies comes from a book written by Maurteen's grandfather that has 'lain up in the thatch these fifty years' (Yeats, *CPl*, 55). The grandfather/author is remembered as impossibly unworldly:

> he was no judge of a dog or a horse,
> And any idle boy could blarney him[.] (Yeats, *CPl*, 56)

Maurteen is confidently philistine on the worthlessness of such books when set beside the rewards of his life of labour:

> Had I
> Or had my father read or written books
> There were no stocking stuffed with yellow guineas
> To come when I am dead to Shawn and you. (Yeats, *CPl*, 55)

And if Maurteen is there to teach Mary the prudential lesson not to waste time on such books, Father Hart warns of their dangers. In orthodox Christian terms, the fairies can only be evil spirits, followers of Satan's rebellion left wandering the world:

> it was some wrecked angel, blind with tears,
> Who flattered Edain's heart with merry words. (Yeats, *CPl*, 56)

In the context of a Celticism which privileged the spiritual and the cultural over the material, and an archaic pagan spirituality over conventional Christian belief, the attempted dissuasions of a Maurteen or a Father Hart could only have enhanced the attractiveness of the lure of the fairies. Yet there is an unexpected dimension to Father Hart's vision of things when he encourages the wavering Mary to a demonstrative expression of her love for Shawn:

> My daughter, take his hand – by love alone
> God binds us to Himself and to the hearth,
> That shuts us from the waste beyond His peace,
> From maddening freedom and bewildering light.
> (Yeats, *CPl*, 62)

This is unusual in its direct identification of erotic love with the love of the Creator, and enforces its image of the world beyond love with key Yeatsian terms. 'Maddening freedom' and 'bewildering light' sound forward in Yeats's poetry to the doom of the heroic life expressed in 'September 1913' with its 'delirium of the brave', or 'Easter 1916': 'And what if excess of love / Bewildered them till they died?' (Yeats, *VP*, 290, 394). The choice of Mary Bruin becomes, as it were, a choice of Achilles between the ordinary fulfilments of a long life and a short-lived tragic destiny. What is more, the exchanges between Shawn and Mary following these lines make it clear that love is not merely the domesticating spirit Father Hart imagines which binds to God and home:

> SHAWN. Would that the world were mine to give it you,
> And not its quiet hearths alone, but even
> All that bewilderment of light and freedom,
> If you would have it.
> MARY. I would take the world
> And break it into pieces in my hands
> To see you smile watching it crumble away. (Yeats, *CPl*, 62)

In love too there lurk the heroic aspirations, the sublime destructiveness supposed to be its antithesis.

The opposing values of *The Land of Heart's Desire* are in real conflict and a real drama results. The removal of the quicken bough which serves as protective talisman at the door-post, the ill-omened giving away of milk and fire on May Eve, above all Mary's culminating invocation at the height of her dissatisfaction – 'Come, faeries, take me out of this dull house!' (Yeats, *CPl*, 61) – all of these create the conditions for the entry of the fairy child. Even as the offstage song the child sings charms the audience with its lyric grace,

> The wind blows out of the gates of the day,
> The wind blows over the lonely of heart
> And the lonely of heart is withered away. (Yeats, *CPl*, 63)

the child enchants the onstage audience, armed and all as they are against her. In her beauty and apparent vulnerability she appeals to their protective instincts, and in her uncanny way she gives them flattering self-images. She can even persuade the priest to take down the crucifix with her estranging revulsion against its appearance:

> What is that ugly thing on the black cross? (Yeats, *CPl*, 65)

(Significantly, it was this incident, the reference to the body of Christ as a 'tortured thing', which was felt to be too shocking to allow the play into the repertoire of the Irish National Theatre Company in 1902.[8])

There is captivating charm in the fairy child, but there is terror too. Yeats makes use of a doubleness of representation here comparable to that in *A Midsummer Night's Dream*. While Shakespeare plays with the pretty diminutiveness of Cobweb and Peaseblossom, the delicate and ornate artifice of the fairies' natural world, Oberon and Titania are gods of power whose dissension causes cosmic chaos. Similarly, Yeats's fey child, as she faces the impotent Father Hart, transmutes into a being quite other than the vulnerable creature who invited indulgent pity:

> Because you took away the crucifix
> I am so mighty that there's none can pass,

Unless I will it, where my feet have danced
Or where I've whirled my finger-tips. (Yeats, *CPl*, 68)

In the contest for the spirit of Mary Bruin which follows, all the Christian exhortations of the priest, all the courageous love of Shawn, cannot withstand the magnetic force of the fairy. Mary dies and the child exits triumphant.

To those left on stage the pathos of the death and its spiritual significance make for a catastrophe. 'Come from that image', says Bridget as the stricken Shawn bends over his dead wife:

body and soul are gone.
You have thrown your arms about a drift of leaves,
Or bole of an ash-tree changed into her image.
FATHER HART. Thus do the spirits of evil snatch their prey
Almost out of the very hand of God. (Yeats, *CPl*, 71–2)

That gloomy sense of tragic defeat is modified for the theatre audience by a choric reprise of the fairy lyric with dancing figures outside:

The wind blows out of the gates of the day,
The wind blows over the lonely of heart,
And the lonely of heart is withered away (Yeats, *CPl*, 72)

The song, in Yeats's most accomplished early style, has no less eerie grace the second time we hear it. But, as with the last repetition of the refrain in 'The Stolen Child', it sounds a different note in the new context. The release into the land of heart's desire, the removal of the world's sorrow, is a denaturing of the human expressively rendered as desiccation: 'the lonely of heart is *withered* away'. The play, slight as it is, dramatises the tension between two opposed orders of being, the one a state of mortal limitation and change but also of life and love, the other an alienated state of changeless beauty in nature, and it ends with that tension unresolved.

The Travelling Man

The Travelling Man had an odd genesis which has been illuminatingly reconstructed by James Pethica.[9] Based on a legend Gregory collected on Slieve Echtge and included in *Poets and Dreamers*, it was initially written as a collaborative effort with Yeats in early November 1902 when, following the success of *Kathleen ni Houlihan*, they had been working together on a number of new plays including *Where There is Nothing* and *A Pot of Broth*. Yeats was not happy with the result, and after an inconclusive exchange of views between the co-authors, there was a second attempt at the play re-written in the pagan mode Yeats favoured. This version, first apparently called *The Country of the Young*, and then *The Wild Horse*,[10] may have been composed at Coole in March 1903 but was abandoned not long after. At Yeats's urging in 1905, Gregory completed the play, with Yeats supplying the 'Rider's Song', and this was the only part of the play which she acknowledged as specifically his.[11] It was published first in 1906, collected in *Seven Short Plays*, and finally produced at the Abbey in 1910. In itself it is hardly one of Gregory's best works, but it is interesting for the light it throws on her distinctive characteristics as a writer, her collaboration with Yeats and thus on *Kathleen ni Houlihan*.

The original story tells of a poor homeless girl who meets the Saviour, is sent to the house of a man whose wife has just died and eventually marries him. When in due course the Saviour comes to the house 'with the appearance of a poor man', she denies him the few grains of wheat for which he asks: 'Wouldn't potatoes be good enough for you?' At this, he takes nine grains and leaves, causing all the rest of the wheat to disappear. The woman realises who he is and follows after him, begging forgiveness. Christ points the lesson of her ingratitude: 'From this out, whenever you have plenty in your hands, divide it freely for My sake' (Gregory, *CP*, III, 374). The play elaborates on the little folk-story, giving the woman (identified only as Mother) a child old enough to act as interlocutor and to be told the tale of the meeting with 'the King of the World'. The occasion is the anniversary of the woman's coming to the house and she is making a special cake in anticipation that on one of these anniversaries the King may return as he promised he would. When she goes out to borrow some white flour for the cake, the Travelling Man enters and plays with the Child, disrupting the orderly home, taking down special crockery from the dresser. The Mother is appalled when she returns to find her child in the arms of a beggarman, and is all the more outraged when she discovers that he has assisted in messing up her house. She refuses him a share of the cake that is being prepared, offering him cold potatoes instead. He leaves, is pursued by the Child who eventually comes back to say that the Travelling Man has walked across the flooded river. At last the Mother realises what she has done. 'He is gone, he is gone, and I never knew him! He was that stranger that gave me all! He is the King of the World!' (Gregory, *CP*, III, 28).

In gathering folklore with Yeats in the summer of 1897, Gregory commented in her diary that 'we found startling beliefs & came to the conclusion that Ireland is Pagan, not Xtian'.[12] Yeats, to a much greater extent than Gregory, *needed* to believe that Ireland was pagan not Christian, and he tried his best to move their collaborative play in that direction. The evidence of the paganised second version of the play, *The Country of the Young*, shows Yeats's effort to reconceive it in his terms.[13] The first appearance of Christ to the Mother is replaced by the recollected vision which she had when very young of a wild black horse, followed by the apparition of a young man with a silver bridle for it. It is the memory of the wild horse, the hope of catching it, and of seeing the young man return which has haunted her all through her married life. The central part of the story, with the exit of the Mother, the entrance of the Travelling Man and the play with the Child, is much as in the original and final version. But the ending is totally changed. After the Travelling Man is driven out, the play closes with the Child seeing the black horse again, a vision which significantly and, as she feels it, tragically, the Mother can no longer see.

Gregory's *The Travelling Man*, as it ended up, shows little sign of the pagan dimensions that Yeats wanted. It is true that the action is set at Samhain, the pre-Christian equivalent to Hallowe'en, and supernatural appearances other than that of Christ might well be expected. The Edenic vision of the Golden Mountain and its garden with a tree 'that has fruit and flowers at the one time', its four gates of gold, silver, crystal and white brass, could come from any mythological tradition. But the King of the World who first appears to the Mother with a crown 'made of the twigs of a bare blackthorn' (Gregory, *CP*, III, 22) can be none other than Christ with His crown of thorns. And throughout the action the Travelling Man is identified as the outcast and protector of outcasts. The Mother recalls how she was driven out originally 'because of some things that were said against me'. She did not dare to ask for shelter because she feared 'they might think some shameful thing of me, and I going the road alone in the night-time' (Gregory, *CP*, III, 21–2). She was then ashamed to be taken for someone like the people she supposes to be the natural companions of the Travelling Man as she drives him out:

> Go out of this now to whatever company you are best used to, whatever they are. The worst of people it is likely they are, thieves and drunkards and shameless women.

To which Christ, associate of publicans and sinners, assents:

> Maybe so. Drunkards and thieves and shameless women, stones that have fallen, that are trodden under foot, bodies that are worn with fasting, minds that are broken with much sinning, the poor, the mad, the bad ... (Gregory, *CP*, III, 28)

Yeats, full of the Nietzschean afflatus of *Where There is Nothing*, would have re-written these lines as follows:

> Those that like breaking the things about them the way a child likes to be breaking them: homeless happy people, flowing hearts in broken bodies: the saints, the poor, the mad, the bad, they are my friends.[14]

Nothing better marks the contrast between the orthodoxy of Gregory's Christian vision and the apocalyptic anarchism of Yeats.

The Travelling Man is, as it is subtitled, a 'Miracle Play'. Gregory's play follows the spirit of the original source in providing a folklorised version of Christian legend. The fable is domesticated to a peasant setting, and localised in the area around Coole. The mythical Slieve-na-nOr, the Golden Mountain, is imagined as close to the real Slieve Echtge where the source story was heard. The rising river which the Travelling Man eventually crosses so miraculously is at Ballylee, the site of what was to be Yeats's tower. Yeats too, in *The Land of Heart's Desire*, uses this combination of real locale and fabulous action: the play is set at least nominally in the 'Barony of Kilmacowen, in the County of Sligo' (Yeats, *CPl*, 53). But Yeats makes no effort to give the illusion of a solid offstage topography, as Gregory does. Everywhere in *The Travelling Man* specifying detail is used to create a texture of actuality: the Child interrupts the Mother every time she mentions a recognisable name – 'I know Kilbecanty. That is where the woman in the shop gave me sweets out of a bottle' (Gregory, *CP*, III, 22); the class-consciousness of the Mother – 'Did ever anyone see the like of that! A common beggar, a travelling man off the roads, to be holding the child!' (Gregory, *CP*, III, 26); the exceptional occasion represented by her baking with white flour – 'It is not often in the year I make bread like this' (Gregory, *CP*, III, 27).

The didactic spirit of *The Travelling Man* involves bringing home to an audience its Christian anti-materialist message by the simple homeliness of its setting. Its sentimentalism derives from the conscious effort of a sophisticated writer to mimic the naive style of folk-tale and folk-belief. Yeats never tried, or was never able, to mask the sophistication of his writing, to 'get down out of that high window of dramatic verse'[15] which remained his natural medium. The peasants of *The Land of Heart's Desire* speak a full Yeatsian blank verse liable to ludicrous bathos when it has to descend to the exchanges of the dinner-table: 'The butter is by your elbow, Father Hart' (Yeats, *CPl*, 59). But there are essential differences of substance as well as style in the way in which Yeats in *The Land of Heart's Desire* and Gregory in *The Travelling Man* imagine the incursion of the extraordinary upon the ordinary figured in the motif of strangers in the house. For Yeats the fairy child beckons towards a world of the uncanny which is at once strange and beautiful, attractive and terrible; to escape into it is not only to leave the clogging materialities of the human world but the nurturing ties of life and love as well. Gregory's Travelling Man, by contrast, represents the deepest and most authentic truth of being which passes unrecognised by those absorbed in the false values of day-to-day living. Yeats's play has an ending which can be read as tragic catastrophe or happy release; *The Travelling Man* concludes with a vision of transfiguration. These differences, which reflect the divergent beliefs and imaginative bent of the two authors, need to be registered when we look at *Kathleen ni Houlihan* as a collaborative creation.

Kathleen ni Houlihan

Kathleen ni Houlihan is, of course, radically unlike either *The Land of Heart's Desire* or *The Travelling Man* in that it did have political meanings written into its pre-script. Yeats spoke of its source in a famous passage of his letter of dedication to Gregory in the 1903 'Plays for an Irish Theatre':

> One night I had a dream almost as distinct as a vision, of a cottage where was well-being and firelight and talk of a marriage, and into the midst of that cottage there came an old woman in a long cloak. She was Ireland herself, that Kathleen ni Houlihan for whom so many songs have been sung and about whom so many stories have been told and for whose sake so many have gone to their death.[16]

Yeats here actualises in the supposedly real-life dream the convention of the *aisling*, the dream-vision of Ireland which was the main form of political poetry in Irish for some 150 years from the middle of the seventeenth century.[17] Moreover the motif of the *puella senilis*, the old woman transformed into the young girl with the walk of a queen and used in the dramatisation of the vision, had much older sources again. It has been traced back to the Celtic ur-myth of blood-sacrifice to the sovereignty goddess Eire in which the danger or death of a young man can rejuvenate the old crone to make her a fit mate for a new sovereign.[18] The many cognate female figurations of colonised Ireland as the Poor Old Woman, or Dark Rosaleen, would have given instant recognition value to Yeats's and Gregory's Kathleen ni Houlihan.

This in itself alters the dynamics of the play in relation to other versions of the stranger in the house. Elsewhere the strangeness of the stranger allows for varying sorts of recognition and misrecognition by characters on stage or by the audience in the auditorium, with meanings potentially deployed in the gap between recognition and misrecognition. With Ibsen's stranger in *The Lady from the Sea*, with Hilde Wangel or the Rat-wife, the audience fumble to identify the outsider as the characters do: good/bad, real/imaginary, natural/supernatural. In *The Land of Heart's Desire* the audience know the fairy child for what she is; the cottagers may suspect, but are bewitched into taking her for what she seems to be. The play's double ending combines the horror of the characters' belated recognition of what they see as evil with some element of continuing attraction on the part of the audience. There is no such dubiety in *The Travelling Man*: Christ is unmistakably Christ and unmistakably good in his disguise as beggar; the Mother's failure to identify him is only designed to enforce her mortal fallibility when the truth of the final transformation is declared. *Kathleen ni Houlihan*, as written and produced for a convinced nationalist audience, is closer to the condition of Gregory's *The Travelling Man* than Yeats's *The Land of Heart's Desire*, but its action and political effects derive from the interaction of its two authors.

'All this mine alone', wrote Gregory assertively of the first scene of the play up to and including the entrance of Kathleen on the earliest surviving draft.[19] Even without such evidence, this draft was easily identified as hers, with its concrete characterisation of the peasant family as they mull over the good fortune of Michael's approaching marriage: the story of how the dowry was bargained for, the hopes for extending the farm and for educating the second son for the priesthood. This is a Gregory genre scene with the typical concerns of the Irish country family etched in. It may even be thought characteristic that where Yeats's Bridget, the mother in *The Land of Heart's Desire*, has no function in the play but to be 'old and bitter of tongue', Gregory's Bridget reminds her husband forcibly of her contribution to their marriage when he momentarily slights her for having come to him as a dowry-less wife.

> If I brought no fortune I worked it out in my bones, laying down the baby, Michael that is standing there now, on a stook of straw, while I dug the potatoes, and never asking big dresses or anything but to be working ... (Gregory, *SW*, 303)

The pride of Augusta Gregory in the role of working woman speaks out of such lines.

The ground of stage reality established in this specificity of family life offers a resistance to the metaphorical when Kathleen enters. To the nationalist audience of the time already, much less to those at the other end of the century with ninety years' more familiarity with the still further hackneyed tropes of Irish political rhetoric, there must have been something almost obtuse in the Gillanes' non-recognition of the old woman's figures of speech:

> BRIDGET. What was it put the trouble on you?
> OLD WOMAN. My land that was taken from me.
> PETER. Was it much land they took from you?
> OLD WOMAN. My four beautiful green fields.
> PETER (*aside to* BRIDGET). Do you think could she be the widow Casey that was put out of her holding at Kilglass a while ago? (Gregory, *SW*, 306)

But the misrecognition of the allegorical Kathleen ni Houlihan as an actual dispossessed widow is only partially a misrecognition. A homology is enacted here between the national expropriation of colonial conquest and the local evictions familiar to any nineteenth-century peasant family. The gap between literal and figurative meaning is bridged so that one appears as the other writ large: Ireland's loss of sovereignty over her four provinces, her four green fields, is felt upon the pulse as the dispossession of a widow Casey from her holding at Kilglass.

If the first scene of *Kathleen ni Houlihan* Gregory claimed as 'all mine alone', the rest of the play she acknowledged as 'This with W.B.Y.'[20] and it is to Yeats the speeches of Kathleen are generally attributed. Certainly her vatic utterances are stylistically distinct from the homely Gregory dialect of the Gillane family. Yet even if the conception and execution of the character of Kathleen were mainly Yeats's, the effect of her interaction with the people of the cottage, her role in the play's action, may be largely influenced by Yeats's collaborator. James Pethica convincingly argues that the form of the play's nationalism may be more due to Gregory than to Yeats.[21] *Kathleen ni Houlihan* is strikingly linked by Lucy McDiarmid to an imaginative pattern running right through Gregory's writing in which imprisoned or executed patriots are the occasion of expressive power for women.[22] Certainly the emphasis on self-sacrifice in the play is consistent with the mood of Gregory's remarkable essay, 'The Felons of Our Land', published in *The Cornhill Magazine* in 1900, celebrating the tradition of Irish rebel ballads. That essay also suggests how far Gregory's religion as well as her nationalist conviction inform

Kathleen ni Houlihan. 'To the spiritual mind,' she remarks in her conclusion, 'the spiritual truth underlying each development of Christianity is always manifest.' But, she goes on to argue, there is 'a significant contrast in the outward form in which religion appears to the peasant of England and the peasant of Ireland'.

> To the English peasant the well-furnished village church, the pulpit cushion, the gilt-edged Bible, the cosy rectory, represent respectability, comfort, peace, a settled life. In Ireland the peasant has always before his eyes, on his own cottage walls or in his white-washed chapel, the cross, the spear, the crown of thorns, that tell of what once seemed earthly failure, that tell that He to whom he kneels was led to a felon's death.
>
> (Gregory, *SW*, 278)

Gregory's was not the religion of the Irish peasant. In this passage she positions herself with the readers of the *Cornhill* as one of the 'spiritual mind[s]' to whom 'the spiritual truth underlying each development of Christianity is always manifest'. But there is no doubt where her emotional allegiance lies between the English and the Irish peasant, and there is a strong political thrust in identifying the 'felons of our land' with the felon/founder of the Christian religion. Here, as much as in Yeats's dream, is the germ of *Kathleen ni Houlihan*.

If Gregory's diaries of the 1890s record her gradual development from the Liberal Unionist position of *A Phantom's Pilgrimage, or Home Ruin*, her pamphlet opposing the Home Rule Bill of 1893, to the (implicitly) revolutionary nationalism of 'The Felons of Our Land', they testify also to her steady if undemonstrative Anglican belief. Augusta Persse had reacted against the evangelicalism of her mother's conviction in salvation by faith alone,[23] and her life throughout this period in its church-going (Westminster Abbey when in London) and its good works (the Gort workhouse, the promotion of Irish goods from the local convent, the poor of Southwark) reflects her Broad Church practice. Her nationalism and her religion bear the stamp of the same principles: self-abnegating commitment to duty, service and the advancement of the causes to which she had given her loyalty. All this was compatible with a hard-headed practicality and a considerable degree of egotism, but self is smuggled in under the self-protecting mode of altruism: her books are designed to preserve the memory of her husband, to promote the cause of Irish culture; she stays on in London society (which she quite obviously enjoyed) in order to make a position for Robert when he is grown-up. Her sense of family duty, her Christian and her nationalist faith, are all distinguished by the same resolute single-mindedness and directed energy.

Yeats's nationalism, by contrast, was always deeply conflicted and his attitude towards Christianity seems to have oscillated between indifference and distaste. His restiveness with the simple Christian moralism of *The Travelling Man*, his need to paganise it or to twist it towards heterodoxy, are characteristic. So it seems probable that the elements of *Kathleen ni Houlihan* which most align it with scriptural parable bear the stamp of Gregory rather than Yeats. The Old Woman goes about the countryside looking for friends in her trouble much as Christ called disciples. 'There was one that had strong sons I thought were friends of mine, but they were shearing their sheep, and they wouldn't listen to me' (Gregory, *SW*, 305). The call is the test, like the invitations in the parable of the rich man's feast, and those too caught up in their worldly material lives fail it. The demand of Kathleen has the absolutism of Jesus, when she refuses the offer of alms: 'If anyone would give me help he must give me himself, he must give me all' (Gregory, *SW*, 308). This Christian ideal of complete self-sacrifice is hardly likely to have come from Yeats the maker of multiple, often stridently assertive, selves.

For the play's original audiences the religious colouring of the figure of Kathleen would have given her an unquestionable authority and legitimacy comparable to that of the 'King of the World' in *The Travelling Man*. As a result, other potentially more sinister elements in the figure, which might well be Yeatsian, are muffled or overwritten. It is Michael, on the point of marriage, who is to be drawn away by the old woman, just as it was Mary Bruin the newly married bride who falls under the spell of the fairy in *The Land of Heart's Desire*. In both plays marriage stands metonymically for all the human ties which bind us to one another and to the world, counterpoised with the otherness of an otherworld. In *The Land of Heart's Desire* to yield to this otherness is death, and in *Kathleen ni Houlihan* there is an erotics of death in the attraction of the old woman. 'It is not a man going to his marriage that I look to for help' (Gregory, *SW*, 308), she hints darkly. 'With all the lovers that brought me their love I never set out the bed for any' (Gregory, *SW*, 308). Within the tradition of female personifications of Ireland, the object of desire could be abused as a faithless whore who has given herself to strangers, as well as pitied for her abandoned loverless state.[24] In the Yeats–Gregory play she is, at least vestigially, a romantic *belle dame sans merci*, the woman who lures man away from sexual consummation towards death.

That dimension to the figure is both enacted and glorified in the play's climactic ending. The original script apparently called for Michael to remain standing on the threshold, caught between the claims of Delia, his bride-to-be, and the old woman. But Maud Gonne, playing Kathleen, significantly and characteristically insisted that this was a weak ending and it was changed in rehearsal to have him rush out following the strains of the Old Woman's song:

> They shall be speaking for ever,
> The people shall hear them for ever. (Gregory, *SW*, 309)

Bridget and Delia were left in a tableau embrace of consolation.[25] Men must die and women must weep. This is then sacralised by the play's famous last line as Peter asks the younger son Patrick who has just come in: 'Did you see an old woman going down the path?' To which comes the reply: 'I did not, but I saw a young girl, and she had the walk of a queen' (Gregory, *SW*, 311).

Such an ending is characteristically Yeatsian in so far as he favoured strong closure and revelatory last lines in his dramaturgy. The action of *Calvary* concludes with Christ's bitter cry from the Cross, 'My Father, why hast Thou forsaken Me?' (Yeats, *CPl*, 456), given quite new meaning by the succession of nay-sayers in the play who have refused the sacrifice of redemption. The last scene of *The Resurrection* rings out with the cry of the Greek, 'The heart of a phantom is beating! The heart of a phantom is beating!' (Yeats, *CPl*, 593). What is untypical of Yeats in the ending of *Kathleen ni Houlihan* is the lack of emotional ambiguity which it generates. The transformative epiphany of the rejuvenated Kathleen gives unequivocal validation to the sacrifice of Michael. The audience sees the cost in the broken lives of Delia and Bridget, perhaps, but the cost is well worth it, for assuredly there, outside the door though invisible, is the young girl with the walk of a queen. This in its apotheosis of the stranger in the house approximates much more closely to the vision ending of *The Travelling Man* than it does to the two-way facing dramatics of the changeling in *The Land of Heart's Desire*. To that extent, whoever wrote which bit, *Kathleen ni Houlihan* may be accounted a product of Gregory's rather than Yeats's imagination.

'All art,' Synge was to say, 'is a collaboration' and there were many more collaborators besides Yeats and Gregory in the theatrical event of the first production of *Kathleen ni Houlihan*. Adrian Frazier has shown just how far the play fulfilled the aesthetic and political demands set out by Frank Fay, the need for a drama to 'send men away filled with the desire for deeds'.[26] Antoinette Quinn argues convincingly for the ideological significance of Maud Gonne's performance, and for the production by Inghinidhe na hEireann within the context of their political objectives.[27] The theatrical realisation of *Kathleen ni Houlihan* was not in the hands of Yeats and Gregory. It was not first produced by the Irish Literary Theatre over which they had primary control, neither of them were involved with rehearsals and Gregory did not even attend the performances.[28] The theatrical event represented by *Kathleen ni Houlihan* as performed in St Teresa's Hall, Clarendon Street, in April 1902 by a nationalist company of amateur actors with the expectations of an audience attracted by such a company, cannot be considered wholly the creation of either Yeats or Gregory or both.[29] What is at issue here is the political meaning which the play generated and the potential for such meaning which the text offered.

Again and again the testimony was to the extraordinary kinetic impact of the play. This was without doubt the play which Fay had demanded, sending 'men away filled with the desire for deeds'. Stephen Gwynn's reaction is often taken as representative when he recalled wondering 'whether such plays should be produced unless one was prepared for people to go out and shoot or be shot'.[30] Lennox Robinson was convinced that *Kathleen ni Houlihan*, along with Gregory's popular *The Rising of the Moon*, 'made more rebels in Ireland than a thousand political speeches or a hundred reasoned books'.[31] The play's power could work surprisingly even with those of very unnationalist convictions. Gregory recorded the reaction of Shaw watching a London performance in 1909: 'When I see that play I feel it might lead a man to do something foolish.' She was, she said, 'as much surprised as if I had seen one of the Nelson lions scratch himself'.[32] What was there in *Kathleen ni Houlihan* to move even the normally immovable G.B.S.?

The effectiveness of the play in part derives from the very concrete ordinariness of the peasant setting as established by Gregory in the first scene. This makes for the kind of literalism in the allegory attested to by Patrick Pearse. In his 1916 essay 'The Spiritual Nation' he wrote of how in his childhood he believed in the actual existence of a woman called Erin, 'and had Mr Yeats' "Kathleen ni Houlihan" been then written and had I seen it, I should have taken it not as an allegory, but as a representation of a thing that might happen any day in my house'.[33] The liaison between the realised typicality of the Gillanes' cottage as 'home' and the strange Old Woman that visits it facilitates this sort of child-like literal reaction. What is more, the representativeness of the Gillanes as a peasant family gives to the play its popular and populist quality. In the Yeatsian imagination it is normally the exceptional heroic figures who are susceptible to the dream of a transcendent, immortal destiny – Cuchulain being the archetype of such a hero. Although Mary Bruin the changeling bride may not seem to fit such a pattern, even she (with her husband Shawn) can articulate a vision of love quite antithetical to the values of ordinary hearth and home. But the call of Kathleen ni Houlihan, like the call of Christ, can come to anyone and everyone. Though Michael must forsake the common good of marriage, family, house and comfort in the self-sacrificial act which marks him out from those who cleave to such things, his action in doing so is paradigmatic, indeed exemplary, rather than the tragic doom of the special hero. His role therefore is openly available to any audience member, if gender-skewed towards males. The challenge is to all, and the reward is the infinitely desirable transformation of old woman into young girl.

That transformation, miraculous, instantaneous, brought about by the willingness of the young man to lay down his life, is infinitely desirable for a nationalist community as it figures a revolution capable of restoring the country from its oppressed state of colonisation to renewed sovereignty. But the trope of strangers in the house as embodied in *Kathleen ni Houlihan* brings out the peculiar nature of that imagined dream of liberation. In so far as the original myth of the king's marriage to the sovereignty goddess Eire can be construed as a ritual both of kingship and of fertility, the blood sacrifice restores the land to health and establishes the legitimacy of the true king whom she marries. But in the context of a colonised Ireland, the nature and identity of that true king is highly problematic. In the Norman period, the bardic poet might celebrate the prowess of his individual chieftain, treating the invader/occupiers as no different from other rival chieftains to be outmatched in valour. But from the seventeenth century on, with Gaelic culture and the clan system definitively broken, the *aisling* poets increasingly had to look outside the country for liberation and for the true sovereign. Hence the repeated focus on the various Stuart kings and pretenders under their several aliases; hence the constantly renewed hope of succour from France or Italy or Spain: 'Oh! the French are on the sea, / Says the *Shan Van Vocht*'; 'There's wine ... from the royal Pope / Upon the ocean green; / And Spanish ale shall give you hope / My Dark Rosaleen!'[34]

This produces the special complexity of *Kathleen ni Houlihan*'s image of strangers in the house. It is strangers in the house which have put the Old Woman wandering in the first place, the colonial invaders who have taken away her land. She acts as stranger in the house of the Gillanes, disturbing and troubling them with the imagination of a pristine Ireland of the past which might be realised again in the future. The play's climax comes with the news that the French have landed in Killala Bay, that the 1798 Rebellion is about to start. These strangers to Ireland need to invade in order to make possible the liberation/restoration of Kathleen ni Houlihan as sovereign Ireland. But who gets to marry her? There is a telling political ellipsis in the way the original structure of the myth is re-embodied in Yeats–Gregory's play. Michael must forego the sexual consummation of marriage to die instead for Kathleen. The stranger French are necessary catalysts for the expulsion of the stranger English. What then? The power of *Kathleen ni Houlihan* derives not only from the potency with which it imagines revolution as a miraculous transformation, but the skill with which it leaves unanswered the question of what is to follow the revolution.

The Shadow of the Glen

If the performance of *Kathleen ni Houlihan* in April 1902 brought together a new combination of forces and gave a new direction to the dramatic movement, the production of *The Shadow of the Glen* in October 1903 threatened to tear it apart. *Kathleen ni Houlihan* had created an alliance between the 'literary' aspirations of Yeats and Gregory's Irish Literary Theatre (which by 1901 had run its allotted three-year course), and the more earnestly nationalist politics of Inghinidhe na hEireann and the Fay brothers. The Fays had provided the makings of the Irish acting company that the Irish Literary Theatre had so obviously lacked. Out of the amalgam of literature and theatre, culture and politics came the Irish National Theatre Society. But hardly was it formed than it started to disintegrate; fusion and fission were never far apart in the early Irish theatre movement, given its volatile constitutent elements. The performance of Synge's *The Shadow of the Glen* in a bill which ironically, or provocatively, included *Kathleen ni Houlihan*, resulted in a walk-out by prominent nationalists, some of them the very members of Inghinidhe na hEireann who had performed Yeats's and Gregory's play eighteen months before. As Antoinette Quinn puts it, 'Maud Gonne's exit from the premiere of Synge's play was as conspicuous as her entrance at the premiere of *Kathleen ni Houlihan* the previous year.'[35] What was it in Synge's re-drawing of the stranger in the house which produced such a political reaction so antithetical to *Kathleen ni Houlihan*?

Synge's Tramp who comes to the cottage of Nora and the supposedly dead Dan Burke is a stranger, addressed by no other name, but he is a very un-mysterious stranger. He knows the neighbourhood, he knows the local news, he knew the recently dead shepherd Patch Darcy who died spectacularly mad in the hills. He is familiar with the outside world beyond the cottage and its potential for supernatural terror; he, like Nora Burke, walks in due dread. When the Tramp hints that Nora might be afraid as a lone woman to let a man like himself into the house, she shrugs off fear of what any mere man might do to her: 'It's other things than the like of you, stranger, would make a person afeard.' Tramp assents 'with a half-shudder': 'it is surely, God help us all' (Synge, *CW*, III, 37). The account of the death of Darcy which follows on from this exchange is intended to illustrate the difference between the terrors of the uncanny which the Tramp fears when he first hears 'queer talk' in the dark night on the mountains – '"Merciful God," says I, "if I begin hearing the like of that voice out of the dark mist, I'm destroyed surely"' – and the acceptable voice of a real if mad man, retrospectively recognised when Darcy's dead body is found: 'Then I knew it was himself I was after hearing, and I wasn't afeard any more' (Synge, *CW*, III, 39). The Tramp, in his ordinary human fear of the *unheimlich*, cannot be its representative, as the fairy child is in *The Land of Heart's Desire*, or the Old Woman in *Kathleen ni Houlihan*. That natural/supernatural ambiguity of being which plays around other strangers in the house is removed. The Tramp is not a Travelling Man who will shortly shed his disguise and start to walk across rivers; he is just what he seems, a tramp.

The wooing speech with which he draws Nora to accompany him at the end of the play, the land of heart's desire which he offers her, are equivalently unmetaphorical.

> Come along with me now, lady of the house, and it's not my blather you'll be hearing only, but you'll be hearing the herons crying out over the black lakes, and you'll be hearing the grouse, and the owls with them, and the larks and the big thrushes when the days are warm, and it's not from the like of them you'll be hearing a talk of getting old like Peggy Cavanagh, and losing the hair off you, and the light of your eyes, but it's fine songs you'll be hearing when the sun goes up, and there'll be no old fellow wheezing the like of a sick sheep close to your ear. (Synge, *CW*, III, 57)

The world of natural delights here offered, the prospect of an escape from age and ageing, may appear to resemble Yeats's fairy invocation to the land 'where nobody gets old and bitter of tongue'. But Nora's reply is rooted in an unedited reality of actual climatic conditions and their likely results: 'I'm thinking it's myself will be wheezing that time with lying down under the Heavens when the night is cold'

(Synge, *CW*, III, 57). What the Tramp has to give is a mental attitude, a way of coping with time, mortality, the weather, not a means to transcend them:

> You'll be saying to yourself one time, 'It's a grand evening by the grace of God,' and another time, 'It's a wild night, God help us, but it'll pass surely.' (Synge, *CW*, III, 57)

The Tramp and Nora, like the other characters Dan Burke and Mike Dara, live in a material world which is not ultimately transformable.

Take away the capacity for transformation, the dimension of the metaphorical, and what remains is a representational version of an Irish country cottage visited by a real tramp off the roads. But in the conditions of the time this scene could not be representational without being held to be representative. What seems extraordinary in the reaction to *The Shadow of the Glen* was the speed with which it was turned into a debate over the arranged marriage of convenience, the sexual morality of Irish women, and by extension the nature of the Irish national character. John B. Yeats already, in a positive evaluation of the play on the day it was due to be produced, wrote of it in *The United Irishman* as an attack on 'our Irish institution, the loveless marriage'.[36] *The Irish Times*, with its very different politics, published a disapproving review the following day deploring the way in which this objective was carried out:

> Mr Synge has distinct power, both in irony and dialogue, but surely he could display them better in showing in some other way – the way that should above all cast no slur on Irish womanhood – the wrong of mercenary marriage.[37]

Implied here is an imperative to defend the purity of Irish female reputation, whatever the truths of social actuality. There might well be arranged marriages in Irish rural life, Arthur Griffith, the play's most vehement critic, could concede, but the principles of monogamy and sexual fidelity are maintained. Whatever the real-life equivalent of Nora does, said Griffith, 'she does not go off with the Tramp'.[38]

It is significant that this is the culminating objection to Nora's behaviour. It is bad enough that she entertains the Tramp alone at the wake, that she may be suspected of adultery with Patch Darcy, that she obviously had a pre-arranged agreement to marry Mike Dara after her husband's death, but to go off with a Tramp! Class outrage here gives a new pitch of feeling to moral outrage. In the context of *The Travelling Man*, the Mother's attachment to her dresser and delf, her class-conscious revulsion at a beggar holding her child, might be the tokens of her spiritual blindness, though when the play was finally staged at the Abbey one reviewer at least had every sympathy with her distrust of a disreputable tramp.[39] But Nora in her willingness to accept the companionship of an itinerant – and it is no more willed a choice than that – betrays the bourgeois ideology which is integral to an urban middle-class construction of the national ideal.

The figure of the stranger in the house accorded with the Celticism of Yeats, Gregory and the early theatre movement in so far as it set the pull of otherworldly transcendence within a stylised ground of family normality. That dynamic might be rendered as the dangerous attraction of faery in *The Land of Heart's Desire*, or valorised as spiritual or politico-spiritual ideal in *The Travelling Man* or *Kathleen ni Houlihan*. The cottage room was emblem for a reassuringly familiar model of human life, limited yet comfortable, its material pleasures not undervalued except by the ultimate exacting standards of the absolute claims made by the strangers from outside. The sacrifice of a Michael Gillane in giving up home and marriage was a sacrifice all the more ennobling for the substantial value of what he gave up. In *The Shadow of the Glen* Synge doubly deconstructed this trope of the good relinquished for the best. His family was not, like the Gillanes, a married couple whose family happiness echoed their material prosperity and vice versa. He portrayed instead a dysfunctional marriage, as childless as it is loveless, with bare material subsistence its only motivation for the wife: 'What way would I live and I an old woman if I didn't marry a man with a bit of a farm, and cows on it, and sheep on the back hills' (Synge, *CW*, III, 49). And the drive to leave the home is not one of self-abnegation but of self-fulfilment. The renunciation of the sexual consummation of marriage for the higher sublimation of dying for Kathleen ni Houlihan was edifying, admirable, magnificent. But escape from the bed of an impotent old husband – 'he was always cold, every day since I knew him, – and every night' (Synge, *CW*, III, 35) – to the prospect of outdoor sex with a younger man – 'there'll be no old fellow wheezing the like of a sick sheep close to your ear' (Synge, *CW*, III, 57) – was quite another thing again. Where Yeats and Gregory move through metaphor and allegory towards a transcendental metamorphosis which the nationalist audience could ecstatically applaud, the secularising, materialising spirit of Synge's play produced exactly the opposite effect.

There was no doubt a degree of overreaction to *The Shadow of the Glen*, given the muted little comedy of mood that it is; the play seems to have gone down better in later performances so that even Joseph Holloway, that geigercounter of nationalist sensibility, could conclude that 'there is very little harm in this strangely conceived domestic scene set in peculiarly real, Irish everyday talk'.[40] But the issues raised by the play are significant because they reflect how drama was construed by the audiences of the time. With the drive towards an Irish national theatre, any stage space was liable to be read as microcosm of the nation. The peasant country cottage in particular, for the Dublin-centred gaelicising nationalists, was that place of origin which in its pristine simplicity typified their imagined community. This was quite consistent with its normative function within a drama which showed it invaded and transformed by the stranger from without. Nationalist Ireland had to be capable of imagining itself as at once already spiritually and socially wholesome (to counteract colonial misrepresentations to the contrary), and about to be transformed by revolutionary liberation. Synge's cottage, his not-strange-enough Tramp with the very limited form of liberation he offers Nora, seemed a hideous travesty of all that. The concern of the next chapter will be with the clash of author/audience perspectives enacted in the full-scale engagement of *The Playboy* production.

3 Shifts in perspective

'Synge seemed by nature unfitted to think a political thought', wrote Yeats in 'J.M. Synge and the Ireland of his Time'.[1] This statement has by now been frequently and convincingly contested. There is, to begin with, the biographical evidence of Synge's political actions and opinions, his interest in socialism in the 1890s, his reading of Marx and his ringing declaration to his nephew E.M. Stephens: 'A radical is a person who wants change root and branch, and I'm proud to be a radical.'[2] There is the social criticism voiced in his articles for the *Manchester Guardian* on the Congested Districts which Yeats sought to suppress from Synge's posthumous *Collected Works*. Synge was nationalist enough to join Maud Gonne's militant Association Irlandaise in Paris in 1897, if only very briefly, and like many Irish nationalists he was fervently pro-Boer in the Boer War.[3] Yeats's apolitical version of Synge has been challenged both by those who seek to uncover in his work a politics to be distrusted, and those who find in him a politics they admire. For Seamus Deane, for instance, Synge's cult of the heroic is politics by other means: 'The attempt to recover a new ideal of heroism from the reintegration of the shattered Gaelic culture with the presiding English polity is no more than the after-image of authority on the Anglo-Irish retina.'[4] Declan Kiberd has countered Deane's view with a politically concerned and committed Synge whose sensitive awareness of the consequences of colonialism animated a decolonising vision ahead of its time.[5]

And yet there is more to Yeats's observation about Synge's inability to think a political thought than merely Yeats's own strategic need to create an artist-martyr misconceived by nationalist philistines. Particularly for someone as politically attuned as Yeats,

Synge's apparent imperviousness to the likely impact of his work could seem naive, even obtuse. A case in point is the sketch for a 1798 play which Yeats adduces in the 'J.M. Synge and the Ireland of his Time' essay as an illustration of Synge's political innocence.[6] It was apparently written on the urging of Frank Fay as part of a campaign to 'try to get an intelligent popular audience in Dublin':

> If you could give us a drama of '98 as much alive as *In the Shadow of the Glen* and *Riders to the Sea* showing what the peasantry had to endure. I believe that there were whole districts in which there was not a woman unviolated. I think Yeats in *Cathleen* has pointed out the right road for plays of that time. The leaders only give you melodrama; it is a picture of the smaller tyrannies that their followers had to endure we want. (Synge, *CW*, III, 214)

Synge, with some doubts, dutifully responded with the scenario for a play. Sure enough, it is about the victims of rebellion at grassroots level, centring on the threat of rape to two women. But one of the women is a 'Rebel' and one a 'Papist' (Synge's terms in the scenario), their fears of violation are from the soldiers of opposed sides and they have a 'violent quarrel' about religion. It is true that Synge planned to show the Protestant woman drawn by sympathy to helping the Catholic woman carry her wounded son to safety; still, it can hardly have been what Fay had in mind as a strong patriotic follow-up to *Kathleen ni Houlihan*. Did Synge really think that such a play would win friends for the Abbey in the nationalist community, or was it a sort of sardonic joke at the expense of Fay's piety? It might well have been quite seriously intended. The sketch has many of the hallmarks of Synge's achieved work: its iconoclastic ironies; its anti-heroic slant; its anarchic scepticism. There is a sense in Synge of a sort of helplessness in the face of the drives of his own imagination, as if he could not himself understand why the convinced cultural nationalist that he was, with a genuinely sincere admiration for the Irish peasants, should have produced plays about them which were satiric to the point of caricature.

All this makes exceptionally difficult the issue of the political intentions of *The Playboy*. Edward Hirsch argues that the play represented an assault on the audience's ideological preconceptions, an assault characteristic of modernism.[7] It is a plausible view, and his analysis particularly of the conflicting modes of the play, the initial markers of realistic representation subverted by a fantastic theatricality, is an acute perception of *The Playboy*'s formal instability.[8] Yet when Hirsch speaks of an assault on the audience the aggressive intention implied seems at odds with what we know of Synge's attitude towards the play in production and after. There appears to have been little of the self-conscious wilfulness of the modernist writer there. His letter to Molly Allgood (the original Pegeen Mike), the morning after the first night, is oddly matter-of-fact, more concerned with missed lines and individual performances than at having provoked a riot: 'I think with a better Mahon and crowd and a few slight cuts the play would be thoroughly sound.' About the audience reaction he only remarks coolly, 'It is better any day to have the row we had last night, than to have your play fizzling out in half-hearted applause. Now we'll be talked about.'[9] Any publicity is good publicity. His attempts to defend the play, first (in the theatre programme note) on the grounds of its realism, then (in an evasive letter to *The Irish Times*) on its mixture of the fantastic and the serious, seem maladroit rather than part of a modernist agenda of subversion. It was left to Yeats to fight the public battle of the play with all the consummate artistry and strategic disingenuousness of the brilliant frondeur he was. There is no doubting the modernist credentials of *his* assault upon audiences.

Synge's conscious intentions may well be beside the point: the presentation of the play was an intensely political event and the fall-out from it cannot be shrugged off as mere misreading by a politically hypersensitised audience of a highly original work of theatre. What made *The Playboy* the political battleground it so instantly became? It is important to pinpoint the specific elements within the text which so outraged the Abbey spectators on 26 January 1907 and nationalist-minded audiences in Ireland, England and America for years after. We need to reconstruct as precisely as possible the perspective which they brought to the play in order to be able to see its offensiveness as they did. But it is equally important to try to read the play for the alternative perspectives, the other hypothetical audiences to which it reaches out. This is a play, after all, that may have provoked its original audience to fury, but has gone on to hold the stage in Ireland and internationally with an enduring power that no other Irish drama has yet matched. What was it in Synge's conception and realisation of *The Playboy* which could produce both the original object of violent invective and its afterlife of theatrical canonicity? To come at this clash of perspectives on the play it is necessary to go back to the flash-points of nationalist reaction: shifts, crimes, setting. This is to be a chapter on sex, violence and geography in *The Playboy*.

Shifts

'Audience broke up in disorder at the word shift.'[10] The famous telegram to Yeats announcing the riots may appear to us now, as it seemed to some people at the time, merely the measure of the absurdly disproportionate overreaction in *The Playboy* riots. It is, however, worth going back to the word itself to examine its provocativeness. The line which finally brought the house down comes in Act III, when Christy re-enters having apparently succeeded in killing his father, and the Widow Quin is trying to persuade him to run from the lynch-mob that is forming. When Christy will not abandon his hopes of winning back Pegeen with his renewed parricidal prowess, the Widow Quin remarks with understandable irritation:

> WIDOW QUIN (*impatiently*). Isn't there the match of her in every parish public, from Binghamstown unto the plain of Meath? Come on, I tell you, and I'll find you finer sweethearts at every waning moon.
> CHRISTY. It's Pegeen I'm seeking only, and what'd I care if you brought me a drift of chosen females, standing in their shifts itself maybe, from this place to the Eastern World.
> (Synge, *CW*, IV, 165–7)

Outbreak of pandemonium.

It was not, in fact, the first but the third time that the word had been used in the play. Pegeen in Act II, finding the Widow Quin roistering with Christy and the girls, had scornfully dismissed the Widow's request for a pennyworth of starch as the blatant pretence it was: 'And you without a white shift or a shirt in your whole family since the drying of the flood' (Synge, *CW*, IV, 105). The Widow herself later, as though in disproof of Pegeen's class-contemptuous insult on the poverty of her wardrobe, pictures her daily life 'darning a stocking or stitching a shift' (Synge, *CW*, IV, 127). All three instances illustrate how embedded the word is in the intricate assonantal sounds and balanced rhythms of Synge's prose; it is clearly chosen as much for reasons of euphony as for any associations it may have had. But whereas in the first two mentions of the shift it is only an item of laundry or of mending, in Act III the shifts actually appear on women's bodies. The animal physicality of those bodies is enforced by the rhyme word chosen to describe their aggregation, 'a *drift* of chosen females, standing in their shifts itself'. 'Drift' (= 'herd') was previously mentioned in the play as part of Shawn Keogh's dowry for Pegeen Mike, 'the drift of heifers I'm giving' (Synge, *CW*, IV, 155). If Synge thought that he was reducing the offensiveness of the passage by at least covering up the women in Christy's imagined nation-wide beauty contest – up until his final typescript version he had them fully 'stripped' (Synge, *CW*, IV, 154) – he was much mistaken.

The word was a talking-point in the letters of outrage that immediately followed the production. Someone writing to *The Freeman's Journal* signing herself 'A Western Girl' was especially shocked:

> Miss Allgood (one of the most charming actresses I have ever seen) is forced, before the most fashionable audience in Dublin, to use a word indicating an essential item of female attire, which the lady would probably never utter in ordinary circumstances, even to herself.[11]

Oddly enough, here it is the use of the word by Sara Allgood (playing the Widow Quin) which is picked out rather than the later more inflammatory speech of Christy. The offence is against the modesty of the performer as well as that of the audience. Why should the word in itself have been judged so immodest, and how could Sara Allgood have named this 'essential item of female attire' in a more modest way? The *OED* history of the usage of 'shift' supplies an answer.

The *OED* definition 10 for 'shift' is as follows:

> A body-garment of linen, cotton, or the like; in early use applied indifferently to men's and women's underclothing: subsequently, a woman's 'smock' or chemise. Now *rare*. In the 17th c. *smock* began to be displaced by *shift* as a more 'delicate' expression: in the 19 c. the latter has, from the same motive, given place to *chemise*.

What we see here is that successive words, first smock, then shift, have been fetishised by intimate contact with the (female) body, and thus have come to be banished from polite discourse in favour of something felt to be more discreet. The use of the word by the likes of Pegeen, Christy and the Widow Quin might well be historically authentic, as Synge himself maintained. Living as they do in remote parts of the west, they would quite plausibly have kept the more old-fashioned word which was disappearing from usage elsewhere. But for the largely middle-class Dublin audience and for the 'Western Girl', western and all as she is, 'shift' is already indelicate, vulgar, to be replaced by the more genteel 'chemise'. The shift as shibboleth marks off the difference between the world of the urbanised and modernising audience and the country life which both the audience and the author are bent on figuring in their different ways.

'On the French stage,' Synge wrote to Stephen McKenna in the wake of the dispute over *The Shadow of the Glen*, 'the sex-element of life is given without the other ballancing [*sic*] elements; on the Irish stage ... people ... want the other elements without sex. I restored the sex-element to its natural place, and the people were so surprised they saw the sex only.'[12] This appears to be a sane analysis of the shocked reaction to the sexuality of *The Playboy* which, in many respects, seems now so innocent. In the 1911–12 US touring productions of the play, the nationalist Irish-Americans were incensed by Pegeen spending the night unchaperoned in the house with Christy.[13] But the text makes it quite clear that they sleep chastely in separate rooms. Christy and Pegeen's relationship throughout is an eminently proper boy-and-girl romance with marriage the only consummation imagined. Nationalists of the time were exaggeratedly aware of the decorum of sexual relationships, particularly of female sexuality, whether this is given a sociological explanation in a new repressive control of women in post-Famine Ireland, a religious etiology in the puritanical traditions of the Irish Catholic Church, or seen as the mirror-process of anti-colonial national image-making, the Irish replicating and outdoing the Victorianism of the English Victorians.[14] Whatever the causes, the image of woman, so central to nationalist iconography, was an insistently desexualised one, and in such a context Synge's drift of females in their shifts were scandalously erotic.

Yet Synge's rendering of the sexuality of his stage figures was not just the natural restoration of balance to the drama which he makes it out to be in his letter to McKenna. If his audience was shocked by the physicality of his peasant women, he was in some measure excited and liberated by them. There are signs through *The Aran Islands* that for Synge, repressed product of his late-Victorian middle-class upbringing that he was, there was an attractive lack of physical self-consciousness in the island women. At times this is aestheticised, as in the passage so reminiscent of Joyce's later wading girl in *A Portrait of the Artist as a Young Man*:

> as I walk round the edges of the sea, I often come on a girl with her petticoats tucked up round her, standing in a pool left by the tide and washing her flannels among the sea-anenmomes and crabs. Their red bodices and white tapering legs make them as beautiful as tropical sea-birds, as they stand in a frame of seaweeds against the brink of the Atlantic.
>
> (Synge, *CW*, II, 76)

There are attempts to idealise his attraction to the Aran women and align them with metropolitan models of liberation: 'The women of this island are before conventionality, and share some of the liberal features that are thought peculiar to the women of Paris and New York' (Synge, *CW*, II, 143). But in some incidents Synge betrays ingenuously the suberotic frisson which unaccustomed physical proximity brought him. In Part II of *The Aran Islands*, for example, he recounts an incident from his second visit to Inishmaan when he was staying again with the McDonagh family:

> I had some photographs to show them that I took here last year, and while I was sitting on a little stool near the door of

> the kitchen, showing them to the family, a beautiful young woman I had spoken to a few times last year slipped in, and after a wonderfully simple and cordial speech of welcome, she sat down on the floor beside me to look on also.
>
> The complete absence of shyness or self-consciousness in most of these people gives them a peculiar charm, and when this young and beautiful woman leaned across my knees to look nearer at some photograph that pleased her, I felt more than ever the strange simplicity of the island life.
>
> (Synge, *CW*, II, 106)

'Strange simplicity' here reveals more than merely the young Synge sublimating his frustrated desire in a language of euphemism. It is the key to one element, one impulse underlying his drama. His stage scenes of country life allowed him to imagine an arena of uninhibited physicality as antithetical other to the world of middle-class repressions which he (and his potential audiences) occupied. Where the nationalists sought to project on to the peasants an idealised and asexual being, a life of the chemise rather than the shift, Synge was equally projecting from within a bourgeois consciousness in insisting on the primitive embodiedness of his characters. Christy may soar in metaphorical eulogy of Pegeen – 'Amn't I after seeing the love-light of the star of knowledge shining from her brow, and hearing words would put you thinking on the holy Brigid speaking to the infant saints' – but the Widow Quin is there to remind an audience of Pegeen's quite unsaintlike corporeality: 'There's poetry talk for a girl you'd see itching and scratching, and she with a stale stink of poteen on her from selling in the shop' (Synge, *CW*, IV, 125–7). The Widow herself is crucial in the play for the grotesque dimension of sexuality which she represents, and its associations with violence.

Imagine the married life of the Quins: 'Marcus Quin, God rest him, got six months for maiming ewes' (Synge, *CW*, IV, 59), and the Widow Quin, relict of the same. Her claim to fame is that she killed her husband; but not, Pegeen hastens to make clear to Christy in Act I, in any very creditable fashion:

> She hit himself with a worn pick, and the rusted poison did corrode his blood the way he never overed it and died after.

> That was a sneaky kind of murder did win small glory with the boys itself. (Synge, *CW*, IV, 89)

This, as it were, routine and semi-accidental murder of a husband suggests a scarifying degree of domestic violence by both married partners. In the same scene, as the competition for ownership of Christy hots up, Pegeen's abuse of the Widow attains a quite baroque level:

> Doesn't the world know you reared a black ram at your own breast, so that the Lord Bishop of Connaught felt the elements of a Christian, and he eating it after in a kidney stew?
> (Synge, *CW*, IV, 89)

Her witch-like unnatural practices, her pick-swinging marital past, turn her into a monstrous figure of perverse sexual destructiveness – 'a widow woman has buried her children and destroyed her man' (Synge, *CW*, IV, 89, 131).

And yet the Widow is rendered natural and real within the dramatic world of *The Playboy*, and is in many ways the most humane and sympathetic character in the play. She turns her widowed situation into a subject of restrained pathos in her wooing of Christy in Act II:

> I'm above many's the day, odd times in great spirits, abroad in the sunshine, darning a stocking or stitching a shift, and odd times again looking out on the schooners, hookers, trawlers is sailing the sea, and I thinking on the gallant hairy fellows are drifting beyond, and myself long years living alone.
> (Synge, *CW*, IV, 127)

The wilder flights of sexual fantasy, the self-widowed woman with black ram as unholy succubus, are earthed in a homely reality all the more disconcerting for its physical immediacy. The domestic scene of 'darning a stocking or stitching a shift' lends credibility to the shocking (for a 1907 audience) explicitness of the woman's longing desire for the 'gallant hairy fellows' out on the sea. In passages like this, the Mayo of *The Playboy* is constituted as a place where women wore shifts, had bodies under them, and bodily desires which they were prepared to express with a shameless lack of restraint. For Synge, and the audience he imagined for the play, this might represent the exhilarating otherness of the peasant milieu, a site for the reality and joy which he insisted in the 'Preface' that the drama should combine. For the first-night audience which the play actually addressed, its strangeness was an ugly monstrosity which they vehemently resisted.

For the purpose of this chapter's analysis, it is possible to separate out the several sources of offence of the play, its sexual explicitness, its representation of violence and its location in the West of Ireland. But the more pervasively destabilising quality of *The Playboy* was its refusal to observe the proper separateness of these several subjects. If we accept Mary Douglas's thesis in *Purity and Danger* that the idea of impurity arises from a confusion of categories, then *The Playboy* was a very impure, a very dangerous, play indeed.[15] As the repressed physicality of the sexual was allowed to appear from under the normal decencies of its covering, so sex was proximate to violence and both made manifest in the actuality of a specific location. Again and again necessary distinctions, differences and the ideological labelling that went with them were jumbled in unsorted contiguity. Such contamination of confused categories was a deeply disturbing affront to the middle-class nationalist community whose self-image depended on just such moral classification. But for Synge and the implicit Syngean perspective on the play, the embodied and anarchic Mayo made it a carnivalesque of the imagination.

Crimes

From the very beginning there was a suspicion of some extra dimension of significance in the story of the father-killer and the community that hero-worships him. 'Perhaps,' said the puzzled *Evening Mail* reviewer, 'it is an allegory, and the parricide represents some kind of nation-killer, whom Irishmen and Irish women hasten to lionise. If it is an allegory it is too obscure for me. I cannot stalk this alligator on the banks of the Liffey.'[16] Critical interpreters since have not held back from speculation on metaphoric, symbolic or even allegorical schemes of meaning underpinning *The Playboy*. Christy is a parody version of Oedipus, a mock Christ or Cuchulain, and the reception of his crime by the people of Mayo echoes with analogues of mythic narratives.[17] The schema which Declan Kiberd brings to bear upon the play is drawn from postcolonial theory. 'The tripartite structure of [the] play,' Kiberd maintains, 'corresponds very neatly with Frantz Fanon's dialectic of decolonisation, from occupation, through nationalism, to liberation.'[18] Kiberd's reading places *The Playboy* as a decolonising text misread by a generation of nationalists still trapped in the need to conceive of themselves in terms of the binary oppositions set up by the colonial process, like the onstage audience of Mayo-ites unable to follow Christy Mahon through to the final stage of liberation which he achieves at the play's end. I will be returning to the metaphoric suggestiveness of the action of *The Playboy*; but first it is necessary to retrace the origins of the narrative and what it is in Synge's treatment that made it so inflammatory.

The story of the man who killed his father and was sheltered from the law by the Aran islanders had already been folklorised into oral narrative by the time Synge heard it on Inishmaan, some twenty-five years after the event, and seems to have been regularly retold for visitors.[19] Although Synge is careful to distinguish it as an 'anecdote', not a 'folktale', told him by the oldest man on the island as an actual happening within his memory, it evidently has the set-piece form of the much-repeated story:

> He often tells me about a Connaught man who killed his father with the blow of a spade when he was in passion, and then fled to this island and threw himself on the mercy of some of the natives with whom he was said to be related. They hid him in a hole – which the old man has shown me – and kept him safe for weeks, though the police came and searched for him, and he could hear their boots grinding on the stones over his head. In spite of a reward which was offered, the island was incorruptible, and after much trouble the man was safely shipped to America. (Synge, *CW*, II, 95)

The event which provided the basis for the Aran story took place on 28 January 1873 when William Maley, from the Calla district of Galway near Clifden, hit his father Patrick Maley with a spade in a dispute over who had the right to cultivate a tiny potato-garden on the family farm.[20] Maley was a recently married man of thirty-eight who had spent several years at sea in America, and one of the points at issue in the fatal argument seems to have been money sent home by the son to the father. When Patrick died some hours later and the police had been summoned, William disappeared from sight. Rumoured to be hiding in Deer Island at one point, and apparently actually arrested on Aran, he nonetheless contrived to escape in spite of the £20 reward offered for his capture.[21] His description continued to appear as 'not arrested' through the 1873 issues of *Hue-and-Cry*, the Irish police gazette; in 1877 there must have been information on his whereabouts in the United States because there were moves to have him extradited, but it does not appear that he ever stood trial.[22]

The coroner's jury at the inquest on Patrick Maley took a lenient view and returned a verdict of manslaughter, which is presumably why *Sinn Fein* could claim that *The Playboy* was a distortion of the facts: 'out of a tragic accident, a playwright makes unnatural murder, out of human sympathy he makes inhumanity'.[23] Parricide, however, was not in fact such an uncommon crime, and Synge may just possibly have conflated the Maley story with a quite different incident which happened in June 1898 at the very time when he was staying on Aran for his first visit. This was the case of Michael Connell, oldest son of Thomas Connell, who murdered his father in a fit of violent rage on their family farm in Ballyheigue, Co. Kerry. From this event Synge might have taken the Kerry setting, and the idea of the aggrieved farm-bound son turning finally against his unjust father. When explaining why he should have beaten his father's head to a pulp, besides attacking his mother, Connell

> said he was not insane, but that the family had been treating him very badly. From inquiries it was elicited that the old man had promised the farm, the stock of which is five cows, to the eldest son some time ago, but failed to keep his promise.[24]

There was no question of Michael Connell being sheltered from justice: he promptly gave himself up to the police. But a third, much more publicised case, that of James Lynchehaun from 1894, also has a bearing on Synge's *Playboy* version of the father-killing and its reception. Lynchehaun's crime was a very different one: arson and violent assault on the Englishwoman on whose estate he lived in Achill Island. But his escape from police custody when on remand and the three months he spent in hiding as the 'Achill troglodyte' may have coloured the Inishmaan telling of the story of the parricide concealed (as Lynchehaun was) in a hole at times under the very feet of the searching policemen. Certainly Lynchehaun's subsequent, even more sensational, history of prison escape (1903) and trial for extradition in the United States (1904) influenced Synge's writing of *The Playboy*.[25]

In relating the story of the father-killer in *The Aran Islands*, Synge comments, 'This impulse to protect the criminal is universal in the west' and he gives it an orthodox explanation in the 'association between justice and the hated English jurisdiction' (Synge, *CW*, II, 95). As such the resistance to law-enforcement and the hatred of informers could be acceptably sanctioned within an anti-colonial construction of Irish character. But the issue of crime was an intensely touchy one, and Synge's representation of the crime of parricide in *The Playboy* proved wildly provocative. The fact that the people of Mayo were shown hero-worshipping a parricide was, notoriously, one of the main sources of offence to the play's nationalist critics. And it did not help that organs of the Unionist press, while hardly sympathetic to the play, took it as evidence for their denigratory view of the Irish. So *The Freeman's Journal* protested vigorously at the 'calumny on the Irish people':

> Let us remember this calumny runs on old and familiar lines. It has ever been the custom of traducers of the Irish people to charge them with sympathy with all forms of crime. Over and over again this same lie has been made the justification for Coercion. To those who think that the calumny in Mr. Synge's play may be safely condoned as too grotesque to be offensive may be commended the views of the 'Irish Times', which commends the squalid and repulsive travesty as 'remorseless truth'.[26]

The Irish people are traduced in being charged with sympathy for *all forms of crime*. It was crucial to the nationalist position to discriminate between forms of crime which were legitimate, in so far as they represented the justifiable struggle against an oppressive colonial power, and those which had no such legitimacy: sexual offences, domestic violence, crimes against property without political motivation. A standard British strategy in sanctioning imperial rule was to claim the Irish as naturally, irremediably, anarchic and lawless. Nationalists sought to counter this with a self-image of the Irish as inherently law-abiding, honest and upright – 'the people that hate crime probably more than any people in Europe'[27] – with the one honourable exception of political struggle.

The Lynchehaun extradition trial in Indianapolis in 1904 illustrates this very well. Lynchehaun's appallingly brutal attack on Agnes McDonnell, murderous in intent though the victim survived, involved biting off her nose and gouging out one eye. With a background of personal animosity behind the attack, no countenance could be given to a crime such as this. So, when in Chicago in 1903 Lynchehaun approached Michael Davitt, the nationalist founder of the Land League who had served time in prison for his political beliefs, Davitt repulsed the attempt to claim kinship or recognition; indeed he reported Lynchehaun to the local authorities, thus initiating the process by which the British sought to have him extradited. But in the extradition proceedings themselves the following year, Lynchehaun's crime was completely refigured as a politically motivated one. All trace of personal animus against Mrs McDonnell was removed, and the assault became a group plan of local tenants and the Irish Republican Brotherhood of which Lynchehaun now claimed to be a leader. The action was part of a campaign 'to regain the lands of Ireland for the Irish, to drive out the landlords, and to establish a republican form of government in Ireland'. The brutal violence of the attack was excused as part of the inevitable excesses of revolution, Mrs McDonnell being accorded the dignity of comparison with Marie Antoinette. In both cases, argued Lynchehaun's defence lawyer, if 'you look at it from the civil side it was a cruel case, but if you look at it from the political side it was a natural act'.[28]

This played well in Irish-American Indianapolis and the case for extradition was rejected, but Lynchehaun may have remained a queasy subject for Irish nationalists in Ireland when Synge chose to introduce a reference to him into the text of his play, and into the defence of the play's authenticity. Sara Tansey is reminded by another of the hero-seeking village girls in Act II that she was 'the one yoked the ass cart and drove ten miles to set your eyes on the man bit the yellow lady's nostril on the northern shore' (Synge, *CW*, IV, 97). The notoriety of the case and the detail of the biting of the nose would have made the allusion unmistakable to the original audience.[29] What is more, Synge specifically cited the Lynchehaun case as one of the incidents which had suggested the idea of peasant willingness to shelter the criminal to him.[30] This took the phenomenon of sympathy with crime into an uneasy borderline between politically acceptable and unacceptable lawbreaking.

It is a borderline which the play throughout, in fact, refuses to recognise. In the opening scene Pegeen Mike celebrates the lost local patriots of the past:

> Where now will you meet the likes of Daneen Sullivan knocked the eye from a peeler, or Marcus Quin, God rest him, got six months for maiming ewes, and he a great warrant to tell stories of holy Ireland till he'd have the old women shedding down tears about their feet. (Synge, *CW*, IV, 59)

Whatever the nationalist antagonism towards the police might have been, there is a disconcerting violence of detail in 'knocked the eye from a peeler', and in Marcus Quin's exploits the activities of 'Captain Moonlight', the agrarian secret societies which respectable nationalists were at such pains to disavow, are associated with the honourable traditions of patriotic rhetoric. Worse was to come, though, when Christy Mahon, replacement hero for the Daneen Sullivans and the Marcus Quins, was interrogated as to his crime. One of the men in the pub, Philly O'Cullen – characterised in one of the drafts of the play as 'elderly, thin and political' (Synge, *CW*, IV, 60) – suggests appropriately political crimes that Christy may have committed. He thinks that 'Maybe the land was grabbed from him, and he did what any decent man would do?' (Synge, *CW*, IV, 71), or that Christy went out fighting for the Boers like members of the Irish Brigade in the South African War. Yet with equal and undiscriminating relish the villagers can suggest rape, murder, forgery or bigamy in their party-game of guess-the-crime. The Mayo people are indeed represented as admiring all forms of crime, not just those which are politically defensible.

Killing your father, some sort of ultimate act in the defiance of taboo, tops the bill.

The killing of the father itself was a dangerously unstable image as it stood between the metaphoric and the actual, the idealised and the abhorred. As some sort of primal act of defiance of authority, it could not but attract political interpretation in a colonial context. It is this allegorical potential which the *Evening Mail* reviewer sensed and shied away from.[31] To accept that the father-killer could be read as a liberator was to face the fact that the liberator could also be a man who hit his father over the head with a spade in an argument over an arranged marriage. Once again there was an unthinkable confusion of categories. Ireland as colonised country had the sacred right to resist, to destroy its tyrannic parent, the colonising power of England; but the Irish people were deeply, piously submissive to the authoritarian, patriarchal model of the family sanctioned by their authoritarian and patriarchal Church. It is hard to see how such a provocative dramatic design, exposing as it does the conflict between the would-be revolutionary aspirations of nationalism and its intense social conservatism, could have been conceived by Synge in political innocence.

Declan Kiberd argues that it was not, and that Synge had a political objective in the play: to uncover the impotent psychic violence of the colonised state, and to lead an audience stage by stage with Christy, through a heroised enthusiasm equivalent to romantic nationalism, towards the true liberation of independent self-making. For Kiberd, the father and son going out at the end in their reversed roles 'constitute the image of a revolutionary community, while the villagers lapse into revivalism'.[32] In this reading the original audiences, like the villagers, were unable to respond to the challenge of a political vision beyond the colonising/nationalist face-off. However, the action of *The Playboy* hardly works with such a clear progressive dialectic nor with such a politically engaged commitment as Kiberd's analysis implies. There are moments of vision in the play, clearings of consciousness, which represent points of changed awareness for the characters and the audience: Christy's discovery of the need for self-sufficiency as the crowd turn on him – 'if it's a poor thing to be lonesome, it's worse maybe go mixing with the fools of earth' (Synge, *CW*, IV, 165); Pegeen's shocked recognition of the reality of violence brought home to her in Christy's second 'murder' – 'there's a great gap between a gallous story and a dirty deed' (Synge, *CW*, IV, 169). Yet these moments never steady into the stages of gradual revelation. They are too caught up in the play's heavily ironic mode of representation which allows no attitude, no emotion or idea to go unchallenged. So it is also with the afflatus of Christy's exit, his final 'victory' over his father:

> Ten thousand blessings upon all that's here, for you've turned me a likely gaffer in the end of all, the way I'll go romancing through a romping lifetime from this hour to the dawning of the judgement day. (Synge, *CW*, IV, 173)

It is hard to see that the Mahons, with their power positions of bullying and being bullied now merely switched, can really represent an exemplary 'image of a revolutionary community', or that we can accept Christy's exhilarated playboy rhetoric at face value here any more than earlier in the play. Synge's play about the hero-worship of a parricide may not have been the maliciously provocative attack which nationalists took it to be at the time, but it is hardly the systematically Utopian text of Kiberd's politically benevolent reading either.

In a letter to Stephen McKenna, Synge made it clear that Irish attitudes towards law and order, the colonised context, were not determinant in the play's conception.

> *If* the idea had occurred to me I could and would just as readily [have] written the thing, as it stands, without the Lynchehaun case or the Aran case. The story – in its ESSENCE – is probable, given the psychic state of the locality. I used the cases afterwards to controvert critics who said it was *impossible*.[33]

The psychic state of the locality may be the hero-hunger of a Pegeen Mike in need of the likes of Daneen Sullivan, Marcus Quin or Christy Mahon to animate her deprived world with wonder. But the measure of the difference between the situation in *The Playboy* and any actual Irish situation, as the play's critics were quick to point out, is Christy's status as stranger and the consequent glamorisation of violence. William Maley was sheltered by people on Aran to whom he was related; Lynchehaun was protected by a whole network of extended family. As much as resistance to the alien law of a colonial authority, the Irish disposition to shield the criminal had to do with kinship loyalties common in almost any rural community. By contrast Christy is imagined to be a hero exactly because he is a complete outsider, his 'deed' something that happened in a 'distant place', 'a windy corner of high distant hills' (Synge, *CW*, IV, 75).

The strangeness of Christy and the estrangement of the Mayo village in which he finds himself mark the play's plot as the comic device it is. The community in which the terrified and guilty young man is greeted with astonished admiration when he is driven to confess his crime, in which because he has killed his father he is judged to have 'the sense of Solomon', has all the exaggerated topsy-turvydom of fantastic comedy. This is indeed, as Synge affirmed to McKenna, an imaginative conception which is quite independent of, quite other to, the Irish conditions which first suggested it. And yet, though under the pressure of journalists in the wake of the riots Synge called the play an 'extravaganza', the comedy of the parricide is hardly an innocent fantasy. It is not only the fact of Christy's supposed deed and the people's inverted attitude of respect for it which is disturbing. The language of *The Playboy* is pervaded by a sportive violence no less unsettling for its casualness. Images of hanging, of madness, of grotesque cruelty are the mere subject of amused anecdote. 'You never hanged him', says Pegeen when speculating with the others on just how Christy may have killed his father, 'the way Jimmy Farrell hanged his dog from the licence and had it screeching and wriggling three hours at the butt of a string, and himself swearing it was a dead dog, and the peelers swearing it had life' (Synge, *CW*, IV, 73). Jimmy Farrell, the owner of the dubiously dead dog, later in the play recalls with relish an instance of the dangers of madness: 'I knew a party was kicked in the head by a red mare, and he went killing horses a great while, till he eat the insides of a clock and died after' (Synge, *CW*, IV, 137). The Widow Quin, touching on the same subject, warns Old Mahon, whom she has convinced of his insanity, that he should disappear unobtrusively from the scene, 'for them lads caught a maniac one time and pelted the poor creature till he ran out raving and foaming and was drowned in the sea' (Synge, *CW*, IV, 145).

This is no realistic picture of Irish country life as it is lived; the high colour of violence throughout is a feature of the grotesquely fantastic version of reality which the play presents. And yet the carnival nature of *The Playboy* is such that this mode of fantastic grotesquerie is never freed into the pure unreality of farce either. This is true above all of the play's central representation of Oedipal conflict. Synge makes of Christy's story a ludic version of the Oedipus myth. Nothing could better illustrate the horrors of the threatening father-figure than Christy's picture of the gigantesque Old Mahon

> and he after drinking for weeks, rising up in the red dawn, or before it maybe, and going out into the yard as naked as an ash tree in the moon of May, and shying clods again the visage of the stars till he'd put the fear of death into the banbhs and the screeching sows. (Synge, *CW*, IV, 83–5)

It is this terrifying projection of the son's fear which Christy must face in his act of rebellion with the loy. But the other side of the Oedipal horror is also represented in the play, in equally parodic/grotesque form. The source of the quarrel between father and son is the threat of an arranged marriage for Christy with the Widow Casey – not his actual mother but his foster-mother whom

> all know did suckle me for six weeks when I came into the world, and she a hag this day with a tongue on her has the crows and seabirds scattered, the way they wouldn't cast a shadow on her garden with the dread of her curse.
> (Synge, *CW*, IV, 103)

(Although it is never directly stated, it is implied that Christy's own mother died in childbirth: Old Mahon in a moment of maudlin self-pity remembers how 'it was I did tend him from his hour of birth' (Synge, *CW*, IV, 137)). Christy flies from the Widow Casey, the fully monstrous mother, only to encounter an attractively disguised version of her in the Widow Quin.

The Playboy is a comedy and it plays comic games with the tragic legend of Oedipus: Christy does *not* succeed in killing his father, he does *not* marry either of the available mother-substitutes, tempted as he may be momentarily by the seductive offer of the Widow Quin. Yet to give such a mock version of the Oedipus legend is not wholly to disarm it of its terrors. It is some sort of ultimate tragic trauma, perhaps, for the son to discover that he has killed his father and slept with his mother. But there is a nightmare quality also in the father who is repeatedly killed and will not stay dead. 'Are you coming to be killed a third time' (Synge, *CW*, IV, 171), asks Christy in bewildered disbelief, as his father crawls on to the stage in the last scene, a survivor of the second attempt on his life, as of the first. There is a similar unsettling phantasmagoria in the image of the monstrous mother successfully escaped in Kerry who nonetheless reappears in only slightly disguised form in Mayo.

Synge's imagined West of Ireland, where violence is not only condoned but positively appreciated as a spectator-sport, serves as dramatic scene for certain adolescent rites of passage: Christy's transformation into a 'likely gaffer in the end of all', master of future fights with his father, Pegeen's desolated recognition of the loss of her hero, real or legendary. Synge is romantic ironist enough to represent individuals in the end as lonely creatures trapped within the constricting forms of the social. But Christy's progress through the play can hardly be convincingly read as a paradigm of colonial/nationalist/decolonised consciousness, and may be related only tangentially if at all to the socio-political realities of turn-of-the-century Ireland. The incidents of the parricides in Galway or in Kerry, the Lynchehaun case in Achill, authorised the conception of a primitive place where conventional attitudes towards crime and violence are freed from normal restraint, just as the unselfconsciousness of Aran women suggested the characters' sexual uninhibitedness. Synge did not intend to mock or satirise the real peasant communities which sponsored this fictive scene; there is instead a sort of glory in its violent otherness. What the West of Ireland gave him was a remote space where his grotesque action could be rendered with a sort of deadpan surface realism and at least a show of plausibility. It was this show of plausibility which enraged his critics, suggesting as it did that the real west resembled his carnivalesque version of it. For there were political issues at stake in that western setting also.

Setting

On the first night of *The Playboy* W.G. Fay, who had some difficulty remembering his lines throughout ('W.G. was pretty fluffy', commented Synge with annoyance in that morning-after letter to Molly Allgood[34]), substituted the words 'Mayo girls' for 'chosen females' and thus, according to Joseph Holloway, inveterate disapprover, made it more 'crudely brutal'.[35] Why should this fluff in the lines have made matters worse? The letter from the 'Western Girl', which protested the mention of the shift, provides a partial answer. She angrily disputed Synge's claim to authority: 'I think I know the West of Ireland as well as Mr. Synge does, and I can state that in no part of the South or West would a parricide be welcomed.'[36] The protesters in the theatre itself repeatedly shouted 'That's not the West of Ireland.'[37] The Mayo setting, the reference to the half-clad Mayo girls, were so inflammatory because the West of Ireland represented a contested site in the colonial/nationalist struggle. If the British represented the Irish as inherently crime-loving and lawless, the West of Ireland, the most remote and least Anglicised part of the country, was thought of as the most endemically anarchic. For the nationalists, exactly reversing this cultural geography, the West became the preserve of uncontaminated Gaelic purity where, setting aside the necessary resistance to colonial power, a naturally high respect for law and order was maintained. If Mayo was the home of Lynchehaun, it was also the home of Michael Davitt and the starting-place of the Land League, the home of John MacBride who contested a parliamentary by-election in Mayo *in absentia* while fighting in South Africa for the Boers against the British. MacBride is in fact referred to, although not named, in the play: 'maybe', suggests Philly, Christy 'went fighting for the Boers, the like of the man beyond, was judged to be hanged, quartered and drawn', a reference which one early draft made more explicit: 'Maybe he went fighting for the Boers the like of Major MacBride, God shield him, who's afeard to put the tip of his nose into Ireland fearing he'd be hanged, quartered and drawn' (Synge, *CW*, IV, 71, 70). In setting the action in Mayo Synge brought into the play all the political and cultural baggage that went with that location.

It may have been all but accidental that Synge set his play in Mayo, an area of Ireland that he knew less well than Wicklow, Aran or

Kerry, but where he happened to be travelling in the autumn of 1904 when he first began to work on *The Playboy*. The following year, however, the poor north-western regions of Mayo were among the 'Congested Districts' which he toured with Jack Yeats as part of their joint commission from *The Manchester Guardian* for a series of illustrated articles. It was then that he acquired a detailed knowledge of the Belmullet peninsula, the setting for the play, and was able to give a convincingly specific location to the action. Belmullet (the little town where Synge stayed on both his visits to Mayo) is at the most extreme north-western tip of Ireland, a convincingly long walk for Christy and Old Mahon from the south-western county of Kerry which is their imagined home. In *The Playboy*, as in his Wicklow plays, Synge took care to give to his action a local habitation and a name: the characters' references to places are convincingly authentic for people living in the Belmullet peninsula. Pegeen Mike orders her trousseau from Castlebar, the nearest major town; Shawn Keogh will call a piper from Crossmolina or from Ballina, some 25 or 30 miles east of Belmullet; Christy imagines honeymoon outings with Pegeen Mike on Neifin, the mountain to the south-east, or in Erris to the north; when settled with her he will spend his nights poaching salmon in the Owen (= Owenmore river) or the Carrowmore lake.

Synge's realisation of the setting for *The Playboy* as convincingly local locality goes beyond the mere introduction of a few plausible Mayo place-names. He set out to create not just a mapped reality of place but the mental landscape of a small community who inhabit a given neighbourhood. Shawn Keogh is 'Shawn Keogh of Killakeen' (an invented rather than real place-name), no doubt to differentiate him from the five other Shawn Keoghs of the area, as Michael James is Michael O'Flaherty, son of James O'Flaherty, and his daughter Margaret O'Flaherty is Pegeen Mike. Within this sort of infinitely intermarried society, patronymics or toponymics have to be used to distinguish all the people who share the very few family names. Michael James's pub, *The Playboy*'s only stage setting, is the focus-point of the neighbourhood, the one commercial establishment of the area. The measure of its isolation is the fact that there is 'not a decent house within 4 miles, the way every living Christian is a bona fide save one widow alone' (Synge, *CW*, IV, 67), that is to say, everyone in the community (with the exception of the Widow Quin) count as 'bona fide' travellers for the purposes of the licensing laws, and can drink out of hours as only those more than 4 miles from their home were allowed to do. But this is a purely legal fiction, as we learn in Act II when Christy, taking Michael James's information at literal face value, assumes that the girls have come a full four miles to hear his story:

> PEGEEN (*turning round astonished*). Four miles!
> CHRISTY (*apologetically*). Didn't himself say there were only bona fides living in the place?
> PEGEEN. It's bona fides by the road they are, but that lot come over the river lepping the stones. It's not three perches when you go like that ... (Synge, *CW*, IV, 107)

Synge here renders what it is to live in a place, to know it as an actual inhabited location, short-cuts and all, not as the space mapped by roads and licensing laws.

In so far as the localisation of the setting represented a realising technique, in so far as the play worked to make its milieu more credibly that of a small community out on the Belmullet peninsula, Synge exacerbated the complaint of inauthenticity against him. If the play purported to be set in a real place, if the speech and mentality of the characters mimicked that of people living in a real place, then their failure to resemble the real people of Mayo, or rather to resemble what the Dublin Abbey audience held the Mayo people to be, was all the more objectionable. But Synge uses space and locality in *The Playboy* for purposes of estrangement as much as for realising verisimilitude. His characters are grounded in their own known neighbourhood which is given concrete substance as they live plausibly within it. As they reach out beyond it, though, towards areas outside their immediate experience, their orientation becomes vague, fantastic, bizarre by the standards of any likely audience looking on. The representation of place in *The Playboy* thus provides a significant testing-point for the perspective on it which the text implies. On the Dublin stage of the Abbey, and on other stages where audiences had vested political interests in what the West of Ireland was like, it was rejected as a travesty, a falsification of the Mayo it claimed to be. How was an audience expected to see the imagined space of *The Playboy*? From what vantage-point are they supposed to look on at the Mayo characters looking out from their restricted locale?

Within the neighbourhood there are the allusively familiar places around – Killakeen, Killamuck, the Stooks of the Dead Women (which Synge in fact transplanted up from Kerry like so much else in the play) – grafted on to the actual topography of North Mayo and its place-names, Belmullet, Crossmolina, Castlebar. Outside that scope, the imagination of space becomes fluctuating and indeterminate. Geographical orientation, east and west, are used gesturally and figuratively rather than literally. Pegeen has fantasies about Christy's past life as 'the like of a king of Norway or the Eastern world' with no very defined sense of where either place might be, just as Philly conjectures that he may have been 'off east', fighting for the Boers to indicate the exoticism of the action rather than the actual site of the war. The 'western world' which lends to the play's title its grandeur of sweep has a similar deliberate imprecision. It may plausibly be taken to be the West of Ireland, whether the county of Mayo, the province of Connaught, or the whole western seaboard. But it is also contaminated by allusions in the play to the 'Western States', where Shawn wants his rival Christy to go, the glorified America of emigrant fantasy 'where you'll have golden chains and shiny coats and you riding upon hunters with the ladies of the land' (Synge, *CW*, IV, 115). For latter-day audiences the phrase may have resonances of the whole configuration of Europe and North America now known as the 'western world'. In Synge's contemporary context it may have had an added mythological dimension, associated with the fairy world of the west, Tir-na-nOg. This swirl of mixed reference is experienced from outside the world of the speakers, not intended from within.

Such an outside perspective is essential again and again to the comic appreciation of the characters' flights of geographic fantasy. Pegeen in Act III rejects with heavily ironic scorn the pleas of her about-to-be-ex-fiancé Shawn, pleas based largely on his property and the consequent desirability of the match:

> I'm thinking you're too fine for the like of me, Shawn Keogh of Killakeen, and let you go off till you'd find a radiant lady with

> droves of bullocks on the plains of Meath, and herself
> bedizened in the diamond jewelleries of Pharaoh's ma.
> (Synge, *CW*, IV, 155)

The diminutively local 'Shawn Keogh of Killakeen' is here wielded as sardonic title; the 'droves of bullocks' stand as ironic counterpart to the 'drift of heifers' which Shawn has just reminded them he has to offer as dowry. The plains of Meath, the rich grazing county on the opposite eastern side of Ireland from the desperately poor land of Mayo, are appropriately antithetical. But the grandeur of the 'diamond jewelleries' and the wild exoticism of 'Pharaoh's ma' are flights way beyond anything conceivably real. Time and space categories are collapsed or elided in the characters' speech. Christy, thinking that Pegeen has turned against him in Act II, resolves that 'it'd be best, maybe, I went on wandering like Esau or Cain and Abel on the sides of Neifin or the Erris plain' (Synge, *CW*, IV, 109). We can see what brings Esau to mind, deprived of his birthright, and Cain, doomed to banishment east of Eden; but Cain *and* Abel? Presumably they come in together as a fixed unit, 'CainandAbel', from Christy's aural memory of sermons which would have been his main source of scriptural knowledge. The construction of the simile leaves these figures of the Pentateuch wandering around the actual North Mayo countryside with the desolate Christy Mahon.

The mental mapping of Synge's characters goes beyond sublunar geography towards an imagination of heaven and hell. Christy fervently implores the Widow Quin to help him win Pegeen at the end of Act II, with promises of prayers in recompense:

> I'll be asking God to stretch a hand to you in the hour of death,
> and lead you short cuts through the Meadows of Ease, and up
> the floor of Heaven to the Footstool of the Virgin's Son.
> (Synge, *CW*, IV, 131)

Such baroque phrasing no doubt derives plausibly enough from the florid language of Catholic prayer. But the 'short cuts' represent the domesticating countryman's touch. Even in Heaven, Christy is sure that you can be shown a short-cut if you know a well-disposed native of the place. Christy's most elaborate imagination of Heaven comes in his famous image of Helen of Troy. In the love-duet with Pegeen Christy pictures her in an assured future of their love together:

> If the mitred bishops seen you that time, they'd be the like of the holy prophets, I'm thinking, do be straining the bars of Paradise to lay eyes on the Lady Helen of Troy, and she abroad pacing back and forward with a nosegay in her golden shawl.
>
> (Synge, *CW*, IV, 149)

In Synge sexual attractiveness is often thus measured in terms of the desires of celibate male frustration. Here the envy of an imagined bench of bishops contemplating the beauty of Pegeen is projected up to the holy prophets in Paradise. But notice that, in this Syngean afterlife, the Christian heaven is next door to the Elysian fields in which the Lady Helen of Troy walks; and the ascetic denizens of heaven are imprisoned there, raging for the sensual liberty which Helen enjoys. Through the wild indecorum of Christy's vernacular geography of heaven, Synge exposes and subverts the traditional opposition of classical Hellenism to the revealed religion of Judaeo-Christianity.

The audience perspective on this is necessarily an outside one, based on a wider and more orthodox geography or cosmology. It is impossible to enjoy the fantastic imagination of the 'radiant lady on the plains of Meath' unless there is some sense of the unlikelihood of her being 'bedizened with the diamond jewelleries of Pharaoh's ma'. With no awareness of the heterodoxy of Helen's classical Elysium bordering the prophets' Paradise, the subversive power of the image would be lost on us. The imagination of the people in Synge's plays is freed up to construct the world differently, overriding normal distinctions of space and time so that Esau, Cain *and* Abel may seem to people Neifin and the Erris plain. The experience of that freedom as freedom is only available to those who ordinarily observe such distinctions as normal, for whom this is another construction of the world from their own.

This would no doubt have been true for the original Abbey audiences. But for them this only related the characters to the tradition of the stage Irishman whose ignorance is exploited for the condescending merriment of the English. In such a view the geographical mis-orientations of Synge's Mayo people were like Irish bulls, designed to illustrate the child-like illogicality of the natives. *The Playboy* was rejected all the more vehemently as it seemed to collude with such colonial stereotyping. Synge's version of North Mayo may, on the face of it, seem not unlike the West Cork of Somerville and Ross where the English Resident Magistrate Major Yeates stands in for the viewpoint of the English *Badminton Magazine* readers (where the Irish R.M. stories were first published) in marking off the zany abnormality of Irish peasant behaviour. *The Playboy* is different not only in the absence of any audience sponsor equivalent to the R.M. within the text, but in the subversiveness of its imagined scene. Somerville and Ross, for all their enjoyment of the otherness of the Irish and their sense of identification with them, reaffirm as reassuringly normal the R.M.-like perspective of their English readership. The peculiarities of place in Synge's peasant Mayo, by contrast, and the mentality of the people who live there, challenge an audience to maintain their sense of extra-theatrical normality, their orderly middle-class construction of the world in which east is east and west is west. The breakdown of conventional order and orientation is experienced with a bewilderment partly felt as liberation. It is this liberatory dimension in the play's imagination of place which justifies the conception of *The Playboy* as carnival.

Carnival and the sacred

There is one objection to *The Playboy* made by its rioting critics which has not yet been considered: its profanity. In advance of the first production, Yeats and Gregory were fully aware of the need to tone down the language of the play, but they were neither of them directly involved in rehearsals and Synge, who was in charge, had an author's reluctance to cut his own lines. So few if any of the characters' oaths were thinned out; and there were a lot of them to thin. In Act I alone there are no less than thirty-three invocations of the name of God, some of them quite spectacularly inappropriate:

PEGEEN (*with blank amazement*). Is it killed your father?

> CHRISTY (*subsiding*). With the help of God I did surely, and that the Holy Immaculate Mother may intercede for his soul.
>
> (Synge, *CW*, IV, 73)

It is pious custom to acknowledge the assistance of the Lord in any action you have achieved, and equally to pray for the soul's rest of anyone departed this life. But when the dead man is your own father whom you have dispatched from this life, then both the requested intercession of the Virgin and the devout humility before God's aid seem somewhat out of place. This is an Irish bull with a topspin of sacrilege. Yet Act I, in which it appears with all the other profane 'Glory be to God's, was applauded by the first-night audience, so much so that the directors sent Yeats that very premature early telegram: 'Play a great success'. Things were to get worse as the play went on.

Synge and his play, Yeats as sponsor and spokesman, were attacked for the foreignness, the inadequacy and inauthenticity of their representation of Irishness. Coded into that antagonism was a subtext of sectarian suspicion which was always there but seldom voiced. No one ever quite said that Synge was a Protestant defaming Irish Catholicism; at one debate on the play a self-proclaimed Protestant nationalist deplored the fact that 'Protestants calling themselves Nationalists should be responsible for [*The Playboy*'s] production'.[38] Lip-service had to be paid at least to the ideal of nationalism as an interdenominational creed, and only D.P. Moran of *The Leader*, the most vituperative but perhaps the most honest of the nationalist editors, was occasionally explicit in aligning confessional and political allegiance.[39] Still, Synge's profanity coming from a Protestant writer was bound to have been an added source of offence to the largely Catholic audiences of the Abbey. For it was not only the set-piece ironies of pious habits of language in flagrantly impious contexts like Christy's confession which were sources of provocation. More pervasively there was the merely mechanical use of mouth-filling oaths as rhythmic counters to round out a line or give emphasis to an intonation. Synge wrote as the unbeliever he was, and gave to his characters a colourful language of the sacred emptied out of belief.

One of the sorest of sore spots in this most provocative of texts was Michael James's betrothal blessing on Christy and Pegeen. Michael James, staggering home in his cups from the wake in Act III, is reluctantly pressured into accepting Christy instead of Shawn Keogh as son-in-law. The speech is worth quoting at length to illustrate its multiple sources of offence and the way they are combined.

> MICHAEL (*standing up in the centre, holding on to both of them*). It's the will of God, I'm thinking, that all should win an easy or a cruel end, and it's the will of God that all should rear up lengthy families for the nurture of the earth. What's a single man, I ask you, eating a bit in one house and drinking a sup in another, and he with no place of his own, like an old braying jackass strayed upon the rocks? (*To Christy.*) It's many would be in dread to bring your like into their house for to end them maybe with a sudden end; but I'm a decent man of Ireland, and I'd liefer face the grave untimely and I seeing a score of grandsons growing up little gallant swearers by the name of God, than go peopling my bedside with puny weeds the like of what you'd breed, I'm thinking, out of Shaneen Keogh. (*He joins their hands.*) A daring fellow is the jewel of the world, and a man did split his father's middle with a single clout should have the bravery of ten, so may God and Mary and St. Patrick bless you, and increase you from this mortal day.
>
> (Synge, *CW*, IV, 157)

The Irish patriarch so drunk he has to be propped up by the couple he is about to bless no doubt was an objectionable spectacle to start with. The drunkenness and the cowardice of the 'decent man of Ireland' (who has all too obviously only accepted Christy because he is scared to reject him) are much too close to the stereotypical stage Irishman for comfort. The traditional Irish family values he preaches, the God-given responsibility of procreation, are unsettled by the strident sexuality of the braying jackass (an image of the single life Synge picked up on Aran where it was used in reproof of his own celibacy). This is followed by the eugenics of violence which makes the 'puny weed' Shawn Keogh an unfit mate, where the children of the supposedly ferocious Christy will be 'gallant little swearers by the name of God'. In this extravaganza of profanity upon profanity, the specifically

Irish form of the benediction must have added a last touch of outrage for the original audiences. The litany of God and Mary and St Patrick is derived from the standard sequence of greetings in Irish: 'Dia dhuit', God be with you, 'Dia is Muire dhuit', God and Mary be with you, 'Dia is Muire dhuit is Padraig', God and Mary and Patrick be with you. The authority of the Almighty Father and his Irish attendant saints is here invoked by a father in honour of the supposed father-killer. It is no wonder that at one performance an outraged spectator shouted out at this scene, 'If that is Irish, then I'm an Englishman.'[40]

Could such a speech, with its dizzying incongruities and its interlaced blasphemies so calculated to offend, have been conceived without malicious political intent? In suggesting the carnivalesque nature of the play, it has been no part of the design of this chapter to prove Synge's *Playboy* innocent, only innocent as charged with the deliberate intention of making a travesty of the Irish and all that they held sacred. That was the effect of the play but not its objective. Travesty, rather, is endemic in carnival where the sacred is systematically profaned, the physical is permitted its riot, the images of the holy are deliberately guyed and mocked. It was not for nothing that Synge labelled the scene of Michael James's blessing 'Rabelaisian' (Synge, *CW*, IV, 297): it has the true exuberant unrestraint of Rabelais. What made the carnival mode of *The Playboy* so distinctive – and so inevitably offensive to the Abbey audience – was the way it was disguised beneath an appearance of social realism and the way Ireland, the West of Ireland, was thus made to appear as a 'natural' site of carnival.

When Christy enters the pub in Act I, he has been walking 'wild eleven days', a plausible length of time to cover the more than a hundred and fifty miles from Kerry up to the Belmullet peninsula. He 'killed' his father, he tells the Mayo people, on 'Tuesday was a week', that is the Tuesday before last. Assuming that he does not count in the day of the assault itself, his eleven days' walking will have brought him to the O'Flahertys on a Saturday night; which sounds right, given the sports the following day which are likely to have been held on a Sunday in unsabbatarian Ireland. In other words the action of the play occupies a single weekend. It is the very least of *The Playboy*'s secularising spirit that we never hear of anyone going to Mass, and that the priest Father Reilly is never seen, only endlessly cited by the all but imbecile Shawn Keogh.[41] The Saturday night and Sunday morning occupation of Michael James and his cronies is not mass-going but attending the extravagantly bibulous wake of Kate Cassidy (of which more shortly). The quite exceptional character of Christy's visit, the festive structure of the action culminating in the sports, are masked beneath what look like just another couple of days in the lives of the local people of 'a wild coast of Mayo' (Synge, *CW*, IV, 55).

George Brotherton, drawing on M.M. Bakhtin, has usefully detailed the features of Christy which mark him as a type of Carnival King, crowned for a time by the people, only to be uncrowned, abused and scourged by them at carnival's end.[42] As with other Lords of Misrule, Christy is a specially unlikely, unlordly figure whose temporary achievement of sovereignty is an inversion of the lowly position he normally occupies. When he achieves his moment of apotheosis, raised aloft on the shoulders of the crowd after his victory in the mule-race, Old Mahon can not believe the evidence of his own eyes, so improbable does it seem that his son, 'the loony of Mahon's', should be thus fêted. Christy, in one early title for the play 'The Fool of Farnham' (Synge, *CW*, IV, 294), is metamorphosed into the hero of Mayo's Feast of Fools. Though such a carnival form underpins the play and gives it its structure, it is a rite buried within a dramatic mode which does not declare its own ritual nature.

The festive is always offstage in *The Playboy*, apprehended at an oblique angle to the represented action. The drama of the sports is enacted through the narrative of the excited onlookers who watch it from the window of the pub high above the strand where it goes on below. The set fills briefly with Christy's adoring followers carrying in his prizes, only to empty again, leaving him alone for his love-scene with Pegeen. Where Boucicault made the set-piece of the wake one of the theatrical high points of *The Shaughraun*, in *The Playboy* it only reaches us through the celebratory reminiscence of Michael James. Yet the carnival grotesque is no less vividly itself for coming to us through language rather than representation. Michael James regrets not having taken Christy with him to Kate Cassidy's wake,

> for you'd never see the match of it for flows of drink, the way when we sunk her bones at noonday in her narrow grave, there were five men, aye, and six men, stretched out retching speechless on the holy stones. (Synge, *CW*, IV, 151)

If the sports are one kind of carnival climax, this is another: with its excesses of consumption and evacuation, its outrageous proximities of physical life and death, of the profane and the sacred, it is what Bakhtin calls 'grotesque realism'.[43] Where Boucicault with his staged spectacle domesticated the Irish wake, tamed it to the tastes of his audience, Synge made of the burial of the unseen and unknown Kate Cassidy an anarchic defiance of every sort of decorum.

The long colonial history of Ireland, its ever-strengthening nationalist movement at the turn of the century that sensed victory near at hand, demanded pure polarities, a kind of cultural Manichaeism. There were to be no shadings, no crossovers, no hybridities in the antitheses which separated men from women, east from west, the English from the Irish, sacred from profane. Synge's version of carnival in *Playboy* collapsed all these categories into one another. In a number of respects, however, the play does not correspond to Bahktin's concept of carnival which has so dominated thinking on the subject in the later twentieth century. Its form is not overtly fantastic. If Synge marked some of its scenes as Rabelaisian, the play as a whole has none of the demonstratively fantastic gigantism of Rabelais. The strangeness of its imagined setting is all the stranger for its appearance of ordinary social reality. It is not anti-hegemonic in thrust; it does not unequivocally celebrate the 'body of the people' as Bakhtinian carnival is said to do. Even though Synge was at pains to acknowledge his 'collaboration' with the Irish country people, his debt to the 'popular imagination that is fiery and magnificent, and tender' (Synge, *CW*, IV, 54), he remained satirically distrustful of communal values, even where a primitive community of the people was involved. In form and style, also, *The Playboy* does not fully conform to Bakhtin's model of carnival, not least in being a play. For Bakhtin the novel, with its hybrid capaciousness, its juxtaposition of a full range of diverse modes of discourse, is the main vehicle for the dialogic imagination, activating the heteroglossia of language. In its dramatic genre, in its surface realism and its homogeneousness of language, *The Playboy* may appear monologic rather than dialogic. However, the discursive dialogue of Synge's play operates between the language, the mentality and behaviour of the stage characters, and those of an implied audience. The Dublin nationalists who first watched the play in the Abbey in 1907 could not be expected to take the view of such an implied audience; their very concept of the nation involved an idealising vision of the difference between their own modern middle-class lives and a pure, crimeless peasantry of the West of Ireland. As a result they were bound to repudiate *The Playboy* as malicious travesty. But another perspective was available for those who could see in the grotesque otherness of the play's imagined world a carnivalisation of their own.

4 Class and space in O'Casey

D.J. O'Donoghue, writing two years after Synge's death, expressed a common nationalist viewpoint when he described how the plays reflected 'an exotic and alien mind'. 'I have never been able to regard Synge as one who, living amongst a people, grows to be one of them, identifies entirely with them, and voices their thoughts and emotions, and interprets their every movement.'[1] Synge remained the Anglo-Irish gentleman outsider, by his own admission forced for his knowledge of the people to eavesdrop on 'what was being said by the servant girls in the kitchen' (Synge, *CW*, IV, 53). With O'Casey's tenement plays it was different from the beginning. O'Casey was perceived as writing from within; he was praised for the immediacy, the authenticity and reality of his representation of slum life. *The Shadow of the Gunman* was 'a gramophone record of the Dublin accent and the Dublin tenement and the Dublin poor'.[2] 'Mr O'Casey lived among the people he portrays, and he makes his audience live among them, too', wrote the *Irish Times* reviewer of *Juno and the Paycock*.[3] In *The Plough and the Stars* (which won admiring reviews before it hit trouble at its fourth performance), 'It is as if the author had taken us by the hand and brought us down to this tenement ... and told us to watch what was going on.'[4]

After the production of *Juno*, Joseph Holloway recorded in his journal:

> O'Casey is amused when he hears people say, who never were in a tenement, that his plays are photographic of the life he depicts. They not knowing anything at first hand of what they are talking.[5]

But the phenomenal success of these plays involved exactly this disparity of knowledge, and by implication of class, between playwright and audience. O'Casey offered something new on the Abbey stage, a picture of Dublin's urban poor, of the lives of the tenement streets which were literally just around the corner from the Abbey Theatre, but where most of the audience would never have set foot. There had been tenement plays before O'Casey, notably *Blight* in 1917, by Oliver St John Gogarty and Joseph O'Connor, which was the first Abbey production O'Casey himself ever saw.[6] But *Blight*, subtitled *The Tragedy of Dublin*, was a problem play in the style of Shaw's early *Widowers' Houses*, exposing the social ills of the tenements to fuel a campaign for urban renewal.[7] O'Casey's tenement drama, by contrast, was felt as slice-of-life naturalism, with all the contemporaneity of immediate events rendered from within by the self-educated slum dramatist.

This image O'Casey took to himself with pride. In a famous passage of his third-person *Autobiographies* he wrote:

> It had often been recorded in the Press, by those who could guess shrewdly, that Sean was a slum dramatist, a gutter-snipe who could jingle a few words together out of what he had seen and heard. The terms were suitable and accurate, for he was both, and, all his life, he would hold the wisdom and courage that these conditions had given him.[8]

Such a vision of O'Casey as the working-class writer who himself emerged from the tenements he so brilliantly dramatised in his first three produced plays, the so-called 'Dublin trilogy', was fostered by the *Autobiographies*, endorsed by the first generation of critics of his work and is probably still the popular belief of most theatre audiences. However, biographical scholarship since the 1960s has shown how misleading this notion is in a number of ways.[9] O'Casey's parents, Michael and Susan Casey, were not working class, but lower middle class: Michael was a clerk with the Protestant Church Missions, O'Casey's older sister Bella was a trained National School teacher. The young John Casey had a much less deprived childhood and much more regular education than he is prepared to admit in the *Autobiographies*. And he did not grow up, he did not live for most of his pre-playwriting days, in the tenements. His father was the chief tenant, even perhaps the sub-landlord of the four-storey house where he was born, 85 Upper Dorset St.[10] Though the North Dublin flats and houses the family lived in were often small and cramped by today's standards, they could not be called slums in comparison with the horrific conditions registered in the 1914 Dublin Housing Inquiry Report on the tenements.[11] The only time O'Casey ever spent in what could credibly be called a tenement was the period of five months in 1921–2 when he shared a room in 35 Mountjoy Square, on which experience he based *The Shadow of a Gunman*.[12]

On closer examination, it appears that rather than the working-class autodidact from the slums of his self-representations, O'Casey belonged to that commoner type, the writer from a middle-class family gone down in the world. Count up the authors of the later nineteenth century alone who had financially insolvent or inadequate fathers: Ibsen, Strindberg (even if his failed father may have been a Strindbergian invention), Chekhov, Shaw, Yeats, Joyce. O'Casey was unlike these – and like Synge – in losing his father at an early age by death, but the social consequences were comparable to those of paternal failure. Just nine years younger than Synge, O'Casey curiously had exactly the same position in his family, as the youngest of five surviving children with, in each case, three older brothers and a sister. However, the Synges and the Caseys came from the opposite edges of the middle-class social bands. Mrs Synge, when her barrister husband died in 1872, was left in reduced but still comfortable circumstances with £400 a year in rents.[13] Synge himself was to have an annual income of £40 from inherited capital, enough with help from his mother to support him through long unproductive years in Germany, France and the Aran Islands. Michael Casey's annual salary, by comparison, was £70 and his death in 1886, when O'Casey was just six, brought the family perilously close to subsistence level, even with two sons and a daughter earning. A comparison with the Shaws, closer in class to the Caseys than the Synges, brings out just how near to the bottom of the bourgeois heap O'Casey's family were. Shaw and O'Casey at different times both briefly attended the same school, the Central Model School, Marlborough Street. For Michael Casey to send his children there was an effort, a measure of his educational ambition, because it involved the payment of some fees and was a cut above the National School which was the alternative. For Shaw attendance at the school (if only for six months) was social degradation, as he confessed in the remarkable late essay entitled 'Shame and Wounded Snobbery: A Secret Kept for 80 Years': the reason was that the Model School took Catholic as well as Protestant pupils.[14]

O'Casey, then, was not, technically, working class in origins; he did not grow up illiterate or uneducated; he did not come from the tenements. Yet the exposed position of his family on the very margins of the lower middle class, and the physical proximity of the places they lived to the actual slums made of O'Casey's social consciousness something quite different from that of a Synge or a Shaw, a Yeats or a Joyce. His was no case merely of *vie en Bohème* or shabby gentility. He did at times endure real poverty and the menace of the tenements was readily before him. It is out of this experience that the three plays of the Dublin trilogy were created, and they are informed by the complex emotions and attitudes of that class identity. The stage space of the tenement, the grand Georgian town house designed for gracious living honeycombed with the working-class families of the poor, that image so integral to the impact of O'Casey's plays with middle-class theatre audiences, was constructed by a playwright who did not himself come from within that milieu but who knew it from uncomfortably close quarters. To understand *The Shadow of a Gunman*, *Juno and the Paycock*, *The Plough and the Stars*, and their reception, it is necessary to understand the conflicted class attitudes that shape them.

Class constructions

The six volumes of O'Casey's *Autobiographies* are more or less worthless as sources for the facts of his life. Notoriously without dates, freely inventive in style and substance, they constitute a heavily ornamented fantasia on biographical themes rather than any sort of verifiable narrative. Published between 1939 and 1954, well after O'Casey's international fame as a dramatist was established, the past was reconceived throughout to correspond to the needs of the then present: the need to settle old grudges, to justify opinions, to dramatise the story of the poor boy from the slums struggling towards creative fulfilment. As such retrospective re-creations, they cannot be trusted as providing the raw material for the 1920s plays. The existence of those plays and their familiarity to readers are among the *données* of the *Autobiographies*; at one point in *Inishfallen, Fare Thee Well*, there is a fantasy of Fluther Good appearing fighting drunk in Yeats's Merrion Square salon as though the fictional Fluther were as real, if not more real, than the effete Yeatsian groupies O'Casey so despised (O'Casey, *A*, II, 234). Yet O'Casey's autobiographical self-mythologising does provide a sense of the emotional strands within his constructed persona and its class formation. As such the *Autobiographies* supply a suggestive background for the reading of the Dublin tenement plays.

In the first volume, *I Knock at the Door*, O'Casey does not try to conceal the original lower-middle-class status of his family, the Cassides as he calls them. If anything he highlights it and the fall into poverty brought about by his father's death. A set-piece description of the fully furnished Victorian parlour in the chapter on 'His Father's Wake' is to stand in contrast to the stark surroundings of later dwellings; and the elaborate funeral of his father – 'Hearse, mourning-coach, cabs, and cars' (O'Casey, *A*, I, 41) – is strikingly unlike the pathetic/grotesque spectacle of his mother's funeral, thirty years and three volumes later, where he has to borrow cash from the local shopkeeper to pay the undertakers before they will carry the coffin out of the house. It is above all Michael Casside's books which are enumerated as indicators of his class and educational status: 'a regiment of theological controversial books ... a neatly uniformed company of Dickens', Scott's, George Eliot's, Meredith's and Thackeray's novels; Shakespeare's Works; Burns', Keats', Milton's, Gray's, and Pope's poetry' (O'Casey, *A*, I, 27–8). The dying father is horrified by the idea that his son, unable to attend school because of his eye disease, will 'grow up to be a dunce' (O'Casey, *A*, I, 28). One major drive of the *Autobiographies* is to prove that Johnny did not grow up to be a dunce, that he vindicated the values figured in his father's library of books, that he was capable of re-gaining the middle-class status which by the father's death the family had lost.

Reading, learning, the culture of books and knowledge, are

held to fiercely as the measure of the boy Johnny's potential or actual superiority to those around him.[15] In his first job, smarting under the humiliation of his poverty and his position as the lowest kind of office-boy in Hymdim and Leadem's (the chandler's company Hampton-Leedom), his revolt takes the form of a challenge to one of the bosses to a competition in learning: 'I'll bet I know more'n you do' (O'Casey, *A*, I, 275). The spirit of this challenge is repeated throughout the sequence of the *Autobiographies*. Johnny is driven to reclaim lost status not in terms of social hierarchy or position in employment (about which he is uniformly satirical), but as the distinction of knowledge and culture, a truer and more authentic ground of superiority. His hunger for books is a recurrent motif; every gain or loss of income is calculated in terms of the number of second-hand books that can be bought or must be done without. Whatever his material deprivations, the need for reading is represented as an appetite to be satisfied at all costs.

In this O'Casey distinguishes himself from other members of the family. The picture of the young Johnny Casside is a conventional-enough portrait of the artist in embryo. As the youngest son protected by his mother, the runt of the litter with the handicap of his bad eyes, he is cast as the atypical member of the family whose physical weakness will be counterpoised by the creative achievements of his mind. Within this pattern, O'Casey's portrait of his older siblings is not a kindly one. Their physical strength, their appetites and needs, are resented as they are associated with the degradation of the family. So, for example, Ella's (the real-life Bella's) marriage to a common soldier, which led to her having to give up her position as a teacher is rendered by O'Casey with a sort of prurient disapproval of its sexual motivation, her desire for her 'drummer boy'.[16] The mother's grim verdict on the marriage – 'You've made your bed, an' you'll have to lie on it' (O'Casey, *A*, I, 68) – is as though endorsed and vindicated by the outcome when the husband turns into a wife-beater, goes mad and leaves her a destitute widow with five children. 'She had married a man who had destroyed every struggling gift she had had when her heart was young and her careless mind was blooming' (O'Casey, *A*, I, 446). It is a similar situation with the two older, hard-drinking, brothers Tom and Mick, who give up careers in the post office to join the army. Their drinking, their fecklessness, Tom's marriage to a lower-class woman (particularly savagely treated by O'Casey), all contribute to a picture of people who have let the family down, betrayed their own higher potential.

This culminates in the episode in *Inishfallen, Fare Thee Well* where Sean (after the death of his mother) is forced to leave the house he has lived in so long by a confrontation with Mick, the degraded drunken brother:

> From the corner of an eye he saw the tousled figure staggering into the room, knocking clumsily and intentionally against the table at which Sean was sitting, while an envious, dirty hand, sliding along it, sent the little ink-bottle flying to the floor. Sean said nothing, but sat quietly where he was.
>
> – Writin', be God, again! murmured the blurred voice of his brother; some fellas are able to give themselves airs! Scholar, is it? Scholar, me arse! Well, th' ink's gone, so wha'll we do now? Here's one who's forgotten moren' some'll ever learn. There's a man here. Takes a few dhrinks, but a man, all th' same; a man with two good mitts. Writin'! If I was someone, I'd thry to be a man first! But Sean sat still, quiet, where he was.
>
> (O'Casey, *A*, II, 31)

The whole scene is a moral justification of the teetotal Sean, the quiet, studious, creative writer, with his middle-class values of books and education, against the machismo of the drunk who revenges in jealous resentment of his brother's superiority the awareness of his own degenerate state.

But if this is one strand of the *Autobiographies* by which Johnny/Sean, unlike his siblings, will win through against all the odds to the assured position of well-read and cultured writer, there is another conflicting pattern which emerges when he becomes a navvy. As someone from a Protestant lower-middle-class family background, O'Casey need never have worked as an unskilled labourer. His second job as described in the *Autobiographies*, like his first, was with an all-Protestant firm (Jason's = Eason's); in both cases sectarian hierarchy assured him a position among the white-collar staff, a caste above the

Catholic vanmen and messenger-boys. Too restless, too insubordinate, to hold down such jobs – he only lasts a week at Jason's – O'Casey in the *Autobiographies* elides what must have been a prolonged period of unemployment before he went to work for the GNR, the Great Northern Railway, in 1903.

Sean's initiation into manual labour is signalled as a new epoch in 'At the Sign of the Pick and Shovel', the opening chapter of *Drums Under the Window*, the third volume of the *Autobiographies*. The description of his first day at work highlights his comic inadequacy, his total physical unfitness to handle pick or shovel, as the marks of his previous class background. But within the course of a single paragraph, he is transformed:

> His body now became flexible, his arms strong, his legs firm in tackling shovel, pick, crowbar, rope, scaffolding-pole, wheelbarrow, hod, or sledge with the best of them . . . and, at last, [he] found himself the one man in the gang who could mount a ladder with a hod carrying near eight stone in it, balancing it with equal ease on right shoulder or on left[.]
> (O'Casey, *A*, I, 409)

The few pages at the start of this chapter are practically all we hear of O'Casey's nine years' service with the GNR, and doubts have been cast on how continuously he worked in this time.[17] But in the *Autobiographies* it makes for a new pride in physical work, a new political role as activist in the labour movement, and a new dimension to the persona of Sean. From this point on, the experience of the labourer becomes a criterion of value, a hallmark of authentic being. It is by these standards that the largely middle-class leaders of the Republican movement are found wanting:

> Few of those whom Sean knew could handle a pick or shovel, tie a knot, do a bandage round a serious wound, slash a gutway in a hedge, light a fire and cook a simple meal in a wet field with a keen wind blowing. About these things they knew next to nothing. (O'Casey, *A*, I, 550)

Hence his identification with the workers against the Republicans: 'Few of the Republicans were of his kinship. Here, in these houses in the purple of poverty and decay, dwelt his genuine brethren' (O'Casey, *A*, I, 552).

In this context, it is noticeable that O'Casey exactly transvalues those characteristics which he used to stigmatise members of his own family. His sceptical critique of de Valera at the beginning of *Inishfallen, Fare Thee Well* is typical:

> Sean couldn't see an excited De Valera rushing round a hurling field . . . or slanting an approving eye on any pretty girl that passed him; or standing, elbow on counter in a Dublin pub, about to lower a drink, with a Where it goes, lads. . . . He knew, like Griffith, next to nothing about the common people.
>
> (O'Casey, *A*, II, 4)

It is the sexual desire of his sister, the thoughtless physicality and irresponsible thirst for drink of his brothers, which O'Casey reprobates in them as a betrayal of the principles of mental culture which he alone in the family upholds. Yet middle-class political leaders such as de Valera and Griffith are to be distrusted because they lack the common touch, unearthed in the sport, the pubs and the sex which are the real life of the real people. The Johnny/Sean of the *Autobiographies* is at once the son of his lower-middle-class father, clinging to the idea of books as source of independence and integrity which will ultimately distinguish him from his downsliding siblings, and the creature of his working experience, militantly committed to the values and the interests of his fellow workers.

There is a familiar conflict in the psychology of the working-class writer who belongs to the category Richard Hoggart in *The Uses of Literacy* calls 'the uprooted and the anxious'.[18] To want to be a writer is to aspire beyond one's social origins, to aspire to be middle class both in economic and cultural terms. Yet solidarity with the class from which the writer comes, sympathy and commitment to the proletarian life which is the subject of writing, makes for anxiety and instability of class consciousness. It is a drama played out in English and Scottish literature in varying forms, from the novels of D.H. Lawrence, through the drama of the 1950s' 'angry young men' to the poetry of Tony Harrison and the fiction of James Kelman. In O'Casey this conflict has an added dimension because of the degree to which he cherishes middle-class values as a lost family legacy, while at the same time identifying with the working classes all the more aggressively because it is an elected identification.

This is particularly clear in *The Harvest Festival*, the only survivor of the early O'Casey plays rejected by the Abbey. The hero, Jack Rocliffe, a heavily idealised self-portrait, is a young labour activist who dies a martyr's death in the cause of the workers. He is significantly better dressed than the average worker, and speaks with no trace of the dialect which his fellow-workers (and his mother) have. His account of his own history is suggestive:

> well-dressed as I am, & well fed as I appear to be, I have shared the workers' shame. After my father died, when I was but five years of age, I lived for ten years on a cup of tea & a few cuts of dry bread daily, with a few potatoes on Sunday in honour of the Christian Festival, and becoming sickly and delicate on the dainty food I was receiving, charitable people took pity on me and gave me bottles of medicine to give me an appetite.[19]

This is the Dickensian model of the middle-class child who falls out of the system for accidental reasons, experiencing as a result the life of the working class to which he does not actually belong: note the disjunction in 'I have *shared* the workers' shame.' In *The Harvest Festival*, and in many other of his writings, these mixed emotions and conflicted class-consciousness too often produced only a melodrama of self-justification. In the Dublin tenement plays they resulted in a drama shaped and informed by the conflict.

A room of one's own: *The Shadow of a Gunman*

> My bed was along the north wall of the room, and Sean O'Casey's bed was more or less in the middle. There was a door in the south wall. I think that there would have been about three feet between the head of Sean's bed and the centre of the room when we slept, and there would have been the same distance between his feet and the door.[20]

So, in a translated version of the original Irish, Michael O'Maoláin described the actual setting on which *The Shadow of a Gunman* was based. O'Casey shared O'Maoláin's one-room flat, the 'return room' as it is called in *The Shadow*, on the ground floor of 35 Mountjoy Square for a period of five months in the winter of 1920–1. O'Maoláin, otherwise Michael Mullen, was a fellow Gaelic League enthusiast; he had worked closely with O'Casey in the labour movement, and served with him on the Council of the Irish Citizen Army. It was here that O'Casey experienced the Black-and-Tan raid which provides the main incident for *The Shadow*, and which was to be written up separately as the chapter on 'The Raid' in *Inishfallen, Fare Thee Well* (an account in which O'Maoláin is airbrushed out altogether).

Although Donal Davoren, O'Casey's *Shadow* stand-in, was regarded by most early reviewers as a very unconvincing character and since then has generally been seen as a mere feed for the star comic part of Seumas Shields (the equivalent of O'Maoláin), the conception of the play was originally centred on Donal. As O'Casey described the play, then called *On the Run*, to Lennox Robinson while at work on it in October 1922: 'It deals with the difficulties of a poet who is in continual conflict with the disturbances of a tenement house, and is built on the frame of Shelley's phrase: "Ah me, alas, pain, pain ever, forever".'[21] Although at this stage O'Casey may have been following Gregory's advice to him to 'cut out all expression of self, and develop his peculiar aptness for character drawing',[22] *The Shadow* is, in its way, as autobiographical as *The Harvest Festival*, or as *Red Roses For Me*, O'Casey's later reworking of the same materials. Davoren is shown composing O'Casey's own poems, and the design of the play is to illustrate how essential it is for a writer in a working-class environment, as for a woman writer, to have a room of his/her own. On this O'Casey wrote feelingly not only from his relatively brief experience of Mountjoy Square, but from the conditions of 422 North Circular Road where he lived while writing all three of the Dublin plays, a house which was not a slum tenement and where he did have a room of his own, but where he was very aware of the disturbing presence of other flat-dwellers around him.

Davoren is distinguished from the ordinary tenement people by his lack of belief in religion or politics, his greater education – like Jack Rocliffe in *The Harvest Festival* his speech has very few of the marks of dialect – and his preoccupation with literature. In recasting himself and his room-mate as Davoren and Shields, O'Casey exaggerated the differences between himself and O'Maoláin who was, by his own account, almost as interested in books as O'Casey was.[23] Shields has to be literate enough to spot Davoren's quotations from Shelley and Shakespeare, but for the most part he is characterised as an ignorant philistine to Davoren's sensitive poet. 'In him,' as the introductory stage direction has it, 'is frequently manifested the superstition, the fear and the malignity of primitive man.'[24] And this 'primitive man' is, of course, a man of the Dublin tenements. It would certainly not have suited O'Casey's purposes in the play to show him as the Irish-speaking native of Inishmaan O'Maoláin actually was. It is the essence of the situation that Shields is at home in the tenement, Davoren is not.

Davoren's predicament, the running gag of the play, is his constantly frustrated need to be alone and undisturbed to get on with the writing of his poetry. He is chained to the room as Shelley's Prometheus is to the rock, ('Ah me! alas, pain, pain ever, pain for ever!') and the casual but incessant comers and goers of the building are the vultures gnawing at his peace. In Act I it is, at first, the efforts to wake Seumas Shields, then his irrepressible conversation when woken, the entrances of Shields's breezy pedlar-partner Maguire, and of his belligerent rent-demanding landlord; even when Shields is gone, there follows a whole succession of visitors: Minnie Powell, Tommy Owens, Mrs Henderson and Mr Gallogher. The interruptions go on into the night in Act II, with the ever-present Shields, the addition of still more of the tenement population in the Protestant loyalist Grigsons, and finally the Auxiliaries as the ultimate intruders. The keynote is provided in the early exchange between the caged and tormented Davoren and the lackadaisical Shields:

> DAVOREN (*pacing the room as far as the space will permit*). What in the name of God persuaded me to come to such a house as this?
> SEUMAS. It's nothing when you're used to it; you're too thin-skinned altogether. (O'Casey, *SP*, 9)

Whatever the degree of theatrical sympathy or identification with Davoren and his aestheticising beliefs, the tenement characters come before the audience as they do before Davoren as figures of another life. The authorial stage directions describing Minnie Powell in Act I, for instance, reproduce the condescension of Davoren. She suddenly switches topic, 'for like all of her class, MINNIE is not able to converse very long on the one subject' (O'Casey, *SP*, 11). Like all of *her* class, that is, not mine the playwright's or yours the reader/audience's. The Dogberry style of humour of Mr Gallogher's letter to the Irish Republican Army, with its would-be legalese and malapropistic language, makes use of Davoren as audience sponsor in the awareness of how absurd it is. O'Casey himself wrote a letter, equivalent to Mr Gallogher's, on behalf of tenants threatened by a landlord asking about procedures in the Republican courts in October 1921. It is a measure of how distant the comically contrived situation of the play is from reality to read the serious formal reply to O'Casey from Austin Stack, Minister of Home Affairs in the underground Dáil Éireann.[25] The tenement people of *The Shadow* display themselves before Davoren, as O'Casey displays them for an audience; they are 'characters' in the otherness of the life they represent. Their splendid comic vitality, their wonderful idiosyncratic speech and behaviour is dependent on the outwardness with which they are constructed.

To Davoren is attributed authority partly owing to his superior education and partly to his imagined status as gunman on the run: the two are linked together. Donal has just the glamour for Minnie Powell that Christy Mahon has for Pegeen Mike, the potent combination of 'savagery and fine words'. The comedy of cross-purposes is similar in that neither Christy nor Davoren are the heroes they are thought to be by the strange community into which they come, the one only a pretend parricide, the other the mere shadow of a gunman. But they are made different by the class gap which is posited between Donal and the tenement people. Christy and Pegeen speak the same language, have the same points of reference, even if Pegeen initially misreads Christy as the playboy of her fantasy. Minnie, by contrast, speaks deferentially to 'Mr Davoren' (as do the other people of the tenement), and in her first conversation with him shows the difference between her class values and his: she regards wild flowers as weeds, and naively believes all love-poems must be addressed to a real-life girl-friend of the poet. Her credulity in taking him to be a gunman is associated with her working-class lack of sophistication. She takes away as souvenir of their brief encounter the piece of paper on which their two names are given the (to her) talismanic status of being typed together.

Minnie is initially to Davoren just one more of those hundred-and-one disturbers of his poetry-writing peace. Her blithe unawareness of his point of view is written into their opening exchange when she comes to borrow some milk:

> MINNIE. ... I shouldn't be troublin' you this way, but I'm sure you don't mind.
> DAVOREN (*dubiously*). No trouble in the world; delighted, I'm sure. ...
> MINNIE. ... Do you be alone all the day, Mr Davoren?
> DAVOREN. No, indeed; I wish to God I was.
> MINNIE. It's not good for you then. I don't know how you like to be by yourself – I couldn't stick it long. (O'Casey, *SP*, 11)

But by the end of the play, of course, Minnie's disregard for private space, here placed as a class-marker, comes to be viewed very differently. In Act II when she 'rushes into the room ... only partly dressed' (O'Casey, *SP*, 37) to warn Davoren of the coming raid, she saves the situation by cool-headedly and self-sacrificingly removing the bag of bombs which the men have only just discovered. The ignorance of the value of privacy, the lack of respect for Davoren's much-needed room of his own, are turned into a heroic ideal of communal solidarity.

This turnaround makes of Davoren a self-portrait very different from anything else in O'Casey. O'Casey never made any secret of his own physical cowardice; it is registered repeatedly in the *Autobiographies*. In the ironically entitled chapter, 'I Strike a Blow for You, Dear Land', for instance, he tells how Johnny is caught up in an anti-Boer War demonstration and, more or less by accident, knocks a soldier off his horse. In what reads very like a wish-fulfilment fantasy sequence he is rewarded with seduction by a nubile young nationalist girl who is impressed by his bravery. Though he goes along happily enough with the agreeable outcome, he is aware that 'He was no soldier. Never would be – he felt it. There was no use trying' (O'Casey, *A*, I, 368). In the *Autobiographies* generally, O'Casey contrives to make of his cowardice something like an anti-heroic badge of honour, discretion as the better part of valour, and in plays such as *The Harvest Festival* and *Red Roses for Me* he produces idealised self-portraits in which he can play the hero, as courageous as he is clever. Nowhere else does he leave an autobiographical character as bleakly exposed as he does Davoren, 'poltroon and poet', at the end of *The Shadow*.

Self-criticism and self-irony did not come easily to O'Casey, and it may be that he did not consider Davoren sufficiently like himself to feel impugned by the character in the play. What is significant is the way in which Davoren's class pretensions, the values for which he stands, are challenged by the tenement environment. At the start of the play, the contrast between Davoren and Shields works to highlight the brutality, ignorance, superstition and boastfulness of the latter. By contrast, Davoren is sensitive, freethinking, educated, literary, all qualities that the playwright implicitly endorses. But as the action proceeds, the vigour of Shields's self-assurance, his unputdownable comic verve, increasingly make Davoren look merely wispy and inadequate. When it comes to the crisis over the bombs both behave with equal pusillanimity, both are paralysed with fright and let Minnie take on the responsibility. (As O'Maoláin put it tellingly of the comparable moment in the real raid, 'I admit I wasn't Cuchulain at the gap, but O'Casey was terror in the shape of a man.'[26]) Shields's cowardice is particularly repulsive, praying only that Minnie won't split on them: 'God grant she won't say anything!' (O'Casey, *SP*, 42). Yet, though Davoren has a full sense of the moral obloquy of letting Minnie suffer for them, it does not help him to do anything. The two are condemned equally. If anything Davoren comes worse out of it; the anti-heroic Shields at least has the cowardice of his lack of convictions. Davoren is left, spouting his literary quotations from Shelley and the Bible still, in what seems like just one more posture as 'poltroon and poet'.

If *The Shadow* at the beginning dramatises half-comically, half-seriously the plight of the writer in the tenement, the need for a room of his own, the life of the tenement invades the room and overwhelms the writer. The sharp particularity of comic characterisation in the Falstaff-like Shields, in the patriotic hero-worshipper Tommy Owens or the Bible-thumping drunk Adolphus Grigson leave

Davoren looking pretentious and insipid. The one room which the poet hopes vainly to keep as his own space, when invaded by all his heterogeneous neighbours becomes a theatre of the whole tenement beyond its bounds. The act of writing, which is an impulse to control, construct and compose, is undone by the sheer anarchic energy of life which acts as its disruptive antithesis. The early reviews of *The Shadow* both criticised and admired the play for its dramatic shapelessness. It was only a series of sketches strung together, not a properly well-made play, the reviewers repeatedly commented; but this was appropriate to its subject, a guarantee of its authenticity as the true picture of the inchoate tenements. The very failure of Davoren, the O'Casey surrogate writer, to keep separate the room of his own becomes the distinctive triumph of O'Casey the maker of tenement plays. And in the heroic self-sacrifice of Minnie Powell is adumbrated a communal ethic of the tenement which stands against the bourgeois individualism of personal values and private space. That is an issue that was to be developed as a central theme of *Juno and the Paycock*, associated with the politics of gender and the family.

Women and family values: *Juno and the Paycock*

Minnie Powell saves the skins of Davoren and Shields in *The Shadow*; the only person who even tries to help and support her is Mrs Henderson. The men boast and blow, but it is the women who show the real courage of suffering and endurance. This was perceived as the pattern of the Dublin plays from early on, and O'Casey's cult of the woman went on to become a cliché in criticism of his work. It is noticeable that in this, as in many other respects, the three plays of the 'trilogy' are atypical of O'Casey's drama as a whole. Certainly nobody would think of O'Casey as a feminist on the basis of *The Harvest Festival* or *Red Roses For Me* with their positively Christ-like heroes, *The Silver Tassie* with its predatory wives and sex-object girlfriends, or the later plays in which male sexuality (*Cock-a-Doodle-Dandy*) and male-led activism (*The Star Turns Red*) are so often associated with liberation. Even within the Dublin plays, the issue of gender is oversimplified in the traditional view of women as heroes, men anti-heroes. *Juno*, with its most fully central and most fully heroic heroine figure, may be taken as a test-case for exploring the relation of gender to the questions of class and space with which this chapter is concerned.

One of the things which is distinctively new and different about *Juno* is its lack of an authorial stand-in, even such a critically conceived stand-in as Donal Davoren in *The Shadow*. This has decisive consequences for the rendering of the working-class mother Juno Boyle. The heroic figure of Juno is related to O'Casey's own mother as she came to be realised in the *Autobiographies* and as she was fictionally imagined in *The Harvest Festival*, the infinitely hard-working, resolute, compassionate spirit of the home and family. But in these other works O'Casey, or the O'Casey lookalike Jack Rocliffe, is always there to be the object of the blindly admiring mother's protection – blindly admiring, for her incomprehension of her son's actions and ideas is often stressed. In the *Autobiographies* O'Casey's very moving tribute to his mother at her death involves a ritual which turns her into an honorary member of the labour movement in which he believed:

> Over the white shroud, over the coffin, he draped the red cloth that had covered the box on which she had so often sat. It would be her red flag, ignorant as she was of all things political, and seemingly indifferent to the truth that the great only appear great because the workers are on their knees; but she was, in her bravery, her irreducible and quiet endurance, the soul of Socialism[.] (O'Casey, *A*, II, 25)

We are given a glimpse of the mother–son disagreement over politics in *The Harvest Festival*, with Mrs Rocliffe's explanation for her son's having stopped attending church: 'He talks about the Gospel of Discontent, and when I say that he should try to be content with his lot, he laughs, and puts his arms around me an says, "You don't understand, mother, you don't understand".'[27] The working-class mother fails to understand the truth of the political principles so evident to the enlightened, educated son (and by implication to the readers/audience), though she may embody those principles as the 'soul of socialism' in her very unconsciousness.

In *Juno*, in place of the heroic Jack Rocliffe, or the autobiographer Johnny/Sean, there are only weak children who inadequately represent the causes they support, in Mary's case the Trades Union, in Johnny's Republicanism. The dramatically strong Juno is given the best of her exchanges with both of them on their political beliefs. With Mary, who is made to appear vain and frivolous, spending her time on strike trying to decide which ribbon she should wear in her hair, Juno questions the logic of the dispute over which Mary is striking:

> MRS BOYLE. I don't know why you wanted to walk out for Jennie Claffey; up to this you never had a good word for her.
> MARY. What's the use of belongin' to a Trades Union if you won't stand up for your principles? Why did they sack her? It was a clear case of victimisation. We couldn't let her walk the streets, could we?
> MRS BOYLE. No of course yous couldn't – yous wanted to keep her company. Wan victim wasn't enough. When the employers sacrifice wan victim, the Trades Unions go wan betther be sacrificin' a hundred. (O'Casey, *SP*, 49)

Mary here may have political logic on her side: Juno's attitude threatens the very basis of all industrial action. But in the dynamics of theatrical dialogue it is the mother who is given the lines.

'It doesn't matther what you say, Ma – a principle's a principle' (O'Casey, *SP*, 49). It is the same tag which Johnny mouths boastfully in proud proclamation of the ideals for which he was wounded in the Easter Rising and again on the Republican side at the start of the Civil War in 1922: 'I'd do it agen, ma, I'd do it agen; for a principle's a principle'.

> MRS BOYLE. Ah, you lost your best principle, me boy, when you lost your arm; them's the only sort o' principles that's any good to a workin' man.
> JOHNNY. Ireland only half free'll never be at peace while she has a son left to pull a trigger.
> MRS BOYLE. To be sure, to be sure – no bread's a lot better than half a loaf. (O'Casey, *SP*, 65)

Once again Juno's working-class pragmatics enforced by the common sense of the homely proverb undermine Johnny's posturing. We are likely to be suspicious of the validity of such loudly proclaimed principles even before we know that Johnny has betrayed them by informing on his comrade Robbie Tancred. An audience is encouraged to join in Juno's general scepticism about 'principles' in themselves. The effect of this is the more striking, given O'Casey's own personal addiction to acting on principle. This is the man who (according to the *Autobiographies*) gave up his job in Eason's rather than remove his cap when being paid his week's wages, who lost his job in the GNR because he would not renounce his membership in the Union, who resigned from his beloved Irish Citizen Army rather than accept that Countess Markievicz might belong both to the ICA and the Irish National Volunteers. Surely Mrs Casey, Juno-like, must have had a number of occasions to regret her son's adherence to the proposition that 'a principle's a principle'. But in *Juno* there is no compellingly self-justifying son to represent the O'Caseyan point of view, and the anti-intellectual, apolitical mother has it all her own way.

For much of the play the conflict of principles is not between unthinking mother and thinking son as in *Autobiographies*, but between caring wife and care-free husband. If Juno stands as an archetype of the working-class mother, the Captain is a comic embodiment of the shiftless working-class father, a kind of walking illustration of Oscar Wilde's proposition that work is the curse of the drinking classes. In the first act in particular the audience is allowed to glory in the Captain's ignorance, his self-glorifying fantasies, his workshy evasiveness. The opening authorial stage direction introducing Mary may present her aspiration to education as admirable: 'Two forces are working in her mind – one, through the circumstances of her life, pulling her back; the other through the influence of books she has read, pushing her forward' (O'Casey, *SP*, 47). This is not the view of her father, who complains of his daughter to Joxer that 'she's always readin' lately – nothin' but thrash, too. There's one I was lookin' at dh'other day: three stories, *The Doll's House*, *Ghosts*, an' *The Wild Duck* – buks only fit for chiselurs!' (O'Casey, *SP*, 59). It is a great laugh-line in the theatre not only for the splendid absurdity of Ibsen's sombre problem plays taken for children's stories, but for the temporary comic release into Boyle-like philistinism for an audience normally respectful of the highbrow culture Ibsen represents. An audience has to be educated enough to find the Captain's misrecognition of the plays' titles funny; the laughter derives from a vicarious enjoyment of Boyle's ignorant derisiveness. Literature in his world is represented instead by the unending stream of cliché/quotation served up by Joxer as the emollient offerings of the parasite, garbled literary hand-me-downs from Burns or Scott, Thomas Davis or William Carleton.[28] Once again an educated audience is allowed to revel in this travesty of cultured citation.

The Captain stands for drink, talk, the public-house, the pleasure principle; Juno stands for work, the home, the family, the reality principle. At first the basic dynamics of comedy may seem to align an audience with the former against the latter. It is significant that one of Juno's constant, and constantly thwarted, objectives is to ring-fence the Boyles' two-room flat against the intrusive Joxer. Joxer, 'an oul' front-top neighbour' (O'Casey, *SP*, 76), is always lurking somewhere about the house with his signal song, 'Are you there, Moriarty?' to establish when the coast is clear for him to sneak back in. The buttydom of the Captain and Joxer is an all-male camaraderie of the tenement and beyond it the pub, Foley's or Ryan's, the two locals at the imagined corner of the street. This homosocial bond, in some productions played even with a touch of the homoerotic, is set against the husband/wife relationship and its responsibilities which the Captain so signally flouts. As befits her name, Juno's territory is the home, the room we see on stage, which she has to hold together against the depradations of the strutting paycock and his tenement cronies.[29]

Act I ends with the illusion of migration out of the tenements for the reintegrated Boyle family to 'somewhere we're not known' (O'Casey, *SP*, 67), with the prospect of the Captain living on his unearned capital as model husband and father, having renounced Joxer for ever; Act II by contrast serves to crystallise what is at issue in the scene which they continue to inhabit. The party in celebration of the supposed inheritance, the spending-spree on furnishings and consumer goods all on borrowed money advanced from the pawnbroker's, represent the thoughtless extravagance of a class too poor ever to have learned the habits of saving. With all its splendid comic energy, Mrs Gogan's arabesque reminiscences, the party-piece songs and recitations, this is a temporary gaiety under threat from the realities that impinge so starkly with the entrance of Mrs Tancred mourning her son. Presented in this scene is a proximity of death and life, of sacred and profane, distinctly different from the *Playboy* carnivalesque. For here the categories are not confused, the solemn funeral rites and the anguish of human grief still the party-spirit into sobriety. A theatrical space is cleared for Mrs Tancred's great threnody over her murdered son.

What is more, the exchange between the Captain and Juno on the death of Tancred, after the mourners have left, is a key moment in the enunciation of the values that stand between them.

> BOYLE. ... We've nothin' to do with these things, one way or t'other. That's the Government's business, an' let them do what we're payin' them for doin'.
>
> MRS BOYLE. I'd like to know how a body's not to mind these things; look at the way they're afther leavin' the people in this very house. Hasn't the whole house, nearly, been massacreed? There's young Dougherty's husband with his leg off; Mrs Travers that had her son blew up be a mine in Inchegeela, in County Cork; Mrs Mannin' that lost wan of her sons in an ambush a few weeks ago, an' now, poor Mrs Tancred's only child gone west with his body made a collandher of. Sure, if it's not our business, I don't know whose business it is.
>
> (O'Casey, *SP*, 80–1)

Boyle's self-image as righteously indignant taxpayer calling on the government to do its duty is splendid; but Juno's speech is at the heart of the matter. Suddenly the population of the tenement swells with names we have never heard before; the offstage house fills with the bodies of the maimed, the mourning wives and mothers of the Civil War. In a speech which is convincingly demotic in phrasing and syntax – 'Mrs Tancred's only child gone west with his body made a collandher of' – she expresses her belief that we are members of one another: 'Sure, if it's not our business, I don't know whose business it is.' This is the tenement ethic at its most positive, just as Boyle's self-preening irresponsibility, which is seen as equally typical, is the tenement spirit at its worst.

Juno is no saint of the slums; within minutes of this proclamation of concern for Mrs Tancred and the other victims of war she can relapse into the hard politics of blame: 'in wan way, she deserves all she got; for lately, she let th' Diehards make an open house of th' place' (O'Casey, *SP*, 81). She is as class-conscious as the next within the closely observed pecking order of the tenement. She is sycophantically ingratiating with the schoolteacher and would-be lawyer Charles Bentham, and when he deserts Mary can understand his social squeamishness about the family: 'I don't blame him for fightin' shy of people like that Joxer fella an' that oul' Madigan wan – nice sort o' people for your father to inthroduce to a man like Mr Bentham' (O'Casey, *SP*, 85). O'Casey feeds no illusions about a one-class egalitarianism of the poor in the tenements; no one is so low in the order of things that they cannot find someone else to regard as lower, and the nearer the bottom you are, the more important the preservation of differentials. The character of Juno is tougher than the *mater dolorosa* she has sometimes been made to seem on stage.

But in the final act the antithesis between herself and the Captain does become absolute. In her support for Mary in her pregnancy, in the anguish of her feeling at Johnny's death and in her powerful reprise of Mrs Tancred's prayer, 'Take away this murdherin' hate, an' give us Thine own eternal love!' (O'Casey, *SP*, 100), she incarnates and expresses as a woman the ethics of caring and compassion, of family values extending into a broader human solidarity. By contrast, Boyle is the type of the hopeless and heartless male in his vicious reaction to the news of Mary's seduction – 'when I'm done with her she'll be a sorry girl' (O'Casey, *SP*, 92) – and in his final appearance, too drunk even to register the fact that his son is dead: 'The blinds is down, Joxer, the blinds is down!' (O'Casey, *SP*, 100) he says, staring at them without even taking in the implication of their lowering. It is this which makes the Captain and Joxer, so hilarious in the earlier acts, in their last drunken entrance an obscenely un-comic cross-talk act on which the play fittingly ends.

Juno closes thus with a strong emotional drive which divides sympathies along gender lines. But the play as a whole works against any simple moral or ideological polarisation. *Juno* is a theatrical invitation to an audience to watch this space, a space which can never be viewed or valued in one way for long. The very idea of it as tenement flat, as the living space of the four adult Boyles, makes it a place where their different lives co-exist in the friction of enforced proximity. The inner room which Johnny so feverishly tries to turn into sanctum and sanctuary with the light burning before the image of St Anthony is also the changing-room into which the grumbling Captain is banished to take on and off his moleskin trousers at need. The snatched attempt at a moment of intimacy by Jerry Devine pleading for Mary's love – 'Don't be so hard on a fella, Mary, don't be so hard' – is rendered ludicrous by the re-entrance of Boyle: 'What's the meanin' of all this hillabaloo?' (O'Casey, *SP*, 57). Juno's always renewed efforts to give the flat the order and integrity of a family home are inevitably denied by the Captain and Joxer's impulse to open it out into an extension of the pub. The metamorphoses of the room speak its changing nature and status, from the naturalistic representation of the subsistence living space of Act I, through the artificial, all-but-surreal transformation of it in the party-time of Act II, to the stripped and dismantled stage set of the final act. An audience views it across an implied class gap which allows/demands that it be seen from no one fixed position. The comic catharsis of escape into the know-nothing hedonism of the Captain and Joxer is succeeded and challenged by the compassionate humanity of Juno. The tenement culture of backbiting and begrudgery, every inch of imagined social superiority in constant contention, is also the culture of sharing and mutuality, going out beyond the bourgeois limits of home and family. In *Juno*, as in the other two Dublin plays and virtually nowhere else in his work, O'Casey was able to make of his own ambiguous inside/outside perspective on the tenements an immanent dramatic tension, a fully realised theatrical scene.

City and nation

The dramaturgy of O'Casey's urban plays is in some ways not so different from that of the earlier Abbey rural settings, the scenes of Synge or Gregory. The box-set which enclosed the space of the country cottage could be, and no doubt was, reused with a minimum of adaptation to make up the one room on view in O'Casey's first two tenement plays. (*The Plough and the Stars*, which moves out into the pub and then on to the streets, is a somewhat different matter: more of that in the next chapter.) But there are fundamental differences in the relation of O'Casey's stage space to what is imagined offstage, and to the extra-theatrical realities. The country cottages of Synge, of Gregory, of Yeats in *The Land of Heart's Desire* are placed in the remotest of country districts, on Aran, in Connemara or Mayo, in the Wicklow glens. Their distance, their separateness from the urban theatrical milieu in which they are viewed, are essential to their nature as dramatic representation. The life lived there is conceived as simple, primitive, timeless, and as such can have the status of paradigmatic microcosm of the nation as a whole. The reduction in scale down to the offshore island, the small village, the one family, the setting in a topographical beyond and an archaic present, make for an originary model of the community. If Synge's plays were offensive as they failed to correspond to the ideological configuration for this model which the audiences demanded, they still worked on the same principle. The execrated Mayo of *The Playboy*, no less than the acclaimed Aran of *Riders to the Sea*, is a place defined by its otherness.

O'Casey's tenement scenes, by contrast, were experienced by their first audiences in the 1920s as a world of the here and now. There was, to start with, the topical immediacy of the events they represented, the Black-and-Tan terror of *The Shadow*, the horrors of the Civil War in *Juno*, played on the stage of the Abbey within two years of the events themselves. These were conditions which all Dubliners knew more or less at first hand. And though the largely middle-class Abbey audiences might never have been in a tenement to check the supposed photographic realism of the plays (as O'Casey so wryly remarked), the tenements were part of a known urban scene felt as familiar. The inner-ness of the inner-city slums, their proximity to the very theatre itself, were as much distinct features of the O'Casey plays as the far-out-ness of the earlier Abbey dramas. In neither case was the life or milieu represented that of the audience. But the Dublin trilogy showed Dubliners the life of their own city, and whereas Synge's vision of the West was distrusted in part because of his class background, O'Casey's supposed tenement origin was the guarantee of the authenticity of his drama.

'Mr O'Casey lived among the people he portrays, and he makes his audience live among them, too': the *Irish Times'* reaction to *Juno* quoted at the beginning of this chapter was the tribute paid to the plays in review after review. It was fourth-wall naturalism of a special sort, admired not just for its dramatic skill in creating a life-like illusion but for its near-literal reproduction of the life of the people itself. It was, according to Lennox Robinson, 'reporting of the highest kind, almost of genius'.[30] Such was the justification, the positive value, of plays that defied generic boundaries, calling themselves tragedies even though they were bursting with the life of comedy, plays without the plotted shape of well-made action which Dublin reviewers in the 1920s still normally expected. The heterogeneous and anarchic form of O'Casey's drama was admired because it was held to mirror the disorderly formlessness of the tenements.

The emphasis on photographic realism in the Dublin trilogy was clearly not altogether a mistake. O'Casey does appear actively to have researched his subjects in order to achieve authenticity. There is a very funny (and telling) incident recalled by Maire Keating, the girlfriend to whom he dedicated the volume containing his first two plays, about his decoy propositioning of a prostitute on the Dublin quays just to get details for the characterisation of Rosie Redmond.[31] The characterisation of the plays involves a mimicry of individual idiolects and physical mannerisms for comic purposes: Seumas Shields's stuttering repetitions, the shoulder-shrugging Joxer's 'face like a bundle of crinkled paper' (O'Casey, *SP*, 52), the Captain's strutting walk and puffed-out cheeks, were all almost certainly modelled on real-life originals.[32] But the impression of surface naturalism and eidetic reproduction masks the high theatricality of the plays, their use of the standard routines of comedy and the operatic climaxes of melodrama. And the spectacle of the tenements, supposedly seen as they were, in fact depended on the vantage-point of class difference, a gap not only between the characters and the audience but between the characters and the author also. Marx's dictum, used by Edward Said as the epigraph to *Orientalism*, applies to the people of O'Casey's tenements: 'They cannot represent themselves, they must be represented.'[33] Though in the Dublin trilogy O'Casey succeeded in removing any self-surrogate, the plays work as an act of writer's ventriloquism for a social group that cannot speak for itself.

The impulse to give voice to the voiceless was inherent in the literary revival, the national theatre movement, from the beginning. Yeats's famous injunction to Synge to go to Aran and 'express a life that has never found expression' (Synge, *CW*, III, 63) is symptomatic. In O'Casey what stood revealed was not a previously unexpressed community on the rural periphery, Corkery's Gaelic-speaking 'hidden Ireland', but a hidden Ireland at the heart of the city. The O'Caseyan tenement room is thus a metonym for society at large that is different from the dramatic spaces of Synge, Gregory or Yeats. In the plays looked at in chapter 2 featuring the stranger in the house, there is a simple set of equivalences by which family = house = community = nation. In the case of O'Casey's rooms that are only spaces within a house, with families that can hardly sustain separate identities in the larger social aggregation of the tenement, and with tenements that are themselves but a section of the city, there can be no such clear-cut progression of significance. The wholeness of the country cottage which could figure a putative wholeness of the nation is replaced with a fragmentariness which can represent a people only in refracted shards, if at all. It is partly the poverty of the poor and their powerlessness which mean that they are always seen as victims or at best observers of social structures and forces that reach on up beyond them. There is also their very plurality which stops any one person, any one family attaining a central or even a representative significance. The imagined rise and real fall of the Boyles could provide a narrative rhythm for *Juno*, but it could hardly figure in any direct way the life of the nation as a whole. In the first two plays of the Dublin trilogy Irish audiences were delighted with this new city-centred drama which, in its proletarian otherness, disrupted previous conventions of Irish theatrical representation. With *The Plough and the Stars*, which more directly and polemically challenged the self-images of the post-revolutionary nation, it was to be otherwise.

5 Reactions to revolution

'then and not till then, let my epitaph be written'.[1] The Irish nationalist imagination was a prolonged waiting upon the 'then' of Robert Emmet's speech from the dock, the revolutionary Year One when Ireland would once again take her place among the nations of the earth. The many failed rebellions, of which Emmet's was one of the more pathetic, were dress-rehearsals for the real thing which would eventually arrive. When it came it would be dramatic, transformatory, as the ending of *Kathleen ni Houlihan* was: the *puella senilis* would be *senilis* no longer but would appear as the young girl with the walk of a queen, rejuvenated by the selfless sacrifice of her patriots. With the Easter Rising of 1916 such a moment seemed to have come at last. It was an event planned with conscious theatricality, and if the initial Dublin audience reaction was derisive, within years it grew to be regarded by Irish nationalists as the great drama which Pearse and the other leaders had planned it to be. How was the theatre to stage a staged real event, the revolution which *Kathleen ni Houlihan* had imagined as myth? Still more problematically, how was the theatre to deal with the aftermath of that six-day dramatic scene of revolution, the prolonged, bitter and messy guerilla war of 1919–21, or – worse still – the infinitely more embittering and messier civil war of 1922–3, in a country divided between those who maintained that the revolution was over and others who passionately held that the struggle had to continue? The events that succeeded 1916 left Irish people with a chronic sense of disillusionment in the disparity between revolutionary ideal and actuality, and it left the theatre with a crisis of representation: how to represent both the revolution and reactions to it in postrevolutionary Ireland.

'We in Ireland,' wrote F.S.L. Lyons, 'are all in a sense children of the revolution ... and for the past sixty years scholars and statesmen alike seem to have been mesmerised by the Easter Rising of 1916.'[2] Or, as Alan Simpson put it more pungently, 'We have had our brains washed, as Pearse intended, by the para-theatre of the 1916 Proclamation.'[3] Lyons was speaking as one of the revisionist school of historians working to change the situation he described, to turn Irish historical studies away from its obsession with a narrative of national revolution to an analysis of the underlying social, economic and cultural experience. Alan Simpson, director of Behan and of Beckett, could be taken to represent a movement within Irish drama against the Pearsian 'para-theatre', a postrevolutionary theatrical revisionism. Such a movement began early on. *Kathleen Listens In*, O'Casey's one-act 'political phantasy' of 1923, imagined Kathleen, daughter of the O Houlihans, not mysteriously transformed by independence but positively oppressed by liberation and the contending suitors for her hand to whose voices she has to 'listen in': the Freestater and the Republican, the Farmer and the Businessman.[4] *The Shadow* and *Juno* dramatised the 'Troubles' of 1919–23 as a chaotic terror of noises off, and *The Plough* was to act as iconoclastic reconception of Easter 1916 itself. Denis Johnston, as an emerging young playwright later in the 1920s, sought in *The Old Lady Says 'No!'* for the means to render the complexities and complacencies of Free State Ireland so unlike the revolutionary imaginings of a Robert Emmet. Still in the 1950s, the renewed IRA Border campaign signalled that this same irredentist movement had not gone away, and Brendan Behan, as a former convicted Republican terrorist, was in a position of exceptional authority to show it in action. *The Hostage*, with its crazy brothel-cum-IRA-safe-house, is a metaphor for Ireland thirty-six years after Independence. All three playwrights, O'Casey, Johnston and Behan, were engaged in demythologising, de-dramatising revolution, denying it the miraculous transformatory powers which it claimed for itself in the light of the intractable, untransformed political realities it had left behind.

This theatrical revisionism was not only a political reaction against the unfulfilled promises of revolution. It was a search for new dramatic forms and idioms, new audiences appropriate to the postrevolutionary situation. In origin the Irish Literary Theatre had pledged itself to 'that freedom of experiment which is not found in theatres in England';[5] it was to be artistically as well as nationally independent. But by the 1920s this had settled down into a tradition of mirroring a jog-trot form of nationalism, the representative family in the representative village or small town, in a jog-trot form of naturalism, a conventionally crafted plot overlain with a surface realism of colloquial dialogue. The political unease of people disillusioned with the outcome of revolution was matched by a restiveness with the formulaic quality of plays following pre-revolutionary Abbey models. The Dublin Drama League, founded in 1918 to put on productions of non-Irish plays on the Abbey's non-playing nights, represented an attempt to open up Ireland and Irish theatre to new dramatic forms. 'Seeing foreign plays,' argued Lennox Robinson, the moving spirit behind the League, 'will not divorce minds from Ireland ... but being brought into touch with other minds who have different values of life, suddenly we shall discover the rich material that lies to our hand in Ireland.'[6] The plays performed at the Drama League may have influenced O'Casey – according to one account he attended about 60 per cent of their productions[7] – and certainly had a formative effect on the plays of Johnston. But Robinson's defensive tone, even in 1918 when setting up the League, suggests the atmosphere of national isolationism likely to greet Irish plays influenced by avant-garde styles from abroad. Abbey audiences, raised on a diet of Abbey plays, looked to find in their national theatre comfortable images of their own Irishness of a recognisable sort. They rejected *The Plough* as anti-nationalist; they never got to see Johnston's expressionistic *The Old Lady Says 'No!'* because the Abbey directors rejected it for them.

Where were O'Casey and Johnston, or later Behan, to find audiences receptive to their new styles of representing postrevolutionary Ireland? The answer was either in small arthouse theatres set up in Dublin as alternative to the Abbey – the Gate which put on *The Old Lady Says 'No!'* as one of its landmark early productions in 1929, or the Pike where Alan Simpson directed Behan's *The Quare Fellow* in 1954 – or in London where O'Casey's *The Silver Tassie*, another Abbey *refusé*, was staged in 1929, and where Joan Littlewood's Theatre Workshop productions of Behan were to bring him international fame. If the Abbey as national theatre came to stand for an officially national ideology and a conservative dramaturgy, then alternative views of Ireland had to find alternative venues: the Dublin wits recognised this polarity when they christened the Gate and the Abbey Sodom and Begorrah. But production outside the country could bring charges that the Irish playwright was adapting to English playing styles and English audience preconceptions, reverting to stage Irishry. Hence the suspicious unease of Irish reactions to Behan's collaboration with Littlewood.

The three plays looked at in this chapter, *The Plough and the Stars*, *The Old Lady Says 'No!'* and *The Hostage*, are used to illustrate three attempts to find a politics, a style and an audience appropriate for postrevolutionary Irish drama. To what extent are the plays' reactions to revolution politically reactionary, counter-revolutionary? The nationalist objectors to *The Plough* in 1926 clearly thought O'Casey, in satirising the Easter Rising, attacked the very basis on which the independent state was established, and more recent critiques of the play have been equally resistant to its revisionist ideology. The struggle of Johnston in *The Old Lady* was not only to express the politics of Free State Ireland but to find, in the wake of Joyce, a dramatic style capable of representing the urban realities of modern Dublin. The theatre history of *The Hostage*, with its first Irish-language version as *An Giall* and its shape-changing progress from London to Paris, New York and San Francisco, brings up sharply the question of who created or controlled its images of Ireland: playwright, producer or audience. Politics, style and audience in these three plays are not distinct but interlocked issues in the dramatisation of independent Ireland.

Politics: *The Plough and the Stars*

'You have disgraced yourselves again', thundered Yeats at the fourth-night Abbey audience which had disrupted *The Plough*, and by his 'again' he paired the 1926 event with the *Playboy* riots of nearly twenty years before. But the reaction to *The Playboy* was unlike *The Plough* in being to a considerable extent predictable. Synge had been a controversial and (with the one exception of *Riders to the Sea*) an unpopular playwright from the production of *The Shadow of the Glen* on. Up to 1926 O'Casey had been the darling of the Abbey and the Abbey audiences alike. In *The Shadow* and in *Juno* he had mocked political pieties, as he was to do in *The Plough*. The anti-heroic sentiments of Seumas Shields had been enjoyed, if not positively approved:

> I'm a Nationalist right enough; I believe in the freedom of Ireland, an' that England has no right to be here, but I draw the line when I hear the gunmen blowin' about dyin' for the people, when it's the people that are dyin' for the gunmen! With all due respect to the gunmen, I don't want them to die for me. (O'Casey, *SP*, 28–9)

The very terms over which a deadly civil war had been fought out, with all the terrible consequences shown in *Juno*, could be turned into the absurdity of Captain Boyle's posturing defiance of his wife (in her absence of course): 'Today, Joxer, there's goin' to be issued a proclamation be me, establishin' an independent Republic, an' Juno'll have to take an oath of allegiance' (O'Casey, *SP*, 62). Both the earlier Dublin plays had upstaged the violence of the national struggle, rendering it only as it was experienced by bystanders and victims. Yet when *The Plough* repeated many of the same techniques, expressed many of the same views, the audience objected violently. Why?

Not all the audience objected violently. The play's first performance was well received; the protest did not gather momentum until the fourth night, and there was an element of political faction to the demonstration led by women of strongly Republican sympathies.[8] There was an anti-Free State edge to some of the hostile criticism. Hanna Sheehy-Skeffington, for instance, the most articulate of the demonstrators, shouted 'The Free State Government is subsidising the Abbey to malign Pearse and Connolly.'[9] But whatever the element of political bias in the protests – the Republicans claiming the moral high ground as true heirs of 1916 reproaching the backslidings of the Treaty-instituted government – the memory of the Rising was by this stage a potent icon which nobody in the independent Ireland of 1926 could be seen to treat disrespectfully, whatever their current politics. And there they all were in the theatre, as living reminders of the event, the mothers, widows, sisters of the martyrs to the national struggle: Mrs Pearse, both of whose sons had been executed, Mrs Tom Clarke, whose husband had been the oldest of the signatories of the Proclamation, the sister of Kevin Barry, the 'lad of eighteen summers' whose hanging was the stuff of popular ballad, and Mrs Sheehy-Skeffington, widow of the pacifist Francis Sheehy-Skeffington who was arrested and shot during the Rising on the orders of a deranged British army officer.[10]

The different reaction to *The Plough* as against the earlier two O'Casey plays was partly a question of distance in time; the Rising was close enough to be freshly remembered and felt by participants and survivors, but far enough away to be hallowed in memory. *The Shadow*, produced in 1923, and *Juno*, in 1924, found war-weary audiences responsive to O'Casey's ironic and disillusioned versions of contemporary events. Those events were very immediately contemporary: the raids of the Black and Tans had been going on just two years before the first performance of *The Shadow*, the Civil War ended only a year before *Juno*. But by 1926 the Easter Rising was ten years back in time and, whatever the political divisions that remained over subsequent events in the split between Treaty and anti-Treaty factions which emerged out of the 1919–21 War of Independence, all were bound to look back reverently to the memory of 1916. 'In no country save in Ireland,' declared Mrs Sheehy-Skeffington in a letter to the press, 'could a State-subsidised theatre presume on popular patience to the extent of making a mockery and a byword of a revolutionary movement on which the present structure claims to stand.'[11] The attack on the foundational myth of 1916 brought out a mood of national defensiveness. 'There is an effort abroad to destroy Nationalism and supplant it with internationalism', claimed one anti-*Plough* protester.[12] The successful production of *Juno*, which was then running in a London West End theatre, left Dubliners suspicious that O'Casey was playing to English prejudices, and that the row over *The Plough* would be exploited for publicity effect over there. An editorial in the *Evening Herald* urged the need for theatre censorship, arguing that 'by far the worst kind of play is that which shows Irishmen up to the ridicule of foreigners'.[13] National self-image was now bound up in the rite of becoming which was the Easter Rising.

The Plough relates to the Rising as Tom Stoppard's *Rosen-*

crantz and Guildenstern Are Dead relates to *Hamlet*. The high familiar drama is seen from backstage, from the wings, from the viewpoint of bit-players and spear-carriers rather than principals. The conscious theatricality of the Rising involved *mise-en-scène* as well as costume and script ('the para-theatre of the Proclamation'). Occupying the GPO, with its pillared neo-classical façade at the dead centre of Dublin's central shopping street, was a grand manifestation of the revolutionary design, however mad it might have been as a military strategy. O'Casey and the Abbey would, of course, never have been capable of showing that show direct, but repeatedly and systematically in *The Plough* he gives us backwards glimpses of it. The leaders of the Rising are never shown on stage: all we see are intermittent appearances of the back of Pearse's head in Act II. As Stoppard estranges the well-known fragments of the *Hamlet* text which erupt from time to time into his extra-*Hamlet* play, so the collage of quotation from Pearse's speeches overheard from within the pub is subjected to ironic scrutiny. The dramatised events of Easter Monday morning, already by 1926 so famous, including the appearance of the troop of British cavalry, are narrated in the distanced style recommended for Brecht's *Verfremdungseffekt*. The Covey describes the Lancers coming down Sackville Street

> Throttin' along, heads in th' air; spurs an' sabres jinglin', an' lances quiverin', an' lookin' as if they were assin' themselves, 'Where's these blighters, till we get a prod at them?' when there was a volley from th' Post Office that stretched half o' them, an' sent th' rest gallopin' away wondherin' how far they'd have to go before they'd feel safe. (O'Casey, *SP*, 144)

The key moment of the Proclamation itself is similarly rendered as the subject of excited gossip:

> THE COVEY. An' then out comes General Pearse an' his staff, an', standin' in th' middle o' th' street, he reads th' Proclamation.
> MRS GOGAN. What proclamation?
> PETER. Declarin' an Irish Republic.
> MRS GOGAN. Go to God! (O'Casey, *SP*, 145)

The sheer demotic animation of the language subverts the high stylised dignity claimed by the ritual of the Proclamation.

It was Acts II and III of the play which caused most offence, and it is in these acts that O'Casey brings his bystanding non-participants closest to the sacred drama of the Rising. To do so, he had to move his action closer into the centre of the city and move his characters out of their tenement. The house which provides the setting for most of *The Plough* was based on 422 Nth Circular Road, where O'Casey was then living, suitably downgraded socially to make it more convincingly a slum. But it also had to be imagined as nearer to the GPO action than the 20 minutes walk away it actually was, if the reports fresh from the fighting and the sense of loot available just around the corner were to be made vividly credible. Although the exact placing of the pub in Act II is never stated, its design is also to show the public event of the meeting just beyond the foregrounded space of the tenement characters' carry-on. Whereas in *Juno* and *The Shadow* O'Casey had confined his people to one room, with all outside events, all political effects coming in at them as passive observers or uncomprehending victims, *The Plough* sends them out into the streets, into the pubs, to live in immediate reaction to the big picture which is just off-camera.

The effect of this is at its most astringently satiric in Act II because of the deliberate contamination of the metaphoric and the material in its juxtaposition of the political meeting and the pub-talk. The sacramentalist strain is heavily represented in O'Casey's malicious selection from Pearse's greatest hits: 'The old heart of the earth needed to be warmed with the red wine of the battlefields ... And we must be ready to pour out the same red wine in the same glorious sacrifice, for without shedding of blood there is no redemption!' (O'Casey, *SP*, 129). It is real whiskey not sacramental blood/wine which the people in the pub are drinking, and the link between the political rhetoric and the thirst for alcohol is made directly. As Peter Flynn puts it, ordering for himself and the no-longer-teetotal Fluther, 'A meetin' like this always makes me feel I could dhrink Lock Erinn dhry!' (O'Casey, *SP*, 128).

The commonest objections to this act were to the presence of the prostitute Rosie Redmond and the introduction of the Tricolour, the national flag, into a pub. Once again, though, it may have been the inclusion of the two together which caused the deepest disturbance. The three soldiers of the Irish Citizen Army and the Irish Volunteers bearing the two flags, the ICA's Plough and the Stars which gave the play its name and the Tricolour of the Volunteers, come into the pub late in the act. Their ritualised chorus of dedication to the cause uses the traditional feminisation of the figure of Ireland.

> CLITHEROE. You have a mother, Langon.
> LIEUT. LANGON. Ireland is greater than a mother.
> CAPT. BRENNAN. You have a wife, Clitheroe.
> CLITHEROE. Ireland is greater than a wife.
>
> (O'Casey, *SP*, 141)

It is just so that Michael in *Kathleen ni Houlihan* leaves behind mother and bride-to-be to give himself for the strange old woman that is Ireland. In Yeats's and Gregory's play, however, there was no Rosie Redmond on the scene to emerge from the snug with Fluther after the soldiers leave with their flags, suggesting that Ireland might be greater than a mother or a wife but not than a drunken night with a whore. It was not just prudishness or national paranoia that made the 1926 Irish audience react as they did to Act II of *The Plough*: the very iconography of the nationalist imagination, sacralised in the Rising, was literally desecrated in the secular and mundane setting it is given.

The pub of the second act created one sort of image of the informal life of the people immediately adjacent to the public arena of politics which is just beyond its window. The street scene of Act III outside the tenement equally set up a space between the action of the Rising, not far away, and the domestic interiors which were all the earlier plays had shown. The terms of the Proclamation appealed to one people, one nation: 'Irishmen and Irishwomen: In the name of God and of the dead generations from which she receives her old tradition of nationhood, Ireland, through us, summons her children to her flag and strikes for her freedom.'[14] O'Casey, in his oblique representation of the Rising, brings out the disparateness, the disunity, the fragmented incoherence of the people reacting to the event. Already in the previous tenement plays the imagined urban scene, in its formless heterogeneity, did not sit with the unitary idea of the nation as family figured in the country cottages of the early Abbey drama. In *The Plough* O'Casey moved from a kaleidoscopic to a prismatic design in representing the human and political variegation of his people. He tenants his house with characters illustrating a chosen spectrum of differing political attitudes: Peter Flynn's do-nothing nationalism of Moore's Melodies and gorgeous uniforms, the Covey's doctrinaire anti-nationalist socialism, Clitheroe of the workers' Citizen Army, the Protestant Bessie Burgess with her belligerent Unionism. The strains of 'Tipperary' from the Dublin Fusiliers marching off to embark for the Western Front are there to remind us, as background to the Rising, of that greater war in which so many Irishmen were fighting for England rather than against her.

The third act, with its comings and goings of the people of the tenement, some sallying out to the looting, some in retreat from the fighting, performs most powerfully to dismantle the aspirational idea of the single nation which the Proclamation proclaimed. With the backdrop of the house itself, the image of multi-inhabited plurality, O'Casey works up the dramatic dissonance between the several characters, the several scenes which simultaneously occupy the stage. There is the animosity between the fighting men and the looting non-combatants which is expressed as class hatred. Brennan is indignant that Clitheroe only fired warning shots at the looters:

> CAPT. BRENNAN (*savagely to* CLITHEROE). Why did you fire over their heads? Why didn't you fire to kill?
> CLITHEROE. No, no, Bill; bad as they are they're Irish men an' women.
> CAPT. BRENNAN (*savagely*). Irish be damned! Attackin' and' mobbin' th' men that are riskin' their lives for them. If these slum lice gather at our heels again, plug one o' them, or I'll soon shock them with a shot or two meself!
>
> (O'Casey, *SP*, 154)

Brennan and Clitheroe both belong to the Citizen Army, the workers' militia, but when the workers do not support what the rebels are doing for them they are written out of the nation and become disposable 'slum lice'. The mixed mode of the tenement drama itself is represented in this act by the pathos of the consumptive Mollser alongside the boisterous comedy of the looting: Bessie and Mrs Gogan's habitual feuding turned to a co-operative raid on the shops; Fluther, having given a 'shake up' to a local pub, returning roaring drunk in possession of a half-gallon of whiskey.

To this anarchic dramatic mélange is added the terrible melodrama of the reunion of the Clitheroes, and the plight of the wounded Langon. O'Casey here takes on a stock theatrical situation, the conflict between love and duty, and turns it into something different. To start with, Nora's hysterical language, compounded of the Magnificat and the Prodigal Son, is almost as embarrassing to the audience as it is to Clitheroe:

> Jack, Jack, Jack; God be thanked . . . be thanked . . . He has been kind and merciful to His poor handmaiden . . . My Jack, my own Jack, that I thought was lost is found, that I thought was dead is alive again! . . . Oh, God be praised for ever, evermore! . . . My poor Jack . . . Kiss me, kiss me, Jack, kiss your own Nora! (O'Casey, *SP*, 154)

An audience, however sympathetic, may well be with Clitheroe here in shrinking away from Nora's public demonstration of her feelings: 'for God's sake, Nora, don't make a scene'. This area of discomfort is counterpointed with others. There is the raw quality of the language of the wounded Langon, whose situation makes it so urgent for Clitheroe to leave:

> Oh, if I'd kep' down only a little longer, I mightn't ha' been hit! Everyone else escapin', an' me getting' me belly ripped asundher! . . . I couldn't scream, couldn't even scream . . . D'ye think I'm really badly wounded, Bill? Me clothes seem to be all soakin' wet . . . It's blood . . . My God, it must be me own blood! (O'Casey, *SP*, 155)

This does more than provide a grim contrast to the metaphorical and sacramental blood of the Pearse speeches of Act II – 'the red wine of the battlefields' – and a grisly literalisation of Langon's rhetorical cry in that earlier scene: 'Wounds for th' Independence of Ireland!' (O'Casey, *SP*, 141). It renders with crude force an ordinarily unheroic reaction to violent physical pain. And presiding over the whole scene from an upper window is the triumphalist Bessie Burgess, whose motto is always to kick a good man when he is down as you will never get a better chance:

> Th' Minsthrel Boys aren't feelin' very comfortable now. Th' big guns has knocked all th' harps out of their hands. General Clitheroe'd rather be unlacin' his wife's bodice than standin' at a barricade . . . An' th' professor of chicken-butcherin' there [Brennan, a chicken-butcher in private life], finds he's up against somethin' a little tougher even than his own chickens, an' that's sayin' a lot! (O'Casey, *SP*, 155)

This is a merciless scene, in which ugliness and indecorum deny to the audience any sort of aesthetic catharsis. It acts as the very antithesis of the imagined drama of the Rising where the risen people were to be transformed into one nation by the heroism of blood-sacrifice.

It is not surprising that the Abbey audiences of 1926 should have protested against this polemic iconoclasm, nor yet that latter-day critics of O'Casey should also have reacted against his reaction to revolution. If *The Plough* could be called a revisionist version of the Rising, it has come under attack from those generally opposed to the revisionist enterprise of re-writing Ireland's past. Seamus Deane criticises generally the inadequacy of O'Casey's political thinking, his failure to 'develop a critique of Irish history or politics'. The Dublin of *The Plough*, according to Deane, 'is not a city in which politics has any truly social or human basis. Instead, only in repudiation of politics can humanity express itself'.[15] In Deane's view O'Casey sets up a spurious division between a male-represented obsession with empty ideas and ideology and the family-based humanism of the women. Declan Kiberd repeats one of the complaints of the original protesters that O'Casey does not give the leaders of the Rising a look-in: 'he kept them on the edge of his stage and never allowed one of them to make a full statement of the nationalist case'. Kiberd again develops a critique of *The Plough* glimpsed in the 1926 Republican reactions when he argues that it was designed to meet the views of the post-1922 governing classes. 'By depicting his inner-city Dubliners as jabbering leprechauns, [O'Casey] appealed to the new middle-class elites which dominated the Free State and which cast the Dublin proletarian in the role once reserved by the Anglo-Irish establishment for the stage-Irish peasant.'[16]

Given that the Rising and its representation remain a contested area in Irish political life, it is to be expected that *The Plough* should thus continue to be controversial, and that anti-revisionists should resist the sort of contemporary tendencies they see it supporting. It may nonetheless be a mistake to look for an authorial motivation for the politics of *The Plough*, or even the coherent political analysis which Deane and Kiberd fault the play for lacking. *The Plough* is not a fair picture, a politically balanced view of the Easter Rising; O'Casey certainly does not give the leaders the equal air-time which Kiberd wants for them. However, the play is hardly as condescending to the people of the tenement as Kiberd implies with his reference to 'jabbering leprechauns' nor as calculated to comply with the prejudices of the new Free State ruling class. That class itself was probably not so securely in place by 1926 to make a definite target audience; Kiberd is reading back into the 1920s what he sees (and deplores) as the complacently anti-nationalist middle-class audiences of the 1980s and 1990s. *The Plough* in its original context was genuinely provocative rather than cynically exploitative, as the explosively divided response to the first performances of the play suggests. The real power and strength of O'Casey's behind-the-scenes dramatisation of the Rising, for all its occasional uncertainties of touch and often laboured language, comes from a rough dramaturgy which resists the simplifying tropes of revolution.

This is not, as Deane maintains, a matter of promoting a sentimental humanity represented by women and the family over against a stigmatised but unexamined politics of the men. The tenement community cannot be directly equated with the family, as I have tried to show in the previous chapter, and O'Casey's treatment of the women of *The Plough* is even more ambiguous than in his previous plays. Nora Clitheroe was originally conceived as a middle-class woman temporarily misplaced in the tenements, and re-written down into the working classes on instructions from the Abbey's directors.[17] The palimpsest character that results makes for a mixed response. There is some sympathy for Nora's home-making, her desire for privacy with her husband and her attempts to improve the quality of her life in the tenement flat. She is seen to be right about Clitheroe's vanity as the motive for his involvement in the Citizen Army. Yet her desperate possessiveness, the emotional excess of her performance in Act III and her final collapse into madness suggest a fragility in the ideal of home and personal values for which she stands, a weakness associated with what remains of the bourgeois colouring of her character. The anti-type of all this is Bessie Burgess, Bessie who does *not* stand for home and family – she is incensed at Nora's lock on the door in the first act as an insult to her neighbours – whose capacity for compassion and self-sacrifice is equally matched by her capacity for violent political provocativeness.

The last scene of the play, the scene of Bessie's death and what follows it, is most fully representative of the way in which the political ironies of *The Plough* work. The reversal which makes Bessie the virago of Act I into Nora's nurse and defender is expressed most piquantly in having her Protestant hymns, previously sung in drunken defiance, turned into soothing lullabies for her mad Catholic neighbour. It is such a hymn, 'I do believe, I will believe / That Jesus died for me', which she is to sing as her dying credo. But her death is no act of voluntary self-sacrifice. 'I've got this through ... through you ... through you, you bitch, you!' (O'Casey, *SP*, 173), she gasps out in the authentic accents of the woman who tore into Nora in the first act. Bessie voices no Juno-like prayer of general forgiveness; O'Casey keeps his hard edge to the end of this play. The emotional climax of Bessie's death is succeeded by the entrance of Sergeant Tinley and Corporal Stoddart and their singing of 'Keep the Home Fires Burning' in chorus with their fellow British soldiers offstage. The device is borrowed from Shaw's *Heartbreak House*, which ends in the wake of the zeppelin raid with Randall Utterwood playing 'Keep the Home Fires Burning' on his flute. O'Casey's irony, however, is more inward and more deeply expressive for his dramatic situation. The two British soldiers sitting down to tea enjoying the home fire of the woman they have just shot could be read as a fiercely satiric image of colonial occupation. Yet it is hardly felt as such partisan irony. Following as it does on 'Tipperary' sung by Irish soldiers going off to fight at the Front earlier in the play, it works to remind an audience that the emotion which the song expresses is real enough, that in Ireland, as in France, these men are far from home and entitled to such consolation as they can get from the sentimental strains of Ivor Novello.

In the final scene, and in the play as a whole, O'Casey uses a technique of organic ironies. Through it he holds in dramatic tension the human conflicts endemic in the Irish situation, conflicts between private and public life, between the several religious and political factions, between the Great War beyond Ireland and the little war within. *The Plough* represents a reaction to revolution which is not counter-revolutionary in political intention. It does not offer a considered critique of the Rising. What it disassembles rather is the unifying, harmonising and idealising thrust of the narrative of the Rising as national icon. It presents a view from the streets and the pubs suggesting the intractable materials on which the Proclamation summoning the children of Ireland to its flag has to operate. Not one flag but two to start with, the Plough and the Stars as well as the Tricolour, and children that include the Coveys and the Uncle Peters, the Fluthers and the Bessies, the Rosie Redmonds and the Mollsers, as well as the dedicated soldiers of the Volunteers and the Citizen Army. 'Make a nation of that lot', is the challenge the play throws down to the revolution.

Style: *The Old Lady Says 'No!'*

The Old Lady Says 'No!': the title is expressive in all sorts of ways. Johnston put about the story that it was 'written by somebody on a sheet of paper attached to the front of the first version, when it came back to me from the Abbey', and that the 'old lady' who so offhandedly rejected his play was Lady Gregory.[18] Although late in life Johnston even doctored one of his own manuscripts to make good this legend, the facts appear to be as follows: it was a second version of the play not a first which was definitively turned down by the Abbey in 1928; it was Yeats not Gregory who was mainly responsible for the rejection; and Johnston's animus against the 'old lady' derived not from the rejection of the play itself but from her withdrawal of an Abbey subsidy promised for the production of the play elsewhere.[19] Whatever the actual details, the title was made multiply significant. Lady Gregory, one of the Abbey's *ancien régime* directors, stood for the theatre's nay-saying conservatism in its rejection of Johnston's avant-garde modernist drama. At the same time, the old lady who said no was the 1920s Kathleen ni Houlihan, the play's character of the aged Dublin Flower Woman who identifies herself by mouthing snatches from Yeats's and Gregory's famous play. *The Old Lady* pioneered a new style of dramatic representation in defiance of the fossilised national theatre, while what it represented was the failure of postrevolutionary Ireland to become the young girl with the walk of a queen.

Johnston approached the subject with a very different background from O'Casey. From an upper-middle-class Protestant family, with a father who was to become a judge in the Irish Free State, he himself trained as a lawyer at Cambridge and Harvard and continued to practise as a barrister throughout the early stages of his playwriting career. It is symptomatic of their class difference that, where O'Casey had to write the Clitheroes down into the working classes to make their dialogue sound convincing, Johnston had to commission an actress friend to sketch in the dialogue of the two working-class girls who appear briefly in *The Old Lady*.[20] Johnston came to the theatre as a highly educated literary intellectual, fired by his experience of contemporary experimental plays from the Dublin Drama League in which he worked as actor and director. Style, modes of expression, ways to modernise Irish theatre were thus primary preoccupations for Johnston as they had not been for O'Casey. The aim of *The Old Lady* was to produce a play freed up by the example of the later Strindberg, exploiting the expressionist techniques of Kaiser, Toller and the early O'Neill, a play that had assimilated the lessons of *Ulysses*.

Although Johnston formally disavowed many of these influences in his 1960 introduction to the play, he made clear there its modernist theatrical aesthetic:

> We were tired of the conventional three-act shape, of conversational dialogue, and of listening to the tendentious social sentiments of the stage of the 'twenties, and we wanted to know whether the emotional appeal of music could be made use of in terms of theatrical prose, and an opera constructed that did not have to be sung. Could dialogue be used in lieu of some of the scenery, or as a shorthand form of character-delineation? Could the associations and thought-patterns

> already connected with the songs and slogans of our city be used deliberately to evoke a planned reaction from a known audience? (Johnston, *Old Lady*, 52–3)

The technique of the play is one of collage, beginning with the parody historical melodrama of Robert Emmet made up of fragments from a whole range of Irish nineteenth-century patriotic poets from Thomas Moore to John Todhunter. The breakdown of this absurd playlet, when one of the Redcoats arresting Robert Emmet deals him an over-enthusiastic blow on the head, provides the basis for the play proper: the actor in Robert Emmet costume (minus his boots) wandering round 1920s Dublin in a state of concussed bewilderment, a 'delirium of the brave' in a sense unintended by Yeats. This allows the play's action the shape-changing fluidity of Strindberg's *Dream Play*, where the only unity is provided by the mind of the dreamer and his obsessions.

If O'Casey's tenement house provided a different sort of metonym for the nation from the traditional country cottages of the early Abbey, then *The Old Lady* with its shifting mindscapes is a radical attempt to render the multifariousness of the urban experience. It is here that Joyce's precedent was so important. *Ulysses* had not only shown Dublin as a modern city but as the very stuff of modernist representation, not just an agglomeration of people, buildings, institutions, but an intertextual site of multiple co-existing languages in voice and print. It is this Joycean texture of the city for which Johnston tries to find a theatrical equivalent in *The Old Lady*. The Speaker/Emmet, in his efforts to return to Rathfarnham, scene of the stalled play, and be reunited with his lover Sarah Curran, struggles to give coherence to the bewildering array of life-forms that he encounters. In the street-scenes of Part One these include a social cross-section of passers-by, from the Flapper and Trinity Medical Student to Carmel and Bernadette from Phibsboro' (the characters with the ghosted-in dialogue), each with their own preoccupations; in the interiors of Part Two there is the arriviste salon of the Free State Minister for Arts and Crafts, where Emmet is politely welcomed, and the O'Casey style of tenement in which the young man whom the Speaker has apparently shot dies interminably. And repeatedly there are the phantasmagoric/symbolic figures, the speaking Statue of Grattan, the taunting flower-seller, the Syngean Blind Man, who reappear to haunt the Speaker's consciousness. No scene, no characters stay put as in traditional representational drama; they are continuously refigured in choric and choreographed forms as theatrical manifestations of contemporaneity.

In political terms the play works to undermine the postures of nationalist revolution centred on Emmet. The Speaker's main antagonist in the play is the Statue of Grattan, who speaks for the tradition of constitutionalist nationalism, while Emmet represents the spirit of armed rebellion. Though the Speaker sees on the Statue the face of Major Sirr, the army officer come to arrest him, presumably viewing anything less than outright revolution as a complicity with colonial authority, Grattan is given the stage best of their exchanges:

> GRATTAN. Full fifty years I worked and waited, only to see my country's new-found glory melt away at the bidding of the omniscient young Messiahs with neither the ability to work nor the courage to wait.
> SPEAKER. I have the courage to go on.
> GRATTAN. Oh, it is an easy thing to draw a sword and raise a barricade. It saves working, it saves waiting. It saves everything but blood! And blood is the cheapest thing the good God has made. (Johnston, *Old Lady*, 71–2)

With the old tattered Flower Woman crying out from the base of the statue a mocking version of lines from *Kathleen ni Houlihan* – 'Me four bewtyful gre-in fields. Me four bewtyful gre-in fields' (Johnston, *Old Lady*, 71) – this is a strongly subversive attack on Emmet's romantic revolutionism. Johnston, through Grattan, highlights the main casualty of Emmet's rebellion, the mob-murder of Lord Kilwarden, 'the justest judge in Ireland' (Johnston, *Old Lady*, 71). As with the later 'murder' of the young man Joe, the Speaker is forced to face the unintended violent consequences of his romantic ideals. Johnston, through the figure of Grattan, privileges the eighteenth-century Patriot tradition, expressing a Burkean distrust of revolution.

Yet the play as a whole is not simply resistant to the revolutionary idealism of Emmet. It is poised somewhere between satiric debunking of the claims of the revolution and satiric exposure of the society that has failed to live up to those claims. Much of Part One exposes the unreality of the Speaker's histrionic posturing, the inadequacy or irrelevance of his vision to the people of contemporary Dublin. Robert Emmet having to queue for a tram or bus to take him to Rathfarnham ridicules the costumed pastness of the figure by privileging the social actuality of the audience's present.[21] The street-crowd turns on the Speaker when they spot that instead of the traditional high leather boots of all the famous paintings of Emmet, he is wearing the gaudy modern carpet-slippers which have been substituted after his accident. Emmet in slippers is a travesty version of the idol with feet of clay.

Particularly in Part Two, however, the alienated displacement of Emmet in 1920s Dublin reflects more on the city's shallow tawdriness rather than on his misguided romanticism. The salon scene caricatures the post-1922 establishment with its alliance between the gunmen turned government ministers and such Anglo-Irish figures as Lady Trimmer who have thrown in their lot with the new dispensation. 'I've wanted to meet him for such a long time', says Lady Trimmer when Emmet is announced. 'My husband always says that we of the old regime ought to get into touch with those sort of people' (Johnston, *Old Lady*, 96). Neo-colonial re-Anglicisation under a thin Celtic Revival veneer is suggested in the Minister's daughter Maeve reciting A. A. Milne, learned at the Banba School of Acting. High culture is represented by O'Cooney, O'Mooney and O'Rooney, recognisably based on O'Casey, the artist Patrick Tuohy, and the novelist Liam O'Flaherty.[22] The mishmash of modern Ireland is expressed in the operatically deployed cacophany of simultaneous voices, where the Speaker tries to go on with his nineteenth-century style declamation, the General sings 'She is far from the land where her young hero sleeps' (Moore's Melody on Emmet and Sarah Curran), O'Cooney and the Minister reminisce about the good old days of the Troubles, while O'Mooney and O'Rooney continue with the chatter of the salon.

Johnston borrowed from expressionism the basic organisational principle of the quest, in which representative scenes of modern life are visited and found wanting in the quester's search for some sort of validating significance. As *The Old Lady* progresses, the Speaker's desperate desire to re-find Sarah Curran, to get back to Rathfarnham and his part in the play, take on this sort of moral urgency. Emmet's Utopian longings are treated the more sympathetically as they accord with the playwright's own needs to find a new style to express his vision. The Ireland of *The Old Lady* is a country burdened by its past history and overwritten by its past writers. In his initial ideas for the play, Johnston thought of including not just one talking statue but a whole cast of the statues of Dublin arguing out their several views of the country. Equally crucial to the conception of *The Old Lady*, and more prominent in the finished play, was the dance of shadows, the writers whose words continue to echo through Dublin's literary consciousness: Yeats, Joyce, Wilde, Shaw. If the actual subject of *The Old Lady* is the problematic state of post-revolutionary Ireland, it is no less expressive of the problematic state of being a post-revival would-be Irish dramatist. The Blind Man in his pastiche Synge-style links the thanatocracy of the dead patriots and their pernicious legacy for the present with the dead weight of Ireland's literary heritage:

> It takes a dark man to see the will-o'-the-wisps and the ghosts of the dead and the half dead and them that will never die while they can find lazy, idle hearts ready to keep their venom warm ... In every dusty corner lurks the living word of some dead poet, and it waiting for to trap and to snare them. This is no City of the Living: but of the Dark and the Dead!
>
> (Johnston, *Old Lady*, 109)

The drive of *The Old Lady* is to exorcise that ghost-haunted nightmare of history and to find a new modernised version for Emmet's revolutionary vision of Ireland. This is the aim of the ritual of commination, with its Blakean style proverbs of Hell, intended to invoke a new heterodox spirituality. It is the design of the Speaker's concluding salute to Dublin:

> Strumpet city in the sunset
> Suckling the bastard brats of Scots, of Englishry, of Huguenot.

Brave sons breaking from the womb, wild sons fleeing from their Mother.
Wilful city of savage dreamers,
So old, so sick with memories!
Old Mother
Some they say are damned,
But you, I know, will walk the streets of Paradise
Head high, and unashamed.
There now. Let my epitaph be written.

(Johnston, *Old Lady*, 122–3)

This paean to Dublin as whore challenges the nationalist puritans who denied (in the wake of *The Plough*) that there was such a thing as a streetwalker in her streets. With its Irish as 'bastard brats' of mixed ancestry it derides the ethnic Celticist strain of the nationalist vision. 'Old Mother' Ireland, with her sons in flight from her, suggests Joyce's sow that eats her own farrow. And yet this latter-day Kathleen ni Houlihan will be transfigured, she will 'walk the streets of Paradise Head high, and unashamed'. In such a gesture of affirmation, the writer's act of confidence – 'I know' – enables Emmet's vision to be renewed and reincarnated. In this modernist prose poem, the conditions set by the speech from the dock 'when Ireland takes her place among the nations of the earth' are fulfilled: 'There now. Let my epitaph be written.'

The Old Lady, with its extraordinary density of allusion and citation, risks collapse under the weight of its own intertextuality. There is a kind of damaging knowingness of the over-educated in the constant barrage of references, to European as well as Irish canonical and non-canonical texts. But whatever its ultimate limitations, the play suited perfectly, indeed helped to shape what became the Gate Theatre house style. The figure of the Speaker – not Robert Emmet, but an actor playing Robert Emmet – was a magnificent vehicle for the histrionicism of the flamboyant Micheál MacLíammóir. The fluid dramaturgy of the play gave full scope to the inventive panache of his producer partner Hilton Edwards, synthesising lighting, movement, choric speaking and set design as never before in Irish theatre. *The Old Lady* was to become a sort of flagship for the Gate, as *The Plough* after its initial rough ride was to become the Abbey's most loved and most often-revived play. The plays are antithetical in so far as the self-conscious theatricality of *The Old Lady* constantly calls in question the stability of any form of representation, while the naturalistic surfaces of *The Plough*, its scenic design and acting style, insist on their actuality. But in another sense there is a marked continuity between the two. Johnston develops systematically what is latent in O'Casey's play. Where O'Casey intercut quotations from Pearse's speeches as part of the ironic design of the pub scene, Johnston extends the principle of collage right through his play from the scrap-book pastiche of the opening playlet. Where *The Plough* uses the tenement house and its varied tenants to undermine the centralising and unifying drama of the Rising, Johnston sets the visionary Emmet against a cinematic montage of the whole city of Dublin. Both plays offer a retrospect on revolution in terms of what it did not achieve, what it failed to transform as promised. But where *The Plough* gains its strength from its reactive relation to the Rising, Johnston in *The Old Lady* seeks a new modernist style which may give to postrevolutionary Ireland appropriate theatrical life and even a renewal of revolutionary purpose.

Audience: *The Hostage*

In Act II of *The Hostage*, when Meg finishes singing 'Who fears to speak of Easter Week', she comments 'The author should have sung that one.'

> PAT. That's if the thing has an author.
> SOLDIER. Brendan Behan, he's too anti-British.
> OFFICER. Too anti-Irish, you mean. Bejasus, wait till we get him back home. We'll give him what-for for making fun of the Movement.
> SOLDIER (*to audience*). He doesn't mind coming over here and taking your money.
> PAT. He'd sell his country for a pint.[23]

These exchanges write into *The Hostage* all the major talking-points about the play: the controversy over the nature of Brendan Behan's collaboration with Joan Littlewood and her Theatre Workshop company in its creation; Behan's politics as a former IRA man; his public reputation as a drunk; his exploitation of stage Irishry for English audience consumption. And they illustrate also the house-style of the production which did so much to shape the play: sub-Brechtian, jocular, interactive, anti-illusionist. A play which began life in Irish, commissioned by Gael-Linn and performed in the tiny Damer Hall in Dublin, but which went on to international success in England, France, America in a heavily adapted English-language version raises the issue of the audience for Irish drama in a specially acute way.

The original *An Giall* was fairly obviously indebted to O'Casey, as more than one of the reviewers of the first production pointed out. Behan himself came from the northside inner-city Dublin area which O'Casey's plays had made famous, and *An Giall* is set in the familiar 'bedroom in an old tenement in Dublin' (Behan, 29). But 'The Hole', the suggestive name of the brothel-cum-IRA-hideout, is intended to dramatise the gap in time between O'Casey's Ireland of the 1920s and Behan's contemporary scene. Monsúr, the fanatical Englishman converted to Irish nationalism who is the Hole's owner, represents the crazy delusion of a latter-day Republicanism frozen in time, still in the 1950s fighting out the battles of 1916–23. The degeneration of the Republican stronghold into whorehouse, the antics of the 'new IRA' officers, puritanical and amateurish, judged by the hardbitten 'old IRA' veteran Pat who runs the whorehouse, all provide a sceptical view of the continuation of the freedom struggle against the British. On this Behan, previously convicted for Republican violence both in England and in Ireland, was seen to speak with authority. His name as a dramatist was made with *The Quare Fellow* in which he had exploited his inside knowledge of Mountjoy jail to show the atmosphere in the prison on the day of an execution. *An Giall* also dramatised a waiting-on-death situation, this time the hanging for political offences of an IRA volunteer in Belfast; it is as a bargaining weapon against this execution that the British soldier Leslie is captured as hostage and ends up in The Hole. The backdrop of the renewed activities of the IRA border raids of the 1950s gave the play a topicality equivalent to O'Casey's Dublin trilogy, but where O'Casey's plays had reflected the revolution which had just gripped and transformed the nation as a whole, *An Giall* could represent the IRA action as the work of a lunatic fringe.

The Dublin ex-con Behan, with his Irish practised in prison, was a rare bird indeed, and the production of *An Giall* was enthusiastically received as a landmark in Irish-language drama. However, *The Irish Times* reviewer concluded his accolade by saying he 'hoped that Mr Behan translates his play into a language which more people can understand and more theatregoers enjoy'.[24] This was, of course, exactly what Behan was to do when he provided Littlewood with the version which she staged as *The Hostage* at the Theatre Royal, Stratford East, later in 1958. The critical arguments have been over the changes made from the Irish to the English version of the play: whether they represent a distortion of the original for commercial purposes or a theatrical enrichment, and what is the status of the text of *The Hostage* that resulted. How far is it Behan's own play and how far a collaborative product substantially ghosted by Littlewood and the Theatre Workshop company? It is an argument with significant political dimensions.

An Giall followed a relatively simple plotline concerned with the caricatured Monsúr, the relationship between Pat, Monsúr's former IRA lieutenant, and his 'almost' wife the whore Kate, the boy-and-girl affair between the two young orphans, the English Leslie and the Irish servant-girl Teresa, as a version of the standard national romance. In the English-language text this is substantially embroidered and theatrically re-cast. Where *An Giall* simply listed a series of offstage whores and pimps as the lodgers of The Hole – 'Ropeen and Colette ... The Mouse, Clod, Scholar and Bo-Bo' (Behan, 37) – *The Hostage* writes in parts for Ropeen and Colette and adds in an extra selection of oddballs and deadbeats for good measure. There is Mr Mulleady, the 'decaying civil servant', who turns out to be a police undercover agent, and Miss Gilchrist, hymn-singing social worker and fan of the Royal Family. The racial, sexual and international mix is still further enriched by having Colette bring home a Russian sailor and the male whore Rio Rita pick up a black customer, 'Princess Grace' – a topical joke soon after the famous, and famously blonde, film star Grace Kelly had married Prince Rainier of Monaco. Finally, the more or less naturalistic style of *An Giall* was radically changed to accommodate an onstage pianist and the interspersal of songs throughout, and the recurrent disruption of stage illusion in ensemble participation.

All these alterations have been seen by some Irish critics as a betrayal of the Irish original. Ulick O'Connor, Behan's first biographer, is particularly vehement in his condemnation:

> *The Hostage* as it was performed in the West End and Paris version is a blown-up hotch-potch compared with the original version which is a small masterpiece and the best thing Behan wrote for the theatre ... *An Giall* had its roots in Ballyferriter, the Blaskets and the Atlantic; *The Hostage* in a commercial entertainment world Brendan had no real contact with.[25]

The later academic critic Richard Wall, translator of *An Giall* and editor of both texts, is more measured in his judgement but to similar effect: '*The Hostage* clearly lacks the integrity of *An Giall*; its tone is much coarser' (Behan, 19). What is interesting about this debate is the emphasis such critics lay upon an authorially controlled text as a criterion of value. *An Giall* is privileged as more authentic, and more authentically Irish, not only because it was written in the Irish language, but because it is considered to be more completely Behan's own creation. In allowing it to be adapted to suit Littlewood's style of direction, which included varying the text to suit specific audiences, Behan betrayed the integrity of his own work. The Irish dramatic tradition in the modern period from the founding of the Abbey Theatre (with its three playwright directors) has always been dominated by authors and by language. In spite of Synge's dictum about all art being a collaboration, there has been little willingness to see a theatre work as collaborative construct among author, director, theatre performers and audience, the model on which companies such as the Theatre Workshop were based. Thus Behan's *Hostage* 'under Littlewood' was a self-undoing. Going with this suspicion of a playscript outside the control of the playwright is an uneasiness with the marketing of the Irish drama for foreign tastes. Ulick O'Connor again:

> In the Dublin version [i.e. *An Giall*], the brothel was a bawdy, ramshackle Dublin 'kip', peopled by amiable eccentrics of the

> sort that Joyce wrote about in *Ulysses* and Gogarty in his ballads. In the Littlewood production it has become less a brothel than a platform for the queer camp current at the time.[26]

Native forms of Irish self-representation, sponsored by the respectable precedents of Joyce or Gogarty, are contaminated by the alien influences of a decadent cosmopolitanism.

The view from the other side complements the Irish perspective. In her account of the origins of *The Hostage* Littlewood significantly writes out *An Giall* altogether. As she tells it, the play was an original commission for the Theatre Workshop, based on the incident of a British soldier hostage killed in Cyprus, combined with Behan's own anecdotal memories of a Dublin pubcrawl in his IRA days while nominally in charge of a hostage. 'There's a play in it', she describes herself saying to Behan: 'Write it.'[27] *Joan's Book,* with its subtitle, 'Joan Littlewood's Peculiar History as She Tells It' hardly promises factual accuracy, and here her chronology is clearly astray: she has the exchanges leading to the writing of the play take place in the wake of the launch of *Borstal Boy,* which was not in fact published until after *The Hostage* had been staged. What is significant is the way she remembers the play's origins and the way she represents Behan's role in writing it: the drunken Irishman constantly defaulting on his promises to supply a script; the Theatre Workshop team having to improvise the show which was so spectacularly successful.[28]

The play may well have had its origins in the death of a hostage outside Ireland, a British officer taken hostage not in Cyprus but in Egypt during the 1956 Suez crisis who died smothered in a cupboard as Leslie does in *An Giall.*[29] The point of Littlewood's story, however, like the aim of so much in her production of *The Hostage,* was to internationalise the play's theme, to turn it from a play about Republicanism and the continuing Irish question to a play about colonialism and armed conflict throughout the world. The continuing rearguard struggle of Britain as an imperial power is registered in references to Kenya and Cyprus. It is not only latter-day Irish Republicans whose ideas are outdated; the play exposes the absurdity of national defence systems in the age of the atomic bomb. As Pat says when asked to explain why the IRA of the 1950s is different from the independence movement in which he fought: 'It's the H bomb. It's such a big bomb that it's got me scared of the little bombs' (Behan, 85). Tuning the play to the tastes and convictions of a British left-wing audience in this way allowed Littlewood to play down the potentially sensitive issue of the anti-English hostility to be expected from Behan the convicted Republican terrorist. The programme notes for the first production of *The Hostage* obviously sought to allay such fears:

> Brendan Behan . . . has hatred for the political forces which divide and subject Ireland: but for the people – even if those people are the subject of antagonistic political forces – he has only love and understanding. If a stranger attacks Britain, no one will support this country more than Brendan Behan . . .[30]

More than one Irish critic has bridled at this, and has cited it as evidence that Littlewood fundamentally misrepresented Behan in *The Hostage*, while he may have been too drunk to notice.[31] Yet even as *An Giall* the play had attracted some criticism in Dublin that it was 'Pro-British',[32] and the character of Leslie, the 19-year-old English conscript so innocent of the national conflict in which he has become a pawn, is indeed an attractive one. The sympathy for English people which Littlewood attributes to Behan he did indeed show generously through *Borstal Boy*, particularly in his sense of affinity with the boys from English working-class backgrounds very like his own. The socialist inflection to *The Hostage* was there already in *An Giall*. So, for instance, Leslie's satiric scorn at the idea that the British government will change their minds about the execution of the Belfast prisoner because of the risk to a squaddie-hostage like himself was included almost word for word in the Irish-language text:

> You're all cracked if you think that Private Leslie Alan Williams 53742981662 is causing anxiety to the Government over in England. Do you think they're sitting around their clubs in the West End crying about me? Do you think the Secretary of State for War will be saying to his wife tonight: 'Oh, Isabel Cynthia my darling, I'm not able to sleep at all, thinking about poor Williams.' Well, I heard before that the

> Irish were silly, but I didn't know 'till now how silly they were. (Behan, 66–7)

In many respects, Littlewood, rather than changing or traducing Behan's politics, developed them out of latency. There was a Christian anarchist vein running through Behan's work, a taste for, a sympathy with, all who failed to fit approved social and political categories: the sad and the mad, the odds and the sods. This makes the enlarged cast of *The Hostage* with its whores, blacks and gays authentically Behanesque, not just the 'queer camp' of the London King's Road that Ulick O'Connor deplores. The dance which accompanies one of the last songs of Act III is a genuine climax to Behan's play, not just Littlewood's version of Behan's play:

> As the song goes on, the whores and the queers sort themselves out into a dance for all the outcasts of the world. It is a slow sad dance in which ROPEEN dances with COLETTE and PRINCESS GRACE dances first with MULLEADY and then with RIO RITA. There is jealousy and comfort in the dance.
> (Behan, 160)

The politics of *The Hostage* may be Behan's own politics, more or less, but there was much in the presentation and reception of the London production to make Irish critics' suspicions understandable. To start with there was the type-casting implicit in the reviews. So, for example, there was Kenneth Tynan's famous and often-quoted *Observer* review of *The Hostage*: 'Its theme is Ireland, seen through the bloodshot eyes of Mr Behan's talent.'[33] Behan is allowed to be talented, but the deftly inserted epithet makes it the talent of an Irish drunk. Penelope Gilliatt enthused about the writing: 'Language hasn't had an outing like this since *The Quare Fellow*. The English habitually write as if they were alone and cold at ten in the morning: the Irish write in a state of flushed gregariousness at an eternal opening time.'[34] The associations of the Irish with language and drink in such national stereotyping confirms expectations of what Irish drama should be like. I will be coming back to these English preconceptions, and their effect on the reception of Irish playwrights, in later chapters. In the case of *The Hostage*, it was the songs and dances in particular that were specifically marketed for their Irishness. The show started as it meant to go on:

> As the curtain rises, pimps, prostitutes, decayed gentlemen and their visiting 'friends' are dancing a wild Irish jig, which is good enough reason for MEG and PAT to stop their preparations and sit down for a drink of stout. (Behan, 82)

Welcome to the come-all-ye, audience.

The theory of the action suspended for the songs, the direct interaction between performers and audience, the topical jokes, is the Brechtian theory of alienation. The audience are challenged to think rather than merely empathise, to be always aware of being in a theatre watching a performance with consequences for the extra-theatrical world outside. What in fact tends to be the result in the Littlewood–Behan *Hostage* is a nudge-nudge, wink-wink cosying up to the audience rather than an abrasive or provocative stimulus. This is particularly true of the now embarrassingly dated treatment of homosexuality. 'We're here because we're queer / Because we're queer because we're here' runs the chorus of the trio by Rio Rita, Mulleady and Princess Grace. 'The trouble we had getting that past the nice Lord Chamberlain', minces Princess Grace (Behan, 159). The political songs, whether genuine Republican populist stuff like Pat's 'On the Eighteenth day of November' celebrating a particularly bloody ambush of the Black and Tans in Cork in 1920, or Monsewer's pseudo-Kipling parody 'The Captains and the Kings', become showstopping set-pieces which have had all the political harm taken out of them. The audience are drawn into a singalong effect which includes them with the ensemble all united in party harmony.

The play's last unexpected song (Behan's idea, according to Littlewood[35]) is intended to reverse this effect. After the shattering sequence of Leslie's stylised death, shot down in the melée of the attempted rescue, followed by Teresa's moving tribute, 'He died in a strange land, and at home he had no one. I'll never forget you, Leslie, till the end of time', comes the last surprise as

> LESLIE WILLIAMS *slowly gets up and sings:*
> The bells of hell,

Go ting-a-ling-a-ling,
For you but not for me ... (Behan, 167–8)

This *can* work, as it is intended to work, to deliberately undermine the catharsis achieved in the emotional moment of the death, and to remind us that 'it's not in the play-world that people are dying, but out there in the real life of the audience and the distressful country beyond'.[36] But it can also act as a last let-off, a release for the audience into the reassurance that it has only been make-believe after all, and that the violent forces at work in the Irish–English situation can be dissolved into a jolly Irish–English song-and-dance routine.

An Giall/The Hostage, like *The Plough* and *The Old Lady* before it, represents a sceptical reaction to the dramatics of revolution. The play in both its forms clowns around the solemnity of Republican rhetoric, turns the grand tropes of national liberation into music-hall farce, even if in the end a tragic farce. But the history of the play in production, its reception and critical reputation, are in some ways as significant as its politics. *An Giall* was close kin to an O'Casey play, a tragicomedy that upstaged the claims of militant Republicanism to speak for a people so well able to speak in unruly fashion for themselves. As a play in Irish, and one in more-or-less old-fashioned naturalistic mode, it had nowhere much to go beyond the restricted Irish-speaking audiences of Ireland. To reach a wider and more sophisticated audience, the shift to London and the Theatre Workshop idiom was a logical move. In the theatrical era of Brecht, *The Hostage* was a version of Ireland in a suitable modern style, just as *The Old Lady* had been in the late 1920s. Yet such an adaptation to the theatrical milieu of London's left-wing fringe could be read from within Ireland as a betrayal, not only a backsliding on Behan's former political principles as a convinced Republican, but selling out to English – then French and American – audiences the integrity of the representation of Ireland in a tarted-up (in every sense) display of stage Irishry built upon Behan's own public notoriety. As with the other two plays considered in this chapter that struggle to find a politics, a style, an audience in the wake of revolution, the struggle is as significant as the degree of the success.

Unfinished business

The chapter on O'Casey, Johnston and Behan in Philip Edwards's *Threshold of a Nation* is entitled 'Nothing is Concluded'. Edwards argues that their plays' lack of closure expresses the continuing and insoluble political problems they dramatise: 'Their burden is that there is no solution and no end to Ireland's difficulties.'[37] That was written twenty years ago now, and neither Ireland's difficulties nor the attempt by playwrights to come to terms with them on stage have ended in that time. This chapter could be continued all but indefinitely with a sequence of plays from the 1970s on which have followed the precedents set by *The Plough*, *The Old Lady* and *The Hostage*. Behan's play in the 1950s might suggest, relatively reassuringly, that the continuing anti-British struggle of the IRA was a crazy, if disastrous, leftover of the past. Since 1969 no such reassurance could be credible in the light of the renewed violence in the North, the deadly seriousness and efficiency of the war being waged between paramilitary terrorists (on both sides of the sectarian divide), the police and the British army. For dramatists from Ulster in particular there has been a felt urgency to respond to the urgencies of the violence, to find if not political solutions at least a way of resisting theatrically the stark polarities of the conflict. Friel's *Translations* looked at in the first chapter, and the whole Field Day Theatre Company that it inaugurated have been the most prominent examples of this movement of resistance, the need to find or make audiences receptive to new ways of representing Ireland. Three other Ulster plays can be used as brief final illustrations of the issues explored in this chapter, as they continue on in contemporary Irish theatre.

Friel's *The Freedom of the City* (1973) was written in immediate angry reaction to the events of Bloody Sunday in Derry the previous year. The play is powered by the outrage felt in the nationalist community at the findings of the Widgery Tribunal, which cleared the British soldiers of blame for the shooting of thirteen unarmed civil rights marchers. Friel satirically guys the tribunal in the play for what he sees as its palpably prejudiced attempt to cast the victims of the shootings as terrorist suspects. *The Freedom of the City* shows three street demonstrators who, blinded by tear gas, find themselves accidentally holed up in the Mayor's parlour of Derry's

Guildhall, are taken for a terrorist occupation and gunned down when they come out. It met a hostile press reaction in Britain where it was viewed as nationalist agit-prop. But Friel's play, as well as showing up the Widgery-like tribunal that investigates the deaths with obvious prejudice, satirises equally the spurious uses made of the event from the nationalist side, the romantic Republican ballads turning the victims into martyrs, the political capital made from their deaths in the media. The play is staged in fluent mock TV-documentary style, starting with the images of the dead bodies so horrifically familiar from the Bloody Sunday killings. It is like O'Casey, however, in its rendering of the three representative urban figures whose lives are sacrificed and traduced by the need of the contending political forces to believe in their own false melodramas.

Stewart Parker's *Northern Star* from 1984 goes right back for its images of revolution to the 1798 Rebellion and the Presbyterian United Irishman leader Henry Joy McCracken. Parker's play is comparable to *The Old Lady* in its self-conscious awareness not only of the burden of Irish history, but of the weight of Irish dramatic self-expression. The progress of McCracken, from the confident idealism of the early United Irishman to the despair of the failed rebellion and the gallows, is matched by a successive pastiche of theatrical styles from the breezy comedy of Farquhar and Sheridan to the last grim Beckettian apocalypse. Parker, like Johnston before him, writes the intertextuality of his inheritance as Irish playwright into the terribly repeated and unfinished matrices of Irish history. *Northern Star* won considerable acclaim when originally produced in Belfast and Dublin, and has been successfully revived in Ireland since, but, again like *The Old Lady*, the density of Irish-specific quotation and allusion have prevented its finding audiences outside the country.

In the continuing dialogue of Irish drama reflecting the continuing attempt to come to terms with the unfinished business of revolution, Frank McGuinness's *Carthaginians* (1988) takes off from O'Casey and Friel, with a suggestion of Behan. Like Friel's *Freedom of the City* it is about the after-effects of Bloody Sunday in Derry. For its central metaphor it develops the Rome/Carthage analogy for Britain/ Ireland from *Translations*: McGuinness's Carthaginians are the bereaved and deranged Derry figures who occupy a graveyard waiting for the dead to rise. In the bizarre collocation of characters and the fluidity of their gender roles, there might be a recollection of Behan, whose last unfinished play *Richard's Cork Leg* was an extravaganza in a graveyard. The centrepiece of the action in *Carthaginians* is the gay Dido's play-within-the-play, *The Burning Balaclava*, a splendid parody of O'Casey and the imitative derivations from O'Casey that have turned his situations and emotions into theatrical cliché. The characters all called Doherty, the apolitical mother of the politically engaged son with her devotion to the Sacred Heart, the cross-party love affair between the Catholic Republican and the Protestant daughter of the RUC police officer, send up the hackneyed images of conflict which have become the stock-in-trade of the Irish dramatist through the time of the Northern 'Troubles'. McGuinness tries to escape from the stale inadequacies of such forms of representation; the play looks for a new poetry of the theatre to express the bombed-out after-battle experience of Derry, some way of working through mourning and loss towards renewal and resurrection.

This chapter's concern has been with the dramatic reactions to revolution since 1922. To react to revolution as O'Casey did in its immediate aftermath was to challenge the transformations it had promised in the light of the disillusioning realities that followed. If modern urban postrevolutionary Ireland was to be adequately represented, some style had to be found other than the revivalist mode of country cottages figuring the nation; such was Johnston's objective in *The Old Lady*. The aim of *The Hostage* was to dramatise for an audience outside Ireland the continuing fallout from a revolution which some Irish people persisted in believing unfinished. But that persistent belief in the unfinished nature of the Irish revolution, even if still held only by a minority of the island's population, has come since 1969 so to dominate the consciousness of Ireland at home and abroad that it represents a new difficulty, a new challenge for Irish drama. For many people the romantic conception of the 1916 Rising may now seem remote and irrelevant in the context of late twentieth-century Ireland. Yet equivalent ideas of revolution still animate the actions of Sinn Fein/IRA and must be met as a continuing political reality. Contemporary Irish playwrights have felt the pressure to respond to that situation and, however often it has been attempted before, to find different ways of staging it and different audiences to understand it. That is one of the forms of the politics of Irish drama with which this book is concerned. There are others, in plays less obviously concerned with national politics, plays such as Yeats's *Purgatory* and Beckett's *All that Fall*, the subject of the next chapter.

6 Living on

The plays in the previous chapter were concerned with reactions to revolution by those disenchanted with its outcome, disillusioned with its failure to deliver a promised metamorphosis, with its protracted aftermath of violence. The viewpoint of the plays was of those who might have hoped for a revolution capable of transforming lives in need of transformation, who saw with dismay the fragmented shards of a nation in place of a dreamed-of unity. But what of the people who had nothing to gain, everything to lose from revolution, the colonial class of past dispossessors who stood to be themselves dispossessed? How did the Ascendancy look when it was no longer in the ascendant, the minority Protestant community in a time when power had been ceded to a Catholic nationalist majority? Yeats's *Purgatory*, Beckett's *All that Fall*, provide two very different dramatic versions of that situation. They are both in the most literal sense postcolonial plays, concerned with the period after Independence and the outcome for those who had held power and position before 1922. *Purgatory*, written in 1938 in Yeats's mood of extreme revulsion from contemporary Irish society, broods on the ruined house that stands for the lost class of the landed Anglo-Irish. In *All that Fall*, nearly twenty years later, Beckett recreates the suburban Foxrock which he recalled from the 1920s, where a general atmosphere of entropy and decay is associated with the dwindling condition of shabby-genteel Protestantism in an Irish Free State. Each play can be construed as some sort of verdict on the postcolonial society and on those who live on within it.

Yet if *Purgatory* and *All that Fall* reflect such social and political issues, they do so only obliquely and the obliqueness in itself is of significance. For these two plays are significant not only for their contrasting dramatisation of the postcolonial situation, but as they are symptomatic of the off-centre position which Yeats and Beckett share in relation to Irish drama. The Irish drama considered in this book is posited on the idea that Ireland is out there to be represented, analysed, interpreted for audiences at home and abroad, and that its Irishness is essential to its drama. It is a body of plays recognised for their Irishness internationally as well as nationally, a tradition of drama with an identifiable intertextual line of descent. Beckett could hardly be expected to figure centrally in such a tradition, Beckett who fled from Ireland, from what remained of the Irish literary revival, from a geographical or cultural location for his art. In his 'Homage to Jack B. Yeats', he stated his placeless aesthetic: 'L'artiste qui joue son être est de nulle part'[1] – 'The artist who stakes his whole being comes from nowhere.' Yeats, though, should surely occupy a dominant position in a book on the politics of Irish drama. After all, if something as multiply determined as a theatre movement can be said to have an architect, then Yeats was the architect of the Irish national theatre movement. He gave an enormous amount of his political energies to the 'theatre business, management of men' he professed to dislike, and as much of his creative energies to the production of plays on specifically Irish themes. Yet, arguably, Yeats's plays, as well as Beckett's, appear anomalous within the context of an Irish drama which depends upon an assumed otherness of Ireland and the need to represent that otherness.

In so far as Irish drama is centrally concerned with the explanation and interpretation of Ireland there is a bias towards the representational within it. Yeats always fought against this from the very beginnings of the Irish Literary Theatre, opposing Moore and Martyn's preference for an Ibsenite drama of contemporary realism. He chafed even under the necessity, urged by Synge and Gregory, of sticking with their distinctive mode of home-grown peasant drama, aspiring to a theatre where the great European classics and his verse plays would be equally well played.[2] His objective throughout was a mythic and visionary drama in which Irish materials were a means towards the expression of deeper and non-nationally specific truths. By 1919 he had given up: in his open 'letter to Lady Gregory' he turned away from the 'People's Theatre' they had both done so much to create and which had been such a paradoxically disappointing success to Yeats. 'I want,' he said in a famous sentence, 'to create for myself an unpopular theatre and an audience like a secret society where admission is by favour and never to many.'[3] In his last play, *The Death of Cuchulain*, he makes the Old Man as producer speak for his own aesthetic of belligerent dissidence, in violent revolt against an acknowledged mainstream of representational drama: 'I have been asked to produce a play called *The Death of Cuculain*. ... I have been selected because I am out of fashion and out of date like the antiquated romantic stuff the thing is made of' (Yeats, *CPl*, 693).

Beckett in some sense moved in the opposite direction from Yeats in his attitudes towards Irish drama. The man whose early attitude to the national theatre was expressed in *Murphy*, where the protagonist decreed in his will that his remains should be flushed away in the Abbey's 'necessary house', preferably during a performance,[4] appears to have mellowed towards the playwrights who in his youth stood for national kitsch. In a very frequently rehearsed comment of 1956, refusing a centenary tribute to Shaw, he remarked that he would 'give the whole unupsettable apple-cart for a sup of the Hawk's Well, or the Saints', or a whiff of Juno, to go no further'.[5] It was apparently 'a mutual admiration for the plays of Synge' which helped to draw Beckett closer to Roger Blin when it was first proposed that Blin should direct *Godot*,[6] and his later plays have frequent echoes of Yeats. However, *All that Fall*, written in 1956, is atypical of Beckett's work in the degree to which it reflects a quite recognisable Irish social reality. And even in it, there is a sort of tongue-in-cheek parody of the tradition of Irish dramatic representationalism.

Yeats's brief verse tragedy for the theatre and Beckett's (for him) quite extended prose tragicomedy for radio are works very fundamentally unlike one another. They present wholly diverse images of living on into post-Independence Ireland. Beckett's play might almost be read as a deliberate antidote to Yeats's, mocking the high gothic melodrama of *Purgatory* with the ordinariness of its suburban scene, the uncatastrophic character of its characters' reduced lives. Beckett fills in the Ireland that Yeats writes out, the petite bourgeoisie deliberately excluded from the Yeatsian 'dream of the noble and the beggarman'. In dramaturgical terms, equally, the plays might stand as representative of the playwrights' antithetical methods: the heroic mode of Yeats against Beckett's anti-heroism, Yeats's pure tragic form set beside Beckett's generically mixed tragicomic vision. Still in the end there are affinities between *Purgatory* and *All that Fall*, affinities that help to define the qualities which Yeats and Beckett share and which differentiate them from other Irish dramatists. The plan of this chapter is to analyse first *Purgatory*, then *All that Fall*, as diverse dramatic versions of Ireland's postcolonial situation, and then to explore in what ways they might be considered alike, with the significance of such similarity in the context of their relations to Irish drama as a whole.

Purgatory: the tragedy of survival

'Study that house', says the Old Man at the opening of *Purgatory*: what house, what time, what place? The stage direction gives no help towards dating or localisation: 'a ruined house and a bare tree in the background' (Yeats, *CPl*, 681). No doubt an Irish audience watching the play in 1938 must have had in mind the many ruined big houses left after the burnings of 1919–23, and it has been suggested that Yeats may have been thinking partly of Augusta Gregory's family home, Roxborough House, destroyed in 1922.[7] Even if not consciously focused on one house or another, the image would have conjured up generically the landscape reminders of the Troubles as Shakespeare's 'bare ruined choirs where late the sweet birds sang' called to mind the dissolved monasteries. Donald Torchiana, reading back from the 1938 date of composition, calculated the 16–year-old Boy's date of birth as coinciding with the setting up of the Free State in 1922, the burning of the house when the Old Man was 16 happening close to the date of Parnell's death in 1891.[8] In Torchiana's view, the play looks back to Yeats's idealised Georgian Ireland and its narrative of misalliance and degeneracy is a lament for the tragic betrayal of Ascendancy values since then. W.J. Mc Cormack has argued, against Torchiana, that it is the late nineteenth century which is more relevant to *Purgatory*, 'years when Irish politics was more evidently and palpably concerned with social issues rather than nationalist principles'.[9] The fact is that though the mood of *Purgatory* is very much of its time of composition,

Yeats avoided specifying its setting. One incidental reference to the 'guards' in a draft of the play – the Old Man after the murder says 'I'll to a distant place & there / Tell my old jokes among new men. / Until the guards have found me or forget'[10] – was dropped as though this single allusion to the Free State era of the Garda Síochána would have compromised the play's timelessness. *Purgatory* speaks *out* of the postcolonial situation, not directly *about* it.

The difficulty in dating the action of *Purgatory*, however, highlights a sort of historical slippage in retrospects on the 'twilight of the Ascendancy' as one nostalgic popular history calls it.[11] When did the Anglo-Irish fall from power? In 1922 with the setting up of the Free State, or in 1903 with Wyndham's Act, the most sweeping of the Land Acts which effectively dispossessed the landowners? In 1869 when the Church of Ireland was disestablished, or in 1829 when Catholics were belatedly emancipated? Or is it necessary to go right back to 1800 when, with the Act of Union, the Ascendancy voted to abolish Ireland's separate Parliament and thus their own power-base? Yet even already at that time, Edgeworth's *Castle Rackrent*, published in the year of the Union, provided a finely satiric rendering of a class in terminal decline, destroyed by their own fecklessness and irresponsibility as much as by the social competition of an upstart middle class. This is a recurrent feature of literary treatments of the Big House from Edgeworth's time down to the novels and plays of Yeats's own: Somerville and Ross's *The Big House of Inver* (1925), Lennox Robinson's *The Big House* (1926), Elizabeth Bowen's *The Last September* (1929). The big house is doomed because its occupants have some inherent tendency towards self-destruction, whether through a wilful blindness to what is going on around them, a failure to fulfil their class obligations to land and peasantry, or a betrayal of their caste by intermarriage or interbreeding with the native Irish.[12] This is a literary trope, a myth of degenerate decline which may be monitory (Edgeworth), pathetic (Robinson), ironic/elegiac (Bowen) or self-accusatory (Somerville and Ross), but is only contingently tied to historical period and actual political event.

The force of *Purgatory* derives from the way Yeats has compressed and concentrated this pattern into his one 'scene of tragic intensity'.[13] With no more than the two characters of unnamed Old

Man and Boy and the ghost presence of the Old Man's mother, it dramatises the tragedy of three generations as a reverie upon a reverie. The Old Man enjoins his son to 'Study that house', but the command is as much to himself and the audience as to the Boy, who cannot be bothered to do more than half-listen. The concentrated obsessive attention on the house issues as all but soliloquy, part expository reminiscence, part brooding meditation:

> I think about its jokes and stories;
> I try to remember what the butler
> Said to a drunken gamekeeper
> In mid-October, but I cannot.
> If I cannot, none living can.
> Where are the jokes and stories of a house,
> Its threshold gone to patch a pig-sty? (Yeats, *CPl*, 681)

A part of the horror of the play is the way in which the Old Man is locked into his reverie, as incapable of relating to the Boy as his own ghost mother, in her reliving of the circumstances of his conception, is incapable of relating to him. The Old Man is driven to go over the facts of his life, of the past of the house and its destruction, just as the unpurged soul of the mother is forced to dream through again her 'crime' of sexual union with the groom. The unexorcised past of the previous generation is replicated in the unfinished business of the present.

A key debate about *Purgatory* is the extent to which the viewpoint of the Old Man is identical with that of Yeats himself. Torchiana is in little doubt about the Yeatsian sympathies in the Old Man's eloquent threnody for the house:

> Great people lived and died in this house;
> Magistrates, colonels, members of Parliament,
> Captains and Governors, and long ago
> Men that had fought at Aughrim and the Boyne.
> Some that had gone on Government work
> To London or to India came home to die,
> Or came from London every spring
> To look at the may-blossom in the park. (Yeats, *CPl*, 683)

The ringing sentence which the Old Man retrospectively passes on his own father at the end of this passage, Torchiana concludes, is 'certainly Yeats's own voice':[14]

> to kill a house
> Where great men grew up, married, died,
> I here declare a capital offence. (Yeats, *CPl*, 683)

There are indeed parallels between this and the emotions that animate much of Yeats's later poetry and prose, the sense of desolation and waste in the destruction of the big house. But Torchiana himself refers in a footnote to a passage in Yeats's 'Commentary' on 'A Parnellite at Parnell's Funeral' which places the imagination of Ascendancy gracious living in a different perspective.[15]

In that 'Commentary', an extended context for the poem which was later re-titled simply 'Parnell's Funeral', Yeats placed the death of Parnell as the last of 'Four Bells, four deep tragic notes' (*VP*, 832) ushering in new eras of Irish history. In that view the French Revolution at the end of the eighteenth century brought in one more decisive change:

> The influence of the French Revolution woke the peasantry from the medieval sleep, gave them ideas of social justice and equality, but prepared for a century disastrous to the national intellect. Instead of the Protestant Ascendency with its sense of responsibility, we had the Garrison, a political party of Protestant and Catholic landowners, merchants and officials. They loved the soil of Ireland; the returned Colonial Governor crossed the Channel to see the May flowers in his park; the merchant loved ... some sea-board town where he had made his money, or spent his youth, but they could give to a people they thought unfit for self-government, nothing but a condescending affection. (Yeats, *VP*, 834–5)[16]

Yeats shows here an unexpected capacity for politically critical distance from both the often idealised Ascendancy and his own ancestors eulogised in *Responsibilities*: 'Merchant and scholar who have left me blood / That has not passed through any huckster's loin' (Yeats, *VP*, 269). The 'Commentary' appeared in *The King of the Great Clock*

Tower in 1934, and one suspects that, before the death of Lady Gregory in 1932, Yeats might not have published a passage citing her venerated husband Sir William Gregory, 'the Colonial Governor' returning each year to enjoy the may-blossom in his park, as an example of the limited Garrison mentality.[17] The distinction Yeats makes between the 'Ascendency with its sense of responsibility' and its nineteenth-century descendants opens up a significant gap between the Old Man's elegy for empire and the authorial viewpoint in *Purgatory*, linked as the two passages are by their shared instance of the return visits every spring to the may-blossom in the park. The Old Man's lines, for all their beauty, can be read as a sentimental back-projection, an idealisation of the graciousness of a life from which he has been by birth and upbringing excluded. With Yeats's judgement on the 'Garrison' shadowing the Old Man's paean to the 'magistrates, colonels, members of Parliament', the eloquence of the speech is placed as typical of the dramatic character. There is ironic room to see him for what he is rather than a mere mouthpiece for his creator.

The question of the degree of Yeats's identification with the Old Man has been particularly fraught because of the connection between the play and the politically distasteful eugenics which Yeats entertained apparently quite seriously at this time. *Purgatory* appeared originally with *On the Boiler* as a designed combination, and the eugenicist message of the pamphlet chimes all too obviously with the burden of the play. The mother's primal crime bringing ruin on the house is misalliance, regarded with the horror almost of miscegenation. The Boy could be taken as representative of the latter-day degenerates whom Irish poets in 'Under Ben Bulben' are urged to scorn:

> Their unremembering hearts and heads
> Base-born products of base beds. (Yeats, *VP*, 639)

The Boy knows nothing of the history of the house and cares less; his conception – 'got / Upon a tinker's daughter in a ditch' (Yeats, *CPl*, 684) – did not even rate a bed, base or otherwise. F.A.C. Wilson even follows through the logic of Yeatsian doctrine to the extent of describing the murder of the Boy as 'a morally desirable' if 'ultimately unavailing act'.[18]

Critics are no doubt right to link the unpalatable politics of *On the Boiler* and *Purgatory*. But even in *On the Boiler*, Yeats allows himself a margin of irony in the title and its explanation:

> When I was a child and wandering about the Sligo Quays I saw a printed, or was it a painted notice? On such-and-such a day 'the great McCoy will speak on the boiler'. I knew the old boiler, very big, very high, the top far out of reach, and all red rust. I wanted to go and hear him for the boiler's sake, but nobody encouraged me. I was told then or later that he was a mad ship's carpenter, very good at his trade if he would stick to it, but he went to bed from autumn to spring and during his working months broke off from time to time to read the Scriptures and denounce his neighbours.[19]

His readers are thus allowed to imagine the poet, 'very good at his trade' of poetry, but here with the mad fit on him preaching the latter-day jeremiads of his 'occasional publication' *On the Boiler*. There is an analogy between the self-ironised persona thus established for the pamphlet and the dramatic character of the play's Old Man with his special psychopathology. This latter can be read as characteristic of the colonial mentality living on into the postcolonial state.

It is crucial to the Old Man to try to separate out the aristocratic from the base in his own ancestry. This, though, he can never do because in his own terms he is inevitably the product of his own mixed birth. We see this when he accuses his hated father of wilfully degrading him:

> That he might keep me upon his level
> He never sent me to school . . .

But when the Boy reasonably questions 'What education have you given me?' his answer in its class contempt is that of his father's son:

> I gave the education that befits
> A bastard that a pedlar got
> Upon a tinker's daughter in a ditch. (Yeats, *CPl*, 684)

The very vehemence of his effort to distinguish pure from impure, the crazed belief that he can cut off the consequences of the original 'crime' by killing the Boy and thus arrest the continuum of time, is a peculiarly Anglo-Irish version of trying to awake from the nightmare of history. Pure and impure are divided along gendered lines: the mother is the focus for the aristocratic state which she betrays by giving herself to the bestial male in whom all the fear of pollution is concentrated. The longstanding tradition of a feminised Ireland allows this to be read as an allegory of the nation in its degenerate, postcolonial state. But it can be seen as representative of something more specific and more inward than that. The crazy and intense emotional illogic of the Old Man, made so dramatically credible, suggests a frenetic effort by the self-divided Anglo-Irish to be convinced in the receding retrospect on their own history that there *was* a time when they were an aristocracy of grace, power and purity, to allay a fear that as a mere garrison class they were always inevitably pre-polluted, pre-doomed.

All that Fall: a lingering dissolution

The tragedy of the Big House and its doom could, in one sense, be described as a sort of consolatory fiction of the Anglo-Irish literary imagination. At least there is grandeur in that destroyed mansion, even a measure of heroic pride in the acceptance of the class as self-doomed. Beckett's Boghill in *All that Fall*, identifiably the writer's own Foxrock, resists such self-aggrandisement. It is true that it begins as though it might be another *Purgatory*, with Schubert's 'Death and the Maiden' heard 'faint from house by way'. 'Poor old woman', Mrs Rooney comments: 'All alone in that ruinous old house.'[20] But from the sound picture built up by the radio play, it is soon apparent that the inhabitants of this outer suburb of Dublin – as Foxrock still was in Beckett's time – do not live in big houses, at least not in the large Georgian country houses which that capitalised Big House conjures up in an Irish cultural context. These are people meeting commuters coming home for their half-day off on the Saturday lunchtime train, getting ready for the races at the nearby (Leopardstown) racecourse: *A Nice Day for the Races* was Beckett's initial mordant title for the piece before hitting on the even more mordant *All that Fall*.[21] This is the petty-bourgeois world of Mr Tyler the retired bill-broker, Mr Slocum the clerk of the racecourse, Mr Barrell the stationmaster – only one letter removed from his original, Mr Farrell the real stationmaster of Foxrock.[22] This is suburban fringe where country, ostentatiously signalled by rural noises, meets city represented by the equally 'exaggerated station sounds' (Beckett, *CDW*, 187), where Christy the carter peddles loads of stydung to the Rooneys for their garden. A whole style of life, a whole social milieu is summed up brilliantly in Maddy Rooney's self-pitying self-description:

> Oh I am just a hysterical old hag I know, destroyed with sorrow and pining and gentility and church-going and fat and rheumatism and childlessness. (Beckett, *CDW*, 174)

The Rooneys and Protestant Foxrock are Beckett's satiric/comic version of Ireland's postcolonial survivors in place of the cursed family of the ruined big house of *Purgatory*.

It is specifically Protestant suburbia which Beckett evokes, at least as far as the central characters are concerned. It would have been the Church of Ireland that Mrs Rooney attended with Miss Fitt, the acquaintance whom she accuses of cutting her when they meet at the station:

> MISS FITT. Mrs Rooney! I saw you, but I did not know you.
> MRS ROONEY. Last Sunday we worshipped together. We knelt side by side at the same altar. We drank from the same chalice. Have I so changed since then?
> MISS FITT (*Shocked*). Oh but in church, Mrs Rooney, in church I am alone with my Maker, are not you?
> (Beckett, *CDW*, 182)

It could only have been in a Protestant church at this time that lay communicants would have drunk from the chalice, as Catholics still took only the wafer, not the wine. Miss Fitt is true to the doctrines of the reformed church in stressing the directness and uniqueness of the worshipper's relationship with God rather than the shared social experience of the Catholic Mass.[23] Theology provides the basis for more of their repartee when Mrs Rooney demands assistance from Miss Fitt in climbing the steps up to the station:

> MRS ROONEY. If you would help me up the face of this cliff, Miss Fitt, I have little doubt your Maker would requite you, if no one else.

> MISS FITT. Now, now, Mrs Rooney, don't put your teeth in me. Requite! I make these sacrifices for nothing – or not at all. (Beckett, *CDW*, 183)

Miss Fitt is indignant at any suggestion of being requited for her good deeds, salvation by works not by grace alone. It is an inspired final joke to have the pious Miss Fitt agree 'resignedly' to give the required help – 'Well, I suppose it is the Protestant thing to do' (Beckett, *CDW*, 183).

This is a 1920s Irish Protestant community: the signs are unobtrusive but they are there. 'Now,' says Mrs Rooney as she and Miss Fitt get stuck on the steps, 'we are the laughing-stock of the twenty-six counties. Or is it thirty-six?' (Beckett, *CDW*, 184). The violently contentious issue of partition, the question of the number of counties of the North potentially to be ceded to the Free State which a Boundary Commission, agreed under the terms of the Treaty, was due to decide but never did,[24] is turned here into an affected ignorance of the details. This is how Beckett's Protestant Rooneys deal with the transfer of the power of the state to their Catholic fellow citizens, not by resistance, nor yet with the sort of brooding self-analysis which lies behind Yeats's anatomy of the Big House and its ills, but with a sort of sneering distaste. The blind Dan Rooney is typical as he gives his account of arriving at the station:

> I got down and Jerry led me to the men's, or Fir as they call it now, from Vir Viris I suppose, the V becoming F, in accordance with Grimm's law. (Beckett, *CDW*, 195)

'As *they* call it now' – 'they' says it all. For the likes of the Rooneys and their fellow-Protestants it is 'they', the Catholic nationalists, who are now in control of the state, and who have decreed that all public signs such as that for the men's toilet should appear in the first national language as 'FIR' not 'MEN', much less 'GENTLEMEN'. Dan, holding up the unfamiliar Irish word between finger and thumb, can only disdainfully reconstruct its meaning from his comparative philology learned long ago in Trinity College, we may presume. The Rooneys have little belief in this official revival of Irish. Dan comments on the peculiarity of his wife's speech:

> MR ROONEY. ... Do you know, Maddy, sometimes one would think you were struggling with a dead language.
> MRS ROONEY. Yes indeed, Dan, I know full well what you mean, I often have that feeling, it is unspeakably excruciating.
> MR ROONEY. I confess I have it sometimes myself, when I happen to overhear what I am saying.

And then comes the punchline to which this whole sequence is building:

> MRS ROONEY. Well, you know, it will be dead in time, just like our own poor dear Gaelic, there is that to be said.
> (Beckett, *CDW*, 194)[25]

The Rooneys' revenge on the postcolonial culture, into which they have lived on, is to treat it with a sort of sardonic and dismissive dissent.

Yeats's *Purgatory* provides calamitous images of a postcolonial state in the ruined house and the dead tree, the self-destroyed Ascendancy class and their degenerate descendants. Beckett characteristically resists such dramatics. If his Boghill/Foxrock is a community in decline, it is in slow and unspectacular decline, a matter of a certain shabby-genteel decrepitude nothing like the Grand Guignol of Yeats's burned-out house and blasted tree. *All that Fall*, like all of Beckett's work, reflects a world of entropy where everything is breaking down or on the point of breaking down: bicycles puncture, cars stall, trains fail to arrive on time. But notice that the expectation is that the train *will* arrive on time, does normally arrive on time. Mrs Rooney insists on an explanation from the stationmaster as to why the 12.30 has been held up. 'Even the slowest train on this brief line is not ten minutes and more behind its scheduled time without good cause, one imagines' (Beckett, *CDW*, 186). The line in question was the Dublin and South Eastern Railway, known to its familiars as the Slow and Easy.[26] Slow and easy it may have been by the standards of the time, but they were quite high standards. The world implied by *All that Fall* is a highly ordered world with a well-developed infrastructure of express trains and commuter trains, timetables and schedules by which its characters live. The play in all its suburban specificity demythologises not only Yeats's romantic Ireland of peasant and gentry but other imagined Irelands as well, such as the comically irregular and whimsically unpunctual rural Ireland of Percy French and Somerville and Ross.

And yet, in spite of the continuing routines of its social activities realised with such brio in Beckett's soundscape, the atmosphere of *All that Fall* is one of running down, ending up. 'It is suicide to be abroad', Mrs Rooney remarks, after she and Mr Tyler have nearly been run over by the motor-van. 'But what is it to be at home, Mr Tyler, what is it to be at home? A lingering dissolution' (Beckett, *CDW*, 175). The lingering dissolution of life in *All that Fall* is made all the more final in prospect because of the infertility, the incapacity for reproduction which is everywhere in the play. The hinny or jennet, such as pulls Christy's cart and may or may not have carried Christ into Jerusalem on Palm Sunday, is a hybrid and so cannot breed; Mr Tyler's daughter has had a hysterectomy: 'They removed everything, you know, the whole ... er ... bag of tricks. Now I am grandchildless' (Beckett, *CDW*, 174). Mrs Rooney's great sorrow is the loss of her one daughter. Yet even as she sobs over the death of 'Little Minnie', it is in terms of the age she would have been had she lived: 'In her forties now she'd be, I don't know, fifty, girding up her lovely little loins, getting ready for the change...' (Beckett, *CDW*, 176). The pathos of the lack of descendants associated with the loss of children is here subverted by the girding up of the loins – for the menopause. If promiscuous breeding, a sexuality heedless of class and caste, is the degeneracy diagnosed in the Anglo-Irish of *Purgatory*, the Protestants of *All that Fall* seem to suffer from the opposite complaint.

Given the relatively low birthrate of the Protestant community and traditional fears of Catholic fecundity, the emphasis on sterility can be read at a sociological level as symptomatic. Beyond that, however, it has been suggested by Terence Brown that the minimal fertility and impotence here and in so much of Beckett's work is a willed denial of reproduction associated with a sort of terminal Protestantism.[27] Politically this could be seen as a death-wish of the defeated, a gloomy pleasure in the prospect of extinction by the disempowered. Theologically it might be Protestant preterite conviction of damnation. As the narrator of 'The End' puts it: 'there's that about the reformed church, you're lost, it's unavoidable'.[28] I will be coming back to damnation presently. But however the preoccupation with the terminal in the play is construed there is in *All that Fall*, almost uniquely in Beckett's work, enough of the mimetic texture of social actuality to give it a cultural and historical context, to allow us to hear–see the characters as typical of their time and place: ageing Free State Protestants living on without heirs and without inheritance.

Affinities

For all their dissimilarities of principle and practice, Yeats and Beckett have been critically considered akin as playwrights. The fullest and most elaborate study is Katharine Worth's 1978 *The Irish Drama of Europe from Yeats to Beckett* which, as the title suggests, places them at the beginning and end of a dramatic tradition, including Wilde, Synge and O'Casey, influenced by a European modernist dramaturgy deriving from Maeterlinck and Gordon Craig. More recently Anthony Roche has traced a line of descent from Yeats to Beckett and argued that Beckett is the 'ghostly founding father' of contemporary Irish drama.[29] Closer to my own view is that of Thomas Kilroy in his essay on the two playwrights:

> Stage imagery which relies, to one degree or another, upon the imported pre-conceptions, the subjective luggage of the audience is of one kind; playwright and audience rely upon a complicity of knowledge. Stage imagery which demands a subjection of the audience's expectations to the severe legislation, the severe mathematics of the stage is of another kind; the imagery is, in a sense, explicit, authoritarian and its immediate authority is that of the stage. The stage imagery of Yeats and Beckett is of this second kind.[30]

Kilroy does not here state directly that most Irish drama relies on stage imagery of the first kind, and that Yeats and Beckett are to be seen as exceptional in making use of the second, but it is implicit.[31] The majority of Irish playwrights have relied on a 'complicity of knowledge' with their audiences, the knowledge of Ireland itself. Though often their object has been to re-make that knowledge, to challenge the preconceptions in stereotype and received understanding, as in the stage interpretations of Ireland considered in the first chapter, the knowledge and preconceptions have to be there to be challenged or re-made. Yeats and Beckett, even where they work with material which is Irish, write a drama which is not in the end determined by its Irishness.

There might have been more obvious pairings than *Purgatory* and *All that Fall* to illustrate the affinities between Yeats and Beckett differentiating them from other Irish dramatists. The minimalist setting of *Purgatory* with its ruined house and bare tree is more suggestive of *Waiting for Godot* than it is of the relatively detailed and crowded background of *All that Fall.* In thematic terms the terrible reliving of sexual encounter as a sort of repeated hell of the posthumous imagination in *Purgatory* can be paralleled in Beckett's *Play*. M, the man forced repeatedly to rehearse with W1 and W2 the script of his double relationship with them, aspires to some future perfect state: 'when will all this have been ... just play?' (Beckett, *CDW*, 313). The desire is like that of Yeats's Old Man to release his mother's soul from its dream, to finish 'all that consequence' (Yeats, *CPl*, 688). More affinities could be found between Yeats's theatre and Beckett's stage drama than with *All that Fall* which, as Beckett's first radio play, is unrepresentative of his work as a whole. Yet it is significant in its very unrepresentativeness as the one piece of Beckett in which he came anyway close to writing a recognisably Irish Irish play. Such similarities as do exist between *Purgatory* and *All that Fall* may provide a testing-ground for the argument that Yeats and Beckett are alike in their difference from other Irish playwrights.

The two plays have so far been considered in this chapter for a common subject: they are both about an Irish colonial mentality in the immediate postcolonial period, about living on into the Irish Free State. Yet at some much more fundamental level they are not concerned with those shaping specifics of historical situation but with a more absolute drama of living on, in or out of the body. For all the meticulousness of Beckett's rendering of Dublin suburbia in *All that Fall*, the technique of the radio play is always to unrealise what it realises. It is like the famous Magritte image where the perfectly painted image of a pipe in alphabet-primer style has the copperplate handwritten legend 'Ceci n'est pas une pipe'.[32] The words and sounds of *All that Fall*, which in their parody of life-likeness gesture towards their own artificiality, are designed to spell out 'This is not Foxrock'.

Beckett takes the conventional code of radio sounds and subjects them to a self-subverting mimicry in Mrs Rooney's descriptive speech:

> The wind – (*Brief wind.*) – scarcely stirs the leaves and the birds – (*Brief chirp.*) – are tired singing. The cows – (*Brief moo.*) – and sheep – (*Brief baa.*) – are hushed and the hens – (*Brief cackle.*) – sprawl torpid in the dust. (Beckett, *CDW*, 192)[33]

Early in the text Mrs Rooney alerts us to the oddity of her speech by means of a question to Christy:

> Do you find anything . . . bizarre about my way of speaking? (*Pause.*) I do not mean the voice. (*Pause.*) No, I mean the words. (*Pause. More to herself.*) I use none but the simplest words, I hope, and yet I sometimes find my way of speaking very . . . bizarre. (Beckett, *CDW*, 173)

This linguistic self-consciousness is a way of underlining the deliberately literary and unspeech-like quality to the dialogue.[34] In this context, the exchange between the Rooneys about 'struggling with a dead language' quoted earlier takes on a different significance. The jibe at the deadness of 'our own poor dear Gaelic' is no more than a sideswipe; the 'unspeakably excruciating' experience of struggling with a dead language is a universal one. As all languages are dead like Gaelic, or moribund like English ('it will be dead in time'), to attempt to speak is always to try to animate language already used, if not used up. The condition is not limited to elderly Protestants speaking an old-fashioned Hiberno-English in 1920s Foxrock.

Similarly, though *Purgatory* may have had its emotional source in Yeats's revulsion against the Ireland of the 1930s, his claims for its application were far more sweeping; it contained, he said after its first performance, 'his beliefs about this world and the next'.[35] The condition endured by the soul of the Old Man's mother in *Purgatory* is that of the 'Dreaming Back', the first in the three-phase stage of expiation undergone by souls after death according to *A Vision*.[36] This anguished re-living by the dead of the traumatic sins of their past lives provides the matrix for tragedy in several other of Yeats's plays. In *The Dreaming of the Bones* Diarmuid and Dervorgilla, responsible for the invasion of Ireland, dance penitentially, eternally unforgiven for their crime. In *Calvary*, Christ 'dreams back' his progress to crucifixion, encountering the nay-sayers who reject his sacrifice, Lazarus, Judas, the Roman soldiers: at the end of the play the words from the Cross, 'My Father, why hast Thou forsaken Me?' (Yeats, *CPl*, 456) ring out as a cry of despairing failure. In *The Words upon the Windowpane* the unappeased spirits of Swift, Stella and Vanessa speak out their tragedy through the voice of the medium at the séance. Although with *The Dreaming of the Bones* the colonial history of Ireland provides one instance of the tragic irreversibility of consequences inscribed in this figure of eternal recurrence, the figure itself is far more basic and more universal in the Yeatsian imagination.

The Old Man expounds formally the purgatorial doctrine of *Purgatory*:

> The souls in Purgatory that come back
> To habitations and familiar spots.
> . . . Re-live
> Their transgressions, and that not once
> But many times; they know at last
> The consequence of those transgressions
> Whether upon others or upon themselves;
> Upon others, others may bring help,
> For when the consequence is at an end
> The dream must end; if upon themselves,
> There is no help but in themselves
> And in the mercy of God. (Yeats, *CPl*, 682)

The Old Man assumes that his mother's crime comes within the first category, that the consequence of her transgression was his own tainted inheritance. He imagines that by killing his son he can stop pollution from being transmitted further, that he has 'finished all that consequence' and freed his mother's soul. He is proved wrong. The hoof-beats come again as the start of the repeated action of the disastrous bridal night, and prayer is all that is left to him:

O God,
Release my mother's soul from its dream!
Mankind can do no more. Appease
The misery of the living and the remorse of the dead.
(Yeats, *CPl*, 689)

Although notionally the 'Dreaming Back' is one stage in a process which leads to eventual purification in the state called the 'Marriage', there is no prospect of the soul in the play reaching such a state. This is a purgatory with no promise of paradise beyond. And in so far as the consequence of the soul's transgression is seen ultimately as upon herself, not upon others, it is outside history. Though ruined house and bare tree may betoken the catastrophic state brought on by a self-betraying Ascendancy, the sin and guilt are inward, spiritual, beyond redemption by anything but the intervention of an unseen and perhaps unreachable God.

Purgatory is a ghost play about those who walk again; *All that Fall* is about those who walk again, and again, and again. *Purgatory* is a drama of the undead; *All that Fall*, like so much of Beckett, is a representation of the pre-dead. There is only one direct reference to the afterlife in *All that Fall* when Dan suggests that he and Maddy should proceed on with their walk home 'you forwards and I backwards. The perfect pair. Like Dante's damned, with their faces arsy-versy' (Beckett, *CDW*, 191). Dante's *Inferno* is invoked to suggest a hell of the here rather than the hereafter. The image of the pair of bodies tied together back to back is evocative not only of the Rooneys in *All that Fall*, but of so many of Beckett's pseudo-couples, inseparably linked yet incapable of direct communication, the torture of life in the flesh exacerbated rather than alleviated by its being shared. There is no one shaping sin of the past which Beckett's characters must live through repeatedly and try vainly to expiate. Instead the only sin is the sin of having been born at all, and the ordinary circumstances of life are rendered as a hopeless and continuous re-enactment. The awful sameness of commuting drives Mr Rooney to think of retiring: 'Never tread these cursed steps again. Trudge this hellish road for the last time' (Beckett, *CDW*, 190). But then he remembers the 'horrors of home life':

> the dusting, sweeping, airing, scrubbing, waxing, waning, washing, mangling, drying, mowing, clipping, raking, rolling, scuffling, shovelling, grinding, tearing, pounding, banging and slamming. And the brats, the happy little healthy little howling neighbours' brats. Of all this and much more the week-end, the Saturday intermission and then the day of rest, have given you some idea. But what must it be like on a working-day? A Wednesday? A Friday? What must it be like on a Friday? And I fell to thinking of my silent, backstreet, basement office, with its obliterated plate, rest-couch and velvet hangings, and what it means to be buried there alive, if only from ten to five, with convenient to the one hand a bottle of light pale ale and to the other a long ice-cold fillet of hake. Nothing, I said, not even fully certified death, can ever take the place of this. (Beckett, *CDW*, 193–4)

'Fully certified death' is what Beckett's people aspire to achieve and it is what life so cruelly and, as it seems, endlessly denies them.

The theology of Yeats and of Beckett is violently, even polemically heterodox. It is significant that in writing *The Dreaming of the Bones*, his play which is most closely modelled on a Japanese Noh play, Yeats wrote out the happy ending of the original. In *Nishikigi* the Buddhist priest *is* able to give release to the souls of the dead lovers. His counterpart in Yeats's play, the young man who has taken part in the Easter 1916 Rising, withholds the forgiveness which would release Diarmuid and Dervorgilla and pronounces perpetual sentence upon them:

> O, never, never
> Shall Diarmuid and Dervorgilla be forgiven. (Yeats, *CPl*, 442)

Purgatory produced a scandal at the time of its first production because of its idiosyncratic doctrine. There is in it, indeed, little sign that the purging of sins, the very purpose of purgatory in traditional Christian theology, will ever be accomplished. The action of the Old Man in killing his son as an attempt to free his mother is blasphemously unlike any gesture which an orthodox believer might offer to assist dead souls out of purgatory.

Beckett's assault on traditional belief is even more direct in *All that Fall*. Not long before the end, Mrs Rooney quotes the biblical text on which the incumbent clergyman is to preach the following day, and which gives the play its title: '"The Lord upholdeth all that fall and raiseth up all those that be bowed down"' (Beckett, *CDW*, 198). After a moment's silence the Rooneys greet this with 'wild laughter', as of derisive disbelief. Sure enough, the last line of the play, the explanation of the accident which delayed the train, serves as a horribly literal disproof of the Providential promise of the Scriptural text. 'It was a little child, Ma'am' the boy Jerry explains to Mrs Rooney:

> It was a little child fell out of the carriage, Ma'am. (*Pause.*) On to the lines, Ma'am. (*Pause.*) Under the wheels, Ma'am.
> (Beckett, *CDW*, 199)

The thriller-like question with which Beckett leaves his listeners in *All that Fall* is did he, didn't he? Did Dan Rooney push the child out of the railway carriage? The text has salted down the clues to suggest he may have. He is most anxious that Mrs Rooney should not hear the circumstances of the accident that held up the train. He reacts violently to Jerry producing an object which he has dropped, an object which might have been a plaything of the dead child. And earlier in the play he has admitted reflectively to an impulse towards murder: 'Did you ever wish to kill a child?' he asks Maddy after facing down the Lynch twins who habitually pelt them with mud:

> Nip some young doom in the bud. (*Pause.*) Many a time at night, in winter, on the black road home, I nearly attacked the boy. (*Pause.*) Poor Jerry! (*Pause.*) What restrained me then? (*Pause.*) Not fear of man. (Beckett, *CDW*, 191)

Dan Rooney has been much vilified by critics of the play, whether they judge him actually guilty of murder or merely of a life-denying spiritual aridity.[37] What is interesting, though, is the suggestion of mercy killing in the formulation 'nip some young doom in the bud'. The impulse to murder the child, as Dan sees it, is an impulse to spare it the horror of a full life: you try to nip in the bud something you know will be disastrous if it is allowed to develop. Any young human life is bound to become a human doom.

It is such an impulse which *All that Fall* and *Purgatory* have in common. The Old Man kills his son partly out of terrible twisted feelings of hatred and self-hatred: the Boy is his father, is himself at 16, the age when he killed his father. But there may also be in this twisted skein of emotion a desire to extricate the boy from the cycle of degradation to which he himself has been doomed. Immediately after the killing, as he sings a snatch of lullaby, there is a moment of anguished tenderness in death, replacing the abrasive aggression of his relationship with his son in life:

> 'Hush-a-bye baby, thy father's a knight,
> Thy father's a lady, lovely and bright.'

He justifies what he has done:

> I killed that lad because had he grown up
> He would have struck a woman's fancy,
> Begot, and passed pollution on.
> I am a wretched foul old man
> And therefore harmless. (Yeats, *CPl*, 688)

It is as though he has taken to himself as scapegoat all the sins that his son would have committed had he lived.

What are we to make of this infanticidal psychopathology which seems in both plays to have its origins in a revulsion against bodily life so strong that murder is justifiable to prevent its continuation? In the case of Beckett, it may be attributable to the Protestant background which many critics have argued colours his imagination throughout, producing the ascetic reaction against life in the body, the preoccupation with salvation and damnation, the alienation of Godless despair.[38] Beckett's philosophical pessimism lies at the dark underside of Protestant belief. The individual conviction of sin beyond redemption by those fallen out of grace can bring a despairing vision of the world from which the only escape is a deliberate ending of the cycle of human life itself. Hence perhaps the impulse to 'nip some young doom in the bud' in *All that Fall*.

There is a comparable horror of the bodily and the sexual in

Purgatory. Even when the Old Man in nostalgic mode is remembering the vigorous life of the past associated with the now blasted tree, he evokes it in suggestive terms:

> I saw it fifty years ago
> Before the thunderbolt had riven it,
> Green leaves, ripe leaves, leaves thick as butter,
> Fat, greasy life. (Yeats, *CPl*, 681–2)

The epithets for the leaves curdle from appreciative delight to a sort of disgusted revulsion at their materiality. The bare tree, which at the start of the play has appeared with the ruined house as the emblems of destroyed life, at the end after the murder of the Boy stands alone transfigured in white light:

> Study that tree.
> It stands there like a purified soul,
> All cold, sweet, glistening light. (Yeats, *CPl*, 688)

This, as the Old Man imagines it, represents his mother's soul purged from the degradation of the bodily and the sexual, rescued from life and its contaminations. The fact that he is mistaken in this illusion, that 'she must animate that dead night / Not once but many times' (Yeats, *CPl*, 689) only emphasises the play's sense of the overwhelming doom of attachment to the body and bodily desire. That is only one side of a Yeatsian dialectic which has as its opposite a celebration of wilful sexuality, and even in *Purgatory* he thought of giving to the Old Man a Crazy Jane-like song to sing at the ironic moment when the ghosts of his parents are re-conceiving him.[39] But the completed *Purgatory*, like *All that Fall*, makes of life in the body an original sin, living on a protracted damnation.

It is possible to read *Purgatory* and *All that Fall* as representations of, reactions to the experience of postcolonial Ireland, but such interpretations feel like under-readings. Even as representational a play by Beckett's standards as *All that Fall* is not intended primarily as a representation of the life of 1920s Foxrock. When Mr and Mrs Rooney meditate on the anguish of struggling with a dead language, it is not just the peculiarly fossilised English of a colonised Ireland that they are talking about. It is the inevitable deadness of all language which torments them. Similarly Yeats's pathology of the self-destroying Anglo-Irish Ascendancy in *Purgatory* is in the last analysis a metaphor for something other than itself. By contrast with this drama of the absolute in Yeats and Beckett, most of Irish theatre has been concerned to put upon the stage social and psychological scenes that are specifically and symptomatically Irish. Boucicault and Shaw, Gregory and Synge, O'Casey, Johnston and Behan in the plays considered so far, Friel, Murphy, McGuinness and Barry in the plays to be looked at in later chapters, create a drama embedded in the shaping realities of Ireland's life. What makes Yeats and Beckett appear anomalous in the context of this sort of Irish dramatic tradition is their common belief in a visionary theatre. In Yeats's and Beckett's drama, for all Yeats's early ideals of an Irish national theatre, there is a shared urge to reach some sort of quick of being, a life of the spirit beyond the specificities of place and culture. These are two Irish dramatists whose likeness is defined by their common unlikeness to other Irish dramatists.

7 Versions of pastoral

The year 1964 is often taken as a new beginning in Irish theatre, with the Dublin premiere of Brian Friel's first major success *Philadelphia Here I Come!*[1] The decade certainly saw the emergence of a fresh generation of playwrights, Brian Friel, Tom Murphy, Hugh Leonard, John B. Keane, Eugene McCabe, Thomas Kilroy, who between them changed the character of Irish theatre. After the social conservatism and economic and cultural isolationism of the previous decades, this was a time of remarkably rapid modernisation in Irish society.[2] Whether the playwrights gave their plays urban or suburban settings (as Kilroy and Leonard did) or, as in the case of the others, preferred traditional subjects in Irish rural and small-town life, there was a new acerbity of social analysis, different angles and some marked changes in dramatic style and technique. In this pattern of theatrical development and innovation, however, it could be argued that, rather than the 1964 *Philadelphia Here I Come!*, Murphy's *A Whistle in the Dark*, rejected by the Abbey and produced to great effect in London in 1961, could be taken as the point of departure for new Irish drama. What is more, Murphy in 1962 had written a play with an astonishingly similar ground plan to that of Friel's *Philadelphia*, the play which was only finally staged as *A Crucial Week in the Life of a Grocer's Assistant* in 1969, five years after Friel's international success. The early playwriting careers of Friel and Murphy make for an intriguing case of interlocking contrasts. For *Philadelphia* and *A Crucial Week* are not their only paralleled plays with chronological quirks between time of composition and production. Murphy's very first dramatic piece, written in collaboration with Noel O'Donoghue, was a one-acter called *On the Outside*, written in 1959, given a radio performance in 1962, but not professionally produced in the theatre until 1974, when it was matched with a second companion piece, *On the Inside*, written by Murphy alone. A pair of Friel one-act plays, *Winners* and *Losers*, with a design once again strikingly comparable to that of Murphy, was produced as *Lovers* initially in Dublin in 1967 and then to considerable acclaim in New York in 1968. There seems to be no question of direct influence, of either playwright consciously borrowing from the other.[3] But a comparison between the two sets of counterpart plays may illuminate both the dramatists' contrasting styles of representing the Ireland of their time, and how those contrasts in style may have contributed to the much more rapid and assured reception of Friel's Irish drama outside Ireland.

Murphy, as a 25-year-old metalwork teacher from Tuam, achieved instant fame with the highly successful if controversial 1961 production of *A Whistle in the Dark* by Joan Littlewood, which transferred from the Theatre Royal, Stratford East to a three-month run in the West End. The controversy was over the play's vision of the Irish in Britain which many people felt could only work to confirm anti-Irish prejudice, but the debate only contributed to the play's success in the theatrical climate of the time. With its frightening picture of an Irish emigrant family in Coventry living in a self-heroised climate of violence, it took its place in the post-1956, naturalistic movement in British theatre: angry young men and women exposing the social underbelly which genteel drawing-room drama had ignored – the Osbornes, Weskers and Shelagh Delaneys. More specifically, though, it was Littlewood's theatre that had brought Brendan Behan to London, and Murphy's Irishness fulfilled expectations set by Behan and earlier Irish dramatists. This was the opening of Kenneth Tynan's review of *A Whistle in the Dark*:

> Thomas Murphy is the kind of playwright one would hate to meet in a dark theatre. I have always been obscurely frightened of loudly singing Irishmen, and of Irish debaters, who corrugating their brows and stubbing my chest with an index finger, beg me to prove them wrong, and I am now convinced that I am scared of Irish dramatists as well. I have not met Mr Murphy, but something whispers that he might

> unnerve me – me, who never flinched from meeting Brendan Behan, even when his shirt was unbuttoned.[4]

On no personal knowledge, Murphy is here constructed as the wild Irish dramatist, outBehaning Behan. And the violence of his play – 'arguably the most uninhibited display of brutality that the London theatre has ever witnessed', Tynan called it, a selling quotation used on billboards and blurbs ever after – was seen as the loosing of raw, primitive Irish energies to shock and stimulate the overcultivated metropolitan audiences of London.

Yet in spite of the fame achieved with *A Whistle in the Dark*, Murphy found it impossible to place his second play, initially called *The Fooleen* and subsequently retitled *A Crucial Week*, in either London or Dublin. *A Crucial Week* fulfilled none of the expectations satisfied by *A Whistle in the Dark*. It was a small-town Irish play in an unacceptable theatrical idiom. *A Whistle in the Dark* corresponded roughly to the fierce naturalism in vogue in Britain at the time of its production. *A Crucial Week* is written in an expressionist style, which has always remained deeply unfashionable in the English-speaking theatre. It opens with a dream-sequence in which John Joe Moran, the 33-year–old[5] grocer's assistant of the title, lying in bed on a Monday morning, is propositioned to elope with the scantily clad figure of his girlfriend Mona, who enters in unreal lighting through the permanently stuck window of his bedroom. Successive episodic scenes then take us through the rest of the crucial week. John Joe's day-time encounters with the oppressive representatives of the small-town life that imprisons him – his whiningly possessive mother, his petty-tyrant employer, his malicious busy-body neighbours – alternate with grotesque fantasies of repression and liberation, driving him to a climactic act of rebellion in which, having thrown up his job and his girlfriend, he broadcasts to the town all its secrets that are normally concealed in whispers. One can well imagine theatre managements of the 1960s regarding this play, with its formal resemblance to pre-Brechtian German Expressionism, as an unproduceable mixture of the offbeat and the banal.

A Crucial Week was provisionally accepted by the 1963 Dublin Theatre Festival, and a London staging was considered by Oscar

Lewenstein;[6] ironically, it was at the 1964 Dublin Theatre Festival that *Philadelphia* was staged, and in a production with which Oscar Lewenstein was also associated.[7] Directed by Hilton Edwards, *Philadelphia* went on to productions in London and New York where it was to achieve a record-breaking run for an Irish play on Broadway.[8] Six years older than Murphy, Friel had much more writing experience by 1964, first of all as a short-story writer for *The New Yorker*, then in radio drama. He had already had two stage plays produced before *Philadelphia*. Where Murphy's career seemed to founder for a time after *A Whistle in the Dark*, from the success of *Philadelphia* Friel went on to build a major international reputation, combining real popular success in the theatre with solid cultural and intellectual credit. In London his plays have regularly transferred to the Royal Court and the National Theatre, when they have not made it to the West End. His work has long been the subject of respectful attention in academic criticism: the first monograph on him appeared as early as 1973;[9] there have been no less than six books devoted to him since 1988.[10]

All these indices of Friel's international reputation are the more striking in comparison with those for Tom Murphy. After *A Whistle in the Dark*, it was seven years before another play of his had a theatre production anywhere. His work has been staged in England and America, but he has never, since *A Whistle in the Dark*, been produced in the West End or on Broadway. *Bailegangaire*, played to enormous acclaim in Ireland by the Druid Theatre Company in 1985 with an outstanding performance by Siobhán McKenna in her last stage role, did not do well when it transferred to the Donmar Warehouse in London. In fact, paradoxically, it was a London revival of *A Whistle in the Dark*, twenty-eight years on, which kickstarted Murphy's reputation again at a time when his finest current work, *Conversations on a Homecoming, The Gigli Concert, Bailegangaire,* could get no more than fringe productions at best outside Ireland. Where Friel's plays have been published by Faber since 1965, it was not until 1988 that Murphy was published by an established house outside Ireland and not until the 1990s that he was given the canonical treatment of publication in Methuen's World Dramatists series. By contrast with the wealth of scholarly study of Friel, there is so far only one full-length book written on Murphy.

That one book, Fintan O'Toole's very valuable *Tom Murphy: the Politics of Magic*, argues that the slowness in the acceptance of Murphy's work was related to its political complexion, its unsympathetically abrasive version of Irish society in its transition to modernity. Though O'Toole makes his case persuasively, it hardly accounts for the disparity between Murphy's and Friel's reputations in Ireland and abroad. Within Irish theatre, the two are commonly regarded as of more or less equivalent importance, the outstanding playwrights of their generation. Both have received many marks of public recognition: Murphy is a member of Aosdána and the Irish Academy of Letters, and has served on the Board of the Abbey Theatre; Friel was an Irish Senator in the 1980s; they have both been awarded honorary degrees from Trinity College, Dublin. The fact that they started so nearly together, and have continued over the years to produce innovative work of distinguished quality, highlights the question of why one should be so much more accessible and acceptable outside Ireland than the other.

It is not my object here to try to answer that question in terms of a detailed analysis of the reception of the two playwrights as such, or of the many variables in the theatrical marketplace that may have led to the greater international fame of Friel. Like the rest of the book, this chapter is predominantly text-based, exploring how the plays considered construct their images of Ireland, rather than their stage history. The comparison of *A Crucial Week* with *Philadelphia, On the Outside/On the Inside* with *Lovers*, allows a close look at the ways Murphy and Friel addressed the subject of Irish society of the 1950s and 1960s. Beyond that, the contrasts in dramatic form and texture of the plays, and their relative international viability, can help to illuminate some of the broad specifications for Irish drama at home and abroad. Ireland, in the cinema as in theatre, has always provided a possible setting and subject for pastoral, a scene distinguished by its otherness and simplicity for the metropolitan audiences who watch it. The comparisons between these early plays of Friel and Murphy can show the different ways in which the two playwrights have resisted or negotiated with these expectations of pastoral in their representation of modern Ireland.

Staying or going: *A Crucial Week*; *Philadelphia*

Emigration is the subject of both *A Crucial Week* and *Philadelphia*, the haemorrhage of people from Ireland which had continued to depopulate the country since the time of the Famine. In the early 1960s, at the point when in fact that demographic pattern was about to change and Ireland's population began to grow again, Murphy and Friel dramatised the communities which drive their young – or youngish – male protagonists to leave. The emphasis in both plays is on deprivation, on the economic, cultural, and spiritual poverty of the Irish small-town experience. The strongly held control of a puritanical Catholic church associated sexual repressiveness with the authoritarian family ethos of home, sexual liberation with fantasies of escape. Class distinctions were the more rigidly enforced in a poor society where only fine shadings of power and position distinguished haves from have-nots. It is the same world represented by Murphy in *A Crucial Week*, Friel in *Philadelphia*, and in a similar mode of satiric scrutiny. The protagonists, John Joe Moran and Gar O'Donnell, stand in for any number of such retarded adolescents, underpaid and undereducated, frustrated and impotent; the plays probe the social causes of their situation. Yet for all their common subject and similar action, *A Crucial Week* and *Philadelphia* in their difference of dramatic style and technique produce radically different theatrical effects.

There is a disconcertingly uncomfortable ugliness to the atmosphere of *A Crucial Week*. Take a single example from the pietistic Mrs Smith early in the play. Mrs Smith is described entering from Mass, 'her voice ... a crying, whining, poverty-stricken tremulo', holding up as instructive *memento mori* to her downtrodden daughter the latest news of 'Molly Byrne, the little poultry girl from the department' who was 'dragged back to the hospital last night':

> they say the hooter on the ambulance never screamed so loud before. And sure all knew the cheap-jack's son was her boyfriend for the last seven weeks. But they strapped the babe down on their tables, and when they opened her up, wasn't she red rotten. Cancer, my dear! Mmmmmm! (Murphy, *P4*, 98)

There is a ghastly authenticity in this, a gleeful exultation in the visceral details of human disaster combined with the hint of sexual misdoings which turns the anecdote into some sort of obscure moral exemplum. It is funny in its own grisly way. But an audience is likely to be left caught uncertainly between laughter and disgust, and a non-Irish audience unfamiliar with this specially Irish form of *schadenfreude* might be simply bewildered.

There is an equally disquieting send-up of the Irish rituals of bereavement in the play's next scene. Pakey Garvey, embittered young emigrant to England, has returned to the town for the funeral of his father, a despised pedlar and drunk who has died at the age of 52. When he goes to pay for the coffin, Mr Brown, John Joe's employer, who is undertaker as well as grocer and general shop-keeper, prepares to go through the rigmarole of condolence, eulogy and regret, but Pakey steadily subverts the formulae. The passage has to be quoted at length to illustrate the pattern of the interchanges.

> MR BROWN. But wasn't it a sad journey you had to make?
> PAKEY. 'Twas.
> MR BROWN. 'Twas.
> PAKEY. 'Twas.
> MR BROWN. 'Twas. 'Twas indeed.
> PAKEY. 'Twas. 'Twas, John Joe?
> JOHN JOE (*trying to restrain his laughter*). 'Twas.
> MR BROWN. It was, sir. (MR BROWN *realizes the mockery, but this is the only way he can play it.*) But he had a good life.
> PAKEY. He had, half-starved. Fond of the bottle too, Mr Brown?
> MR BROWN. He was, he w– Aw!. No now, Patrick. Ah-haa, you were always the joker, always the –
> PAKEY. Not a great sodality man, Mr Brown?
> MR BROWN. Always the joker.
> PAKEY. But maybe he was ashamed of his suit.
> MR BROWN. Well, you never changed. (*Solemn again.*) No, Patrick, your father, Bartley Garvey, could take a drink, and he could carry it. And that was no flaw in Bartley Garvey's character.
> PAKEY (*solemnly*). Musha, poor auld 'Rags'.
> MR BROWN. Ah – well – yes. (Murphy, *P4*, 102–3)

Mr Brown realizes that the usual exchanges of sympathy are not going according to form and switches to the congratulatory noises for the returned emigrant:

> MR BROWN. . . . But you're doing well?
> PAKEY. Oh, yes, Mr Brown.
> MR BROWN. Saving your money, Patrick?
> PAKEY. Oh yes. And when I have enough saved –
> MR BROWN. You'll come home.
> PAKEY. I will.
> MR BROWN. And you'll be welcome.
> PAKEY. And I'll buy out this town, Mr Brown.
> MR BROWN. You will, sir.
> PAKEY. And then I'll burn it to the ground. (Murphy, *P4*, 103)

The comic punch-line hardly brings much release in a sequence like this, the humour has no lift to it. Though we can enjoy the discomfiture of Mr Brown with his hypocritical clichés, the sullen anger of Pakey, the dingy realities that emerge of the life and death of 'Rags' Garvey, inhibit full-bellied laughter. And again a non-Irish audience, unfamiliar with the social rituals mocked, might well see little to laugh at.

When Murphy lifts the stone from off his small-town life in *A Crucial Week* what we see are genuinely creepy creepie-crawlies: from the ludicrous inadequacies of John Joe's love-life – 'an awful bad court', Mona rightly calls him – through his dreadful mother, an unlovely mixture of possessiveness and paranoia, his all-but-lobotomised father, the pseudo-avuncular priest, the whole sniggering, spying chorus of Peteens and Mikeys that crowd John Joe's dreams. When John Joe spills the beans, lets all the skeletons out of the cupboards, what is so awful is the sheer pettiness and convincing specificity of the small-town secrets he reveals at the top of his voice:

> We have flour-bags sewn together for sheets . . . Oh, but we know Mrs Smith doesn't use a sheet at all. Did you know that Mrs Smith? We know that from the day Peter Mullins climbed in your back-room window, because it was the only room in your house he hadn't seen. But he said it was clean, but he wouldn't give you two-pence for the sticks of furniture. And

> what else? Oh, the rig-out Mrs Mullins had on last Wednesday wasn't new at all; a cast-off, bought by her sister in Seattle off one of them cheap-jacks they have over there, for thirty-eight cents. And that she doesn't sleep with Peter; and hasn't for a number of years. Oh, come on, come on, shout out what other valuable newses you want. (Murphy, *P4*, 160)

It is the low-key, unsensational indignity of these revelations which gives this scene its effectiveness in the theatre; the shocked embarrassment of the onstage characters is almost duplicated in the audience.

On the face of it, the subject, setting and design of *Philadelphia* are startlingly like those of *A Crucial Week*. Friel's hero, Gar, is also a grocer's assistant, like John Joe humiliatingly dependent on parent and employer – in Gar's case the same person, his father S.B. O'Donnell. Gar, like John Joe, can get nowhere in his love affair with a girl of rather better family than himself, and this frustration along with all the other constrictions of his small-town life are forcing him to leave. Both plays offer a social anatomy of the life-denying features of the Irish provincial scene: late and loveless marriages, frustrated sexuality, a petit-bourgeois economic situation just above poverty, an unenlightened controlling Church, a meanly conservative social hierarchy, a cultural wasteland. This was a familiarly bleak view of Ireland by the 1960s, familiar from the critical realist traditions of Irish fiction and poetry as well as drama. What Friel had to offer, like Murphy, was an experimentally non-naturalistic mode of representing this scene. But whereas the thoroughgoing expressionism of Murphy's play might have been offputting for potential theatre producers, the single device of the split character of Gar was an acceptably middlebrow deviation from naturalism.

The convention of having Public and Private Gar played by two actors is easily grasped and helps to psychologise the figure. It also adds the potential for a wonderfully playful counterpoint to the drab outer surfaces of Ballybeg social behaviour. The daily spectacle of S.B. coming from the shop, taking his apron off for his tea, is given a running accompaniment from Private Gar in the style of a mannequin parade commentator; the silence of the nightly game of draughts between S.B. and the Canon is broken by Private's mock-epic rendering of it as a heroic battle to the death. At the simplest level, the double Gar solves the basic problem of the dramatist's need to dramatise boredom without boring his audience. It leavens the pedestrianly real with the glorious compensations of fantasy. And the sheer brio of the fantasy is one dimension of the difference in atmosphere between *Philadelphia* and *A Crucial Week*. Take this piece of revenge by Private against the upper-middle-class Senator Doogan who has deftly blocked Gar's hopes of a marriage with his daughter Katie:

> You know, of course, that he carries one of those wee black cards in the inside pocket of his jacket, privately printed for him: 'I am a Catholic. In case of accident send for a bishop.' And you know, too, that in his spare time he travels for maternity corsets; and he's a double spy for the Knights and the Masons; and that he takes pornographic photographs of Mrs D. and sends them anonymously to reverend mother.
>
> (Friel, *SP*, 45)

This sort of passage gives just the sort of comic relief which the dialogue quoted earlier between Pakey and Mr Brown does not. Frustrated humiliation and anger are here happily, safely vented in broad comic caricature. The therapeutic function of laughter, denied in Murphy, is fulfilled in Friel.

The presence of Private Gar, with his outrageous, unspeakable alternative perspectives, can make Ballybeg both funny and fun. With his capacity for an inner reflectiveness, he can also turn it towards a lyrical vision. Private Gar is given an eloquence which by definition he can never have as Public Gar. In an imagined conversation, he can voice, beautifully, poignantly, the childhood memory of fishing with his father, a remembered icon of intimate relationship between them:

> do you remember – it was an afternoon in May – oh, fifteen years ago – I don't remember every detail but some things are as vivid as can be: the boat was blue and the paint was peeling and there was an empty cigarette packet floating in the water at the bottom between two trout and the left rowlock kept slipping and you had given me your hat and had put your

> jacket round my shoulders because there had been a shower of rain. And you had the rod in your left hand – I can see the cork nibbled away from the butt of the rod – and maybe we had been chatting – I don't remember – it doesn't matter – but between us at that moment there was this great happiness, this great joy – you must have felt it too – although nothing was being said – just the two of us fishing on a lake on a showery day – and young as I was I felt, I knew, that this was precious, and your hat was soft on the top of my ears – I can feel it – and I shrank down into your coat – and then, then for no reason at all except that you were happy too, you began to sing: (*Sings*)
>
> All round my hat I'll wear a green coloured ribbono,
>
> (Friel, *SP*, 82–3)

It does not matter that, when finally questioned about it, S.B. has no recollection of this. As Friel himself said about the actual incident from his own childhood on which Gar's recollection is based, 'That's the memory. That's what happened'.[11] In dramatic terms this means that what is not there, what is signally missing from the lived lives of Ballybeg, can yet be there, present theatrically in the meditations of Private Gar.

The very situation of Gar on the eve of departure, as he prepares to remember what he is about to leave, contributes to this doubleness. As he thinks about his evenings with the 'boys', the sheer nullity of their time together boasting about imaginary sexual adventures, he is already moving towards the nostalgia with which those evenings will be remembered:

> No one will ever know or understand the fun there was; for there *was* fun and there *was* laughing – foolish, silly fun and foolish, silly laughing; but what it was all about you cannot remember, can you? Just the memory of it – that's all you have now – just the memory; and even now, even so soon, it is being distilled of all its coarseness; and what's left is going to be precious, precious gold... (Friel, *SP*, 77)

What Private Gar here describes is being enacted for a theatre audience; Ballybeg, the claustrophobically lifeless and loveless small town, is in the process of being re-written as idyll.

Philadelphia is ostensibly all about what makes Ballybeg an impossible place to live in, what forces the likes of Gar to emigrate. It is about deprivation, loss, absence. But what it evokes is the lyrical plenitude of registering loss. So, for example, the absent mother who haunts the text, who stands for all the tenderness, spontaneity and freedom which Gar feels himself to lack, is recreated in idealised form from the glimpsed and fragmentary memories of others. The recollection of fishing with his father may only be a solipsist shrine which can never be validated by anyone else; yet once voiced in the theatre, it can never be unvoiced. And on the point of Gar's going away, the deadeningly ordinary Ballybeg is suffused with a backward glow of charm, to the point where Gar cannot answer his own question:

> PRIVATE. . . . God, Boy, why do you have to leave? Why? Why?
> PUBLIC. I don't know. I – I – I don't know. (Friel, *SP*, 99)

The held ambiguity of that final moment may have allowed many Irish-Americans to enjoy the play in a special way. *Philadelphia* on the face of it affirms for emigrants the rightness of the decision to emigrate; that backward world of Ballybeg has to be left behind. Yet the art of the play can allow also the luxury of enhanced memory of what has been abandoned. All this is done with a sophistication and self-consciousness far beyond any kind of crude strains of 'Galway Bay' pandering to emigrant nostalgia. But emigrant nostalgia is a dimension in the play's imagination of Ballybeg, and undoubtedly was a dimension to its success in America. By contrast *A Crucial Week* casts a cold eye on the Irish small town, but just as cold an eye on the prospect of leaving. John Joe Moran, in what is a not altogether convincing up-beat ending, positively elects to stay in spite of his public doomsday on the town. His most telling statement, though, is a despairing denial of the possibility of significant escape.

> It isn't a case of staying or going. Forced to stay or forced to go.
> Never the freedom to decide and make the choice for
> ourselves. And then we're half-men here, or half-men away,
> and how can we hope ever to do anything. (Murphy, *P4*, 162)

Friel hints at a similar impasse with his prevision of Gar's Philadelpia home, cottonwooled in the smothering love of his Aunt Lizzie, which may be hardly much better than the speechless atrophy of his relationship with his father back in Ballybeg. But *Philadelphia* allows an audience to have it both ways, presenting the ineluctable necessity of leaving the small-town space which is yet graced with charm in memory. The small town of *A Crucial Week*, by contrast, is charmless and graceless, its littleness unrelieved by the prospect of a real elsewhere. While the play could win real appreciation in Ireland when it was eventually produced at the Abbey in 1969 – Murphy's 'blend of sympathy and objective hatred have reached an almost incredible peak of perfection' wrote one theatre critic[12] – it has yet to have a major production outside the country, where such a blend of sympathy and hatred remains unlikely to be appreciated.

A summer birdcage: *On the Outside/On the Inside, Lovers*

One-act plays are hard to place in modern theatre. The days of the curtain-raiser are long gone, evenings made up of a series of unconnected one-act plays are hardly acceptable; there is only the low-level event of a lunch-time show as a slot for the one-act play. So it is not surprising in itself that Murphy and Friel should both have come up with the idea of putting together two one-act plays to create a full-length, more or less unified, theatrical programme. What is interesting is the similarity in formal and conceptual design of the two. Each pair of one-act plays, *On the Outside/On the Inside, Lovers*, is a diptych, a balanced symmetry of matching panels which invites an audience to regard the two together. Murphy and O'Donoghue's *On the Outside* centres on two young men outside an Irish country dance-hall without the 6-shilling price of admission; *On the Inside* presents a group of the more well-to-do people inside the same dance-hall, at the same dance – though there is no overlap of characters. In *Winners*, the first of Friel's two plays that make up *Lovers*, a couple of teenagers, on the point of getting married because the girl is pregnant, spend a summer day together nominally studying for their exams, while a flanking pair of narrating Commentators reveal that the couple died in a boating accident at the end of the day. In *Losers*, the second panel of Friel's diptych, a late middle-aged courtship invigorated by the challenge of a tyrannically spoil-sport invalid mother is transformed into a dead marriage where the influence of the mother has won.

The companionship of the two plays in each case speaks its own message. In Murphy we see the terrible pent-up frustration of Joe and Frank, the excluded lads on the outside of the dance-hall, at being unable to get in, but then we realise that the insiders, the people at the dance caught in the dreary games of Irish parochial catch-as-catch-can, have their problems too. It is like Webster's summer bird-cage in a garden: 'the birds that are without, despaire to get in, and the birds that are within despaire and are in a consumption for feare they shall never get out'.[13] Webster's source for this, Montaigne's lines on bad marriages, appear buried as a remembered gobbet of school French in *Winners*: 'Les oiseaux qui en sont dehors désespèrent d'y entrer; et d'un pareil soin en sortir, ceux qui sont au-dedans.'[14] Friel's two plays set up a comparable paradox. The young lovers who die at the very moment of entering upon their life together are called winners, whereas the losers are the couple who live on to suffer the degeneration of their love into a blighted marriage.

What is distinctive, and characteristic, about Friel's plays is their use of framing narratives. Friel of course began his literary career as a short-story writer – *Losers* is virtually a re-transcription of an earlier short story in dramatic form – and he has remained fond of narrators and narration in the theatre throughout his work as a playwright. The juxtaposition of narrative and drama in *Winners* in many ways anticipates *Dancing at Lughnasa*. In both plays the characters on stage live in an unself-conscious volatility of the present, while a fate-like simultaneous narration fixes them in the tragically final facts of death. The device of the commentators in *Winners*, however, has other uses as well. The Man and Woman who read 'completely without emotion' from something like books of evidence or an inquest report enable Friel to place his two characters precisely in class terms. Maggie lives with her parents in a 'detached red-brick house on the outskirts of the town of Ballymore' (Friel, *Lovers*, 11), where Joe's address is Railway Terrace; her father is a dentist, his mother a cleaning woman. Though the action brings Maggie and Joe vividly before us as individuals, the sociologising commentators make their story and their backgrounds into something generic, representative. The effect in *Losers* is different in that there Andy, the husband, tells the story of his relationship with Hannah, remembering back to their courtship from the blank dead end of their marriage. But in *Losers*, as in *Winners*, the scenes of live action are illustrating insets in a controlling narrative.

Almost all of Friel's plays from *Philadelphia* onwards, have been set in Ballybeg/Baile Beag = Little Town. *Winners*, we can assume, is only set in Ballymore, Big Town, because Friel wants the social stretch from the detached big house to the railway terrace for his lovers to have to cross. The principle throughout is the same: the setting is offered like Thornton Wilder's *Our Town* as a paradigm, a representative example of the universal. The characters are individualised, but with a generic individuation. So Maggie, scatty, unacademic, bursting with an undirected vitality, is complemented by Joe, serious, earnest, purposeful. Hannah in *Losers* who began as the eager lover, fiercely defiant of her religiose mother, grows into a second version of the old woman, while Andy is transformed into a reincarnation of his dead father-in-law. The design of the two plays enforces a comparative and reflective view of the stories as exemplars. What are the prospects for a young couple like Joe and Maggie in a town such as Ballymore, what are their chances of married happiness? Already in the play, when they are at the height of their love for one another, we are shown the pressures upon them of their different class backgrounds and their enforced marriage which provide the occasion for quarrels. Are they not indeed lucky, winners, to have died before the entanglements of life dragged them down to the losing state of Andy and Hannah? The plays' form and technique direct us away from the particular towards the general level at which such questions are asked.

It might be expected that the same would be true of Murphy's *On the Outside/On the Inside* in so far as the double perspective illustrates the two sides of the summer bird-cage, the vanity of human wishes. But it does not come out like that. Murphy puts before us, unmediated, a social scene, the dance-hall culture of de Valera's rural Ireland in its latter days. The specificities of a given community are sketched in casually, by the way: it is a country dance-hall 'an austere building', as the stage direction tells us 'suggesting, at first glance, a place of compulsory confinement more than one of entertainment' (Murphy, *P4*, 167). Joe and Frank have walked out from town, are not quite at home, and are smartingly conscious of their inferiority to the obnoxious Micky Ford who can run a car. It is an INTO (= Irish National Teachers Organisation) dance, and the group we meet in *On the Inside* are largely national school teachers with their special pecking-order of status and respectability. These are social vignettes, precisely evocative of a mode of life in late 1950s Ireland, but it is hard to be sure what more they might signify, of what they might be representative other than themselves.

Joe and Frank, though their plight 'on the outside' suggests exclusion, do not stand in for the socially deprived generally. They are both employed, living at home, keeping only a small proportion of their wages as a kind of allowance/pocket money. Just once in the play, Frank is given something like a speech of social protest:

> The whole town is like a tank. At home is like a tank. A huge tank with walls running up, straight up. And we're at the bottom, splashing around all week in their Friday night vomit, clawing at the sides all around. And the bosses – and the big-shots – are up around the top, looking in, looking down. You know the look? Spitting. On top of us. And for fear we might climb out someway – Do you know what they're doing? – They smear grease around the walls. (Murphy, *P4*, 180)

This has its own power as the passionately intense voice of the humiliated young. But *On the Inside*, which gives us the closest we get to a boss or big-shot in the national school headmaster monitoring the dance from the soft-drinks bar, makes us aware how melodramatic the image of the tank is in relation to the reality. The actual horrors of the dance-hall, inside and out, are the abrasions of the minute class distinctions, the corseting of a rigidly conservative social order, the furtive would-be mutinies against its moral policing.

On the Outside/On the Inside is as much about the problematics of love and sex, Irish style, as *Lovers*. The special anguish of Frank's sense of deprivation in *On the Outside* comes from his inability to meet up with the girl whom he promised to take to the dance; he is to see her at the end snub him for the car-driving Mickey

Ford. In *On the Inside*, amid the wink-and-nudge atmosphere of the dance, Kieran and Margaret, the lovers whose relationship is hanging fire, eventually come to an accommodation that will end in marriage. Kieran expresses his feeling of disenchantment to the cynic Malachy:

> KIERAN. A few years ago: out in the open with it –
> MALACHY. The great outdoors, the furry glen, or forninst the haystack!
> KIERAN. No. But you'd get maybe half a dozen kisses of an evening and you're in love. But then, when the rest of it starts – Yeh know? –
> MALACHY. The rummagin'.
> KIERAN. Yeh. That's all we progress to. Fronts of cars, backs of cars, doorways, steering wheels, gear-levers, and love starts to fade, and we've had our chips. (Murphy, *P4*, 200)

This is saying something very like Friel's *Lovers*, but it is saying it far less tendentiously and in its own more casual language. And that is not the conclusion of the play either. Kieran and Margaret, whose first experience of sex together has been guilt-ridden and uneasy, go off deliberately to 'do it right this time', while Malachy, the big-mouth pretend Lothario, who has lectured the company on the ills of the 'Irish celibate personality', funks a night with a girl when it is offered. 'What is this thing called love?' he asks himself, in the play's closing line, as he stands alone looking at his quarter-bottle of whiskey (Murphy, *P4*, 222).

Both the pieces which make up Friel's *Lovers* are well-made plays, like all his work. The last day in the life of Maggie and Joe in *Winners* is divided into morning and afternoon, Parts I and II. Exposition and development, skilfully shared between the onstage action of the couple and the commenting narrative, come to a climax as the young lovers in the madcap gaiety of confirmed happiness run off to go boating on the lake, and the narrative closes in with the grim details of the inquest that followed their drowning. *Losers* is less formally structured in the anecdotal reminiscence style of Andy's monologue, but it builds no less artfully to the comic catastrophe of Andy's drunken celebration of the decanonisation of St Philomena. By contrast with Friel, Murphy's plays, though finely paced for the theatre, have a much less obvious shape. They are like sketches rather than composed vignettes. The two lads spend the whole of *On the Outside* on the outside of the dancehall; all we see is their vain attempts to find some way of getting in, the repeated frustration of their repeated failure. The play is a sort of *Waiting for Godot* in a minor realistic key. *On the Inside* too has the slightest of narrative lines in the resolution of the relationship of Kieran and Margaret. Most of the play merely observes the scene of the dance with a dryly ironic sense of its mood and atmosphere. Murphy's is an openweave texture of dramatic action; Friel's is closewoven and finished by comparison. The two halves of *Lovers*, separately and together, have the set shape of parable; they are stories disciplined and directed towards meaning. In *On the Outside/On the Inside* meaning is immanent, to be apprehended only in the glancing movement of the drama itself.

Pastoral and anti-pastoral

Ireland is always available as a site for pastoral, in its greenness, its littleness, its location as the offshore-island alternative to the major metropolitan societies of Britain or America. One classic use of Ireland as such a pastoral is John Ford's *The Quiet Man*, where Sean Thornton must go back to his roots in the Irish country cottage White O'Morn to re-discover himself as a man. The idyllic landscape, the quaint customs of courtship, a proper domination of man over woman in marriage, good wholesome fighting as a restorative for the psyche traumatised by the corrupt practice of professional boxing, all these are vested in the Irish scene which is placed as archaic, traditional, originary. It is against this sort of pastoral iconography of Ireland that both Friel and Murphy's early work was written. In place of the rose-tinted views of the returning exile Thornton, they give the grim lookout from within of the Gars and John Joes as they are moved towards emigration by the dingy realities of home. While John Wayne and Maureen O'Hara can easily escape from the benevolently watchful eye of matchmaker/chaperone Barry Fitzgerald, and move to a satisfactory climax with a rain-soaked embrace in a ruined chapel, the social policing of sexual relationships in Murphy and Friel yields only frustration, repression and despair. Even when they traipse out to a countryside barn John Joe remains the 'awfully bad court' of Mona's complaints, the social conditioning of his inhibitions thoroughly introjected: no love among the haystacks here. The happily worldly priest of Ford's film who spends much of his time fishing is turned into the draughts-playing Canon of *Philadelphia* whose inability to provide any sort of genuine spiritual direction is fiercely indicted by Private Gar: 'you could translate all this loneliness, this groping, this dreadful bloody buffoonery into Christian terms that will make life bearable. And yet you don't say a word. Why, Canon? Why arid Canon? Isn't this your job? – to translate?' (Friel, *SP*, 88). The Hollywood pastoral of the Irish rural community in *The Quiet Man* is re-written by Friel and Murphy as a sharply critical anti-pastoral.

Both playwrights give a glum version of the West of Ireland scene so glamorised by Ford. To start with, they use small-town, not rural, settings. Where the pastoral of *The Quiet Man* alternated between the wholesome jollity of the communal and the healing isolation of the cottage in harmony with nature, Murphy and Friel show a claustrophobically closed society with people as estranged from their environment as the most alienated of industrialised city-dwellers. The dance hall in the middle of nowhere is typical of the countryside in *On the Outside*; Andy Tracey in *Losers*, reduced to sitting in his backyard staring through binoculars at nothing, is Friel's sardonic comment on his room with a view. And yet, for all their common reaction against the rural Irish idyll, the differences between the playwrights in theme, style and formal mode make of Murphy's plays true anti-pastorals, Friel's a version of pastoral only disguised as anti-pastoral.

Friel in a significant and often-cited statement denied that the primary subject of attention in *Philadelphia* was a social one: 'I don't think the play specifically concerns the question of emigration. *Philadelphia* was an analysis of a kind of love: the love between a father and a son and between a son and his birthplace.'[15] This is what *Philadelphia* has in common with *Lovers* and what differentiates both plays from those of Murphy. Though it may be lost, silenced or aborted, love haunts Friel's drama as the image of unrealised but actual potential. Gar's romance with Katie Doogan, boyish as it may have been, and easily derailed by her class-conscious father, is animated by genuine feeling. The mother-love for which Gar hungers and which makes him settle for the effusive Aunt Lizzie in all her vulgarity, the unspoken feeling between himself and his father: both are love, all the more plangently felt for the absent presences they are. The grace of Joe and Maggie's moments of young togetherness is what makes them winners in *Winners*, though they die immediately after; the loss of Hannah and Andy's real passion which lives on into its own death leaves them losers. This is a vision of the land of heart's desire in love. It is its own site of pastoral, though the traditional places of pastoral in which it is set thwart rather than enable its realisation.

There is no such soft centre in Murphy's equivalent plays. The fantasy-figure of Mona that entices John Joe in his dreams may beckon towards sexual liberation and social escape, but the bank employee that she is in real life is a much more mundane mixture of ordinary desire and ordinary aspiration to socially approved marriage. The cruel brutality with which John Joe dismisses her seems authorially sponsored in context, a part of the searing truth-telling about his town and its people to which the grocer's assistant is driven:

> You are a silly, stupid bitch. Whore if you could be. What means anything to you? Mummy, big farm, daddy; the priest plays golf with daddy; the bishop knows daddy; money in the bank. Where does John-Balls-Joe come in? For favours, pity? In a few years' time you'll give a nice little 'haw-haw' at all this. In love, Jesus, love! (Murphy, *P4*, 153)

The only love in John Joe's life is his mother's, which operates as a millstone of emotional blackmailing guilt around his neck: 'If I was rich, the first thing I'd do is give a million pounds to my mother. Pay her off' (Murphy, *P4*, 114). The best that the couples of *On the Outside/On the Inside* can achieve is a kind of accommodation with their repressed sexuality. 'What is this thing called love?' asks Malachy: answer, a bad Irish joke. Although the obsessive quest for love and need for love is an increasingly important driving-force in Murphy's drama as a whole, the energy of these early plays goes to demonstrate the deformations of a society in which love is always twisted up with anger, guilt, bitterness. In its dystopic thrust, this is fiercely anti-pastoral.

Literary pastoral has always had its own special language. In classical and neo-classical mode it might be the highly ornate and avowedly artificial strains of Corin and Phyllis. Even in Wordsworthian romantic pastoral, where the aim is to imitate the language of 'men speaking to men', the special simple vernacular of the Cumbrian peasants is mediated by the controllingly authoritative voice of the poet. Pastoral involves a sophisticated and cultivated audience/readership going out to an imagined other place, another language, with its charm dependent on its measured otherness. From at least as far back as Boucicault, Irish dialect has been amenable to such use as a literary variation upon the standard English of an assumed audience. Ireland as pastoral space is marked by the quaintness, the charm, the lyrical otherness of Hiberno-English.

Friel works from within this tradition. He uses a sort of selective speech of the Irish northwest which has enough of the colour of specifically Hiberno-English forms to be heard as a believably local idiolect, but which is completely easy and transparent. 'I didn't find as many about the year' says S.B. commenting on the reduced number of rats in the shop. Nobody needs to have it explained to them that 'the year' = 'this year' in S.B.'s part of the world. But even if they did, there is a gloss on it in Private's mock-ironic reaction: '"I didn't find as many about the year!" Did you ever hear the beat of that? Wonderful! But isn't he in form tonight? But isn't he? You know, it's not every night that jewels like that, pearls of wisdom on rodent reproduction, drop from those lips!' (Friel, *SP*, 48). The absurdly orotund 'pearls of wisdom on rodent reproduction' takes us back up into the wider vocabulary and more formal speech available to an audience of non-S.B.s. It is symptomatic that, in the play's first production, both Public and Private Gar spoke without regional accents in neutral middle-class voices.[16] So it is also with *Lovers*. The Commentators of *Winners*, with their received standard-English narration, frame and counterpoint the vivid colloquiality of the young lovers. In *Losers*, the opening stage direction describing Andy sets up a split level between his awareness and that of the audience: 'Because his mind is simple, direct, unsubtle, he is unaware of the humour in a lot of the things that he says' (Friel, *Lovers*, 52). This includes the recital of the only poetry Andy ever learned at school: 'a thing called

Elegy Written in a Country Churchyard by Thomas Gray, 1716 to 1771, if you ever heard tell of it' (Friel, *Lovers*, 56). The comedy of this would be lost if Friel could not rely on all of his audience having 'heard tell' of Gray's *Elegy*, and appreciate the hilariously inappropriate use to which its sombre sentiments are put as a verbal smokescreen for Andy and Hannah's love-making. Such linguistic distancing techniques allow the dramatist a bridgehead between the special other and distinct world of the rural small/middle-sized Irish town and its language, and the much greater language range of Friel's implicitly metropolitan audiences. In their negotiation between these two language registers, his plays could again be called a version of pastoral.

Murphy's language, by contrast, is much less easy of access. His inclination has been to stick very close to the texture of native idiom, in his first plays even to the quite specific slang of his home town of Tuam. As Fintan O'Toole explains, it is only people of Tuam who call one another 'sham', as Frank and Joe do throughout *On the Outside*, while other words 'whid' (look at), 'buffer' (country-dweller), and 'choicer' (nothing) are similarly local in usage.[17] Murphy often glosses these in parentheses in his scripts but in production relies on actors being able to convey their unfamiliar meaning. He makes frequent use also of scraps of Irish without making allowance for a non-Irish-speaking audience. The derisively contemptuous nickname for the drunken father of Pakey Garvey in the original text of *The Fooleen* was 'Budjail Bui', an Anglicised spelling of 'buidéal bui' = 'yellow bottle'.[18] Even a Dublin audience was going to have trouble recognising just why this was so humiliating, and the text of *A Crucial Week* changes it to 'Rags' for the poor pedlar father, to rhyme cuttingly with 'Bags' for the delivery-boy son. This is not just a matter of a provincial dramatist learning what is viable on stage for a wider audience. Murphy deliberately chooses for his characters an opaque and unfluent language, full of ellipses and quirks of phrasing, a climate of linguistic inadequacy.[19] The aim of such language is not simply to reproduce naturalistically the speech of inarticulate people. That was to some extent the perceived effect of *A Whistle in the Dark* which was acceptable in so far as it conformed to a sort of violent theatre in which action took the place of words. But Murphy from the very beginning was trying to use the broken and irregular forms of live local speech to achieve certain rhythmic patterns beyond or outside conventional stage dialogue. In later plays he was to use laughter, song, story-telling modes as special effects to orchestrate and transcend speech in a non-representational theatre. Yet even if Murphy's object is not to reproduce Tuam Irish-English as she is spoke, it may require an (Irish) audience at least fairly familiar with the groundbase of what such language sounds like to hear and understand the patterns of meaning that are being built upon it. His theatrical style works out from within a local linguistic community; it does not go out to reach, as Friel's does, a wider language world assumed to be outside looking on, listening in.

Pastoral uses its forms of rural difference to articulate values, ideas, concepts which belong within the metropolitan milieu of its producers and consumers. Plays such as *Philadelphia* and *Lovers* work in this way in so far as they address certain traditional intellectual and literary topoi: the relation between the inner and the outer life, memory and experience in *Philadelphia*, love and death, the perversity of desire in *Lovers*. In an academic context, they are eminently teachable plays because of the clarity and resonance of their dramatic form. While engaging audiences with lively and life-like situations, they move towards the paradigmatic and the parabolic. With Murphy the metaphoric or conceptual dimension to the drama, though there, is much more elusive. This might perhaps be attributed to what he emphasises as the emotional origins of his drama: 'In writing a play I attempt to create or recreate the *feeling* of life; *ideas* follow and are developed as appropriate: this is a bonus'.[20] His dramatic situations as a result are not readily translated into other terms. The drunk who has wandered in and out of the inaction of *On the Outside* is left at the end kicking the poster for the dance: a telling image of the absurdity and futility which characterises the whole play but no sort of symbol, much less a statement. Murphy's touch is much less sure when he does attempt a definingly significant dramatic closure. There is a surprise turnaround in the last scene of *A Crucial Life* in which John Joe gives back to his Uncle Alec the little shop which his mother has manipulated her brother into yielding to him; this act of restoration is intended to represent John Joe's capacity for a new beginning after his cathartic night of judgement on the town. This seems unsatisfactory theatrically, coming over as a tacked-on, upbeat ending. Murphy's plays work most powerfully when they suggest their meanings obliquely by the forms of his embodied dramatic gestures.

Underlying the audience expectations of Irish drama which I have here been identifying as 'pastoral' is a microcosm/macrocosm model of relationship between the life of the play and the life of the spectators. What the rural West of Ireland may be for Dublin theatre-goers, Ireland as a whole is to audiences abroad, a place other and different if only by virtue of its littleness, its perspicuousness to audiences who are assumed to inhabit a much larger and more complex society. The dramatic truths which Irish drama can speak are posited upon such an otherness. But they must be speakable in a language which the macrocosm understands and can apply across from the microcosm. This transaction is (in most cases though not all) completely viable in the case of Friel. His Ballybeg is itself an Irish small town of the 1950s or early 1960s with all its specific cultural strictures and limitations; but it is also Littletown, the generic type of all and any such small towns. *Lovers* canvasses two case-histories, characteristic of the bizarre practices of Irish love-making, while also citing them as illustrations of a romantic/metaphysical proposition inscribed in the play's title: love wins only by dying, loses always by living on. To that extent Friel's work could be categorised as pastoral, and owes some of its success outside Ireland to the way it answers to audience needs for Irish drama to act as pastoral. Murphy's plays with a purer, at times even wayward, dramatic autonomy refuse the movement from microcosm to macrocosm, from Irish particular to metropolitan universal. They remain fully resistant to the mode of pastoral, not just because of the greater abrasiveness of their images of Ireland, but in their insistence on being taken on their own terms rather than being translated into the familiar concerns of their audiences.

The comparison of the paired sets of plays in this chapter has been an instrument of investigation, not an attempt at a limiting definition of the work of the two dramatists as a whole. Friel was capable of writing a savagely anti-pastoral play in *The Gentle Island* (1971), though significantly it is a play which has not been very popular either inside or outside Ireland. Murphy, by contrast, has twice returned to adaptations of the genially sentimental *Vicar of Wakefield* and to warmly comic Irish stagings of *She Stoops to Conquer*. Friel may well not have intended for his plays to be viewed as any sort of pastoral. As I mentioned in the first chapter he was nonplussed at the reading of the hedge-school of *Translations* as idyll, and wrote the satiric farce *The Communication Cord* to excoriate such an idealising modern taste for quaint rural *kitsch*. Plays may be consumed as pastorals which are conceived in a very different spirit. A production of *Dancing at Lughnasa* in London could be forced back towards nostalgic period-piece by the expectations of its audiences.[21] What emerges significantly from the juxtaposition of the companion pieces from Murphy's and Friel's early playwriting periods is the way their images of Ireland and the cast of their dramaturgy made the one writer so much more quickly accepted internationally. Tom Murphy did not write the 'Irish' plays that an Irish playwright should. Brian Friel did.

8 Murphy's Ireland

Writing *Bailegangaire* in 1984, Tom Murphy was conscious of the date, the year that Orwell (writing in 1948) projected as the time when everyone would live in fear under the panopticon eye of Big Brother. For the characters in his play, he thought, Orwell got it exactly wrong: these are lives that *no one* is watching.[1] The impulse to bring to mind lost lives, to give voice to the voiceless, has been endemic in Irish drama of the last century. Yeats told Synge to go to the Aran Islands: 'Live there as if you were one of the people themselves; express a life that has never found expression' (Synge, *CW*, III, 63). O'Casey's tenement characters were the urban poor whom the early Abbey drama had ignored in favour of the rural peasantry. Behan brought to the stage for the first time whores and gays, a previously unseen prison population. And in the next chapter I will be looking at the efforts of Frank McGuinness and Sebastian Barry to call back into memory those figures from the beginning of the century, loyalists from north or south, whom the Irish national narrative has written out. What is distinctive about the characters of *Bailegangaire*, and its companion play *A Thief of a Christmas*, is that these are people re-remembered, the early Abbey peasantry whom the playwright himself had initially tried to forget. The two plays represent at once an attempt by a modern playwright to come to terms with the older, by now classic, phase of Irish drama and, in re-figuring it, to work through a past which still lies buried below the surface of an only partly modernised Ireland.

One of the versions of pastoral against which Murphy reacted at the beginning of his career was the theatre of Synge, Gregory, Yeats as he then saw it. The story has been told more than once of how *On the Outside* came to be written, arising out of a casual conversation between himself and Noel O'Donoghue as they hung about Tuam one Sunday morning after last Mass waiting for the pubs to open. O'Donoghue suggested writing a play; Murphy questioned what it would be about. '"One thing is sure," O'Donoghue said, "it's not going to be set in a kitchen!"'[2] By 1959 the country-cottage-kitchen settings of the early Abbey plays seemed clichéd stereotypes, to be avoided at all costs. Even though by his own admission *A Whistle in the Dark*, changing the Irish country kitchen for an Irish emigrant kitchen in Coventry did not advance Murphy all that far from traditional subjects and styles,[3] through the 1960s and 1970s he continued to look for forms of theatrical representation beyond the cottage, outside the conventions of Abbey peasant drama. In several plays such as *The Morning After Optimism* (written in the early 1960s but not produced until 1971), *The Sanctuary Lamp* (1976), *The Gigli Concert* (1983), he experimented with non-mimetic plots and neutral undefined spaces in which some of the characters were Irish, some of them not. In his plays which did have an Irish setting, he sought alternative locations such as the dancehall of *On the Outside/On the Inside*, or alternative modes such as the expressionism of *A Crucial Week* or the epic/grotesque tragedy of *Famine* (1968). The setting of *Bailegangaire*, then, was a deliberate decision to return to what he had previously reacted against: 'The room is a country kitchen in the old style . . . probably the central room of the traditional three-roomed thatched house.'[4]

Bailegangaire is concerned with the re-telling of the story of Mommo the senile grandmother, the story of the laughing-contest fully dramatised in *A Thief of a Christmas*. It contains a few references also to a still earlier episode in the life of Mommo and her sculptor husband Seamus represented in *Brigit*, a television play written before the other two but only broadcast later.[5] The three together make up a trilogy of which *Bailegangaire* is the culmination.[6] It is a play, however, which does not stand in narrative need of its other two parts. *Brigit* is a relatively slight piece and its relation to *Bailegangaire* is quite tangential. *A Thief* is an extraordinary play of considerable potential which has suffered from the memory of a disastrous first production at the Abbey. For the director with the courage and the resources to attempt it, there could be a theatrical tour de force in a staging of the two plays side by side, the large-cast drama of *A Thief* with the three-hander *Bailegangaire*. But *Bailegangaire* subsumes its prequels within itself. It sends an audience unfamiliar with Mommo's story groping to piece it together, drives them to share in the need of Mommo's grown-up granddaughters Mary and Dolly for the always unfinished story to come to an end. In that dynamic is figured a pathology in the relation of Ireland's past to its present which the play works to expose and exorcise. It is with the one rich text of *Bailegangaire* that this chapter will largely be concerned, invoking *A Thief* only for comparative purposes.

If Murphy felt that no one was watching the lives of such as Mommo, Mary and Dolly in 1984, it may have been partly because attention on Ireland was focused elsewhere. The unending attrition of the situation in Northern Ireland made for a constantly compelling subject. Playwrights, whether moved by political conscience and the need to respond to the urgencies of the time or by the ready market for 'Troubles' plays or by both, sought to dramatise the conflict and probe its origins. The end of chapter 5 touched on a few of such latter-day reactions to revolution by Friel, McGuinness, Parker. The effect of these plays, however, looming so large in Irish drama in the 1980s, was to reinforce the imagination of an Ireland shaped exclusively by its history of colonial struggle and sectarian hatred. In *Bailegangaire* it is otherwise. Its rural West of Ireland setting with an almost completely homogeneous Catholic culture means that religious division is not an issue. The obsessively canvassed question of national identity in the colonial/postcolonial context is hardly more significant in the play as such. Yet the three women of *Bailegangaire* stand for much more than themselves as they represent the inadequacies of a modernity still unable to come to terms with the archaic formations of the past, the problems of latter-day Irish women with an inheritance of repressive patriarchy. Murphy's Ireland involves a reconception of the country cottage of Synge, Yeats and Gregory to create an Irish drama which tells a different story from the theatre of national politics.

Retelling the story

The story itself which Mommo tells constantly and never finishes is an odd one: the story of a laughing-contest. It is based, it appears, on an event which actually happened, or at least was told as if it had happened, in a little village near Tuam around the turn of the century.[7] As Murphy dramatises it in *A Thief* it is a competition with fatal consequences, for the local champion laugher Costello, challenged by the Stranger (Mommo's husband), dies of over-exertion at the end. This is supported in *A Thief* by a plot which has most of the village betting on Costello against the publican/gombeen-man John Mahony, who controls all their lives, and who loses out when Costello at the moment of death manages one last laugh winning the villagers their bets. All this plot scaffolding is removed from the version of the story in *Bailegangaire* which Mommo tells as a traditional folk-tale of how Bochtán (= the Poor Man), the original name of the village where the laughing-contest took place, 'came by its new appellation, Bailegangaire, the place without laughter' (Murphy, *P2*, 92). The curse cast upon the villagers as a result of having engaged in the laughing-match is the inability to laugh beyond childhood. However, where the storyteller of the traditional *seanchas* tells it in the first person, pretending that the events actually happened to him/herself, Mommo sticks firmly to third-person narration, refusing to acknowledge that the stranger who started the laughing competition was her own husband, and the stranger's wife herself. A *Bailegangaire* audience that is unfamiliar with *A Thief* is forced to reconstruct as best they can the story mediated through Mommo's compulsive, jumbled, fragmentary telling. The play deliberately risks unintelligibility to gain its effect.

Bailegangaire is a split-level drama: Mommo's tale of the laughing-contest of long ago contrasts with a contemporary present in which her two already middle-aged granddaughters Mary and Dolly have to look after her. As foreground to the play, representationally rendered onstage and offstage, there is the recognisable present of Ireland 1984. Outside the traditional cottage kitchen the cars stream past, coming from the trade union meeting at which the future of the Japanese-owned computer plant down the road is being decided. Dolly with her crash-helmet arriving on her put-putting Honda motorcycle speaks of a world of videos and rubber-backed linoleum throughout the house, the tacky sub-industrialised countryside of modern Ireland. The play works by the counterpoint of these realities, solid, familiar, banal, with the highly wrought grotesqueries of Mommo's story-telling. An audience is made to empathise with the nightmarish, grinding awfulness of Mary's present situation as resident Mommo-sitter: forced to listen to a story which she has heard so often as to know it off by heart from a ga-ga grandmother who will not recognise her, hurtfully taking her for a servant. And yet, of course, those watching the play are hearing the story for the first time and are drawn into it as a bravura performance, want to hear more of it, want to know what it is about and how it ends.

Mommo's is a bed-time story, told to her imagined grandchildren of more than thirty years before: 'Let ye be settling now, my fondlings, and I'll be giving ye a nice story tonight ... An ye'll be going to sleep' (Murphy, *P2*, 91). We listen at first to a highly ornamented rhetoric of story-telling:

> It was a bad year for the crops, a good one for mushrooms, and the contrary and adverse connection between these two is always the case. So you can be sure the people were putting their store in the poultry and the bonavs (*bonhams*)[8] and the creamery produce for the great maragadh mór (*big market*) that is held every year on the last Saturday before Christmas in Bailethuama in the other county. And some sold well and some sold middlin', and one couple was in it – strangers, ye understand – sold not at all. And at day's business concluded there was celebration, for some, and fitting felicitations exchanged, though not of the usual protraction, for all had an eye on the cold inclement weather that boded.
>
> (Murphy, *P2*, 94–5)

It is a rich mix of language, the Irish and the Irishisms blending with an orotund vocabulary of Latinate English, and an audience is borne along on its rhythms, hardly attending to its content. By degrees, though, a story begins to shape up, and it becomes apparent that it is Mommo's own, that the strangers, 'a decent man ... and his decent wife the same', were indeed Mommo and her husband. At moments when the narrative falters and Mary interjects from outside it, pieces of the underlying truth and its pain emerge. 'And how many children had she bore herself?' asks Mommo of the 'decent woman' of her story:

MARY. Eight?
MOMMO. And what happened to them?
MARY. Nine? Ten?
MOMMO. Hah?
MARY. What happened to us all?
MOMMO. Them (*that*) weren't drowned or died they said she drove away. (Murphy, *P2*, 99–100)

We attend in Mommo's speech to an interleaved fabric of times past. There is the folklorised story of the laughing-match which gradually puts itself together: the arrival of the strange couple, unable to get home because of the frost, at the pub in Bochtán; the challenge of the stranger to prove himself a better laugher than Costello, the big-bellied man with the gurgling, infectious laugh; the contest which starts in jest but, as bets are made and feeling grows high, continues literally to the death, ending with Costello's collapse. All this, fully orchestrated in *A Thief*, is re-scored for solo voice in *Bailegangaire*. One of the spellbinding marvels of the play's first Druid Theatre Company production, with Siobhán McKenna playing Mommo, was to listen to her render the whole crowded pub-scene and its inhabitants: not only the two laughing contestants, each with his distinctive laugh, but the stammering publican John Mahony, his buxom wife Rose, and the collection of bystanding locals from the mad Josie – 'Josie was a Greaney and none was ever right in that fambly' (Murphy, *P2*, 113) – to the

> two old men with their heads in the chimbley, each minding a pint of black porter . . . The one of them givin' out the odd sigh, smoking his pipe with assiduity and beating the slow obsequies of a death-roll with his boot. An' the other, a Brian by name, replying in sagacity 'Oh yis', sharing the silent mysteries of the world between them. (Murphy, *P2*, 114)

The tale itself, so vividly recreated in the telling, is cut through with other earlier memories. At a crucial moment of the contest it is the stranger's wife who drives her husband on, in resentment at a long frozen marriage, as Mommo recalls with 'quiet anger':

> But what about the things had been vexin' *her* for years? No, a woman isn't stick or stone. The forty years an' more in the one

> bed together an' he to rise in the mornin', and not to give her a glance. An' so long it had been he had called her by first name, she'd near forgot it herself... (Murphy, *P2*, 140)

Twined into the tangled skein of Mommo's narrative is not only the desolation of her relations with her husband and the catalogue of the losses of her children, but the strange figure of her father, the man with a big stick for whom Mommo is recurrently waiting, and whose Job-like philosophising she recollects:

> 'Oh,' he groaned, 'I have wrestled with enigmals (*all*) my life-long years. I've combed all of creation,' that man intoned, 'and in the wondrous handiwork of God, have found only two flaws, man an' the earwig. Of what use is man, what utility the earwig, where do they either fit in the system?'
>
> (Murphy, *P2*, 165)

The memory Mommo baulks for most of the play, however, is the memory of what happened *after* the laughing-contest. 'Tom is in Galway', is a phrase she repeats again and again, 'he's afeared of the gander'. Tom was the youngest of the three grandchildren – he is to be seen in *Brigit* too afraid of the gander to go outside. The three were left by themselves when their grandparents went off to the market, and while they were delayed by the frost and then the laughing-contest, Tom threw too much paraffin on the fire, was caught by the flames and died of burns in hospital in Galway. It is this death, together with the nearly simultaneous death of her husband (beaten up by the people of Bochtán when he appeared to have won the laughing-match) that Mommo will not face, and that makes her unable to get to the end of her story. It is this too which links the ever-repeated unfinished story with the lives of the two surviving grandchildren, Mary and Dolly, which we are now watching many years later.

Mary, the older unmarried sister, has returned from a nursing career in England to take her turn at looking after her grandmother. Lonely and distraught, at a loss in her life, she is driven to the point of breakdown by the strain of her situation, and is bitterly resentful of

Dolly who has escaped from it. Not that there is much joy in Dolly's life either. She is a grass-widow with several children, living on the weekly wired remittances of her emigrant husband working abroad, revenging in casual sexual encounters his coldness and absence, brutalised by him for her infidelities on his annual Christmas visit home. At the point of the play's action, she is pregnant and desperate at the prospect of her husband's reaction to this manifest proof of unfaithfulness, scheming to get Mary to take on the child as her own, threatening murder or infanticide if she does not. A past affair, whether real or imagined, revealed between the repressive Mary and Dolly's husband adds one more complication to the sense of the tension between them.

At the time of the play's composition, the situation of Dolly in particular and her desperate reaction to her unwanted pregnancy had a special topical resonance in Ireland. If Murphy sought to draw attention to the lives of his women characters whom nobody was watching in 1984, in that year the death in labour of a 15-year-old schoolgirl at the end of a pregnancy completely concealed from her family, and the notorious 'Kerry Babies' case in which not one but two murdered infants were found in a single area of Kerry, highlighted the continuing plight of rural Irish women.[9] In the text of the play there is in fact a reference to the bodies of babies abandoned as those in Kerry were: 'The unbaptised an' stillborn in shoeboxes planted, at the dead hour of night treading softly the Lisheen to make the regulation hole – not more, not less than two feet deep – too fearful of the field, haunted by infants, to speak or to pray' (Murphy, *P2*, 164). And yet, such is the hypnotic power of the story-telling old woman in the bed, her tale could become as engrossingly present as the 'real-life' narrative of Mary and Dolly with all its immediate relevance for a 1980s Irish audience. Indeed, parts of the latter could even seem conventionally fictional, the ordinary stuff of TV drama – the husband of one sister who is in love with the other sister, the proposal for one to take over the other's baby etc. But the contrasting idioms are essential to the play's structure, the clichéd modernity of Dolly and Mary's messy emotional entanglements bound in with the never-ending archaic narrative.

The fraught bonds between the lives of the three women are

vested in the story and its retelling. The story becomes a ritual involving all three: when Mommo drops off to sleep, Mary is able to take over the narrative, repeating Mommo's words in Mommo's own specialist shanachie idiom; when Mommo is momentarily quiescent, Dolly can start her up again with a malicious prompt. For the first half of the play Mary, at the end of her tether, wanting to read, to listen to music, tries desperately to distract her grandmother. But towards the end of Act 1, Mary has an idea: 'We'll do it together ... We'll finish it. ... And if we finished it, that would be something at least, wouldn't it?' (Murphy, *P2*, 125). There is in this notion the attraction for Mary of collaboration with her grandmother – 'we'll do it together' – Mommo who refuses communication with her, refuses her gift of love. But there is also the sense that Mommo's completion of the story would be some way out of the impasse of her own life also. Dolly cannot understand why Mary is suddenly so insistent on the tale being told out. 'I don't know', is all the reply Mary can make, 'I can't do anything the way things are' (Murphy, *P2*, 134). This urge towards narrative closure from then on becomes the dynamic of the play, making for a double onward momentum for an audience. Like Mary, they will Mommo on to get to the end not only to find out what happened, but because of the feeling that to complete the story will be to face the trauma which lies behind its obsessive re-telling, and perhaps thus to allow Dolly and Mary to come to terms with their lives, to free the family from its tragic inheritance.

Returning to the cottage kitchen

Two of the most famous of the Abbey's cottage-kitchen plays lie behind *Bailegangaire*: *Riders to the Sea* and *Kathleen ni Houlihan*.[10] The configuration of characters is that of *Riders*, the one old woman who has survived all her menfolk, left with her two daughters/grand-daughters. There is even a hint in Synge's play of the emotional relationship worked out in depth between Murphy's three characters. Throughout *Riders* it is Cathleen, the older daughter, who is in charge: spinning, baking, arranging the business of the house. Maurya, the mother, is querulous and contentious with Cathleen, resentful of the authority and control which she has taken over. It is to Nora, the younger daughter, that Maurya talks, and it is Nora only, never once

Cathleen, that she addresses by name. In *Bailegangaire* Mary has the older sister's active, managing role, and we see her through the play almost continuously busy with cleaning, tidying, providing Mommo with her tea, her yellow pills, slices of cake – all of which Mommo perversely refuses. Mary is conscious that on her return home, 'I may have been too – bossy, at first' (Murphy, *P2*, 103). Maurya's normal old mother's jealousy of the daughter who has succeeded her as domestic manager, in Mommo takes the more pathological form of refusing even to recognise the granddaughter who cares for her. 'Miss', she calls Mary, in the pseudo-polite, suspicious tone used to an intruding stranger: 'Will you put on the kettle, Miss, will you!', then whispering to Dolly, 'Who is that woman?' (Murphy, *P2*, 110). It is on Dolly, the much less responsible younger granddaughter who only visits her from time to time, that she lavishes her love.

'... who would listen to an old woman with one thing and she saying it over?' (Synge, *CW*, III, 11). Cathleen's purely rhetorical question in *Riders* is given its grim answer in *Bailegangaire* where, night after night, Mary is forced to listen to Mommo's 'one thing and she saying it over'. The obsessive re-telling of the story is a re-living of the past, behind which lies the same history of loss as in Synge. As Maurya awaits the bringing in of the body of her last drowned son Bartley, she speaks over the litany of her dead:

> There were Stephen, and Shawn, were lost in the great wind, and found after in the Bay of Gregory of the Golden Mouth, and carried up the two of them on one plank, and in by that door ... There was Sheamus and his father, and his own father again, were lost in a dark night, and not a stick or sign was seen of them when the sun went up. There was Patch after was drowned out of a curagh that turned over.
>
> (Synge, *CW*, III, 21)

Mommo too, towards the end of the play, is brought to name 'her great contribution to the roll-call of the dead':

> Her Pat was her eldest, died of consumption ... An' for the sake of an auld ewe was stuck in the flood was how she lost two of the others, Jimmy and Michael ... Her soft Willie was

> her pet went foreign after the others . . . soft Willie, aged thirty-four, in Louisaville Kentucky, died, peritonites.
>
> (Murphy, *P2*, 163–4)

But where Maurya is seen as the stoic sufferer struggling with her impersonal and all-powerful adversary the sea, the pain of Mommo's memories is shot through with remorse and guilt. 'Them (*that*) weren't drowned or died they said she drove away.' Mommo sets this aside as best she can – 'Let them say what they like' (Murphy, *P2*, 98) – yet it is the question to which she is forced to return: 'An' *did* she drive them all away – never ever to be heard of, ever again?' (Murphy, *P2*, 164). The hard woman who urged on one of her sons to fight with another when the first had married against her wishes, who forced her husband to carry on with the laughing-contest, who lost both husband and grandson as a result, how much was she to blame in it all? In place of Synge's tragic vision of Maurya as *mater dolorosa* facing an implacable fate dooming to death the riders to the sea, *Bailegangaire* unfolds a vicious cycle of cause and event, character and circumstance, in which the mother is both agent and victim of the curse upon the family.

In *Kathleen ni Houlihan*, the allegorical old woman, the stranger in the house of the Gillanes, explains her need to seek help, the compulsion to look for redress for her wrongs: 'when the trouble is on me I must be talking to my friends' (Gregory, *SW*, 305). This is the symbol of Ireland's preoccupation with its own history, the use of its own history as a mythology to inspire its people. Murphy's play is without explicit allegorical intention, but Mommo in *Bailegangaire* could be seen as his savage comment on Yeats's and Gregory's image: Ireland's is a story told over and over again by a senile mind frozen in the past, a story which she seems incapable of bringing to an end. In *Kathleen ni Houlihan* the sacrifice Cathleen demands of her sons/lovers rejuvenates her: by Michael's emblematic decision to leave his bride Delia and follow the old woman, she is transformed into the young girl with the walk of a queen. The blood-sacrifice of the young men makes possible the restoration of the sovereignty-goddess. In *Bailegangaire*, the old woman is not a mysterious stranger in the cottage kitchen, but the all-too-familiar incubus who has lived there all her life. And if she is responsible for the deaths of her sons and lovers, it brings her no possibility of transformation, but an irreversible old age of guilt-ridden obsession.

Murphy's resistance to the idealising myth of Kathleen ni Houlihan as feminised personification of Ireland takes a different form from that of earlier playwrights. It is not the disillusioned reaction of an O'Casey or a Johnston in the immediate aftermath of revolution, where the deconstructing animus is a tribute to the potency of the original trope of metamorphosis. The refiguring of *Kathleen ni Houlihan* in *Bailegangaire* involves a shift away from the allegorical mode itself. The vividly realised figure of Mommo, convincingly in the throes of senile dementia, with her intermittent aphasia and her oscillation between violent aggression and vulnerability, belongs in a different order of theatrical reality from Yeats's and Gregory's aisling. What is more, even if *Bailegangaire* challenges the mystical Utopianism of the earlier play, it is not just in a spirit of sardonic iconoclasm that Murphy faces up to the terrors and horrors of Ireland. He resists the misogyny of a mother-hatred which is only the reverse counterpart of the mother-idolatry in the Kathleen ni Houlihan tradition: Mommo is not Stephen Dedalus's old sow that eats her farrow any more than she is the about-to-be young girl with the walk of a queen. An audience is made to feel with human compassion and understanding for Mommo's losses, her deprivations of the spirit and the destructiveness they produced. In the attachment of both granddaughters to her, in their involvement with the constantly re-told story, are figured the liveness of the lines linking present to past in Ireland.

A part of the play's power derives from Murphy's ability to remake the images of Synge, Yeats and Gregory in *Riders* and *Kathleen ni Houlihan*. So Mommo is like Synge's Maurya imaginatively extended, with griefs complicated by the awareness that they are partially self-inflicted; she is a Kathleen ni Houlihan *de nos jours*, grotesque and pathetic, a maundering voice whom a contemporary audience, like the characters in the play, has still to attend to and try to understand. But if these two early cottage-kitchen plays supply models of sorts for *Bailegangaire*, the pub-scene of *A Thief* is consciously related to that of *Playboy*. At the start of Murphy's play the wife of the publican is checking off a shopping-list for Bina, one of her grocery customers:

> Six tallow Christmas candles for to put in your windows, a pair of black laces for your Sunday boots, a fine tooth-comb ...
>
> (Murphy, *P2*, 175)

She echoes here almost word for word Pegeen Mike ordering her trousseau at the beginning of the *Playboy*:

> Six yards of stuff for to make a yellow gown. A pair of lace boots with lengthy heels on them and brassy eyes. A hat is suited for a wedding-day. A fine tooth comb.
>
> (Synge, *CW*, IV, 57)

Both sets of lines mis-prepare an audience for a festive event that is not to happen. The wedding with Shawn Keogh for which Pegeen is laying in provisions will not take place, at least in the lifetime of the play that is to follow. And Bina's hopes of a Christmas when exceptional extravagance may be possible – tallow candles for the window, black laces for the Sunday boots – are equally to be disappointed. With the news of the disastrously bad market in Tuam comes the certainty that it will be a 'thief of a Christmas' instead of the expected seasonal celebration. But in both plays, an occasion for saturnalian festivity will come in the unexpected form of the arrival of Christy Mahon, the father-killer, or the Stranger who will challenge Costello to the laughing-contest.

Again the analogies between the two plays are underlined by direct quotations. The first act of *A Thief* ends with an echo of the closing line of the first act of the *Playboy*. Christy, bewildered with his welcome in the Mayo shebeen, had asked himself, 'wasn't I a foolish fellow not to kill my father in the years gone by' (Synge, *CW*, IV, 93). Costello, anticipating an easy victory in the laughing-contest, wonders: 'Why didn't I think of this in the years gone by?' (Murphy, *P2*, 214).[11] The people of Bochtán are hungry for wonders like Synge's villagers; in the second half of *A Thief*, when word of the laughing-match gets round, the pub fills up with as many onlookers as the stage can hold. The laughing contestants become trapped by the people's need for the show to go on, just as Christy becomes the victim of his own notoriety, someone on to whom the Mayo men and women may project their fantasies of anarchy and rebellion. When things go wrong and the sport turns to earnest with Christy's second 'killing' of his father or Costello's collapse, a violent crowd reaction is unleashed. In Synge a lynch-mob looks to hang the man for the deed which had earlier won him hero-worship; in Murphy the Stranger, whom half the pub had been urging on to victory in the laughing-competition, is suspected of being the devil and violently attacked. The Strangers in *A Thief* leave the pub at the end, with just the same reaction of indignant dismissal as the Mahons in the *Playboy*. The exit line of the Stranger's Wife is based on that of Old Mahon: 'An' 'tis glad we are to be goin' from the rogues and thieves that parade Bochtán and the villainy of Galway!' (Murphy, *P2*, 240); 'we'll have great times from this out telling stories of the villainy of Mayo and the fools is here' (Synge, *CW*, IV, 173).

The citations from *Playboy* in *A Thief* and the structural parallels between the two plays are more than the intertextual acknowledgement of a precursor. Murphy in *A Thief* is re-working and extending Synge's peculiar version of carnival, his sort of black rite of comedy. One feature of this re-working is to turn the black blacker. Costello does actually die at the end of *A Thief*, if with an ironic reprise of the comic resurrection motif which runs back from Synge's unkillable Old Mahon to the Shaughraun as live corpse: 'I always had a wish to see a bit of me own Wake' (Murphy, *P2*, 242). Murphy has a more than Syngean relish for the theatrical energies of the saturnalian, the shape and force of carnival twisted towards the tragic/grotesque. But in the second-phase version of it, as narrated by Mommo, Murphy seeks to reinterpret the laughing-contest and to go beyond the tonal range of its Syngean tragicomic mode.

With the re-telling of the story of the laughing-competition, the *Playboy*'s vein of black comedy enters into *Bailegangaire*. For the theme of the contestants' laughter, set by the Stranger's Wife/ Mommo herself, is misfortunes. One after another the hardships of their lives, the most terrible things that have happened them, are offered as subjects of hilarity. The laughter grows in hysterical volume as the pub audience joins in with their share of catastrophes. It was once said that the tragic power of *Riders* depended on showing only the death of the last of Maurya's six sons; the succession of all six of them dramatised on stage would have turned comic. It is such a comedy which Murphy deliberately creates in *Bailegangaire*, for Mommo's enumeration of dead and lost sons, quoted earlier, is her contribution to the stock of laughable disasters. It comes in a climactic speech where Mommo's dead children are joined as a subject for laughter with all Ireland's unwanted, unchristened infants (including those Kerry babies):

> Nothin' was sacred an' nothing a secret. The unbaptised an' stillborn in shoeboxes planted, at the dead hour of night treading softly the Lisheen to make the regulation hole – not more, not less than two feet deep – too fearful of the field, haunted by infants, to speak or to pray. They were fearful of their ankles – Hih-hih-hih. An' tryin' not to hasten, steal away again, leaving their pagan parcels in isolation forever.

And in this same speech, the laughing audience is rendered in a vision of grotesque power:

> The stories kept on comin' an' the volleys and cheers. All of them present, their heads threwn back abandoned in festivities of guffaws: the wretched and neglected, dilapidated an' forlorn, the forgotten an' tormented, the lonely an' despairing, ragged an' dirty, impoverished, hungry, emaciated and unhealthy, eyes big as saucers, ridiculing an' defying of their lot on earth below – glintin' their defiance – their defiance an' rejection, inviting of what else might come or *care* to come! – Driving bellows of refusal at the sky through the roof. Och hona ho gus hah-haa! . . . The nicest night ever. (Murphy, *P2*, 164–5)

What is so terrifying in this speech is not just the weird power of the remembered scene of the afflicted people hysterically laughing at their afflictions, but the triumphalist war-whoop of Mommo at the memory of the defeated Bochtáns, 'Och hona ho gus hah-haa!'[12] her appreciation of it as 'the nicest night ever'.

Black comedy, laughter as exorcism or consolation, has recurred in modern Irish drama from Synge's *Playboy* on through the tragic farce of O'Casey's Abbey plays, the gallows humour of Behan.

The laughter-contest in *Bailegangaire* is a highpoint of that tradition. But within that tradition also there has been a recurrent impulse to escape from the doubleness of the tragicomic mode. 'Take away this cursed gift of laughter and give us tears instead', says Dobelle in Denis Johnston's *The Moon in the Yellow River*, paraphrasing O'Casey's Juno.[13] In Murphy too there is the desire to give full expression to the feeling ironised or cauterised by the laughter of black humour. *Bailegangaire* moves towards an ending where emotion is at last released and a moving tenderness succeeds to the tortured mixture of laughter and despair. At the height of the laughing-match there had been one moment of recognition between husband and wife, recalled by Mommo:

> An' then, like a girl, smiled at her husband, an' his smile back so shy like the boy he was in youth. An' the moment was for them alone. Unawares of all cares, unawares of all the others. An' how long before since their eyes had met, mar gheal dhá gréine,[14] glistenin' for each other. Not since long and long ago. (Murphy, *P2*, 162)

This is matched at the very end, when the story has finally been concluded, when Mommo's formal ending is capped by Mary's recollection of the death of her brother Tom, by Mommo at last giving Mary the recognition she so needs.

The ending offers a multiple image of catharsis. Mommo's story is finished and the horror of its ending has been faced; Mommo and Mary can once again communicate with one another; Mary has agreed to take on Dolly's unborn baby. All three women end up in the bed together, Dolly having drunk herself to sleep. Mommo leads her imagined small grandchildren in the prayers to the Virgin which was their night-time ritual seen in *Brigit*.

> MOMMO. Be sayin' yere prayers now an' ye'll be goin' to sleep. To thee do we send up our sighs. Yes? For yere Mammy an' Daddy an' grandad is (*who are*) in heaven.
> MARY. And Tom.
> MOMMO. Yes. An' he only a ladeen was afeared of the gander. An' tell them ye're all good. Mourning and weeping in this

> valley of tears ... And sure a tear isn't such a bad thing, Mary, and haven't we everything we need here, the two of us. (*And she settles down to sleep*)
>
> MARY. (*Tears of gratitude brim to her eyes; fervently*) Oh we have, Mommo.
>
> *Her tears continue to the end but her crying is infused with a sound like the laughter of relief.*
>
> ... To conclude. It's a strange old place, alright, in whatever wisdom He has to have made it this way. But in whatever wisdom there is, in the year 1984, it was decided to give that – fambly ... of strangers another chance, and a brand new baby to gladden their home. (Murphy, *P2*, 169–70)

Murphy's cottage-kitchen drama ends, not like Synge's *Riders* in a mood of stoic resignation, much less like *Kathleen ni Houlihan* with exhilarated apotheosis, but with a tentative rehabilitation of the damaged family. There are risks of sentimentality here in the ritual of healing and regeneration which the ending offers. But in performance, after the hard day's night of story-telling, all the comic-grotesque horrors of the past, the desperations of the present, which it had worked through, one can only feel that the conclusion, with whatever it offers of reconciliation and renewal, has been theatrically earned.

Refashioning the past

The Irish in their obsession with history are often said, like the Bourbons, to have learned nothing and forgotten nothing. Modern Irish dramatists have tried to belie this reputation by a recourse to history which will enlighten and illuminate the present. This was always a major objective of the Field Day Theatre Company from Friel's dramatisation of the nineteenth-century Ordnance Survey in *Translations* to his treatment of the sixteenth-century Irish leader Hugh O'Neill in *Making History*, from Thomas Kilroy's evocation of the paired Irish lives of Brendan Bracken and William Joyce in *Double Cross* to Stewart Parker's use of the 1974 background of the Ulster workers' strike in *Pentecost*. All these, like other 1980s plays, McGuinness's *Observe the Sons of Ulster*, Parker's *Northern Star*, or Christina Reid's multi-generational *Tea in a China Cup*, adopt the same strategy of recreating the past in order to find a means of better understanding the troubled issues of the contemporary period. Many of them, like *Bailegangaire*, seek to work through the traumas of earlier generations towards a psychotherapy of release. What makes Murphy's play different is that its traumas have little or nothing to do with the colonial matrix of national and sectarian identity which underlies all the other retrospective history plays of the time. His history is not that of Irish against English, Protestant versus Catholic, landlord and peasant; it is above all a history of poverty and its consequences.

Murphy has not completely ignored national politics in his work. The ironically titled *Patriot Game* (1991) staged a version of the Easter Rising in an alienated Brechtian style which nonetheless recognised in its ending the full impact of the event even at seventy-five years distance. But it was his 1968 play *Famine* that dramatised the event which dominates his view of Irish history. *Famine* is an ambitious attempt to imagine the experience of 1846–7, the central years of the potato famine. Although it contains one extended scene in which the assisted emigration scheme of the period is revealed as a conspiracy of heartless landlords to clear their land, and a (for Murphy) atypical representation of the Catholic clergy as champions of the suffering people, it is on the whole not concerned with political analysis of causes and results. It is the psychological experience itself which Murphy seeks to render, the desperate instinct for survival with the terrible destruction of the spirit it brings in the circumstances. The play centres on the figure of John Connor who resolutely, obstinately, continues to believe that there is a means of living through the catastrophe in God-fearing dignity, only to be driven finally to the murder of his wife and son. That tragic action is portrayed as symptomatic not just of the famine but of its long-term consequences for generations to come. In the introduction to the collection *Plays: One* which includes *Famine*, Murphy summed up the thinking behind that play in a passage which is important for the understanding of all his work down to *Bailegangaire*:

> the absence of food, the cause of famine, is only one aspect of famine. What about the other 'poverties' that attend famine? A

> hungry and demoralised people becomes silent. People emigrate in great numbers and leave spaces that cannot be filled. Intelligence becomes cunning. There is a poverty of thought and expression. Womanhood becomes harsh. Love, tenderness, loyalty, generosity go out the door in the struggle for survival. Men fester in vicarious dreams of destruction. The natural exuberance and extravagance of youth is repressed ... What can ... restore mentalities that have become distorted, spirits that have become mean and broken?
>
> (Murphy, *P1*, xi)

It is this Irish inheritance of famine which Murphy explores, that final rhetorical question which he seeks to answer theatrically in *Bailegangaire*.

The historical legacy of poverty in *A Thief* and *Bailegangaire* is not given a precise historical context. There is no secure date for the remembered laughing-contest. The time of *A Thief* is said to be 'about 50 years ago' which, for a play staged in 1985, would take it back fittingly enough to the 1930s, the period of the so-called 'economic war' when Irish agriculture suffered disastrous consequences from the Fianna Fáil government's decision to discontinue payment of the land annuities to Britain.[15] The ages of Dolly and Mary in *Bailegangaire*, thirty-nine and forty-one, would require the laughing-contest to have taken place not much more than thirty years before, in the 1950s.[16] But such literal dating is beside the point with an event from the foggy memory-time of folk-tale. Murphy's stage directions in *A Thief* sketch in the milieu: 'We are dealing with a neglected, forgotten peasantry' (Murphy, *P2*, 175). The crowds who flock into the pub to watch/listen to the laughers at the start of Act II are 'shaped and formed by poverty and hardship. Rags of clothing, deformities. If there is a beautiful young woman present she, too, looks freakish because of her very beauty. The sounds of sheep, goats, sea-birds can be heard in their speech and laughter' (Murphy, *P2*, 215). It is such a mannerist vision of the post-Famine rural people which *A Thief* represents, and to which *Bailegangaire* looks back.

The 'misfortune' with which the laughers begin is indeed the failure of the potatoes, 'the damnedable crop that was in it that year'

(Murphy, *P2*, 163).[17] But this is an Irish country community from after the Famine itself. The Bochtán small farmers like Costello are owner-occupiers of their land, able to mortgage or sell their holdings to the all-devouring John Mahony, if by virtue of their poverty frequently unable to do anything else. There are no longer absentee landlords to blame for their misery; it is one of their own who is exploiting them with a rapaciousness born of intimate proximity to destitution. Costello is valued for his infectious laugh because he is capable of lifting, however temporarily, the atmosphere of melancholy brooding which is all too likely to descend. One of the misfortunes revealed from his side of things is the despairing suicide of his father. The laughing-contest, as a novelty if nothing else, promises a show, an entertainment for the people who, with 'a thief of a Christmas in prospect', are not going to have the money to pay for seasonal festivity. But it brings out within them an inturned competitive agressiveness which easily spills over into violence. For those who have next to nothing, intense energy is invested in identification with their own community, the intercounty, intervillage rivalry which spurs the Bochtáns on in support of Costello, and which makes of the victorious Stranger from Mayo in the next county the target of murderous assault. The whole story of how 'Bochtán – and its *graund* (*grand*) inhabitants – came by its new appellation' (Murphy, *P2*, 92), is told by Mommo in vengeful partisan contempt, echoing her father's vehement abuse of the renamed people of Bailegangaire as 'a venomous pack of jolter-headed gobshites' (Murphy, *P2*, 121). No quarter given or taken in this violent agrarian community which seems to owe nothing of its chronic hatreds to a legacy of colonial occupation or dispossession, everything to an anger of deprivation which has no other outlet.

Poverty produces the intestine aggression that surrounds the laughing-contest; it also contributes to the Irish patriarchal order and its discontents which are on display in *Bailegangaire*. Murphy's decision to write the play for a cast of three women seems to have been as self-conscious a choice as the decision to go back to the previously rejected cottage-kitchen setting.[18] His previous plays had almost all been dominated by men, truculently loquacious men whose absorption in their own fantasies had left them incapable of giving the women characters airtime. *Bailegangaire* allows women space by the simple expedient of keeping men off the stage altogether. It is no very positive feminist statement that results. Mommo mouths the pieties of patriarchy from time to time: 'Oh, men have their ways an' women their places an' that is God's plan, my bright ones', this *à propos* of the father who would 'welt yeh with the stick' (Murphy, *P2*, 115) and who remains the arch-authority behind her story. But submission to such norms within the grind of a subsistence marriage – 'the gap in the bed, concern for the morrow, how to keep the one foot in front of the other' (Murphy, *P2*, 99) – yield the long-fused resentment which explodes at the moment of the laughing-contest when she forces her husband to go on. Beaten in all else, she is determined that here for once she will not yield, and will not allow him to yield. And this is the pattern of her relations with her children also. When the eldest son Pat married against her wishes, she forced her younger son Willie to fight him for two sheep from the family farm which were his due: 'she told him a brother was one thing, but she was his mother, an' them were the orders to give Pat the high road, and no sheep, one, two or three wor leavin' the yard' (Murphy, *P2*, 163). Beneath a formal patriarchy is the emotional authority of the mother which, itself twisted by anger and need, drives men into violence or to exile.

Emigration in Murphy, as we saw already in *A Crucial Week*, is more than a socio-economic problem; it is the symptom of a psychological malaise not to be relieved by mere material prosperity. 'We're half-men here, or half-men away, and how can we hope ever to do anything' (Murphy, *P4*, 162), shouts out John Joe at the climactic moment of his 'crucial week'. *Bailegangaire* shows the lives of the female partners or equivalents to those half-men. There is Dolly, whose husband's regular remittance of £85 a week leaves her well enough fixed financially but no better off any other way. It is a terrifying dysfunction of sexual relations which is revealed in her long speech in Act II where she describes the brutality of her husband's Christmas visits home, and her revenge in loveless intercourse: 'Jesus, men! (*Indicating the outdoors where she has had her sex*) You-think-I-enjoy? I-use-*them*!' (Murphy, *P2*, 150). Mary, the success-story of the family in her nursing career in England, has to return home to satisfy some sort of unfulfilled need. 'Talking with Irish immigrants,'

Murphy said about his own experience of living in England in the 1960s, 'I find that most of them seem to have left their country without a blessing. They appear to impose on themselves a sense of guilt; guilt at having betrayed somebody or let somebody down.'[19] This is the mentality of Mary who has held on for years by way of '*promised* blessing' to the tenuous consolation of a terminally ill patient who had reassured her, 'You're going to be alright, Mary' (Murphy, *P2*, 160). But when she goes back to the home which she feels must be the source of emotional healing, it is to meet with the continued rejection of Mommo's non-recognition.

'What can restore mentalities that have become distorted, spirits that have become mean and broken?' The answer which *Bailegangaire* suggests to begin with is acknowledgement, acceptance. Ireland in the 1980s, under the impact of the continuing political crisis of the North, might be prepared to look back once again at the history of its colonial past to seek clues to the disturbed present of its divided community. But an increasingly urbanised people in an Ireland bent on proving itself a fully modern member of the European Community/Union was less likely to want to confront its inheritance of rural poverty. No one was watching the lives of Mommo, Mary and Dolly, felt Murphy: they were an unfashionable subject for attention. Yet not to acknowledge them, not to listen to Mommo's story, the play implies, was to deny a fundamental truth of Ireland's past and present. By contrast, the telling out of the story and the release which it precipitates represent some sort of model of restoration for the future. It is an acceptance of continuity between the pre-modern and the modern in the country's life; it enables all three characters, to a greater or lesser extent, to accept in one another and their interrelationship an emotional place of origin. In this it is of central importance that they are women. Though they are moved as much by survivor guilt as by any specifically feminine principles of solidarity, in a patriarchal culture where relations between the sexes are so comprehensively maladjusted, the lines of communication between mother and daughter, grandmother and granddaughter, seem to offer a more positive form of filiation.

If *Bailegangaire* is thus, on a thematic level, a refashioning of the past to illuminate the present and offer hope for the future, it is also theatrically a remaking of earlier Irish drama. Yeats sought in Celtic myth truths laid down by a universal Great Memory. The truths told by *Bailegangaire* are of a different order of verity encoded differently. Murphy is closer to Synge than to Yeats in his development of drama out of a localised material of anecdote and folklore. *Bailegangaire* is akin to *Playboy* in the way a germ of supposed fact – the laughing-contest, the sheltered parricide – forms the basis for a dramatic fabulation which escapes altogether from a naturalistic/representational mode. Synge is Murphy's most obvious precursor in their common harnessing of ritual rhythms of action, their use of traditions of oral narrative, and their creation of a special style of enriched dialogue. Murphy alone of Irish dramatists has recreated an original stage dialect 'as fully flavoured as a nut or apple' without a sense of Syngean pastiche.[20] Mommo's narration is a Synge-like rhythmic prose, though based on a dactyllic rather than an iambic beat. What differentiates *Bailegangaire*, however, from *Riders* or *Playboy* is the way in which it distances its archaic mode from a recognisable moment in a historical present. Mommo's extraordinary Syngean language is viable, is not mere stageland Syngesong, because it is heard as the specialist style of the shanachie, set against the more mundane modern articulations of Mary and Dolly. The *Playboy* was set in a placeless place of carnival, *Riders* in the timeless time of tragedy. *Bailegangaire* with its folkloric story-telling reaches back to such prehistories, but from within the historical perspective of a given family and an individual human memory. It is this which helps to make it one of the strongest, deepest and most resonant plays to have come out of Ireland in this last quarter of the century.

9 Imagining the other

Benedict Anderson in *Imagined Communities* defined as essential to nationalism the capacity for imagining a whole community of individuals one would never meet but who were imagined as similar to oneself, similar in attitudes, ideas, the practices of life.[1] That imagined identification (which Anderson associated with the growth of print-capitalism) allowed the idea of the nation as a binding unity to be created. But in post-Independence southern Ireland such an imagined similarity has constantly been verified by social actuality. One of the features of the partitioned post-1922 Free State/Republic, without the six counties of the North, without the substantial number of Anglo-Irish Protestants who drained away in the 1920s, has been its social and cultural sameness. It is not, of course, that Irish society has been without variety or differentiation: everywhere there are and have been class conflicts, gaps between rich and poor, rural and urban, the inveterate rivalries of region with region. Still, in a state where more than 90 per cent of the people share and practise the same religion, a religion, what is more, which has tended to admit of very little variation; in a society where nationalist belief, active or inert, is so widely accepted, so little challenged – in such a state, in such a society, the imagination of anything other than being Catholic and nationalist becomes genuinely difficult. The strenuous effort at imagining the other has been under way in Ireland now for several years, driven in part by the troubled awareness of the continuing disastrous consequences of the polarised inability to imagine the other side in the northern political situation. Frank McGuinness's *Observe the Sons of Ulster Marching Towards the Somme* (1985) and Sebastian Barry's *The Steward of Christendom* (1995) can both be seen as part of this attempt at re-imagining ourselves, not as ourselves alone, sinn féin amháin, but ourselves in our plural difference.

Both plays use as locus for the imagination of the other the period of the First World War, and it is easy to see why. The period from 1914 to 1918 was the time when Irish history and politics were fundamentally recast. The year 1914, with the passing of the Home Rule Bill, had seemed to bring triumph to the constitutional nationalist movement initiated by Parnell and his followers some thirty years before. It was in the afterglow of such a supposed triumph that John Redmond, leader of the Irish parliamentary party, urged Irishmen to join the British Army to fight Germany as a common enemy in defence of little Catholic Belgium. But the revolutionary nationalism of Easter 1916 so changed the concept of Irish patriotism that it left no room for the many thousands of men who had followed Redmond's advice: such men were at best misguided, the dupes of English propaganda. ''Twas Britain bade our Wild Geese go', sang the 1916 commemorative ballad, 'that small nations might be free'

> But their lonely graves are by Suvla's waves or the fringe of
> the Great North Sea
> O, had they died by Pearse's side or had fought with Cathal
> Brugha,
> Their names we'd keep where the Fenians sleep, 'neath the
> shroud of the Foggy Dew.

The huge numbers of Irish soldiers who fell at the Somme or at Suvla Bay in Gallipoli did *not* die fighting in the GPO or under the leadership of the Republican Cathal Brugha in the Civil War of 1922, so their names have no place in the honoured roll-call of the Fenian dead. In the post-1922 Free State period memories of Irish participation in the Great War and the commemoration of the war dead became issues so politically charged that they were dropped from sight and mind in 'a policy of intentional amnesia'.[2]

There was of course one major attempt to dramatise this subject in the 1920s, O'Casey's *The Silver Tassie*, and it was rejected for production in the Abbey most decisively by Yeats. Given his refusal to write about the war himself and his notorious rejection of the poetry of Owen, it is likely that Yeats's objections to *The Silver*

Tassie were as much aesthetic as political. He was indisposed to accept as subject for art a mass conflict in which individual heroism could count for so little. In 'An Irish Airman' it is a 'lonely impulse of delight' which drives Robert Gregory on to meet his fate, not the 'public men' or 'cheering crowds' of imperialist war fever; his country remains 'Kiltartan Cross', his 'countrymen Kiltartan's poor' (Yeats, *VP*, 328). Still Yeats significantly denied that O'Casey *could* have the emotional investment in the Great War which he had in the war of Irish independence: 'you are not interested in the Great War; you never stood on its battlefields or walked its hospitals, and so write out of your opinions'.[3] It is hardly surprising that O'Casey, with two brothers and a brother-in-law who had served in the British Army, coming from a Dublin Protestant community many of whose men fought and died in the war, should have retorted angrily: 'Your statement is to me an impudently ignorant one to make, for it happens that I was and am passionately interested in the Great War.'[4] What is interesting here is not the argument over the play, in which there were elements of wrong-headedness on both sides, but the spirit of Yeats's imaginative isolationism.

For Frank McGuinness 'a curse came upon the Irish theatre with the rejection of *The Silver Tassie*',[5] a curse which his *Observe the Sons of Ulster* set out in some sort to expiate, taking up a half-century later the subject of O'Casey's rejected play. But it is the sons of Ulster, not of Dublin, that McGuinness's play invites us to observe and this involves another dimension of otherness in imagining them. For southern Catholic nationalists Ulster Protestant Unionism is as other as you can get, and though McGuinness comes from the Ulster county of Donegal, it is from a Catholic background on the Republic's side of the border. The play represents therefore a new sort of imaginative reaching out in Irish drama. This is what it shares with Barry's *The Steward of Christendom*, which takes as protagonist not just a southern loyalist of the period of the First World War to match McGuinness's northern ones but a Catholic policeman, defender of the Crown against the forces of nationalist revolution.

The Irish theatrical impulse towards the representation of the unrepresented touched on in the previous chapter was an egalitarian, a democratising one. Playwrights from Synge to Murphy have sought to enlarge the awareness of what constituted the nation by going out to the neglected and forgotten, unexpressed underclasses who deserved a voice. The spirit of McGuinness's and Barry's work, though comparable in its purpose of dramatic recuperation, is different in its need to cross over politically to engage with what has previously been demonised or denied. The great landmark example of this disposition in contemporary Irish literature has been Brendan Kennelly's epic poem *Cromwell* (1983), which grappled with the most execrated figure of the Irish nationalist narrative. Barry and McGuinness in their different ways also seek to escape from the Manichaean construction of Irish history as us and them, or at least to explore imaginatively what makes them them.

The origins of both plays lay in such an imaginative enterprise. *Observe the Sons of Ulster* had its emotional germ in the 1970s, when McGuinness was teaching at the (then) New University of Ulster, the siting of which in solidly Protestant Coleraine rather than predominantly Catholic Derry had caused major political controversy. It was contemplating the Memorial to Ulster's war dead in Coleraine which forced him to imagine what it must have been like for a community to lose a whole generation of young men.[6] What would have been for McGuinness, at least initially, alien territory prompted an empathetic exploration of the deep trauma of the war for Ulster Protestants. *The Steward* is one of the series which Barry calls his 'family plays' in which he has set out to bring to life scenes and figures from among his ancestors. The effect of *Prayers of Sherkin* about a great-grandmother who came from an extreme Protestant sect on a tiny island off the coast of Cork, or *The Only True History of Lizzie Finn* about another member of the family who was a dancer on the English music-hall stage, has been to enlarge and variegate the dramatised experience of Irishness. But the central figure of *The Steward*, the great-grandfather who had been a Chief Superintendent in the Dublin Metropolitan Police and, according to family history, was responsible for the charge on the locked-out workers in 1913 in which four people died, that was something else again. Barry testifies to an initial reluctance to admit to such an ancestor:

> I was in fear of it being discovered that I had such a relative, hiding you might say in my very blood. I was eager to conceal

> him ... He was no cosy name around the fire of family. But a demon, a dark force, a figure to bring you literary ruin.[7]

Yet as he went on with his family plays he came to feel that 'Chief Superintendent Dunne would have to have his go', and in the *Steward* he sought to 'wrench a life from the dead grip of history and disgrace'.[8] It is the otherness of an experience written out of history by Catholic nationalist consciousness which both McGuinness's and Barry's plays go out to recuperate. This chapter is concerned with the strategies adopted and the results achieved in such an imagining of the other, ending with the issue of its political implications.

Observe the Sons of Ulster

If contemplation of the Coleraine War Memorial provided the emotional germ of *Observe the Sons of Ulster*, then the basic structural design of the play must have come from Arnold Wesker's *Chips with Everything* (1958). Whether or not McGuinness had the play consciously in mind, the ground-plan of the two works is too similar for it just to be coincidence. *Chips with Everything* is about a group of nine RAF conscripts doing their military service training. They are all working class except one, the upper-class Pip Thomson who, as an act of rebellion against his hated general-turned-businessman father, has deliberately chosen not to go in for the officer training that is expected for him. With his working-class fellow conscripts he acts as what the training corporal calls an 'agent provocative',[9] trying to stir them into political consciousness. However, his effort at class rebellion fails when his superiors unmask the messianic power motive behind it, and he reverts to type and officer training.

Though *Observe the Sons of Ulster* uses a flashback structure with the protagonist as an old man remembering the past, the configuration of the main action almost exactly duplicates that of *Chips with Everything*. What is significant in McGuinness's play, however, is the way in which he recasts Wesker's plot to explore the specific ethos of Protestant Unionism. Pyper, like his all-but-namesake Pip, is also the odd man out in the group of soldiers starting military training. He is a drop-out from an upper-class Northern Irish family who is much more subtly motivated than Pip: he joins up with a death-wish, having failed as a sculptor, with a disastrous marriage or love affair behind him, with guilty and confused feelings about his own sexuality. But his volunteering as a private is a similar act of class defiance; his aim is to subvert the values for which his family stands, the attachment to king and empire in which his fellow volunteers unselfconsciously believe. He too fails as 'agent provocative'; he like Pip cannot resist the role imposed upon him by his class. As his blacksmith lover David Craig tells him, 'You're not of us, man. You're a leader.'[10] However, Pyper's reversion to type follows a different track to that of Wesker's protagonist. Although he manages to undermine to some extent his comrades' unswerving loyalist faith in the war, the irony of the play is that it is he who is converted to their beliefs. The bonding experience of the trenches takes Pyper through to a shared solidarity with his fellow Ulster Protestants, and after the war it is survivor guilt which animates his determination to return to political orthodoxy. 'The world lay in ruins about my feet. I wanted to rebuild it in the image of my fallen companions. I owed them that much. I came back to this country and managed my father's estates. I helped organise the workings of this province' (McGuinness, 10). Where Pip Thomson the upper-class rebel without a cause is forced back into officer training, Pyper the dissident, the decadent, lives on to become a pillar of the Northern Irish political establishment.[11]

In *Observe the Sons of Ulster* McGuinness seeks an understanding of the psychological, spiritual and political ethos of Protestant Unionism, resisting the crude stereotyping of it which has been all too common among Irish nationalists. At the very simplest level, he resists the homogenising of Northern Ireland into a single place, a kind of extended Belfast of the mind. McGuinness reminds us that there are other places in Ulster besides the one city, and other types of people besides Belfast's shipyard-workers. The sons of Ulster in his play are chosen from a variety of different trades and distributed across the province. Millen the baker and Moore the weaver come from Coleraine in Co. Antrim; Craig, the blacksmith with aspirations to shift into the motor trade, comes from Enniskillen in Fermanagh. Crawford who, as it turns out, is only partly Protestant comes from Derry and wants to be a professional footballer; Roulston the failed preacher (and the only other man of Pyper's social class) is from Tyrone, Pyper himself from Armagh. When the two Belfast shipyard-workers of the group, Anderson and McIlwaine, do finally make their roaring entrance on stage, their difference from the others is marked off by the expression of disgusted recognition from the Coleraine men. 'Belfast,' says Moore with distaste; 'You'd never think it they're that quiet', says Millen with heavy irony (McGuinness, 33). In Part III of the play, 'Pairing', where we see the men in separate pairs back at home on leave after their first tour of duty in Flanders, McGuinness uses some of the most famous landmark places in the province to mark the geographical difference of their origins. We see (or rather are asked to imagine) the stone sculptures of the islands of Lough Erne which Craig shows to Pyper; it is on the Carrick-a-rede rope bridge which swings out over the Atlantic on the North Antrim coast that Millen helps Moore to get his nerve back; and the Belfast men Anderson and McIlwaine stage a two-man march to the Field at Finnaghy where the Orangemen assemble on the Twelfth of July.

The Ulstermen joining the army are bound together by their loyalty to king, country and faith, the loyalty of the 1912 Covenant pledging resistance to the threat of Home Rule. It represents common ground already at first meeting that Craig, Millen and Moore are all 'Carson's men', and have been active in the Ulster Volunteers. This reflects the historical fact that the 36th (Ulster) Division, to which McGuinness's fictional recruits would have belonged, was formed at the start of the war, largely using the existing Ulster Volunteer force.[12] The characters' shared ideology as paramilitaries is taken over into their commitment as regular soldiers to the war. As Craig recalls his involvement with illegal gun-running, the play catches the siege mentality of the former Volunteers, whether in Fermanagh with its mixed population of Catholics and Protestants, or in the virtually all-Protestant Antrim:

> CRAIG. ... Every man had his job to do, even if it was only to keep his eyes opened. We have our fair share of Fenian rats. I did a few runs to collect and deliver the wares. We've a couple of vehicles. Was near enough to your part. I could have supplied yous with stuff.

MOORE. The same stuff was badly needed.
CRAIG. Compared to ours, your part is safe enough.
MOORE. No part's safe this weather. (McGuinness, 26–7)

McGuinness makes little effort to soften the violent sectarianism of his sons of Ulster. There is a scarifying moment when the Belfast men first come in; McIlwaine sniffs out Crawford as a Catholic and launches a brutal attack upon him. The others pull him off, assuring him that Crawford is 'one of ours'. McIlwaine is not convinced: 'He might deny he's a Catholic, but he wouldn't walk in our part of the shipyard' (McGuinness, 34). The play is not in the business of trying to convince an audience that Northern Protestants are broad-minded tolerant guys, if you once get to know them. But it does represent from the inside perspectives very different from those of traditional Republican nationalism. There is, for example, the Ulster folklore version of the Easter 1916 Rising, as given by McIlwaine:

> Did you hear about this boy Pearse? The boy who took over a post office because he was short of a few stamps. . . . He took over this big post office in Dublin, kicks all the wee girls serving behind the counter out on the streets. When the place is empty, him and his merry men all carrying wooden rifles, land outside on the street. Your man reads the proclamation of an Irish republic. The Irish couldn't spell republic, let alone proclaim it. Then he's caught, him and all hands in gaol. He starts to cry, saying he has a widowed mother and he had led the only other brother astray. Anyway, he didn't plan to take over this post office. He walked in to post a letter and got carried away and thought it was Christmas. Nobody believes him. They're leading him out to be shot. He's supposed to see the widowed ma in the crowd. He looks at her and says, pray for me, mother. The ma looks at him, looks at the Tommy, he's guarding Pearse, the old one grabs the Tommy's rifle. She shoots Pearse herself. She turns to the Tommy and she says, 'That'll learn him, the cheeky pup. Going about robbing post offices. Honest to God, I'm affronted.' (McGuinness, 64–5)

This caustically deconstructs the nationalist sacred narrative of the

Rising, including the sacrificial emotions of Pearse's famous poem 'The Mother':

> I do not grudge them: Lord, I do not grudge
> My two strong sons that I have seen go out
> To break their strength and die.[13]

It is a travesty intended as a shock-tactic for a Southern Irish audience brought up on the mythology of the Rising. It serves to remind such an audience that the Battle of the Somme, beginning in July 1916, came hardly three months after the Rebellion, and that Ulster Protestants involved in the greatest and most terrible war in human history can hardly have been expected to think much of the handful of amateur soldiers in green uniforms occupying the GPO. For the people of the Republic the date of 1916 means the Rising; for Ulstermen it is bound to mean the Somme.

Observe the Sons of Ulster not only attempts to reimagine national politics but the politics of gender also, specifically the nature of masculinity. The sons of Ulster gain their strength not from aggression and competitiveness but from male bonding. In Part I, 'Initiation', where they first join up, Pyper plays flauntingly with a homosexual persona as the mark of his difference – 'I have remarkably fine skin, don't I? For a man, remarkably fine' (McGuinness, 17) – and there is by-play between himself and Craig turning on the word 'rare'. The other men regard all this with extreme suspicion, and even after Pyper has proved his worth as a fighter in the war, there is traditional homophobia in Anderson's suspicion of 'something rotten' in the relationship between Pyper and Craig. The movement of the play, however, is to integrate the explicitly homosexual love of Craig and Pyper, with the distorted relationship of Crawford and Roulston, and the more conventional male camaraderie of the other two pairs of soldiers into a single pattern of masculine interdependence. By the end this makes possible the 'Bonding' of Part IV in which Pyper can be reconciled even with his antithetical alter ego Roulston. In the exchange of Orange sashes, in the singing of Protestant hymns, it is the group as a group which is the system of support for all of them. McGuinness's reimagination of the loyalism of the sons of Ulster involves a reconception of manhood to include the tenderness of gay love within the integrating emotions of the company rather than setting it in opposition to the macho brotherhood of the heterosexual males.

The Steward of Christendom

The Steward is, on the face of it, a very different sort of play from McGuinness's, centring as it does on the single figure of Thomas Dunne, the retired Chief Superintendent of the Dublin Metropolitan Police, in its meditative and elegiac mode so different from the astringent tone and tragic intensities of *Observe the Sons of Ulster*. But, as with McGuinness, Barry mediates the action of the past through a remembering present. We see Dunne in his dotage, in the county home in Baltinglass, West Wicklow, recalling with the erratic wanderings of senile dementia his farm childhood in nearby Kiltegan, his idyllically happy marriage ending with his wife's death in child-birth, his loving but variously difficult relationships with his three daughters, his mourning for his son who died fighting in the British Army in the First World War. Above all he remembers with pride his life as a policeman, even though in post-Independence Ireland it brings him brutal contempt from the likes of Mr Smith, the orderly in the home. 'Dublin Metropolitan Police, weren't you, boyo? ... Castle Catholic bugger that you were ... Chief superintendant, this big gobshite was ... that killed four good men and true in O'Connell Street in the days of the lock-out ... A big loyal Catholic gobshite killing poor hungry Irishmen' (Barry, 9).

So how does Barry imagine the life of a Catholic loyalist from the turn of the century through to the 1930s? It is in many ways a life of failure and loss. Though the Kiltegan country childhood (which was Barry's own also) is remembered as an Eden of pastoral sights and sounds, it is an unrecoverable Eden. When Dunne achieves his long-term aspiration of retirement there after a lifetime's service in Dublin, he goes literally mad out of desolation, loneliness and the sense of alienation from his nationalist neighbours. His father was steward of Humewood, the great estate of Kiltegan with its enormous Victorian house, but young Thomas was regarded as the fool of the family, fit only to become a policeman. Though he rose as high as a Catholic could in the force, he is constantly aware that 'there was never enough gold in that uniform. If I had made commissioner I might have had gold, but that wasn't a task for a Catholic, you understand, in the way of things, in those days' (Barry, 11). In many ways, the play could be read as the psychopathology of the Catholic loyalist, going back to his failure to live up to the image of his father. In the infantilist rhapsody which acts as overture to the play, 'Da Da is golden, golden, golden, nothing that Da Da do takes away the sheen and the swoon of gold' (Barry, 6). At the family level the son, despised and beaten by the father, relegated to the police force because good for nothing else, lives out in his gold-poor uniform his inadequacy by the superego standards of his 'golden' Da Da. This personal acceptance of subordinate status out of a failure of personal self-worth can be read as symptomatic of his colonial position, the policeman pathetically obsessed with the trappings of a derived authority, the native agent of empire.

And yet, suddenly and unexpectedly in the first act, comes the hymn of praise which gives dignity and grace to that mentality. 'I loved her for as long as she lived, I loved her as much as I loved Cissy my wife, and maybe more, or differently.' Hearing this for the first time, an audience does not immediately realise who Dunne is talking about. The object of his devotions is never named until the very end of the long speech:

> When she died it was difficult to go from her to the men that came after her, Edward and George, they were good men but it was not the same. When I was a young recruit it used to frighten me how much I loved her. Because she had built everything up and made it strong, and made it shipshape. The great world that she owned was shipshape as a ship. All the harbours of the earth were trim with their granite piers, the ships were shining and strong. The trains went sleekly through the fields, and her mark was everywhere, Ireland, Africa, the Canadas, every blessed place. And men like me were there to make everywhere peaceable, to keep order in her kingdoms. She was our pride. Among her emblems was the gold harp, the same harp we wore on our helmets. We were secure, as if for eternity the orderly milk-drays would come up the streets in the morning, and her influence would reach everywhere, like

> the salt sea pouring up into the fresh waters of the Liffey. Ireland was hers for eternity, order was everywhere, if we could but honour her example. She loved her Prince. I loved my wife. The world was a wedding of loyalty, of steward to Queen, she was the very flower and perfecter of Christendom. Even as the simple man I was I could love her fiercely. Victoria. (Barry, 16)

What is significant about this as a positive evocation of the emotions of empire is the way it links loyalty and order to love, and puts a female figure at its centre. Dunne's worship of Victoria sees her as the ultimate order figure, the order of Christendom whose steward he is. The ultimate master here is a mistress, and her succeeding son and grandson Edward and George only derivative versions of that primal authority. The transcendent adoration of the monarch is the love of husband for wife writ large. Political ideals of order reflect the domestic principles of love and tenderness. In *The Steward* Barry seeks to re-write the traditional nationalist version of Irish history as a tyrannically patriarchal colonial power oppressing a feminised Ireland from the viewpoint of a man who sees his role as servant of a protective matriarchy.

It is the brutal orderly Smith, who had a brother 'shot in the twenties' (Barry, 11), who associates the ex-policeman Dunne with all the horrors of colonial rule back to the execution of Robert Emmet.

> I suppose you held the day of Emmet's death as a festive day. A victory day. I suppose you did. I suppose you were all very queer indeed up there in the Castle. I'm thinking too of the days when they used to put the pitch caps on the priests when they catched them, like they were only dogs, and behind the thick walls of the city hall all the English fellas would be laughing at the screams of the priests, while their brains boiled. I'm thinking of all that. I suppose you never put a pitch cap on anyone. They weren't in fashion in your time.
>
> (Barry, 15–16)

This, though a crude version of nationalist prejudice, is characteristic in making all agents of the Crown equally complicit in the cruelties of colonialism, and all equally alien – 'I suppose you were all very queer indeed up there in the Castle.' Dunne is not disposed to argue with Smith here, continuing through his harangue about the execution of Emmet to meditate appreciatively on the making of a country lamb stew. But at other times he insists on certain essential discriminations to alter the perception of him as the wicked enemy of Smith's imaginings. He was a member of a city police force, not a colonial army of occupation:

> The DMP was never armed, not like the Royal Irish Constabulary. The RIC could go to war. That's why we were taken off the streets during that rebellion at Easter time, that they make so much of now. We were mostly country men, and Catholics to boot, and we loved our King and we loved our country. They never put those Black and Tans among us, because we were a force that belonged to Dublin and her streets. We did our best and followed our orders. (Barry, 11)

There is an element of evasive apologetics here: 'We did our best and followed our orders', traditional line of defence for morally unacceptable actions; Dunne's DMP did not put down the Rising, was not involved in the atrocities of the Black and Tans. But whatever the measure of defensiveness, it does challenge the simple image of heroes and villains in the nationalist telling of the story.

'[T]hat rebellion at Easter time, that they make so much of now.' Barry does not counter the heroic vision of the Rising with a set-piece caricature as McGuinness does; he sidelines it rather, to suggest the perspective of those for whom the Rising was not a central event. The Great War itself, the main subject of *Observe the Sons of Ulster* and its imagination of the other, comes into *The Steward* tangentially through the memory of Dunne's son Willie who died in the trenches. What the play tries to recapture is something of the sense of the many ordinary Irish people for whom the international conflict of the war was more significant than the national struggle of the Rising. Dunne's daughter Annie, who is the most passionately anti-nationalist of the family, protests indignantly that her brother 'gave his life for Ireland'. Her father corrects her 'kindly': 'Will gave his life to save Europe, Annie, which isn't the same thing' (Barry, 20). For an Irishman to have joined the British Army could be construed not just as patriotic but as a commitment beyond insular patriotism. When Dolly, the youngest of the daughters, has been off with a group of other girls saying goodbye to the departing soldiers in 1922, they are regarded by a woman they meet on the bus as 'Jezebels' who deserve to have their 'heads shaved, and be whipped, for following the Tommies'. The bus-conductor intervenes, 'and hadn't he served in France himself, as one of the Volunteers, oh, it was painful, the way she looked back at him, as if he were a viper, or a traitor' (Barry, 31). The play dramatises this painful fissuring in Irish ideological consciousness by which the beliefs and actions of a whole body of Ireland's people – any of the 200,000 men who served in the British Army during the war – are denied or demonised by their fellow citizens.

The Steward is one of Barry's 'family' plays, and it is from within the family that the play's rehabilitation of the Irish Catholic loyalist is effected. If a refigured idea of masculinity is central to *Observe the Sons of Ulster*, *The Steward* equally breaks down gender stereotypes in its exploration of manhood and fatherhood. Though the remembered infancy images, 'Ma Ma's soft breast' and 'Da Da's bright boots', are conventionally polarised, the two together are subsumed within the class of parent and make up a single formative haven of child consciousness. Dunne, as widowed father of his son and three daughters, commits himself to the caring role of the mother as much as the law-giving role of the father. The travail of his long meditation at the end of Act I, as his wife struggles in labour, is a sort of paean to the feminine which matches at the personal level the earlier eulogy of Victoria. There is a troubled awareness of his failure to communicate adequately with his son, his disappointment at the son's not going into the police force. Significantly Willie returns to him as a thirteen-year-old rather than as the young man he was when he died. Still, the last letter written to the father from the front speaks of a relationship of pure love and trust: 'in the mire of this wasteland, you stand before my eyes as the finest man I know, and in my dreams you comfort me, and keep my spirits lifted' (Barry, 58). In the climactic final speech of the play about Dunne's own boyhood what is revealed is the 'mercy of fathers', the unstinting love, the capacity for forgiveness which belongs as much to them as to the mothers. With this subtle and poignant reimagination of the father, Barry replaces the standard image of the policeman, the sadistic agent of a masculine colonising force imposing itself on a feminine colonial other. Instead Dunne, in his rambling reveries of the past, is dramatised as both self and other, masculine and feminine, father and mother, parent and child.

The politics of the other

Like *Bailegangaire*, like many other modern Irish plays, *Observe the Sons of Ulster* and *The Steward* explore history from the vantage-point of a foregrounded or implied present. 'Remembrance', Part 1 of McGuinness's play, shows the Elder Pyper as a very old man who has survived into the time of the 1985 audience, remonstrating with the God who forces him to remember again and again the horrors of the Somme and his lost companions. As he speaks, the silent ghosts of these companions appear to join his own younger self in the reliving of the events which make up the action. It is in de Valera's 1930s Ireland that Chief Superintendent Dunne meanders through memories going back from the handover to the new government in 1922 to the reign of his beloved Victoria and to the dateless idyll of his childhood. Beyond the formal flashback techniques which structure both plays is the impulse towards historical recovery which provided their starting-point, McGuinness's urge to imagine what it was like for a community to be deprived at one time of a whole generation of young men, Barry's felt need to give at least fictional life to his all but forgotten policeman ancestor. The disposition of both playwrights is for some sort of imaginative reparation to these lost figures of Irish history. But the hindsight of present time from which this past is viewed makes of the plays tragedies of loss and waste.

It is impossible for any play about the First World War to be other than doom-laden. The Somme, in which the 36th (Ulster) Division was decimated, is the inevitable fatality waiting for the characters at the end of McGuinness's play as we observe them march towards it. To McIlwaine the shipyard worker is granted a premonition of the scale of that catastrophe which has a specifically Ulster character. Alone with his partner Anderson, he broods on the Titanic, the great supposedly unsinkable ship built in Belfast in 1912 which was lost on its maiden voyage.

> MCILWAINE. It was a sign of what we're in for. What we've let ourselves in for.
> ANDERSON. The bloody *Titanic* went down because it hit an iceberg.
> MCILWAINE. The pride of Belfast went with it.
> ANDERSON. You're not going to meet many icebergs on the front, are you? So what are you talking about?
> MCILWAINE. The war is our punishment.
> ANDERSON. There's more than Belfast in this war.
> MCILWAINE. But Belfast will be lost in this war. The whole of Ulster will be lost. We're not making a sacrifice. Jesus, you've seen this war. We are the sacrifice. (McGuinness, 51)

McIlwaine, like the other men suffering the strain of the war in this 'Pairing' sequence, regains his nerve, and the whole group goes out to fight at the Somme singing the hymns that are their battle-cries, wearing their Orange sashes to the death. However, McGuinness makes us feel that McIlwaine has glimpsed a truth in that passage: the truth that, after the Somme, after the mass mechanised slaughter of the First World War, the petty nationalisms of Unionists and Republicans were to become hollow and unreal.

It has been a commonplace of the analysis of modern Unionism that the shared participation of Northern Protestants with Britain in two world wars has been one of the features which has cemented their political attachment to the Union. *Observe the Sons of Ulster* makes of that commonplace a compelling dramatic reality, but also a diagnosis. McGuinness has commented on the cult of the war dead as a necessary reaction by the people of Ulster to the sheer scale of the catastrophe:

> They could either turn in hatred against the forces who had led these young men to the slaughter or they could . . . celebrate the men's lives and the bravery of their deaths and courage. And they took the second course, not surprisingly, I think, because that possibly made the scale of the tragedy endurable.[14]

There is every sympathy for this feeling but its result, as the play represents it in the figure of the Elder Pyper, is to produce a rigid, fossilised and backward-looking politics. The Younger Pyper sought to escape from his family and class in becoming a sculptor in Paris, but he found that 'when I saw my hands working they were not mine but the hands of my ancestors, interfering, and I could not be rid of that interference. I could not create. I could only preserve' (McGuinness, 56). When after the war he returns to accept the role given him by his caste, his political mission is indeed that of preservation, the reactionary preservation of the status quo. His loyalism, his commitment to the principles of Unionism, is seen as something artificial, a solidarity with those who died, an attempt to expiate guilt. In the last eerie moments of the play, when the ghost of the Younger Pyper joins the Elder Pyper, it is in 'the deserted temple of the Lord' (McGuinness, 80) that he urges him to dance. That deserted temple is the state from which true belief has gone, where the no-surrender stance of Protestant Unionism has become an attitude frozen in the past, dominated by the dead. What the play represents is not just a re-creation of the past but an attempt through that re-creation to understand the pathology of the present; it is as much about 1980s Northern Ireland as it is about the Great War.

If McGuinness's play has a sort of urgency about it which *The Steward* does not, that is because the political crisis which *Observe the Sons of Ulster* addresses by implication is still immediate and intractable. The play seeks to explore and explicate what produces contemporary Unionism, that Unionism which has been one key part to the impasse of Northern politics. Barry's play is, if you like, a purer act of imaginative generosity: it can afford the indulgence of its deeply sympathetic treatment of the lost tribe of southern Catholic loyalists because they are definitively lost. They have no significant part in a modern political landscape. And yet Barry's play also implies a normative political perspective within which the politically other is imagined.

We can see this in the steward of Christendom's feeling for Michael Collins. A disparaging comment about de Valera from Mrs O'Dea (who is clearly no Fianna Fáil supporter), stirs a memory in Dunne: 'I had an admiration for the other man though, the general that was shot, I forget his name.' Even without being able to call his name to mind, he says 'I remember the shock of sorrow when he was killed' (Barry, 28). This prepares us for the long speech describing his 1922 meeting with Collins when he handed over control of the police to him as the head of the provisional government, a speech which forms an equivalent dramatic peak in Act II to the adoration of Victoria in Act I.

> I could scarce get over the sight of him. He was a black-haired handsome man, but with the big face and body of a boxer. He would have made a tremendous policeman in other days. He looked to me like Jack Dempsey, one of those prize-fighting men we admired. I would have been proud to have him as my son . . . He had glamour about him, like a man that goes about with the fit-ups, or one of those picture stars that came on the big ships from New York . . . He was like that, Mr Collins. I felt rough near him, that cold morning, rough, secretly. There was never enough gold in that uniform, never. I thought too as I looked at him of my father, as if Collins could have been my son and could have been my father. (Barry, 50–1)

With the whole psychodynamics of Dunne's relations with his father which the play has established, the way his career in the police force has been a search for the 'golden' authority he felt he lacked as son, this speech is of key importance in suggesting an alternative filiation in which Collins could have been both the son whom Dunne lost to the war and a father to sponsor his own sense of identity. What the ousted policeman of the Crown is allowed here to glimpse is the other forward-moving track of history from which he is excluded, an exclusion he is made to feel as loss.

> I knew that by then most of the men in my division were for Collins, that they would have followed him wherever he wished, if he had called them. And for an instant, as the Castle was signed over to him, I felt a shadow of that loyalty pass across my heart. (Barry, 51)

If *The Steward* goes sympathetically out to the political other in its imagination of an imperial loyalist with a cult of Queen Victoria, it has to show him also capable of appreciating the cult of Michael

Collins which represents some sort of political home base for the implied audience.

These two plays have been outstandingly successful both at home and abroad, in part exactly because they so movingly imagine the lost and unspoken lives they do, and attempt to explore the past in ways enabling to the present. That is why both plays were awarded, or shared in the award, of the Christopher Ewart-Biggs Literary Prize, set up in memory of the murdered British Ambassador to Ireland to recognise outstanding contributions to crosscultural understanding. But we cannot imagine except from where we are. McGuinness and Barry imagine from within the overwhelmingly homogeneous community of post-Independence Ireland and it shows – even when they go out with imaginative magnanimity to the other lives which that community has written out. McGuinness's play sensitively and powerfully recreates the ethos of the sons of Ulster marching towards the Somme; but it is in order to try to fathom what went so terribly wrong as to lead to the dead end of contemporary Unionist politics. The tragedy of Barry's steward of Christendom is that he should have been in the wrong track of history, that he was denied the opportunity of serving Collins as he served Victoria. But it is beyond the powers of even McGuinness's empathetic imagination to imagine contemporary Unionism as anything other than a dead end, an atrophied commitment to a dead past. And Barry's wonderfully tender rendering of his ancestor the Catholic DMP man has to grant him at least an inkling of the greatness of Collins. The greatness of Collins itself goes as unquestioned here as it does in the Hollywood-ised version of Neil Jordan's 1996 film. These are two plays that deserve all the recognition they have had for their capacity to imagine back into existence the realities which the history of nationalist Ireland has forced it, enabled it to leave out of the record. But it is also necessary to recognise the social, human and political actualities from within which that imagining goes on, how McGuinness and Barry recreate the historical past from where they themselves are in history.

Conclusion: a world elsewhere

The Irish plays keep on coming. In July 1997 *The Weir*, a new play by 26-year-old Conor McPherson, opened at the Royal Court Upstairs to such an enthusiastic reception that it transferred to the Royal Court main house in February 1998, to go on to be performed in Brussels and Toronto, a run in Dublin, a return to London, and on to Broadway in April 1999. *The Weir* is not a play about Ireland as such. The title refers to a local weir built by the Electricity Supply Board in 1951 'to regulate the water for generating power' in the western area of Sligo-Leitrim where the play is set.[1] It acts as a metaphor for the controlled release of emotion through talk and story-telling among the five characters, not as a symbol of a stage in the modernisation of Ireland. As McPherson himself says about the play, 'I wasn't concerned with geography or politics. I am from the Republic of Ireland and that's where my plays have their genesis, but not from any need to address anything about my country.'[2] Still, *The Weir* is identifiably, recognisably, an Irish play, and a dimension to its (well-deserved) success comes from that recognisability. The small rural pub scene is familiar from as far back as the *Playboy*. The full-length action, uninterrupted by any interval, consisting in nothing but an evening's drink-talk, has a precedent in Murphy's *Conversations on a Homecoming*. *The Weir* is written in the idiom of the Irish play, relying on certain standard recurrent motifs associated with an Irish rural setting: the opposition of country and city, village and small town; persistent celibacy or late marriage among the men; woman as edgily desired sex-object in a heavily repressed society. This is the more striking coming from McPherson whose earlier plays (*Rum and Vodka*, *The Good Thief*, *This Lime-tree Bower*) showed a much less familiar contemporary urban Ireland of hard men and hard drinking, casual sex and organised crime. In *The Weir* also the one female character Valerie belongs to a Dublin world of the 1990s as a lecturer from Dublin City University who has retreated to the country in breakdown after the accidental death of her child. The remote Irish pub setting, though, remains an archaic place rendering possible and plausible the rehearsal of the set of stories of the supernatural through which the play builds its drama. Its remoteness and difference from the reality inhabited by audiences in London, Brussels, Toronto, New York – or indeed Dublin – is part of what makes it funny and moving, what makes it creditworthy. Ireland in the Irish play is a world elsewhere.

The Irish play is a distinct and distinctly marketable phenomenon. 'It is Ireland's sacred duty,' wrote Kenneth Tynan in 1956 about Behan's *The Quare Fellow*, 'to send over, every few years, a playwright to save the English theatre from inarticulate glumness.'[3] This Irish theatrical rescue operation has been happening with increasing regularity in the 1990s: *The Weir* is only the most recent of a whole series of notable London productions of Irish plays by McGuinness and Barry, Billy Roche, Marina Carr, and Martin McDonagh. In some cases this has also involved a variation on the common pattern of successful Dublin plays transferring to London. *The Steward of Christendom* followed exactly the same trajectory as *The Weir*, initiated at the London Royal Court and only coming to Ireland as part of a triumphant world tour. Martin McDonagh's *The Beauty Queen of Leenane*, though staged first by the Druid Theatre in Galway, is an Irish play made in London by a London-Irish dramatist.

The phenomenon of Irish drama as a commodity of international currency has produced mixed results. It has allowed early success to very talented writers such as McGuinness, Barry, McPherson; it has enabled McDonagh, a playwright of much more doubtful originality, to achieve quite astonishing success by manipulating the formulae of the Irish play. Some Irish plays have travelled better than others: Friel's very sophisticated versions of pastoral are more readily assimilable than the anti-pastorals of Murphy. What is significant in the international reception of Irish drama, beyond the mere vagaries of the theatrical market, is the extent to which it constitutes a separable category, fulfilling its own contrastive function in relation to the metropolitan mainstream. Sebastian Barry was hailed by *Newsweek* as 'the new crown prince of Ireland's majestic theatrical tradition'; the *Guardian* called *The Steward of Christendom* 'an authentic Irish masterpiece', particularly for the quality of its writing: 'I venture to suggest that not even O'Casey or Synge wrote better than this.'[4] The latest successors to Synge and O'Casey are received into the canon by virtue of the difference of their language. For, as Tynan said, without the periodic incursions of the Irish dramatists English theatre would be doomed to 'inarticulate glumness'.

Figured in these expectations of Irish drama may be traces of the Arnoldian notion of the eloquent Celt or his vulgar cousin the Irishman with the gift of the gab. But the idea of Irish drama constructed on difference, its language worked from Hiberno-English variations on the received standard forms which are by implication those of its audience, has been a determining condition within Ireland as much as outside of Ireland. When Synge wrote of his 'collaboration' with the Irish country people in the creation of the language of his plays, when he praised their 'popular imagination that is fiery and magnificent and tender', he was addressing a readership of those like himself distanced from such language by class and education. He would only have spoken the phrases used in the *Playboy* 'in my own nursery before I could read the newspapers' (Synge, *CW*, IV, 53–4), and he is implicitly writing for others who went from nursery to newspapers. Where Irish drama is received abroad as different by virtue of its Irishness, in Ireland that difference is turned on a gap in social milieu between characters and audience. This is true not only of the western peasants of Synge, Yeats, Gregory, the small town denizens of Murphy or Friel, appearing on the stage of the national theatre in the nation's capital, but even of O'Casey's Dublin trilogy where norms of middle-class perception frame the spectacle of the tenements. The spaces of Irish drama, like the language of its people, are predicated as being authentic, truly reflecting the speech and behaviour of a reality out there – hence Synge's strenuous efforts to protest the genuineness of his dialect and audience resistance to those claims. But it is always out there, somewhere other than the metropolitan habitat shared (more or less) by playwright and audience alike.

This is what has made representational styles in Irish drama distinctively unlike their counterparts in European naturalism. Zola aspired to a naturalist theatre which would remake 'the stage until it was continuous with the auditorium', forcing a middle-class audience to see their own lives recreated on stage with scrupulous impartiality.[5] 'Have a look at yourselves,' Chekhov wanted to say to the people who watched his plays, 'and see how bad and dreary your lives are':[6] *your* lives, you in the audience. But the impulse towards an equivalent middle-class naturalism in Ireland was stillborn with the failure of George Moore and Edward Martyn, who favoured such a model, to wrest control of the Irish national theatre movement from Yeats. Although there have been latter-day Irish dramatists such as Hugh Leonard and Bernard O'Farrell who have made middle-class urban and suburban Dublin their subject, on the whole Irish drama has continued to look to social margins for its setting, whether the western country districts or the working-class inner city. It is thus typically other people that a largely middle-class urban audience watches in an Irish play, other people who speak differently – more colloquially, more comically, more poetically. So, for instance, T.S. Eliot in canvassing the issues of a poetic drama could see Synge as a special case: 'Synge wrote plays about characters whose originals in life talked poetically, so that he could make them talk poetry and remain real people.'[7] The naive acceptance that in real life Irish peasants 'talked poetically' by a critic as subtle and sophisticated as Eliot is a testimony to how potent are the conventions of Irish otherness on which the drama is founded.

The recognisable difference of the Irish dramatic scene could be turned towards allegory by Yeats and Gregory with the trope of the strangers in the house, where the country-cottage family stood in for the whole nation's life. In its imagined wildness, it could serve as a site of carnival in Synge's *Playboy*; in its bare simplicity it allowed the uncovering of tragic archetypes in *Riders to the Sea*. In so far as Ireland is posited as a place of the pre-modern, Irish drama has been able to reach down through folklore to underpinning myth and ritual. This was a very obvious feature of the early national theatre movement with Yeats and Synge seeking below the surfaces of Catholic Christian belief a pagan substratum that was primal, deeper, truer. Towards the other end of the twentieth century, the tendency has been developed again, in particular in Friel's later drama. In *Faith Healer*, the circumstances of Frank Hardy's violent murder suggest glancingly the sacrificial death of the king who must be killed to renew the life of his country, a motif much more explicitly dramatised in *Wonderful Tennessee*. *Dancing at Lughnasa* uses its master-image of dancing to link the suppressed harvest festival practices of a pre-Christian Ireland with equivalent African rites of celebration. Yet such ritual patterns remain buried within the representation of a believable social reality. They remain traces of the mythic rendered credible by their semi-archaic Irish setting while still camouflaged within a more or less naturalistic surface. It is in this context that the fully non-representational drama of Yeats, using stylised verse dramaturgy and the (for most audiences) unfamiliar materials of Celtic mythology has failed to win its way into the regular repertory of Irish theatre. The pagan harvest god Lugh might be glimpsed behind the 1930s radio in *Dancing at Lughnasa*, but the figures of Cuchulain and Deirdre on a modern stage tend to remain alien and embarrassing.

The Irish drama has had to be seen to be Irish to be recognised as such, and this has skewed the tradition towards the representational, if not the naturalistic. The tendency has been repeatedly resisted, initially and most arduously by Yeats himself. In a later generation, Murphy with his expressionism, Thomas Kilroy with a radical conceptual drama, Tom McIntyre with a theatre of image and movement, have sought to move away from the conventions of naturalism. But there is a strong pull towards plays which are identifiably Irish by their representation of an Irish scene or subject-matter, the scenes and subjects initially authorised by Synge and O'Casey. So Murphy might begin his career in revolt against the country cottage kitchen setting but return in the 1980s to produce one of the finest country cottage kitchen plays in *Bailegangaire*. McIntyre, so closely identified for so long with a non-verbal dramaturgy, has turned round to writing quite conventionally language-based plays about Kitty O'Shea or Michael Collins. The need for the Irish playwright to write plays about Ireland has made Beckett the odd anomalous figure he is in an Irish theatrical context. Although *All that Fall* mocks up the texture of an Irish social scene, it is to other ends than those of representation. *Waiting for Godot* can be successfully returned to

Ireland with Didi and Gogo played in Dublin tramp, but at the expense of the placeless aesthetic which is so crucial to the play's conception. The mainstream tradition of Irish drama is a representational one to which academic critics try as best they may to assimilate the uncomfortably offstage presence of Beckett, or those older Irish expatriates Wilde and Shaw who equally refused to conform to the requirements for Irish dramatists of writing about Ireland.

Externally, Irish drama is regarded as a thing apart, defined by its national origins rather than by its style or technique. Within Ireland, also, however, there has been a felt need to assimilate into Irish terms theatrical borrowings from abroad. It was one of the aims of the national theatre movement from the start to perform classics of world theatre by way of models for Irish playwrights – hence Gregory's versions of Molière, and Yeats's two Oedipus plays. But Gregory's is a 'Kiltartan Molière' made palatable for Irish audiences by translation into the western dialect she used for her own plays. There has been a similar impulse in the adaptations of Greek tragedy and of Russian drama which have been such a notable feature of Irish theatre of the 1980s and 1990s. Greek tragedy is a sort of common theatrical joint stock, borrowable and adaptable at will in all ages and countries for different local purposes. So *The Riot Act*, Tom Paulin's version of *Antigone*, and *The Cure at Troy*, Seamus Heaney's adaptation of *Philoctetes*, both produced by Field Day, brought a specifically Irish colouring and political moral to their originals. But the perceived affinity between Irish and Russian drama, above all Chekhov, is more remarkable. Versions of *The Three Sisters* and *Uncle Vanya* by both Friel and McGuinness in each case, a *Seagull* by Kilroy, Turgenev's novel *Fathers and Sons* and his play *A Month in the Country* adapted by Friel, all represent a special sort of Hibernicising appropriation of nineteenth-century Russia. In one case, with John McGahern's *The Power of Darkness*, the disguise was so effective that reviewers failed to recognise the play as an adaptation of Tolstoy's melodrama and attacked it as a strained and implausible rendering of Irish life.[8] What should an Irish playwright be doing if not representing Ireland even while adapting Molière or Sophocles, Chekhov or Tolstoy?

'A healthy nation,' wrote Shaw in the 'Preface for Politicians' of *John Bull's Other Island*, 'is as unconscious of its nationality as a healthy man of his bones. But if you break a nation's nationality it will think of nothing else but getting it set again' (Shaw, *CP*, II, 842). The image may be suspect in its assumption that nationality is as natural a feature of the body politic as a skeleton is to the anatomy of the human body, but the point is a telling one nonetheless. No doubt a large part of the anxious obsession with self-representation in the Irish dramatic tradition originates with the colonial and postcolonial condition of the country. If the manifesto-writers of the Irish Literary Theatre in 1897 aspired to 'bring upon the stage the deeper thoughts and emotions of Ireland' it was to help heal those broken bones of national identity. It is a continuation of the same compulsion that has tied so many later Irish playwrights to the task of reflecting, exploring, re-interpreting Ireland's experience of the past and the present. The seismic changes of 1916–23 demanded the reaction of theatrical representation. The long-promised Utopia of national liberation provoked comparison with the reality achieved in an actual Free State with all its limitations. As the partitioned island has continued to manifest symptoms of its fractured state, so the dramatists have returned repeatedly to probe and examine, to attempt therapies of self-analysis. And it has not only been in the politics of the nation that the national life has found its theatrical expression. The dramatised experiences of the past conditioning the present have been as much those of poverty and deprivation with their consequent deformations of mind and spirit, as the oppressions of political domination. The disposition within the drama to represent in Irish life what is symptomatic of Irish life can be attributed in general terms to the colonial/postcolonial consciousness which leaves the question of national identity always an issue.

Ireland's colonial history can be seen, however, as the necessary but not the sufficient condition for Irish drama and its representational character. It has been the aim of this book to analyse the politics of Irish drama as something other than merely the reflection of the political condition of the country. To concentrate on Irish drama as primarily a manifestation of national self-examination is to neglect its crucial international dimension, the fact that it is directed towards audiences abroad as well as at home. That was the rationale for beginning with Boucicault's *Shaughraun* and the tradition of the stage interpretation of Ireland which both predated and has survived the cultural nationalism of the Irish Literary Theatre. Ireland within Irish drama is there to be perceived as John Bull's *other* island, significant in its distinctive otherness. That distance of difference is present even within an Irish context where the mission of Irish drama might appear to be to affirm the lives of the audience in an act of communal self-expression. In Irish theatres too the spectacle of the stage space is shown as something recognisable, yes, but different also and capable of bearing meaning by virtue of its very difference.

What has been produced is the phenomenon of Irish drama as its own special tradition, with a quite marked intertextual line of descent, fulfilling its own role as interpreter of the national life both inside and outside Ireland. I have not sought throughout this book to evaluate that tradition of Irish drama, either to celebrate or criticise it. It is certainly open to criticism. Its bias towards the representational has kept Irish drama formally conservative, resistant to radical theatrical experimentation. Because of the crucial emphasis on its distinct form of Irish English, and its privileging of language, Irish plays and playwrights have neglected or subordinated mise-en-scène. In spite of the special talents of directors from Hilton Edwards to Patrick Mason, Irish theatre has remained author-dominated. It was not accidental that the first three directors of the Abbey were all writers. A case can be made against Irish drama as old-fashioned, wordy, formula-driven, peddling its images of Ireland as a sort of cultural tourism for the home and export markets. Another perspective again can turn all this into occasion for celebration. Irish playwrights have made a quite disproportionate contribution to the canon of world theatre, and Ireland continues to produce a remarkably high number of plays to excite international as well as national audiences. The otherness of Irish voices and Irish subjects, for all their familiarity, still provides a charge of dramatic energy. Within the context of the ever-increasing sameness of global late capitalism and the emptiness of postmodern posturing, Irish drama in its perspicuous difference and the liveness of its political engagements can still produce real theatrical effects. The object of this book has been neither to congratulate nor condemn, but to analyse the multiple politics of Irish drama which has made it what it is.

Notes

INTRODUCTION

1 Christopher Murray, *Twentieth-Century Irish Drama: Mirror up to Nation* (Manchester University Press, 1997).
2 Declan Kiberd, *Inventing Ireland* (London: Jonathan Cape, 1995); Luke Gibbons, *Transformations in Irish Culture* (Cork University Press, 1996); Joep Leerssen, *Mere Irish and Fíor-Ghael* (Cork University Press, 1996), and *Remembrance and Imagination* (Cork University Press, 1996).
3 D.E.S. Maxwell, *Modern Irish Drama 1891–1980* (Cambridge University Press, 1984); Christopher Fitz-Simon, *The Irish Theatre* (London: Thames and Hudson, 1983).

1 STAGE INTERPRETERS

1 Quoted in Townsend Walsh, *The Career of Dion Boucicault* (New York: Dunlap Society, 1915), p. 74.
2 Quoted in Lady Gregory, *Our Irish Theatre* (Gerrards Cross: Colin Smythe, 3rd ed., 1972), p. 20.
3 Bernard Shaw, *The Bodley Head Bernard Shaw: Collected Plays with their Prefaces*, II (London: Max Reinhardt, 1971), p. 808.
4 Brian Friel, 'Talking to Ourselves', interview by Paddy Agnew, *Magill*, December 1980, cited by Marilynn J. Richtarik, *Acting Between the Lines: The Field Day Theatre Company and Irish Cultural Politics 1980–1984* (Oxford: Clarendon Press, 1994), p. 12.
5 Walsh, quoting from the playbill of *The Colleen Bawn*, in *The Career of Dion Boucicault*, p. 74.
6 Playbill reproduced in Richard Fawkes, *Dion Boucicault* (London: Quartet Books, 1979), p. 193.
7 Dion Boucicault, *Plays*, ed. Peter Thomson (Cambridge University Press, 1984), p. 191. All further quotations from *The Shaughraun* are from this edition, with references given parenthetically in the text.

Boucicault was obviously quite hazy about dates: in his open letter to Disraeli, he referred to the 'Fenian insurrection of 1866' (Walsh, *The Career of Dion Boucicault*, p. 137).

8 *New York Herald*, 7 March 1875, cited in John Harrington, *The Irish Play in New York 1874–1966* (Lexington: University Press of Kentucky, 1997), p. 25.

9 See Fawkes, *Dion Boucicault*, p. 195.

10 For details see Robert Kee, *The Green Flag*, II: *The Bold Fenian Men* (London: Quartet Books, 1972), p. 43.

11 Fawkes, *Dion Boucicault*, p. 158.

12 For example, the text of *The Shaughraun* printed in the several standard acting editions, marketed in Britain, does not seem substantially different from the text in Peter Thomson's Cambridge *Plays* edition, which is based on the original New York promptbook.

13 The letter is reproduced in full in Walsh, *The Career of Dion Boucicault*, pp. 137–40.

14 Walsh, *ibid.*, pp. 139–40.

15 Reproduced in Fawkes, *Dion Boucicault*, plate between pp. 126 and 127.

16 On the tradition of the national romance going back to Lady Morgan's *The Wild Irish Girl*, see Leerssen, *Remembrance and Imagination*, pp. 54, 242.

17 Sir Henry Folliott (later Ffolliott) is listed among the English and Scottish families giving extensive grants of land in Fermanagh during the Ulster plantation. See John O'Hart, *Irish Pedigrees*, I (New York: P. Murphy & Son, 1915), p. 818.

18 Luke Gibbons puts almost the exactly opposite argument about Boucicault's Irish heroes whose language, he maintains, is used for 'deception, as a means of sowing *mis*understanding between the Irish and their imperial masters'. See Kevin Rockett, Luke Gibbons and John Hill, *Cinema and Ireland* (London: Routledge, 1988), p. 215. Yet this is only superficially the case: their equivocations and 'Irish Bulls' are ultimately at the service of *éclaircissement* and reconciliation.

19 For a brilliant dramatisation of these events see Donal O'Kelly, *Catalpa* (Dublin: New Island Books; London: Nick Hern Books, 1997).

20 Fawkes, *Dion Boucicault*, p. 193.

21 *Ibid.*, p. 192.

22 The Blaskets are given as the setting for Act I, scene 2, and Act II, scene 6 in both the original New York playbill and the acting editions of *The Shaughraun*. Gerald Griffin had already introduced the Killarney setting for his version of the Colleen Bawn story in *The Collegians*, even though the original murder took place in Garryowen, near

Limerick. The steel engravings of Killarney in Griffin's novel were apparently one of Boucicault's starting-points for *The Colleen Bawn*: see Fawkes, *Dion Boucicault*, p. 114.

23 See, for example, the statistics on performances of Boucicault plays in middle-class and working-class theatres given by Bruce A. McConachie in Thomas Postlewait and Bruce A. McConachie (eds.), *Interpreting the Theatrical Past* (Iowa City: University of Iowa Press, 1989).

24 See Stephen M. Watt, 'Boucicault and Whitbread: the Dublin Stage at the End of the Nineteenth Century', *Eire-Ireland*, 18:3 (1983), 32.

25 Bruce A. McConachie, *Melodramatic Formations: American Theatre and Drama, 1820–1870* (Iowa City: University of Iowa Press, 1992), cited by Harrington, *The Irish Play in New York*, p. 25.

26 Quoted in Gregory, *Our Irish Theatre*, p. 32.

27 W.B. Yeats, *The Letters of W.B. Yeats*, ed. Allan Wade (London: Rupert Hart-Davis, 1954), p. 335.

28 For Shaw's letters to Barker, see *Bernard Shaw's Letters to Granville Barker*, ed. C.B. Purdom (London: Phoenix House, 1956), pp. 22–43; for the letter to Yeats, see Bernard Shaw, *Collected Letters 1898–1910*, ed. Dan H. Laurence (London: Max Reinhardt, 1972), p. 452.

29 *Bernard Shaw's Letters to Granville Barker*, p. 26.

30 *Ibid.*, p. 25.

31 Shaw, *Collected Letters 1898–1910*, pp. 457–8.

32 'George Bernard Shaw: a Conversation', *The Tatler*, 16 November 1904.

33 Shaw, *Collected Letters 1898–1910*, p. 567.

34 See my essay '*John Bull's Other Island*: At Home and Abroad', *The Shaw Review*, XXIII, 1 (1980), 11–16.

35 Joseph Holloway, 'Impressions of a Dublin Playgoer', unpublished manuscript journal, National Library of Ireland, MS 1805, 20 November 1907.

36 See '*John Bull's Other Island*: At Home and Abroad', 14.

37 *Bernard Shaw's Letters to Granville Barker*, p. 45.

38 Shaw, *Collected Plays with their Prefaces*, II, p. 900. All further quotations from *John Bull* are taken from this edition, with references cited parenthetically in the text.

39 Bernard Shaw, *Our Theatres in the Nineties*, II (London: Constable, 1932), pp. 28–9.

40 See Harrington, *The Irish Play on the New York Stage*, p. 41.

41 Martin Meisel, *Shaw and the Nineteenth-Century Theater* (Princeton University Press, 1963), pp. 269–89.

42 Leerssen, *Remembrance and Imagination*, pp. 108–43.

43 Compare the comments of Elizabeth Butler Cullingford, 'Gender, Sexuality, and Englishness in Modern Irish Drama and Film', in *Gender and Sexuality in Modern Ireland*, eds. Anthony Bradley and Maryann

Gialanella Valiulis (Amherst: University of Massachusetts Press, 1997), pp. 164–5.

44 See Martin Meisel, '*John Bull's Other Island* and Other Working Partnerships', *SHAW: the Annual of Bernard Shaw Studies*, 7: *Shaw: the Neglected Plays*, ed. Alfred Turco Jr (University Park and London: Pennsylvania State University Press, 1987), 119–36.

45 The opposition between Dempsey and Keegan corresponds, intriguingly, to a 'dichotomy of the political/worldly versus the spiritual/natural' detected by Lawrence J. Taylor in his analysis of Donegal stories of drunken priests and their miraculous powers: see *Occasions of Faith: an Anthropology of Irish Catholics* (Dublin: Lilliput Press, 1995), pp. 145–66. The teetotal Shaw, of course, was unlikely to portray his saintly Keegan as a drunkard, but in his association with wandering and the natural landscape and in his veneration by the community he does correspond to Taylor's type of the 'silenced' drunken priest. I am grateful for this reference to Lucy McDiarmid.

46 Richtarik, *Acting Between the Lines*, pp. 51–64.

47 Richtarik, *ibid.*, p. 56, quoting from *The Sunday Tribune* and *The Irish Press*.

48 See Leerssen's analysis of Friel's misrepresentations of the Ordnance Survey in *Remembrance and Imagination*, pp. 102–5.

49 Brian Friel, John Andrews, and Kevin Barry, 'Translations and A Paper Landscape: Between Fiction and History', *Crane Bag*, 7.2 (1983), 123–4.

50 See Sean Connolly, 'Dreaming History: Brian Friel's *Translations*', *Theatre Ireland*, 13 (1987), 43.

51 Edna Longley, 'Poetry and Politics in Northern Ireland', *Crane Bag*, 9.1 (1985), 28.

52 J.M. Synge, *Collected Works*, IV: *Plays*, Book 2, ed. Ann Saddlemyer (Oxford University Press, 1968), p. 53. All further quotations from Synge, unless otherwise stated, are from this edition and are cited parenthetically in the text.

53 Brian Friel, *Selected Plays* (London: Faber, 1984), p. 395. All further quotations are from this edition and are cited parenthetically in the text.

54 Cecil Woodham-Smith, *The Great Hunger: Ireland 1845–9* (London: Hamish Hamilton, 1962).

55 Quoted in Richtarik, *Acting Between the Lines*, p. 49.

56 Friel, Andrews, Barry, 'Translations and A Paper Landscape', 123.

57 Key passages from Steiner's work as they influenced Friel are listed by Richard Kearney in *Transitions* (Manchester University Press, 1988), pp. 158–60.

58 George Steiner, *After Babel* (Oxford University Press, 1975), p. 198.

59 Compare *ibid.*, p. 55.

60 William Carleton, *Traits and Stories of the Irish Peasantry* (Dublin: William Curry, 1830; reprinted New York & London: Garland, 1979), II, p. 178.

61 *Ibid.*, pp. 110–11.

62 See Richtarik, *Acting Between the Lines*, pp. 57–8.

63 See, for example, Brian McEvera in *Fortnight*, 215 (March 1985), 19–21, cited by Richard Kearney, *Transitions*, p. 154.

64 Leerssen, *Remembrance and Imagination*, p. 38.

2 STRANGERS IN THE HOUSE

1 Lady Gregory, *Selected Writings*, ed. Lucy McDiarmid and Maureen Waters (Harmondsworth: Penguin, 1995), p. 306. Although the play was always ascribed to Yeats in his lifetime, and appears in his *Collected Plays* in a text from which the one in the Gregory, *Selected Writings*, is derived, I have cited the latter edition throughout this chapter to underline the importance of Gregory's collaboration in the writing. All further quotations from the play are cited parenthetically in the text.

2 *Freeman's Journal*, Tuesday 5 January 1907, cited in James Kilroy, *The 'Playboy' Riots* (Dublin: Dolmen Press, 1971), p. 87.

3 The long-debated joint authorship of the play seems to have been decided by the evidence of an early manuscript draft analysed by James Pethica in '"Our Kathleen": Yeats's Collaboration with Lady Gregory in the Writing of *Cathleen ni Houlihan*', an article originally published in *Yeats Annual*, 6 (1988) and reprinted in *Yeats and Women*, ed. Deirdre Toomey (Basingstoke: Macmillan, 2nd edn 1997), pp. 205–22. However, though the joint authorship is now generally accepted, its implications are not really followed through. For example, Marjorie Howes, in her fine book *Yeats's Nations* (Cambridge University Press, 1996), describes *Kathleen ni Houlihan* as 'written collaboratively by Yeats and Lady Gregory' (p. 74) but then continues with an analysis in which it is referred to exclusively as 'Yeats's play' (pp. 74–8).

4 See Ann Saddlemyer, 'The "Dwarf-Dramas" of the Early Abbey Theatre', in A.N. Jeffares (ed.), *Yeats, Sligo and Ireland* (Gerrards Cross: Colin Smythe, 1980), pp. 197–215.

5 W.B. Yeats, *The Variorum Edition of the Poems of W.B. Yeats*, ed. Peter Allt and Russell K. Alspach (New York: Macmillan, 3rd edn 1966), pp. 86–8. All further quotations from Yeats's poems are taken from this edition, cited parenthetically in the text.

6 In 1895, just the year after the production of the play, the horrific case of the burning of Bridget Cleary in Tipperary was to provide a terrible proof of continuing popular belief in the power of the fairies over a

young wife. See Hubert Butler, 'The Eggman and the Fairies', in *Escape from the Anthill* (Mullingar: Lilliput Press, 1985), pp. 73–4.

7 W.B. Yeats, *Collected Plays* (London: Macmillan, 2nd edn 1952), p. 55. All further quotations from Yeats's sole-authored plays are from this edition, cited pathenthetically in the text.

8 See Hugh Hunt, *The Abbey: Ireland's National Theatre 1904–1979* (Dublin: Gill and Macmillan; New York: Columbia University Press, 1979), p. 38. The play was finally produced by the Abbey in 1911–12 in the season directed by Nugent Monck with the theatre's second company, while the main troupe were touring in America: see Hunt, *ibid.*, p. 97.

9 James Pethica, 'Contextualising the Lyric Moment: Yeats's "The Happy Townland" and the Abandoned Play *The Country of the Young*', *Yeats Annual*, 10 (1993), 65–91.

10 Not, it seems, *The Black Horse*, as Gregory misremembered in *Our Irish Theatre*, p. 64, where she gives a very foreshortened account of the collaboration.

11 'I owe the Rider's Song, and some of the rest to W.B. Yeats.' See Lady Gregory, *Collected Plays*, III: *Wonder and Supernatural*, ed. Ann Saddlemyer (Gerrards Cross: Colin Smythe, 1970), p. 374. All the quotations from *The Travelling Man* are from this edition and are cited parenthetically in the text.

12 Lady Gregory, *Diaries 1892–1902*, ed. James Pethica (Gerrards Cross: Colin Smythe, 1996), p. 151.

13 Pethica transcribes the ts. draft in 'Contextualising the Lyric Moment,' *Yeats Annual* 10 (1993), pp. 85–91.

14 Pethica, citing a revision to the earliest ts. of *The Travelling Man*, *ibid.*, 10, p. 69.

15 W.B. Yeats, *The Collected Letters of W.B. Yeats*, III, ed. John Kelly and Ronald Schuchard (Oxford: Clarendon Press, 1994), p. 322.

16 *Ibid.*, pp. 321–2: for details of the two-volume 'Plays for an Irish Theatre', see p. 320.

17 See Leerssen, *Mere Irish and Fíor-Ghael*, pp. 217–41.

18 See G.F. Dalton, 'The Tradition of Blood Sacrifice to the Goddess Éire', *Studies*, 63 (1974), 343–54.

19 Pethica, '"Our Kathleen"', *Yeats and Women*, p. 409.

20 *Ibid.*

21 *Ibid.*, p. 216.

22 See Lucy McDiarmid, 'The Demotic Lady Gregory', in Maria DiBattista and Lucy McDiarmid (eds.), *High and Low Moderns: Literature and Culture, 1889–1939* (New York and Oxford: Oxford University Press, 1996), pp. 212–32.

23 See her reflections on her mother's death in Gregory, *Diaries*, p. 111.

24 See Leerssen, *Mere Irish and Fíor-Ghael*, p. 217.
25 See Anna McBride White and A. Norman Jeffares (eds.), *Always Your Friend: The Gonne–Yeats Letters 1893–1938* (London: Hutchinson, 1992), p. 150.
26 The quotation is from Frank J. Fay, *Towards a National Theatre*, ed. Robert Hogan (Dublin: Dolmen, 1970), p. 52. See Adrian Frazier, *Behind the Scenes: Yeats, Horniman and the Struggle for the Abbey Theatre* (Berkeley, Los Angeles, London: University of California Press, 1990), pp. 53–8.
27 Antoinette Quinn, 'Cathleen ni Houlihan Writes Back: Maud Gonne and Irish National Theater', *Gender and Sexuality in Modern Ireland*, ed. Anthony Bradley and Maryann Gialanella Valiulis (Amherst: University of Massachusetts Press, 1997), pp. 39–59.
28 See Yeats, *Collected Letters*, III, pp. 166–68.
29 The audience at the hall 'owned by the Carmelites and used by them for giving temperance entertainments' was remembered by George Roberts as a 'very mixed crowd, being made up of members of the Cumann na Gaedhal, the Gaelic League, the National Literary Society, and the usual attendance at the weekly temperance entertainments' – a very broad church. See Robert Hogan and James Kilroy, *Laying the Foundations 1902–1904*, Modern Irish Drama II (Dublin: Dolmen, 1976), p. 12.
30 Stephen Gwynn, *Irish Literature and Drama in the English Language: a Short History* (London: Nelson, 1936), p. 158, cited by Maria Tymoczko in 'Amateur Political Theatricals, *Tableaux Vivants*, and *Cathleen ni Houlihan*', *Yeats Annual*, 10 (1993), 33–64.
31 Lennox Robinson, *Curtain Up* (London: Michael Joseph, 1942), p. 17, also quoted by Tymoczko, 'Amateur Political Theatricals', 59.
32 Lady Gregory, *Seventy Years* (Gerrards Cross: Colin Smythe, 1973), p. 444.
33 Pádraic H. Pearse, *Political Writings and Speeches* (Dublin: Talbot Press, 1952), pp. 300–1.
34 Thomas Kinsella (ed.), *New Oxford Book of Irish Verse* (Oxford: Oxford University Press, 1986), pp. 256, 273.
35 Quinn, 'Cathleen ni Houlihan Writes Back', *Gender and Sexuality*, p. 47. Maud Gonne, arriving late for the first production of *Cathleen ni Houlihan* in the St Teresa's Hall without dressing-rooms, 'caused a minor sensation by sweeping through the auditorium in the ghostly robes of the Old Woman', to the intense disapproval of Frank Fay, who called it 'unprofessional'. See Maire Nic Shiublaigh, *The Splendid Years* (Dublin: James Duffy, 1955), p. 17.
36 Quoted by David H. Greene and E.M. Stephens, *J.M. Synge, 1871–1909* (New York: Collier Books, 1961), p. 151.

37 *Ibid.*, p. 152.

38 Griffith, in *United Irishman*, 24 October 1903.

39 'A "travelling man" is, I take it, a euphemistic way of describing a tramp, be he beggar, pedlar, or tinker, but almost invariably an undesirable who would be more likely to rob a poorbox than perform a miracle. And so when the mother . . . fails to recognise her benefactor until she afterwards hears he has walked over the neighbouring river, her mistake is perfectly natural', *Evening Herald*, 4 March 1910, quoted in Robert Hogan, Richard Burnham, and Daniel P. Poteet, *The Rise of the Realists*, Modern Irish Drama, IV (Dublin: Domen, 1979), p. 26.

40 Robert Hogan and Michael J. O'Neill (eds.), *Joseph Holloway's Abbey Theatre* (Carbondale and Edwardsville: Southern Illinois University Press, 1967), p. 28.

3 SHIFTS IN PERSPECTIVE

1 W.B. Yeats, *Essays and Introductions* (London: Macmillan, 1961), p. 319.

2 See Edward Millington Stephens, 'Life of J.M. Synge', Trinity College Dublin Library ms. 6189–6197, f. 1663. Stephens's work was used extensively by David H. Greene in the biography which was published under their joint names as *J.M. Synge 1871–1909* and which sets out most of the biographical information on Synge's political interests.

3 See Greene and Stephens, *J.M. Synge 1871–1909*, pp. 70–2 for his involvement with the Association Irlandaise.

4 Seamus Deane, *Celtic Revivals* (London: Faber & Faber, 1985), p. 60.

5 Kiberd, *Inventing Ireland*, pp. 166–88.

6 *Essays and Introductions*, pp. 319–20.

7 Edward Hirsch, 'The Gallous Story and the Dirty Deed: the Two Playboys', *Modern Drama*, 23.1 (1983), 85–102.

8 Hirsch's reading is not unlike my own in *Synge: a Critical Study of the Plays* (London and Basingstoke: Macmillan, 1975), pp. 132–45.

9 J.M. Synge, *The Collected Letters of John Millington Synge*: I, *1871–1907*, ed. Ann Saddlemyer (Oxford: Clarendon Press, 1983), p. 285.

10 Gregory, *Our Irish Theatre*, p. 67.

11 Cited in Kilroy, *The 'Playboy' Riots*, p. 10.

12 Synge, *Collected Letters*, I, p. 74.

13 See Dan H. Laurence and Nicholas Grene (eds.), *Shaw, Lady Gregory and the Abbey: a Correspondence and a Record* (Gerrards Cross: Colin Smythe, 1993), p. 74.

14 See J.J. Lee, 'Women and the Church since the Famine', in *Women in Irish Society: the Historical Dimension*, ed. Margaret Mac Curtain and Donncha O Corráin (Dublin: Arlen House, 1978), pp. 37–45, for an

analysis arguing for a socio-economic underpinning to the religious and cultural phenomenon.

15 Mary Douglas, *Purity and Danger* (London: Routledge & Kegan Paul, 1966).
16 Cited in Kilroy, *The 'Playboy' Riots*, p. 13.
17 For an unsympathetic view of such interpretations, see my *Synge: a Critical Study of the Plays*, p. 133.
18 Kiberd, *Inventing Ireland*, p. 184.
19 Two years before Synge's first 1898 visit, Arthur Symons, on a trip to Aran with Yeats, recorded their reception on Inishmaan: '"If any gentleman has committed a crime", said the oldest man on the island, "we'll hide him. There was a man killed his father, he came over here, and we hid him for two months, and he got away safe to America".' Arthur Symons, 'The Isles of Aran', *The Savoy*, 8 (December 1896), 84.
20 See 'Awful Murder of a Father by His Own Son', *Galway Express*, 1 February 1873. The details of this incident were publicised by Gregory Allen in 'An Irishman's Diary', *The Irish Times*, 31 January 1997.
21 See *Return of Outrages reported to the Constabulary Office in Ireland 1873* (Dublin: Alexander Thom for HM Stationery Office, 1874), p. 6.
22 The last reference to the case in the register of state papers in the National Archives (CSORP 16715/1877) concerns the extradition request; the files themselves are unfortunately missing.
23 'The Freedom of the Theatre', *Sinn Fein*, 9 February 1907.
24 'Terrible Tragedy in Kerry', *Freeman's Journal*, 23 June 1898. I owe this reference to R.F. Foster, *W.B. Yeats: a Life*, I, *The Apprentice Mage 1865–1914* (Oxford: Clarendon Press, 1997), p. 598.
25 For a very full account of the Lynchehaun case, see James Carney, *The Playboy and the Yellow Lady* (Dublin: Poolbeg Press, 1986).
26 'The Playboy and the Parricide', *Freeman's Journal*, 29 January 1907, cited in Kilroy, *The 'Playboy' Riots*, p. 19.
27 *The Leader*, 2 February 1907, cited in Robert Hogan and James Kilroy, *The Abbey Theatre: the Years of Synge 1905–1909*, The Modern Irish Drama III (Dublin: Dolmen, 1978), p. 143.
28 Carney, *The Playboy and the Yellow Lady*, pp. 194, 201.
29 James Carney, *ibid.*, p. 208, usefully glosses 'yellow' as 'Synge language for "English" or "Protestant". The word echoes Seán Buidhe, of "Yellow John" which connotes Englishman.'
30 *Freeman's Journal*, 30 January 1907, cited in Kilroy, *The 'Playboy' Riots*, p. 34.
31 Though the Dublin *Evening Mail* was a Unionist paper, and the reviewer on this occasion was visiting the Abbey for the first time, the distrust of the play's suspiciously foreign sophistication – 'Paris Ideas

and Parricides' is one of the headlines over the review – aligns it with nationalist reactions. See 'A Dramatic Freak', *Evening Mail*, 28 January 1907.

32 Kiberd, *Inventing Ireland*, p. 175.

33 Synge, *Collected Letters*, I, p. 333.

34 *Ibid.*, p. 285.

35 Hogan and O'Neill, eds., *Joseph Holloway's Abbey Theatre*, p. 277.

36 Kilroy, *The 'Playboy' Riots*, p. 10.

37 *Ibid.*, p. 43.

38 *Freeman's Journal*, 26 February 1907.

39 See, for example, the analysis by Conor Cruise O'Brien of Moran's article on 'Protestants and the Irish Nation' of July 1901, in *Ancestral Voices: Religion and Nationalism in Ireland* (Dublin: Poolbeg Press, 1994), p. 59.

40 *Daily Express*, 2 February 1907.

41 A 1995 Abbey production, which sought to add an extra mordancy to the play's satire by having a mute Father Reilly repeatedly appear on stage in crowd scenes, only illustrated how deliberate was Synge's strategy in excluding the priest as authority figure.

42 George Brotherton, 'A Carnival Christy and a Playboy for All Ages', originally published in *Twentieth Century Literature*, 37.3 (1991), and reprinted in Daniel J. Casey (ed.), *Critical Essays on John Millington Synge* (New York: G.K. Hall, 1994), pp. 126–36.

43 Mikhail Bakhtin, *Rabelais and His World*, trans. Helene Iswolsky (Cambridge, Mass.: MIT Press, 1968), pp. 18ff.

4 CLASS AND SPACE IN O'CASEY

1 D.J. O'Donoghue, 'The Synge Boom – Foreign Influences', *Irish Independent*, 21 August 1911.

2 P.S. Hegarty, reviewing a revival of the play in *The Irish Statesman*, 7 June 1924, quoted in Robert Hogan and Richard Burnham, *The Years of O'Casey, 1921–1926* (Newark: University of Delaware Press; Gerrards Cross: Colin Smythe, 1992), pp. 146–7.

3 4 March 1924, quoted in Hogan and Burnham, *The Years of O'Casey*, p. 192.

4 *Dublin Evening Mail*, 9 February 1926, quoted by Hogan and Burnham, *The Years of O'Casey*, p. 292.

5 R. Hogan and M.J. O'Neill, *Joseph Holloway's Abbey Theatre*, p. 232.

6 Sean O'Casey, *Letters 1910–41*, I, edited David Krause (New York: Macmillan, 1975), p. 69 n.1.

7 See 'Alpha and Omga', *Blight: A Tragedy of Dublin* (Dublin: Talbot Press, 1917); the play was subsequently collected in *The Plays of St John Gogarty*, ed. James F. Carens [Newark, Del]: Proscenium Press, [1971].

8 Sean O'Casey, *Autobiographies*, II (London: Macmillan, 1963; repr. New York: Carroll & Graf, 1984), p. 231. All further quotations are from this latter edition, with references cited parenthetically in the text.

9 See in particular, Anthony Butler, 'The Early Background' in *The World of Sean O'Casey*, ed. Sean McCann (London: Four Square, 1966), pp. 12–29, and Martin B. Margulies' important short monograph, *The Early Life of Sean O'Casey* (Dublin: Dolmen, 1970). Garry O'Connor, *Sean O'Casey: a Life* (London: Hodder & Stoughton, 1988), has most fully expressed this revised version of O'Casey's background.

10 See Margulies, *Early Life of Sean O'Casey*, pp. 15–16.

11 For details, see David Krause, *Sean O'Casey: the Man and His Work* (London: Macgibbon and Kee, 1960), pp. 5–7, who is one of several O'Casey critics who draw upon the 1914 Report for evidence of conditions in the tenements. Neither O'Casey himself, nor his family, lived in this sort of housing. The term 'tenement' originally meant simply rented accommodation in a house shared by more than one family. As it came to be used emotively in relation to Dublin, and as it is used by O'Casey himself, it referred to the overcrowded slum dwellings of the inner city, often the five-storey Georgian buildings on the north side of the river originally designed as elegant residences for single-family occupancy. It is interesting to note from Holloway's journal that O'Casey's family home is misplaced in Gardiner St., a representative street in this sort of area: see Hogan and O'Neill, *Joseph Holloway's Abbey Theatre*, p. 218.

12 Although Anthony Butler is not prepared even to concede that the houses of Mountjoy Square at the time could be categorised as tenement buildings: see McCann, ed., *The World of Sean O'Casey*, p. 21.

13 Greene and Stephens, *J.M. Synge 1871–1909*, p. 16.

14 Bernard Shaw, *Sixteen Self Sketches* (London: Constable, 1949), pp. 20–9.

15 See John Jordan, 'The Passionate Autodidact: the Importance of *Litera Scripta* for O'Casey', *Irish University Review*, 10.1 (Spring 1980), 59–76, for an analysis of reading and literature as markers of taste and moral standing throughout the *Autobiographies* and the plays.

16 I understand from Christopher Murray, at work on a new biography of O'Casey, that there was an added reason for this disapproval of Bella's marriage by O'Casey and his mother: she was already pregnant at the time.

17 See O'Connor, *Sean O'Casey*, pp. 39–40.

18 Richard Hoggart, *The Uses of Literacy* (London: Chatto & Windus, 1957; repr. Harmondsworth: Penguin, 1992), pp. 291–317.

19 Sean O'Casey, *The Harvest Festival* (Gerrards Cross: Colin Smythe, 1980), p. 17.

20 Michael O'Maoláin, 'The Raid and What Went With It', trans. Maureen Murphy, in Robert G. Lowery (ed.), *Essays on Sean O'Casey's Autobiographies* (London and Basingstoke: Macmillan, 1981), p. 102.

21 O'Casey, *Letters*, I, p. 105.

22 Hogan and O'Neill, *Joseph Holloway's Abbey Theatre*, p. 227.

23 See O'Maoláin, *Essays on Sean O'Casey's Autobiographies*, pp. 106–7. Although O'Maoláin never refers to the fictional portrait of himself as Shields, the tone of the essay suggests he was hurt by it (as well he might be), and there may have been an element of setting the record straight in his emphasis on his own reading.

24 Sean O'Casey, *Seven Plays*, ed. Ronald Ayling (Basingstoke: Macmillan, 1985), p. 3. All further quotations from the plays are taken from this edition, with references cited parenthetically in the text.

25 See O'Casey, *Letters*, I, pp. 94–5.

26 O'Maoláin, *Essays on Sean O'Casey's Autobiographies*, p. 110.

27 O'Casey, *The Harvest Festival*, p. 28.

28 Ronald Ayling's notes to *Seven Plays* very usefully identify the sources of Joxer's quotations.

29 Several critics comment on the appropriateness of Juno's name as 'the guardian of the hearth and the protectress of matrimony'. See Heinz Kosok, *O'Casey the Dramatist* (Gerrards Cross: Colin Smythe; Totowa, NJ: Barnes and Noble, 1985), p. 52.

30 Quoted by O'Connor, *Sean O'Casey*, p. 139, from an article in *The Observer*, 10 February 1924.

31 'He asked her a lot of questions and when he had got most of his information he put on the poor mouth and pretended he had no money. She took pity on the poor starving writer and took him to a cafe and bought him a cup of coffee.' Sean McCann, 'The Girl He Left Behind', in *The World of Sean O'Casey*, p. 35.

32 See O'Connor, *Sean O'Casey*, p. 151, for the origins of the Captain and Joxer.

33 Karl Marx, 'The Eighteenth Brumaire of Louis Bonaparte', in *Surveys from Exile: Political Writings*, II (Harmondsworth: Penguin, 1973), p. 239, cited by Edward W. Said, *Orientalism* (London: Routledge, 1978).

5 REACTIONS TO REVOLUTION

1 Quoted in Robert Kee, *The Green Flag*, I: *The Most Distressful Country* (London: Quartet, 1976), p. 168.

2 F.S.L. Lyons, *Culture and Anarchy in Ireland 1890–1939* (Oxford: Clarendon Press, 1979), p. 1.

3 Alan Simpson, 'O'Casey and the East Wall Area in Dublin', *Irish University Review*, 10.1 (Spring 1980), 49.

4 See Robert Hogan (ed.), *Feathers from the Green Crow: Sean O'Casey, 1905–1925* (London: Macmillan, 1963), pp. 277–99, where this play was first published.
5 Gregory, *Our Irish Theatre*, p. 20.
6 Quoted by Hunt, *The Abbey*, p.115.
7 See Brenna Katz Clarke and Harold Ferrar, *The Dublin Drama League 1919–1941* (Dublin: Dolmen Press, 1979), p. 16.
8 For the fullest account to date of the play's reception and the controversy that followed, see Hogan and Burnham, *The Years of O'Casey, 1921–1926*, pp. 287–325.
9 *Ibid.*, p. 300.
10 See Hogan and O'Neill (eds.), *Joseph Holloway's Abbey Theatre*, pp. 252–5.
11 O'Casey, *Letters*, I, p. 168.
12 Hogan and Burnham, *The Years of O'Casey*, p. 303.
13 *Ibid.*, p. 304.
14 'The Provisional Government of the Irish Republic to the People of Ireland', reproduced in Max Caulfield, *The Easter Rebellion* (London: Frederick Muller, 1964), p. 102.
15 Deane, *Celtic Revivals*, pp. 108, 111.
16 Declan Kiberd, 'The Elephant of Revolutionary Forgetfulness' in Máirín Ni Dhonnchadha and Theo Dorgan (eds.), *Revising the Rising* (Derry: Field Day, 1991), p. 18. See also Kiberd's extended critique of *The Plough* in *Inventing Ireland*, pp. 218–38.
17 In their letter to George O'Brien of 10 September 1925, on first reading the submitted ms. of *The Plough*, Yeats and Lennox Robinson agreed with O'Brien that the love scene between Clitheroe and his wife in Act II 'does not read true. What is wrong is that O'Casey is there writing about people whom he does not know, people he has only read about' (O'Casey, *Letters*, I, p. 146). In her journal for 24 September, Gregory recorded O'Casey's reaction to the directors' reaction to the play: 'He doesn't object to any cuts we make and is re-writing Mrs Clitheroe' (*Lady Gregory's Journals*, ed. Daniel J. Murphy, II (Gerrards Cross: Colin Smythe, 1987), p. 43). The reason for the original judgement on the Clitheroes and the nature of O'Casey's 're-writing' of Nora only came to light with the re-discovery of the 1926 Abbey Theatre promptbook of *The Plough* long mislaid after the 1951 fire – the play had been performed on the night of the fire itself. This promptbook, found by Mairead Delaney, archivist of the Abbey, with the help of Jessie Grene, in December 1997, shows that Clitheroe was originally cast as 'a clerk', and his language, with that of his wife, was first differentiated from the dialect of the working-class characters around them. O'Casey, evidently following the Abbey directors' advice,

changed Clitheroe to 'a bricklayer' and re-wrote the parts of both Clitheroes accordingly. I am very grateful to the Abbey Theatre and to Mairead Delaney in particular for an early opportunity to study the promptbook. For a full account of the promptbook see my 'The Class of the Clitheroes: O'Casey's Revisions to *The Plough and the Stars* promptbook', *Bullán*, forthcoming, autumn 1999.

18 Denis Johnston, *The Old Lady Says 'No'!*, ed. Christine St. Peter (Washington DC: Catholic University of America Press; Gerrards Cross: Colin Smythe, 1992), p. 52. All further quotations are taken from this edition which follows Johnston's last revised text in *The Dramatic Works*, I (Gerrards Cross: Colin Smythe, 1977).

19 For the detail of the doctored manuscript see my 'Modern Irish Literary Manuscripts', in *Treasures of the Library Trinity College Dublin*, ed. Peter Fox (Dublin: Royal Irish Academy, 1986), pp. 230–8, and for a full account of the genesis of the play and its rejection by the Abbey see Christine St. Peter, 'Introduction', *The Old Lady Says 'No!'*, pp. 15–18, 27–45.

20 See Christine St. Peter, '*The Old Lady*: in principio', in Joseph Ronsley (ed.), *Denis Johnston: a Retrospective* (Gerrards Cross: Colin Smythe; Totowa, NJ: Barnes and Noble, 1981), p. 19.

21 Johnston kept updating these scenes to maintain their topicality: so the 1920s' tram is changed to a bus in the 1960s' text, *Collected Plays*, I (London: Jonathan Cape, 1960), and the original popular bands 'Dingle's Band', and 'Clarke Barry', referred to by the characters first called Katie and Lizzie become in the 1977 version the punk-style 'Wet Dreams' and 'Gorgeous Wrecks' discussed by the renamed Carmel and Bernadette.

22 The identifications are those of Christine St. Peter: Johnston, *Old Lady*, 93, 104.

23 Brendan Behan, *An Giall*, ed. and trans. Richard Wall / *The Hostage* ed. Richard Wall (Washington DC: Catholic University of America Press; Gerrards Cross: Colin Smythe, 1987), pp. 140–1. All further quotations from both plays are from this edition with references given parenthetically in the text.

24 *Irish Times*, 17 June 1958, quoted by Michael O'Sullivan, *Brendan Behan: a Life* (Dublin: Blackwater Press, 1997), p. 234.

25 Ulick O'Connor, *Brendan Behan* (London: Granada, 1979, [1st pub. 1970]), pp. 200, 207.

26 *Ibid.*, p. 203.

27 Joan Littlewood, *Joan's Book: Joan Littlewood's Peculiar History As She Tells It* (London: Methuen, 1994), pp. 521–2.

28 *Ibid.*, pp. 525–31.

29 See O'Sullivan, *Brendan Behan: A Life*, p. 224.

30 Quoted by O'Sullivan, *ibid.*, p. 238.

31 See the comments on the programme notes not only of O'Sullivan – 'pure Littlewood at her romantic left-wing best' – *ibid.*, p. 239, but also of O'Connor, *Brendan Behan*, p. 198.
32 See O'Sullivan, *Brendan Behan: A Life*, p. 234.
33 *The Observer*, 19 October 1958, quoted by O'Sullivan, *Brendan Behan: A Life*, p. 239.
34 Quoted by O'Connor, *Brendan Behan*, p. 199.
35 Littlewood, *Joan's Book*, p. 531.
36 Philip Edwards, *Threshold of a Nation* (Cambridge University Press, 1979), p. 237. Compare also the reading of Declan Kiberd, *Inventing Ireland*, p. 528.
37 Edwards, *Threshold of a Nation*, p. 229.

6 LIVING ON

1 Samuel Beckett, 'Hommage à Jack B. Yeats' in *Disjecta* (London: John Calder, 1983), p. 148.
2 See Ann Saddlemyer (ed.), *Theatre Business* (Gerrards Cross: Colin Smythe, 1982), pp. 168–80.
3 W.B. Yeats, *Explorations* (London: Macmillan, 1962), p. 254.
4 See Samuel Beckett, *Murphy* (London: John Calder, 1963), p. 183.
5 Quoted by Katharine Worth, *The Irish Drama of Europe from Yeats to Beckett* (London: Athlone Press, 1978), p. 242.
6 James Knowlson, *Damned to Fame: the Life of Samuel Beckett* (London: Bloomsbury, 1996), p. 453.
7 See Natalie Crohn Schmitt, 'The Landscape Play: Yeats's *Purgatory*', *Irish University Review*, 27.2 (1997), 262–75.
8 Donald Torchiana, *W.B. Yeats and Georgian Ireland* (Evanston: Northwestern University Press; London: Oxford University Press, 1966), pp. 359–60.
9 W.J. Mc Cormack, *From Burke to Beckett: Ascendancy, Tradition and Betrayal in Literary History* (Cork University Press, 1994), p. 345.
10 W.B. Yeats, *Purgatory: Mauscript Materials Including the Author's Final Text*, ed. Sandra F. Siegel (Ithaca and London: Cornell University Press, 1986), pp. 150–1.
11 Mark Bence-Jones, *Twilight of the Ascendancy* (London: Constable, 1987).
12 For Robinson's *The Big House* as a partial exception to this, showing the determination of its heroine to vindicate the principles of her class even after the big house is burned, see Christopher Murray, '*The Big House, Killycreggs in Twilight* and "The Vestigia of Generations"', in Otto Rauchbauer (ed.), *Ancestral Voices: the Big House in Anglo-Irish Literature* (Dublin: Lilliput Press; Hildesheim: Georg Olms, 1992), pp. 109–19.

13 See Yeats, *The Letters of W.B. Yeats*, p. 907.
14 Torchiana, *W.B. Yeats and Georgian Ireland*, p. 362.
15 *Ibid.*, p. 362, n. 30.
16 This passage is discussed at some length also by Mc Cormack, *From Burke to Beckett*, pp. 350–3.
17 For the identification of Sir William Gregory see the entry for 3 June 1922 in *Lady Gregory's Journals* I, ed. Daniel J. Murphy (Gerrards Cross: Colin Smythe, 1978), p. 362.
18 F.A.C. Wilson, *W.B. Yeats and Tradition* (New York: Macmillan, 1958), p. 154.
19 Yeats, *Explorations*, p. 407.
20 Samuel Beckett, *The Complete Dramatic Works* (London: Faber, 1986), p. 173. All further quotations from the play are from this edition, cited parenthetically in the text.
21 For the fullest account of the play and its genesis, see Clas Zilliacus, *Beckett and Broadcasting* (Åbo: Åbo Akademi, 1976), pp. 28–76.
22 See Eoin O'Brien, *The Beckett Country* (Monkstown, Dublin: Black Cat Press, 1986), p. 32.
23 Vivian Mercier, commenting on this passage, suggests that Miss Fitt is theologically lower church than Mrs Rooney: see '"All That Fall": Samuel Beckett and the Bible', in *Modern Irish Literature: Sources and Founders*, ed. Eilís Dillon (Oxford: Clarendon Press, 1994), p. 314.
24 See S.J. Connolly, ed., *The Oxford Companion to Irish History* (Oxford University Press, 1998), pp. 53–4.
25 For an early perception of the significance of this line, see Donald Davie's review of the play on its first transmission, reprinted in Lawrence Graver and Raymond Federman (eds.), *Samuel Beckett: the Critical Heritage* (London: Routledge, 1979), pp. 153–6.
26 See O'Brien, *The Beckett Country*, p. 31.
27 Terence Brown, 'Some Young Doom: Beckett and the Child', in *Ireland's Literature* (Mullingar: Lilliput Press; Totowa, N.J.: Barnes & Noble, 1988), pp. 117–26.
28 Samuel Beckett, *The Expelled and Other Novellas* (Harmondsworth: Penguin, 1980), p. 78.
29 Anthony Roche, *Contemporary Irish Drama: from Beckett to McGuinness* (Dublin: Gill and Macmillan, 1994), p. 5.
30 Thomas Kilroy, 'Two Playwrights: Yeats and Beckett' in Joseph Ronsley (ed.), *Myth and Reality in Irish Literature* (Waterloo, Ont.: Wilfrid Laurier University Press, 1977), p. 186.
31 Kilroy's own *Talbot's Box* (Dublin: Gallery Books, 1979), written close to the time of this essay, achieves an extraordinary theatrical effectiveness from a dramaturgy similar to that he here describes in Yeats and Beckett.

32 See Suzi Gablik, *Magritte* (Greenwich, CT: New York Graphic Society, 1970), plates 109–11.

33 See Zilliacus, *Beckett and Broadcasting*, pp. 62–4, 68–9, on Beckett's handling of radio sound conventions and its realisation by Donald McWhinnie, the producer of the first BBC production of *All that Fall.*

34 See Christopher Ricks's comments on this passage in *Beckett's Dying Words* (Oxford: Clarendon Press, 1993), pp.105–6.

35 Quoted in Torchiana, *W.B. Yeats and Georgian Ireland*, p. 357.

36 For an illuminating analysis of the Yeatsian theology see Wilson, *W.B. Yeats and Tradition*, pp. 140–7.

37 See Brown, *Ireland's Literature*, pp. 121–2.

38 See among others Hugh Kenner, *A Reader's Guide to Samuel Beckett* (London: Thames and Hudson, 1973), p. 134, on the specifically Protestant cast to Beckett's imagination.

39 Yeats, *Purgatory: Manuscript Materials*, pp. 134–5.

7 VERSIONS OF PASTORAL

1 For a discussion of this choice of date see Roche, *Contemporary Irish Drama*, pp. 2–4.

2 See Terence Brown, *Ireland: a Social and Cultural History, 1922 to the Present* (Ithaca and London: Cornell University Press, 1985), pp. 185–204.

3 In the case of *Philadelphia*, it was apparently started in 1962 or 1963, at just the time that Murphy was hawking his unproduced and unpublished script of what was to be *A Crucial Week* round the theatres: see Des Hickey and Gus Smith, *A Paler Shade of Green* (London: Leslie Frewin, 1972), p. 222.

4 Quoted by Fintan O'Toole, *Tom Murphy: the Politics of Magic* (Dublin: New Island Books; London: Nick Hern Books, 1994), p. 9.

5 This is his age in the 1989 text of the play in *A Whistle in the Dark & Other Plays* (London: Methuen, 1989), subsequently reprinted in Tom Murphy, *Plays: Four* (London: Methuen, 1997). In earlier versions, that published as *The Fooleen* (Dixon, Calif.: 1968), and *A Crucial Week in the Life of a Grocer's Assistant* (Dublin: Gallery Press, 1978), he is only 29. I have used the most recent *Plays: Four* text throughout this chapter.

6 O'Toole, *Tom Murphy*, p. 13.

7 The full credits for the production are as follows: 'The first performance of *Philadelphia Here I Come!* was given at the Gaiety Theatre, Dublin, on 28 September 1964 by Edwards MacLiammoir: Dublin Gate Theatre Productions Ltd in association with the Dublin Theatre Festival and Oscar Lewenstein Ltd.' See Friel, *Selected Plays*, p. 26. This is the edition used for Friel's work throughout this chapter unless otherwise stated.

8 For a full account of the New York production see Harrington, *The Irish Play in New York*, pp. 148–56.

9 D.E.S. Maxwell, *Brian Friel* (Lewisburgh, Penn.: Bucknell University Press, 1973).

10 For the most recent, both of which have full bibliographies, see Elmer Andrews, *The Art of Brian Friel* (Basingstoke: Macmillan, 1995), and Martine Pelletier, *Le Théâtre de Brian Friel: Histoire et Histoires* (Villeneuve d'Ascq (Nord): Presses Universitaires du Septentrion, 1997).

11 Brian Friel, 'Self-portrait', *Aquarius*, no. 5 (1972), quoted in Richard Pine, *Brian Friel and Ireland's Drama* (London and New York: Routledge, 1990), p. 19.

12 Quoted from the *Irish Independent* review of November 1969 in Hunt, *The Abbey*, p. 205.

13 John Webster, *The White Divel*, I. ii. 41–4, in *The Complete Works of John Webster*, I, ed. John Lucas (London: Chatto and Windus, 1927).

14 Brian Friel, *Lovers* (Dublin: Gallery Books, 1984), p. 27. All quotations from the two one-act plays are from this edition cited parenthetically in the text. The passage from Montaigne is from *Essais*, III.v, 'Sur des vers de Virgile'.

15 Hickey and Smith, *A Paler Shade of Green*, p. 222.

16 See Christopher Fitz-Simon, *The Boys* (Dublin: Gill and Macmillan, 1994), p. 276.

17 O'Toole, *Tom Murphy: the Politics of Magic*, pp. 42–3.

18 Murphy, *The Fooleen*, p. 10.

19 On this feature of his work, see T. Gerald Fitzgibbon's excellent article, 'Thomas Murphy's Dramatic Vocabulary', *Irish University Review*, 17:1 (Spring 1987), 41–50.

20 Tom Murphy, *Plays: One* (London: Methuen, 1992), p. ix.

21 See Richard Cave, 'The City Versus the Village', in Mary Massoud (ed.), *Literary Inter-Relations: Ireland, Egypt and the Far East* (Gerrards Cross: Colin Smythe, 1996), pp. 295–6.

8 MURPHY'S IRELAND

1 Personal conversation with Tom Murphy, 20 September 1989.

2 Tom Murphy, *On the Outside/On the Inside* (Dublin: Gallery Books, 1976), p. 9.

3 'In writing *Whistle in the Dark* I suppose I cheated. I had told myself it would not be a play set in the traditional Irish kitchen; I didn't go much further when I set it in an English kitchen.' Hickey and Smith, *A Paler Shade of Green*, p. 226.

4 Tom Murphy, *Plays: Two* (London: Methuen, 1993), p. 91. All further quotations from both *Bailegangaire* and *A Thief of a Christmas* are taken from this edition, cited parenthetically in the text.

5 *A Thief of a Christmas* was staged at the Abbey in December 1985, nearly simultaneously with the first production of *Bailegangaire* by the Druid Theatre Company in Galway, though written after it. *Brigit*, written first of the three, was only made as a television play by Radio Telefis Eireann in 1987 and screened in 1988. The text of *Brigit* has not been published, and I am grateful to RTE for allowing me to view a tape of it in their film library.

6 See O'Toole, *Tom Murphy: the Politics of Magic*, pp. 228–31 for an account of the trilogy, and of a differently projected set of three plays out of which it developed.

7 *Ibid.*, p. 231.

8 Murphy supplies explanatory glosses in his text for words in Irish, but in this case the Anglicised Hiberno-English 'bonham' = 'piglet' may not be more comprehensible to non-Irish readers than 'bonav', the pronunciation closer to the Irish 'banbh'.

9 See Wendy Holden, *Unlawful Carnal Knowledge: the True Story of the X Case* (London: HarperCollins, 1994), pp. 101–5. I am grateful to Antoinette Quinn for this reference and for pointing out the relevance of the dating of these events for the play.

10 Though Murphy himself does not acknowledge a conscious influence, Anthony Roche too has commented on Kathleen Ni Houlihan as a dramatic precursor of Mommo and discusses the relationship between *Bailegangaire* and *Riders* in *Contemporary Irish Drama*, pp. 147–9.

11 In the original script used for the Abbey production, the line was even closer to Synge's: 'Now wasn't I the foolish fella not to think of this sport in the years gone by': 'A Thief of a Christmas', unpublished script in the archive of the Abbey Theatre, p. 49. I am grateful to the Abbey Theatre for access to this typescript text of the play.

12 Such, according to Murphy, is the spirit of this ejaculation which Mommo uses repeatedly: in spite of the apparent resemblance of 'och hona' to 'ochón' (= *Ir.* alas), this is not a lament. Tom Murphy, personal interview.

13 Johnston, *Dramatic Works*, II, p. 156.

14 This, one of the phrases Murphy does not gloss in the text, is ungrammatical Irish but seems to mean 'as bright as two suns': I am grateful to Angela Bourke for her confirmation of this reading.

15 See Brown, *Ireland: a Social and Cultural History*, pp. 110–12.

16 This is the dating assumed by Fintan O'Toole in *Tom Murphy: the Politics of Magic*, p. 231. Compare also the analysis of Shaun Richards, 'Refiguring Lost Narratives – Prefiguring New Ones: the Theatre of Tom Murphy', *Canadian Journal of Irish Studies*, 15.1 (1989), 80–100.

17 The 'it' in this line has slipped out of the *Plays: Two* text (which is not

always carefully proofread) and restored from the edition in Tom Murphy, *After Tragedy* (London: Methuen, 1988).

18 See Roche, *Contemporary Irish Drama*, p. 147.

19 Hickey and Smith, *A Paler Shade of Green*, p. 227.

20 The other two playwrights who are often considered to have achieved a comparable style are Synge's near-contemporary George Fitzmaurice and the later M.J. Molloy.

9 IMAGINING THE OTHER

1 Benedict Anderson, *Imagined Communities* (London, New York: Verso, 2nd ed. 1991).

2 R.F. Foster, *Modern Ireland 1600–1972* (London: Allen Lane The Penguin Press, 1988), p. 472.

3 O'Casey, *Letters*, I, 268.

4 *Ibid.*, p. 271.

5 Lecture to McGill Summer School, 1991, cited by Terence Brown, 'Who Dares to Speak? Ireland and the Great War' in Robert Clark and Piero Boitani (eds.), *English Studies in Transition* (London and New York: Routledge, 1993), p. 230.

6 See Brown, 'Who Dares to Speak?' p. 230.

7 Sebastian Barry, 'Following the Steward', foreword to *The Steward of Christendom* (London: Methuen, 1995, repr. 1997), p. vii. All quotations are from this, the most recent edition of the play, and are cited parenthetically in the text.

8 Ibid., pp. viii–ix.

9 Arnold Wesker, *Chips with Everything*, ed. Michael Marland (London and Glasgow: Blackie, 1966), p. 38.

10 Frank McGuinness, *Observe the Sons of Ulster Marching Towards the Somme* (London: Faber, 1986), p. 76. All further quotations from the play are from this edition, cited parenthetically in the text.

11 There is an oddity in the fact that not just one but two Irish plays should, many years later, have drawn upon this 1958 play of Wesker's: Brian Friel's *Volunteers* (1975) has a brain-damaged character called Smiler whose escape attempt from the group of Republican internees working on an archaeological dig in Dublin provides the climax of the play's ending. In *Chips with Everything* the picked-on victim of the conscripts is also Smiler whose similarly aborted attempt at running away ends with an exactly equivalent ritualised return to the group.

12 See David Fitzpatrick, 'Militarism in Ireland, 1900–1922', in Thomas Bartlett and Keith Jeffery (eds.), *A Military History of Ireland* (Cambridge University Press, 1996), pp. 379–406.

13 Patrick Pearse, *The Literary Writings of Patrick Pearse*, ed. Séamas O Buachalla (Dublin and Cork: Mercier Press, 1979), p. 27.

14 Quoted in Myles Dungan, *Distant Drums* (Belfast: Appletree Press, 1993), p. 72.

CONCLUSION: A WORLD ELSEWHERE

1 Conor McPherson, *The Weir* (London: Nick Hern Books, 1998), p. 18.
2 Conor McPherson, 'If You're a Young Irish Playwright, Come to London', *New Statesman*, 20 February 1998. I am grateful to Diane Glasgow for bringing this article to my attention.
3 Quoted from Tynan's *Observer* review of 27 May 1956 in O'Sullivan, *Brendan Behan*, p. 208.
4 Quoted on the back cover of Sebastian Barry, *Plays: 1* (London: Methuen, 1997).
5 Emile Zola, from *Naturalism in the Theatre*, in Eric Bentley, *The Theory of the Modern Stage* (Harmondsworth: Penguin, 1968), p. 351.
6 A.P. Chekhov to Alexander Tikhonov, 1902, quoted in David Magarshack, *Chekhov the Dramatist* (London: Eyre Methuen, 1980), p. 14.
7 T.S. Eliot, *Poetry and Drama* (London: Faber, 1951), pp. 19–20.
8 See my 'John McGahern's *The Power of Darkness*' in *Krino 1986–1996: an Anthology of Irish Writing*, ed. Gerald Dawe and Jonathan Williams (Dublin: Gill and Macmillan, 1996), pp. 80–7.

Bibliography

'Alpha and Omega' [Oliver St John Gogarty and Joseph O'Connor], *Blight: a Tragedy of Dublin* (Dublin: Talbot Press, 1917).

Anderson, Benedict, *Imagined Communities* (London and New York: Verso, 2nd edn 1991).

Andrews, Elmer, *The Art of Brian Friel* (Basingstoke: Macmillan, 1995).

'Awful Murder of a Father by His Own Son', *Galway Express*, 1 February 1873.

Bakhtin, Mikhail, *Rabelais and His World*, trans. Helene Iswolsky (Cambridge, MA: MIT Press, 1968).

Barry, Sebastian, *Plays: 1* (London: Methuen, 1997).

The Steward of Christendom (London: Methuen, 1995, repr. 1997).

Beckett, Samuel, *The Complete Dramatic Works* (London: Faber, 1986).

Disjecta (London: John Calder, 1983).

The Expelled and Other Novellas (Harmondsworth: Penguin, 1980).

Murphy (London: John Calder, 1963).

Behan, Brendan, *An Giall*, ed. and trans. Richard Wall / *The Hostage*, ed. Richard Wall (Washington DC: Catholic University of America Press; Gerrards Cross: Colin Smythe, 1987).

Bence-Jones, Mark, *Twilight of the Ascendancy* (London: Constable, 1987).

Bentley, Eric, *The Theory of the Modern Stage* (Harmondsworth: Penguin, 1968).

Boucicault, Dion, *Plays*, ed. Peter Thomson (Cambridge University Press, 1984).

Brotherton, George, 'A Carnival Christy and a Playboy for All Ages', in

Critical Essays on John Millington Synge, ed. Daniel J. Casey (New York: G.K. Hall, 1994), pp. 126–36.

Brown, Terence, *Ireland: a Social and Cultural History, 1922 to the Present* (Ithaca and London: Cornell University Press, 1985).

Ireland's Literature (Mullingar: Lilliput Press; Totowa, NJ: Barnes & Noble, 1988).

'Who Dares to Speak? Ireland and the Great War' in *English Studies in Transition*, ed. Robert Clark and Piero Boitani (London and New York: Routledge, 1993), pp. 226–37.

Butler, Hubert, *Escape from the Anthill* (Mullingar: Lilliput Press, 1985).

Carleton, William, *Traits and Stories of the Irish Peasantry*, 2 vols. (Dublin: William Curry, 1830; reprinted New York and London: Garland, 1979).

Carney, James, *The Playboy and the Yellow Lady* (Dublin: Poolbeg Press, 1986).

Caulfield, Max, *The Easter Rebellion* (London: Frederick Muller, 1964).

Cave, Richard, 'The City Versus the Village', in *Literary Inter-Relations: Ireland, Egypt and the Far East*, ed. Mary Massoud (Gerrards Cross: Colin Smythe, 1996), pp. 295–6.

Clarke, Brenna Katz and Harold Ferrar, *The Dublin Drama League 1919–1941* (Dublin: Dolmen Press, 1979).

Connolly, S.J, *The Oxford Companion to Irish History* (Oxford University Press, 1998).

Connolly, Sean, 'Dreaming History: Brian Friel's *Translations*', *Theatre Ireland*, 13 (1987), 42–4.

Cullingford, Elizabeth Butler, 'Gender, Sexuality, and Englishness in Modern Irish Drama and Film', in *Gender and Sexuality in Modern Ireland*, ed. Anthony Bradley and Maryann Gialanella Valiulis (Amherst, MA: University of Massachusetts Press, 1997), pp. 159–86.

Dalton, G.F., 'The Tradition of Blood Sacrifice to the Goddess Eire', *Studies*, 63 (1974), 343–54.

Deane, Seamus, *Celtic Revivals* (London: Faber & Faber, 1985).

'Dramatic Freak, A', *Evening Mail*, 28 January 1907.

Douglas, Mary, *Purity and Danger* (London: Routledge & Kegan Paul, 1966).

Dungan, Myles, *Distant Drums* (Belfast: Appletree Press, 1993).

Edwards, Philip, *Threshold of a Nation* (Cambridge University Press, 1979).

Eliot, T.S., *Poetry and Drama* (London: Faber, 1951).

Fawkes, Richard, *Dion Boucicault* (London: Quartet Books, 1979).

Fay, Frank J., *Towards a National Theatre*, ed. Robert Hogan (Dublin: Dolmen, 1970).

Fitzgibbon, T. Gerald, 'Thomas Murphy's Dramatic Vocabulary', *Irish University Review*, 17:1 (Spring 1987), 41–50.

Fitzpatrick, David, 'Militarism in Ireland, 1900–1922', in *A Military History of Ireland*, ed. Thomas Bartlett and Keith Jeffery (Cambridge University Press, 1996), pp. 379–406.

Fitz-Simon, Christopher, *The Boys* (Dublin: Gill and Macmillan, 1994).

The Irish Theatre (London: Thames and Hudson, 1983).

Foster, R.F., *Modern Ireland 1600–1972* (London: Allen Lane: The Penguin Press, 1988).

W.B. Yeats: a Life, I, *The Apprentice Mage 1865–1914* (Oxford: Clarendon Press, 1997).

Frazier, Adrian, *Behind the Scenes: Yeats, Horniman and the Struggle for the Abbey Theatre* (Berkeley, Los Angeles, London: University of California Press, 1990).

'The Freedom of the Theatre', *Sinn Fein*, 9 February 1907.

Friel, Brian, *Lovers* (Dublin: Gallery Books, 1984).

Selected Plays (London: Faber, 1984).

Friel, Brian, John Andrews, and Kevin Barry, 'Translations and A Paper Landscape: Between Fiction and History', *Crane Bag*, 7.2 (1983), 118–24.

Gablik, Suzi, *Magritte* (Greenwich, CT: New York Graphic Society, 1970).

Gibbons, Luke, *Transformations in Irish Culture* (Cork University Press, 1996).

Graver, Lawrence, and Raymond Federman (eds.), *Samuel Beckett: the Critical Heritage* (London: Routledge, 1979).

Greene, David H. and E.M. Stephens, *J.M. Synge, 1871–1909* (New York: Collier Books, 1961).

Gregory, Lady, *Collected Plays*, ed. Ann Saddlemyer, 4 vols. (Gerrards Cross: Colin Smythe, 1970).

Diaries 1892–1902, ed. James Pethica (Gerrards Cross: Colin Smythe, 1996).

Lady Gregory's Journals, ed. Daniel J. Murphy, 2 vols. (Gerrards Cross: Colin Smythe, 1978–87).

Our Irish Theatre (Gerrards Cross: Colin Smythe, 3rd edn, 1972).

Selected Writings, ed. Lucy McDiarmid and Maureen Waters (Harmondsworth: Penguin, 1995).

Seventy Years (Gerrards Cross: Colin Smythe, 1973).

Grene, Nicholas, 'The Class of the Clitheroes: O'Casey's Revisions to *The Plough and the Stars* Promptbook', *Bullán*, forthcoming, 1999.

'*John Bull's Other Island*: At Home and Abroad', *The Shaw Review*, XXIII, 1 (1980), 11–16.

'John McGahern's *The Power of Darkness*' in *Krino 1986–1996: an Anthology of Irish Writing*, ed. Gerald Dawe and Jonathan Williams (Dublin: Gill and Macmillan, 1996), pp. 80–7.

'Modern Irish Literary Manuscripts', in *Treasures of the Library Trinity College Dublin*, ed. Peter Fox (Dublin: Royal Irish Academy, 1986), pp. 230–8.

Synge: a Critical Study of the Plays (London and Basingstoke: Macmillan, 1975).

Harrington, John, *The Irish Play in New York 1874–1966* (Lexington, KY: University Press of Kentucky, 1997).

Hickey, Des, and Gus Smith, *A Paler Shade of Green* (London: Leslie Frewin, 1972).

Hirsch, Edward, 'The Gallous Story and the Dirty Deed: the Two Playboys', *Modern Drama*, 23.1 (1983), 85–102.

Hogan, Robert and James Kilroy, *The Abbey Theatre: the Years of Synge 1905–1909*. Modern Irish Drama III (Dublin: Dolmen, 1978).

Laying the Foundations 1902–1904. Modern Irish Drama II (Dublin: Dolmen, 1976).

Hogan, Robert, Richard Burnham and Daniel P. Poteet, *The Rise of the Realists*. Modern Irish Drama, IV (Dublin: Dolmen, 1979).

Hogan, Robert and Richard Burnham, *The Years of O'Casey, 1921–1926* (Newark, DE: University of Delaware Press; Gerrards Cross: Colin Smythe, 1992).

Hogan, Robert (ed.), *Feathers from the Green Crow: Sean O'Casey, 1905–1925* (London: Macmillan, 1963).

Hogan, Robert and Michael J. O'Neill (eds.), *Joseph Holloway's Abbey Theatre* (Carbondale and Edwardsville, IL: Southern Illinois University Press, 1967).

Hoggart, Richard, *The Uses of Literacy* (London: Chatto & Windus, 1957; repr. Harmondsworth: Penguin, 1992).

Holden, Wendy, *Unlawful Carnal Knowledge: the True Story of the X Case* (London: HarperCollins, 1994).

Holloway, Joseph, 'Impressions of a Dublin Playgoer', unpublished manuscript journal, National Library of Ireland.

Howes, Marjorie, *Yeats's Nations* (Cambridge University Press, 1996).

Hunt, Hugh, *The Abbey: Ireland's National Theatre 1904–1979* (Dublin: Gill and Macmillan; New York: Columbia University Press, 1979).

Johnston, Denis, *Collected Plays*, 2 vols. (London: Jonathan Cape, 1960).

The Dramatic Works, 2 vols. (Gerrards Cross: Colin Smythe, 1977–9).

The Old Lady Says 'No'!, ed. Christine St. Peter (Washington DC: Catholic University of America Press; Gerrards Cross: Colin Smythe, 1992).

Jordan, John, 'The Passionate Autodidact: the Importance of *Litera Scripta* for O'Casey', *Irish University Review*, 10.1 (Spring 1980), 59–76.

Kearney, Richard, *Transitions* (Manchester University Press, 1988).

Kee, Robert, *The Green Flag*, I: *The Most Distressful Country* (London: Quartet, 1976).

The Green Flag, II: *The Bold Fenian Men* (London: Quartet, 1972).

Kenner, Hugh, *A Reader's Guide to Samuel Beckett* (London: Thames and Hudson, 1973).

Kiberd, Declan, *Inventing Ireland* (London: Jonathan Cape, 1995).

'The Elephant of Revolutionary Forgetfulness' in Maírín Ni Dhonnchadha and Theo Dorgan (eds.), *Revising the Rising* (Derry: Field Day, 1991).

Kilroy, James F., *The 'Playboy' Riots* (Dublin: Dolmen Press, 1971).

Kilroy, Thomas, *Talbot's Box* (Dublin: Gallery Books, 1979).

'Two Playwrights: Yeats and Beckett' in *Myth and Reality in Irish Literature*, ed. Joseph Ronsley (Waterloo, Ont.: Wilfrid Laurier University Press, 1977), pp. 183–95.

Kinsella, Thomas (ed.), *New Oxford Book of Irish Verse* (Oxford University Press, 1986).

Knowlson, James, *Damned to Fame: the Life of Samuel Beckett* (London: Bloomsbury, 1996).

Kosok, Heinz, *O'Casey the Dramatist* (Gerrards Cross: Colin Smythe; Totowa, NJ: Barnes and Noble, 1985).

Krause, David, *Sean O'Casey: the Man and His Work* (London: Macgibbon and Kee, 1960).

Laurence, Dan H., and Nicholas Grene (eds.), *Shaw, Lady Gregory and the Abbey: a Correspondence and a Record* (Gerrards Cross: Colin Smythe, 1993).

Lee, J.J., 'Women and the Church since the Famine', in *Women in Irish Society: the Historical Dimension*, ed. Margaret Mac Curtain and Donncha O Corráin (Dublin: Arlen House, 1978), pp. 37–45.

Leerssen, Joep, *Mere Irish and Fíor-Ghael* (Cork University Press, 1996).

Remembrance and Imagination (Cork University Press, 1996).

Littlewood, Joan, *Joan's Book: Joan Littlewood's Peculiar History As She Tells It* (London: Methuen, 1994).

Longley, Edna, 'Poetry and Politics in Northern Ireland', *Crane Bag*, 9.1 (1985), 26–40.

Lyons, F.S.L., *Culture and Anarchy in Ireland 1890–1939* (Oxford: Clarendon Press, 1979).

McCann, Sean (ed.), *The World of Sean O'Casey* (London: Four Square, 1966).

Mc Cormack, W.J., *From Burke to Beckett: Ascendancy, Tradition and Betrayal in Literary History* (Cork University Press, 1994).

McDiarmid, Lucy, 'The Demotic Lady Gregory', in Maria DiBattista and Lucy McDiarmid (eds.), *High and Low Moderns: Literature and Culture, 1889–1939* (New York and Oxford: Oxford University Press, 1996), pp. 212–32.

McGuinness, Frank, *Observe the Sons of Ulster Marching Towards the Somme* (London: Faber, 1986).

McPherson, Conor, *The Weir* (London: Nick Hern Books, 1998).

'If You're a Young Irish Playwright, Come to London', *New Statesman*, 20 February 1998.

Magarshack, David, *Chekhov the Dramatist* (London: Eyre Methuen, 1980).

Margulies, Martin B., *The Early Life of Sean O'Casey* (Dublin: Dolmen, 1970).

Maxwell, D.E.S., *Brian Friel* (Lewisburgh, PA: Bucknell University Press, 1973).

Modern Irish Drama 1891–1980 (Cambridge University Press, 1984).

Meisel, Martin, *Shaw and the Nineteenth-Century Theater* (Princeton University Press, 1963).

'*John Bull's Other Island* and Other Working Partnerships', *SHAW: the Annual of Bernard Shaw Studies*, 7: *Shaw: the Neglected Plays*, ed. Alfred Turco Jr (University Park and London: Pennsylvania State University Press, 1987), 119–36.

Mercier, Vivian, '"All That Fall": Samuel Beckett and the Bible', in *Modern Irish Literature: Sources and Founders*, ed. Eilís Dillon (Oxford: Clarendon Press, 1994).

Murphy, Tom, *After Tragedy* (London: Methuen, 1988).

A Crucial Week in the Life of a Grocer's Assistant (Dublin: Gallery Press, 1978).

The Fooleen (Dixon, CA: 1968).

On the Outside/On the Inside (Dublin: Gallery Books, 1976).

Plays: One (London: Methuen, 1992).

Plays: Two (London: Methuen, 1993).

Plays: Four (London: Methuen, 1997).

Murray, Christopher, *Twentieth-Century Irish Drama: Mirror up to Nation* (Manchester University Press, 1997).

'*The Big House, Killycreggs in Twilight* and "The Vestigia of Generations"', in *Ancestral Voices: the Big House in Anglo-Irish Literature*, ed. Otto Rauchbauer (Dublin: Lilliput Press; Hildesheim: Georg Olms, 1992), pp. 109–19.

Nic Shiublaigh, Maire, *The Splendid Years* (Dublin: James Duffy, 1955).

O'Brien, Conor Cruise, *Ancestral Voices: Religion and Nationalism in Ireland* (Dublin: Poolbeg Press, 1994).

O'Brien, Eoin, *The Beckett Country* (Monkstown, Dublin: Black Cat Press, 1986).

O'Casey, Sean, *Autobiographies*, 2 vols. (London: Macmillan, 1963; repr. New York: Carroll & Graf, 1984).

The Harvest Festival (Gerrards Cross: Colin Smythe, 1980).

Letters 1910–41, I, ed. David Krause (New York: Macmillan, 1975).

Seven Plays, ed. Ronald Ayling (Basingstoke: Macmillan, 1985).

O'Connor, Garry, *Sean O'Casey: a Life* (London: Hodder & Stoughton, 1988).

O'Connor, Ulick, *Brendan Behan* (London: Granada, 1979, [1st pub. 1970]).

O'Donoghue, D.J., 'The Synge Boom – Foreign Influences', *Irish Independent*, 21 August 1911.

O'Hart, John, *Irish Pedigrees*, I (New York: P. Murphy & Son, 1915).

O'Kelly, Donal, *Catalpa* (Dublin: New Island Books; London: Nick Hern Books, 1997).

O'Maoláin, Michael, 'The Raid and What Went With It', trans. Maureen Murphy, in Robert G. Lowery (ed.), *Essays on Sean O'Casey's Autobiographies* (London and Basingstoke: Macmillan, 1981), pp. 103–22.

O'Sullivan, Michael, *Brendan Behan: a Life* (Dublin: Blackwater Press, 1997).

O'Toole, Fintan, *Tom Murphy: the Politics of Magic* (Dublin: New Island Books; London: Nick Hern Books, 1994).

Pearse, Pádraic H., *Political Writings and Speeches* (Dublin: Talbot Press, 1952).

Pearse, Patrick, *The Literary Writings of Patrick Pearse*, ed. Séamas O Buachalla (Dublin and Cork: Mercier Press, 1979).

Pelletier, Martine, *Le Théâtre de Brian Friel: Histoire et Histoires* (Villeneuve d'Ascq (Nord): Presses Universitaires du Septentrion, 1997).

Pethica, James, 'Contextualising the Lyric Moment: Yeats's "The Happy Townland" and the Abandoned Play *The Country of the Young*', *Yeats Annual*, 10 (1993), 65–91.

'"Our Kathleen": Yeats's Collaboration with Lady Gregory in the Writing of *Cathleen ni Houlihan*', in *Yeats and Women*, ed. Deirdre Toomey (Basingstoke: Macmillan, 2nd edition, 1997), pp. 205–22.

Pine, Richard, *Brian Friel and Ireland's Drama* (London and New York: Routledge, 1990).

Postlewait, Thomas and Bruce A. McConachie (eds), *Interpreting the Theatrical Past* (Iowa City: University of Iowa Press, 1989).

Quinn, Antoinette, 'Cathleen ni Houlihan Writes Back: Maud Gonne and Irish National Theater' in *Gender and Sexuality in Modern*

Ireland, eds. Anthony Bradley and Maryann Gialanella Valiulis (Amherst: University of Massachusetts Press, 1997), pp. 39–59.

Return of Outrages reported to the Constabulary Office in Ireland 1873 (Dublin: Alexander Thom for HM Stationery Office, 1874).

Richards, Shaun, 'Refiguring Lost Narratives – Prefiguring New Ones: the Theatre of Tom Murphy', *Canadian Journal of Irish Studies*, 15.1 (1989), 80–100.

Richtarik, Marilynn J., *Acting Between the Lines: The Field Day Theatre Company and Irish Cultural Politics 1980–1984* (Oxford: Clarendon Press, 1994).

Ricks, Christopher, *Beckett's Dying Words* (Oxford: Clarendon Press, 1993).

Roche, Anthony, *Contemporary Irish Drama: from Beckett to McGuinness* (Dublin: Gill and Macmillan, 1994).

Rockett, Kevin, Luke Gibbons and John Hill, *Cinema and Ireland* (London: Routledge, 1988).

Saddlemyer, Ann, 'The "Dwarf-Dramas" of the Early Abbey Theatre', in A.N. Jeffares (ed.), *Yeats, Sligo and Ireland* (Gerrards Cross: Colin Smythe, 1980), pp. 197–215.

(ed.), *Theatre Business* (Gerrards Cross: Colin Smythe, 1982).

Said, Edward W., *Orientalism* (London: Routledge, 1978).

St John Gogarty, Oliver, *The Plays of St John Gogarty*, ed. James F. Carens ([Newark, DE]: Proscenium Press [1971]).

St. Peter, Christine, '*The Old Lady*: in principio', in *Denis Johnston: a Retrospective*, ed. Joseph Ronsley (Gerrards Cross: Colin Smythe; Totowa, NJ: Barnes and Noble, 1981), pp. 10–23.

Schmitt, Natalie Crohn, 'The Landscape Play: Yeats's *Purgatory*', *Irish University Review*, 27.2 (1997), 262–75.

Shaw, Bernard, *Our Theatres in the Nineties*, 3 vols. (London: Constable, 1932).

Sixteen Self Sketches (London: Constable, 1949).

Bernard Shaw's Letters to Granville Barker, ed. C.B. Purdom (London: Phoenix House, 1956).

The Bodley Head Bernard Shaw: Collected Plays with their Prefaces, 7 vols. (London: Max Reinhardt, 1970–4).

Collected Letters 1898–1910, ed. Dan H. Laurence (London: Max Reinhardt, 1972).

'George Bernard Shaw: a Conversation', *The Tatler*, 16 November 1904.

Simpson, Alan, 'O'Casey and the East Wall Area in Dublin', *Irish University Review*, 10.1 (Spring 1980).

Steiner, George, *After Babel* (London: Oxford University Press, 1975).

Stephens, Edward Millington, 'Life of J.M. Synge', unpublished manuscript, Trinity College Dublin Library.

Symons, Arthur, 'The Isles of Aran', *The Savoy*, 8 (December 1896), 73–86.

Synge, J.M., *The Collected Letters of John Millington Synge*, ed. Ann Saddlemyer, 2 vols. (Oxford: Clarendon Press, 1983–4).

Collected Works, 4 vols. (London: Oxford University Press, 1962–8).

Taylor, Lawrence J., *Occasions of Faith: an Anthropology of Irish Catholics* (Dublin: Lilliput Press, 1995).

'Terrible Tragedy in Kerry', *Freeman's Journal*, 23 June 1898.

Torchiana, Donald, *W.B. Yeats and Georgian Ireland* (Evanston, IL: Northwestern University Press; Oxford University Press, 1966).

Tymoczko, Maria, 'Amateur Political Theatricals, *Tableaux Vivants*, and *Cathleen ni Houlihan*', *Yeats Annual*, 10 (1993), 33–64.

Walsh, Townsend, *The Career of Dion Boucicault* (New York: Dunlap Society, 1915).

Watt, Stephen M., 'Boucicault and Whitbread: the Dublin Stage at the End of the Nineteenth Century', *Eire-Ireland*, 18:3 (1983), 23–53.

Webster, John, *The Complete Works of John Webster*, 4 vols., ed. John Lucas (London: Chatto and Windus, 1927).

Wesker, Arnold, *Chips with Everything*, ed. Michael Marland (London and Glasgow: Blackie, 1966).

White, Anna McBride and A. Norman Jeffares (eds.), *Always Your Friend: The Gonne–Yeats Letters 1893–1938* (London: Hutchinson, 1992).

Wilson, F.A.C., *W.B. Yeats and Tradition* (New York: Macmillan, 1958).

Worth, Katharine, *The Irish Drama of Europe from Yeats to Beckett* (London: Athlone Press, 1978).

Yeats, W.B., *The Collected Letters of W.B. Yeats*, III, eds. John Kelly and Ronald Schuchard (Oxford: Clarendon Press, 1994).

Collected Plays (London: Macmillan, 2nd ed. 1952).

Essays and Introductions (London: Macmillan, 1961).

Explorations (London: Macmillan, 1962).
The Letters of W.B. Yeats, ed. Allan Wade (London: Rupert Hart-Davis, 1954).
Purgatory: Manuscript Materials Including the Author's Final Text, ed. Sandra F. Siegel (Ithaca and London: Cornell University Press, 1986).
The Variorum Edition of the Poems of W.B. Yeats, eds. Peter Allt and Russell K. Alspach (New York: Macmillan, 3rd edn 1966).
Zilliacus, Clas, *Beckett and Broadcasting* (Åbo: Åbo Akademi, 1976).

Index